UW-SP Environmental Council

INTRODUCTION

In recent years municipal revenues have clearly failed to keep pace
with the inflationary growth of expenditures. The gap between the
two is most notable in new and expanding communities that must shoulder
the expenses attendant upon municipal growth. Older residents with
fixed incomes find themselves taxed out of their homes, and newcomers
are staggered by the inordinate burden imposed by municipal charges
on their dream house. Small wonder then that the imbalance between
increases in local operating costs and revenues has precipitated taxpayers' revolts in many communities.

Since the root causes of these fiscal stresses have remained unclear,
the public response has tended to be erratic. But whatever their cause,
it is certain that this combination of stress and insecurity militate
against reasoned policy making. The result has been a mounting trend
toward "no-growth" zoning. Certainly much of its vigor is based upon
such considerations as race and class exclusivity, style of life and
environmental amenity as well as fiscal grounds. But the last element
must be resolved as a necessary precondition for broadening the scale
of public thinking.

A new, coordinated approach to relieving the strains of growth and service delivery requires a sound grasp of both the causes of and responses to municipal stress. We hope that this work will be useful
in that effort.

There are few fields that generate as much hard-fought controversy as
those of housing development and municipal cost. Proposals for new
residential units are hailed by some as the final solution to the city
treasurer's problems while others foresee them as the first step on
the path to fiscal disaster. The tunnel vision that typifies both
extremes usually stems from the dearth of adequate and reliable data
on the real dollar impacts of various forms of housing on the municipal
fisc. It is our goal, therefore, to provide some hard data with which
to narrow the understanding gap.

*   *   *   *   *   *

Most of the nation's municipalities rely primarily on local property
taxes and other locally raised revenues to meet the costs accompanying
population increases. In addition to the historic problems of revenue-
sharing, communities are now confronted with pressure from the broader
governmental environment to construct specific housing configurations
for people whose needs and resources cannot be brought into balance
within conventional municipal costs and revenues.

Clearly, some sort of <u>fiscal packaging</u> is needed to bridge the gap
between municipal fiscal stress and the broader societal need, which
may accelerate the drain on communities. Either the state or federal

government must provide operating funds with which to cushion the impact of newcomers upon the communities in which they are located. We are already moving (although slowly) in this direction. For example, major capital improvement grants--water, sewer facilities, etc.--are being provided to developers of certain types of housing. However, such measures have been more talked about than implemented. The initial version of 1972 Housing Act, for example, incorporated a packaging concept, but this feature was written out of the final version of the legislation.

Even if capital grants provisions are made, they will not resolve the problem of operating costs. It is one thing to build a school and quite another to operate it. Construction tends to generate more attention perhaps because its results are tangible, substantial and finite. Yet the carrying costs of capital improvements may represent only a fifth or sixth of the system's actual operating costs.*

Revenue sharing, at least as it is presently structured, represents a step in the right direction. But it does tend to reflect history rather than future need. It gives preferential treatment to those communities whose past census profile evidences need. Future forms could well expand bonus offerings to communities that agree to adopt future development patterns compatible with the national or state needs.

Regardless of which mode prevails--local autonomy regarding a specific housing venture or governmental quota or incentive programs to assure certain housing amenities--we must obtain more adequate data on the actual fiscal levies resulting from development. It is to this end that we have undertaken our study.

*   *   *   *   *   *

Determining the costs attendant upon municipal expansion or upon the addition of specific residential types is a formidable task. We therefore employed a number of investigative procedures.

The first part of the work presents the data obtained from a sample of 7,500 households in various types of housing configuration. It represents an attempt to answer definitively the question of how many school children will be generated by adding a given type of dwelling unit. The first three chapters present some of the highlights of our findings on education costs, social and occupational characteristics

---
*
     Even with current high interest costs involving municipal fund interest charges of 5.5 percent, a high school plant costing $3,000 per student involves interest charges of $165 per year. The same facility's operating cost per student may easily average ten times that amount.

of the residents, origins, commuter patterns, consumer expenditures and general household configuration. Ms. Lynne Sagalyn initiated this element of field work; it was concluded by Duane Windsor, based on a design developed by James Hughes.

Chapters 4, 5 and 6 employ a variety of statistical techniques to focus on the economics of the public sector, with special emphasis upon the importance of growth and population base as determinants of municipal expenditures. Considerable detail is given on the variables associated with per capita expenditure variation. Included is a community analysis of the linkage between population variables and the municipal expenditure patterns associated with them. Of particular note are the relationships between absolute community size and patterns of growth which have been disaggregated here. This section was largely the work of Pat Beaton, Franklin James and Robert Burchell.

Chapter 7 links the field survey data with those on expenditure patterns. It also examines the relationship between per capita expenditures and the consumer's reaction to them as measured by the questionnaire responses. Among the municipal services covered here are: police protection, fire protection, sanitation, recreation, public health, libraries and public education.

The second part of this rather lengthy chapter explores the relationship between consumer satisfaction and the community's size and growth rate. It poses the question: Is there some optimum community size and growth rate that will assure consumer satisfaction? This question generates renewed interest as we move into the era of planned unit development and new towns. Robert Burchell and David Listokin took prime leadership in this section of the study as well as in the concluding chapter.*

We have included an extensive section on methodology as well as a sample of the questionnaire we used in the hope that they will facilitate future research.

Ms. Virginia Paulus, the Center's Librarian, provided indispensable services in developing bibliographical material and background reading resources for the entire group. William Dolphin, our programmer, offered patience and understanding in the fact of the seemingly interminable demands generated in the course of the study. As always the production staff, headed by Ms. Mary Picarella and Ms. Joan Frantz with the assistance of Ms. Connie Michaelson and Ms. Mona Levine, did wonders.

------

*The reader will note that the title page of this volume is quite crowded--and properly so. This study represents a unified effort by the staff of the Center for Urban Policy Research; the breadth of the problems examined demanded a wide variety of talents for this study. Each chapter of the study, while initiated by a specific investigator, was worked on by all of the others.

Professor Norman Walzer, as noted in the text, contributed constructive criticism of initial drafts. The County and Municipal Government Study Commission and its executive director, Eugene Schneider, provided much of the funding and many of the insights for an earlier draft upon which this work is based. This study was part of a contract secured by the Commission from the Department of Housing and Urban Development. Discussion with members of the Department, particularly James Hoben and Wyndham Clark, proved especially useful and insightful.

Our thanks to all of these individuals for their help in securing whatever virtues the study may have--its faults are the authors' own.

George Sternlieb, Director
Center for Urban Policy Research
Rutgers University
New Brunswick, N. J.

TABLE OF CONTENTS

CHAPTER 2- WHO LIVES WHERE--AND WHY

Housing Development
and Municipal Costs

CHAPTER 1

HOUSING DEVELOPMENT AND MUNICIPAL
COSTS: A SUMMARY

A dominant theme at any planning board meeting concerned with
housing proposals is the potential impact on the school system and
municipal services. This emphasis is certainly in line with the
predominance of educational expenditures and municipal operating
costs in determining the property taxes which community residents
must pay. In some suburban communities the cost of education may
make up as much as 80 percent of operating costs, making the focus
on this element particularly important. Even in central cities,
where the costs of education are diluted by the rising pressures of
welfare, police, fire, and other services, education is typically
the largest single item in the operating budget. It is therefore
of utmost importance to municipalities to be able to estimate
effectively the fiscal impact of new residential development.

The literature in this field of municipal finance and urban planning
is relatively sparse and shows highly contradictory results. It
has typically been badly divided between the tightly detailed
empirical case study (the examination of a particular municipality
or a particular housing development which cannot be readily extended
to a different municipality or development) and the broad statistical
analysis of secondary data collected on the state or national level
(which cannot be used at the municipal or development level).
Rarely has the effort been made to integrate these two necessary
elements of the fiscal analysis of housing construction. Hypotheses
generated in case studies must be subjected to empirical tests based
on such secondary data in order to be usable elsewhere. Secondary
data analysis must be related to actual municipalities and housing
developments. Even the case studies have typically dealt only with
educational costs, ignoring most other municipal functions. The
result, of course, has been to make it very difficult for municipal
officials and urban planners to evaluate the impact, on a particular
municipality's budget, of a new housing development before such
housing is actually constructed and inhabited.

The importance of this significant planning problem is clearly
increased by the efforts of the state and federal governments to
"open up the suburbs" as a safety valve for the low and moderate
income residents of core cities. Communities are concerned over the
fiscal effects of an enlarged population with potentially a very
different composition. There appears to have been a distinct
trend toward "exclusionary zoning" partly for the purpose of avoiding the anticipated fiscal pressures of population growth and the
concomitant housing development. Often, given the current inability
to project expected budget costs and revenues, proposed housing
developments are rejected which might, in fact, be sources of

1

revenue in excess of cost. Clearly, exclusionary zoning may be based on other interests as well, but this fiscal barrier is typically the first one encountered. It is a barrier which, more often than not, lacks any foundation in fiscal fact.

The research which is summarized in the following pages has attempted to avoid both micro and macro biases by employing analyses at varying levels of scale. If macro data are employed they are usually composites, via grouping algorithms, of specifically sought, unique entities. Similarly, if the case study approach is utilized the particular case for examination has been isolated as particularly indicative of a larger group of subjects that exhibit similar characteristics.

The summary is deliberately directed to and its format reflects the underlying rationale of the research. *The principal concern of the study was to provide a methodology for estimating the probable fiscal impact on both a municipality's operating budget and educational expenditures of housing developments characterized by various configurational and demographic patterns.* The study was specifically designed to permit any municipality in the State of New Jersey to make at least a rough estimate of the probable municipal and educational costs that will be imposed by a housing development of given characteristics. Such a methodology should obviate the necessity of each municipality having to estimate, via varying criteria, the effects of each proposed housing development upon its municipal fisc. The research is in a form fully replicable in other states and the findings are generalizable to areas beyond New Jersey.

This summary is therefore divided into two parts, i.e., those factors which affect educational and those which affect non-educational costs. The final sections contain a cost-revenue analysis which in very simple form puts to practical use some of the more pertinent findings of the larger study.

EDUCATIONAL COSTS

Despite its significance, the number of students per household which can be anticipated from various forms of housing is a subject which has been surrounded by more diatribe and folklore than by fact. For that reason, one of the major objectives of this research is a clarification of an essential variable: the number of children by school category generated by various forms of suburban housing. The most significant figure used to calculate per capita noneducational costs is total household size. Another objective of this research will be to present the limits of this variable; again the analysis will be by housing type.

2

The main thrust of this section will be to demonstrate the continued validity of both household size and school load multipliers by dwelling type and number of bedrooms. Subsequent portions of this review will deal with the social characteristics of residents by dwelling type and the resident profile and school age children count in several garden apartment developments over time.

Bedroom multipliers are of crucial concern to municipal officials and urban planners interested in analyzing the cost-revenue balance of proposed housing developments. There is an extensive body of literature dealing with this subject. George Sternlieb for Rutgers University (1964)[1] and the L. Robert Rolde Company for NAHB (1962)[2] performed fundamental studies dealing specifically with garden apartments. Since then, a considerable amount of similar work has been done for a variety of housing types.

Ruth Mace and Warren Wicker (1968)[3] and Barton-Aschman Associates (1970)[4] have detailed the cost-revenue implications of single family homes. Paul Holley for ASPO (1966)[5] provided a summary of studies completed on multiple housing types in a variety of geographical locations (Park Ridge, Ill., Fairfax County, Va., Nassau County, N.Y. and nine others). The older studies of high rise structures by Dominic Del Guidice (1963)[6] and Ansel Melamed (1961)[7] are consistently referred to. Carl Norcross for the Urban Land Institute (1968) has evaluated the cost implications and resident profiles of open space communities.[8] Finally, recent studies by governmental planning departments in Westchester County, New York (1971),[9] Arcadia, California (1970),[10] Newton, Massachusetts (1971),[11] and Monmouth County, New Jersey (1973)[12] have looked closely at costs and revenues of garden apartments in a variety of configurations.

The data presented here are based on one of the largest door-to-door cost-revenue surveys ever conducted.* Moreover, the data provide baseline information for multiple municipalities throughout New Jersey. The sample is of a scope and depth to make the results generally useful to local political subdivisions throughout the United States.

*3,600	Garden Apartments	48.0%
1,700	Townhouses	22.7
1,600	High Rise	21.3
600	Single Family	8.0
7,500	Total Units	100.0%

Bedroom Multipliers By Housing Type

The single most common method used to estimate the number of school children in a given development is to apply "school age children multipliers" to the number of additional housing units of various types which will be included in the development. [13] Typically, the size of these multipliers depends on the unit type (single family home, garden apartment, etc.) and on the number of bedrooms provided in each unit. Similar techniques, employing "total household size multipliers," are used to forecast the total additional population in the development. [14] Our initial object is to demonstrate the continuing dominant importance of the bedroom count as a determinant of both the number of school children and the number of people a residential household will contribute to the local population.

Total Household Size

Some of the initial derivatives of this study were multipliers for total household size (i.e., the number of resident persons per dwelling unit), presented here as a function of both housing type and bedroom count (Exhibit 1-1). These numbers may be used to calculate per capita municipal service costs. The equivalents to these household size multipliers for the educational component of development impact are school children per dwelling unit, also available by housing type; these will be discussed subsequently.

EXHIBIT 1-1. TOTAL HOUSEHOLD SIZE BY DWELLING TYPE AND NUMBER OF BEDROOMS

Dwelling Type	Studio	1 Bedroom	2 Bedroom	3 Bedroom	4 Bedroom
Garden Apartments	--	1.902 (n=1,816)	2.805 (n=1,072)	--	--
Townhouses	--	--	2.675 (n= 657)	3.349 (n= 923)	3.741 (n= 109)
High Rise	1.151 (n= 158)	1.817 (n= 553)	2.484 (n= 424)	--	--
Single Family (under $30,000)	--	--	--	3.307 (n= 362)	3.720 (n= 257)

Note: Sample size in parentheses.

Source: CUPR Survey 1972-1973.

High rise and garden apartment units offer a similar configuration of dwelling units, as do townhouse and single family units. In the former, a low number of bedrooms (in most cases two or less) are frequently found, and the units are rented; in the latter, larger bedroom configurations (three to five) are available, and the units are generally owned. We might thus expect some degree of similarity in total household size within the two kinds of housing units.

One and two bedroom garden apartments appear to house approximately 5 to 10 percent more people than do high rise units with an equivalent number of bedrooms. On the average a one bedroom garden apartment houses 1.90 persons, in an equivalent high rise unit the figure is 1.82. A two bedroom garden apartment houses an average 2.80 persons, while in high rise structures there are 2.48 persons per two bedroom unit.

Townhouse units (single family attached) are quite comparable to inexpensive single family homes (under $30,000).* In the three bedroom townhouses, we find 3.35 persons per unit versus 3.31 in single family homes; in the four bedroom townhouses the comparable figures are 3.74 versus 3.72.

Relatively few people are found in smaller townhouses, however; in two bedroom townhouses, the total number of people (2.68) falls almost midway between figures for high rise (2.48) and garden apartment (2.80) units.

If we envision townhouses as the new dwelling choice (as opposed to the modestly priced single family home) for upwardly mobile persons in the early stages of child rearing, and the high rise representing in part a similar choice for mobile singles and young marrieds, then quite possibly the cost-revenue picture of these two newly sought housing alternatives may soon reflect the reduced fertility figures of young, white females (18-34) evident in the 1970 census.** The section on social characteristics of residents will point up significantly different social profiles by housing type which may also contribute to differences between these new versus old shelter choices.

---

*Homes advertised for less than $30,000 for a three bedroom unit during June through September 1972. The addition of a bedroom or other amenities such as central air-conditioning, etc. may increase the selling price of the unit considerably.

**i.e., similar revenue from units based on rent or value; less cost due to both reduced numbers of school children and lower total household sizes.

School Age Children

School load levels are impacted by at least two major variables. The first includes the level of vacancy in apartments which are not being used because they are not contracted for (i.e., vacant and "available for rent," following the census definition) as well as the impact of turnover. An apartment may have been vacated and almost immediately leased by a newcomer. Not uncommonly, however, there is a period in which the apartment stands vacant, while it is being repainted or while previous commitments of the new occupant are being honored, such as selling his previous house or moving from a distant locale.

Garden apartment developments typically have a relatively high tenant turnover. With an average length of stay of approximately three years (roughly borne out by our findings) and a two-week "vacancy" on each move, we would have approximately a 0.75 percent "vacancy" rate. Moreover, some apartment units are always held off the market for one or another reason. Given these factors, after consulting the 1970 census vacancy data figures, we have ascribed a total vacancy of 3 percent for all causes. One may well argue that this figure is too high or too low. The basic numbers, however, are relatively little affected by variations within any reasonable scale.

The second major variable, which may have substantial impact in some states and negligible impact in others, is use of private or parochial schools. In New Jersey, parochial schools absorb approximately 15 percent of all children attending school under age 18. The data presented below reflect the actual experience secured from our interviews, and would seem to be well within the overall state proportion.

Exhibit 1-2 presents public school age children multipliers* by housing type and by number of bedrooms. The numbers pertaining

---

*Based on analysis of actual operating experience, the New Jersey Education Association has adopted a system of weighting average costs of schooling. Weighted enrollments make allowances for the differences in costs of operating kindergarten, elementary, secondary and other programs, thereby providing reasonably comparable data for use with kindergarten through twelfth grade districts. It should be pointed out that there is considerable local variation in the weighting factors. For the examples which follow the weighted figures have not been used. The general weights shown below come very close to actual experience and are thus presented for information purposes.

Level	Weight
Kindergarten	0.5
Elementary	1.0
Secondary	1.3

Most kindergarten pupils attend double shifts, which account for the low weighting. Conversely, high school students require a larger professional staff, including specialists with light student loads.

EXHIBIT 1-2.   PUBLIC SCHOOL ATTENDEES PER DWELLING UNIT
BY NUMBER OF BEDROOMS

Bedroom Type	Grade Level	Pupil Multiplier
Garden Apartment		
One Bedroom	Kindergarten	.005
	Grammar School	.024
	High School	.017
		.046 (n = 1,816)
Two Bedroom	Kindergarten	.032
	Grammar School	.250
	High School	.062
		.344 (n = 1,072)
Townhouses		
Two Bedroom	Kindergarten	.029
	Grammar School	.134
	High School	.057
		.220 (n = 657)
Three Bedroom	Kindergarten	.097
	Grammar School	.450
	High School	.108
		.655 (n = 923)
Four Bedroom	Kindergarten	.125
	Grammar School	.712
	High School	.189
		1.026 (n = 109)
High Rise		
Studio	Kindergarten	.000
	Grammar School	.000
	High School	.000
		.000 (n = 158)
One Bedroom	Kindergarten	.006
	Grammar School	.006
	High School	.000
		.012 (n = 553)
Two Bedroom	Kindergarten	.021
	Grammar School	.115
	High School	.045
		.181 (n = 424)
Single Family*		
Three Bedroom	Kindergarten	.083
	Grammar School	.408
	High School	.135
		.626 (n = 362
Four Bedroom	Kindergarten	.152
	Grammar School	.969
	High School	.172
		1.293 (n = 257)

Notes: 1.   (*) Special Sample of Units < $30,000.
2.   Sample size in parenthesis.

Source: CUPR Survey 1972-1973.

to one and two bedroom garden apartment units are particularly significant. The approximate .04 and .40* school children estimates for these units respectively have withstood the test of time; nearly a decade after the original Rutgers survey, these multipliers remain substantially valid.

The consistent relationship between high rise and garden apartment units for both one and two bedroom units is somewhat reassuring. At the one bedroom level, the number of school age children found in garden apartments (.046) is four times that found in high rise units (.012). In two bedroom units the garden apartment also contains more school age children (.344) than does the high rise unit (.181), this time by a factor of two.

In inexpensive single family homes and townhouses, the consistent and very slight differences in total household size in both three and four bedroom units are not borne out by similar relationships observed for school age children in four bedroom units. At three bedrooms, the townhouse (.655) and the single family home (.626) are almost equivalent; at the four bedroom level the townhouse (1.026) has almost .30 school age children less than the single family home. One possible explanation for this larger difference in the four bedroom units is that a greater proportion of related or unrelated adults live with the modular family in four bedroom townhouses.

In all housing types as bedrooms increase so does the number of school age children. Eight times the number of school age children are found in two bedroom garden apartments as live in one bedroom garden apartments. Three times the number of school age children occupy three bedroom townhouses (.655) as live in two bedroom units (.220); twice the number of school age children live in four bedroom single family homes (1.293) as in three bedroom homes (.626).

Other Development Variables

Do other factors affect both school load and total household size? Do basic characteristics of developments, such as location, size, rental or value levels, race of tenants and so on significantly affect either or both of the above two indices of cost-revenue impact?

To partially answer this question, we have chosen several variables to supplement the basic factor, number of bedrooms per dwelling unit. These are the rent value of the unit relative to comparable units in the county, the location of the unit, and the race of the household

----

*Actually .046 and .344 respectively.

occupying the unit. Two additional characteristics are also
included, i.e., the age of the development and the number of units
included in it.* Each of the latter variables has been said to
influence the number of children and the total population of the
housing development;[15] each may also, in one fashion or another, be
reasonably accurately forecast by a municipality.

---

	*Variable Name	Definition
1.	BR2	Dummy variable indicating two-bedroom units.
2.	BR3	Dummy variable indicating three-bedroom units.
3.	BR4	Dummy variable indicating four-bedroom units.
4.	TH	Dummy variable representing townhouses.
5.	GA	Dummy variable representing garden apartments.
6.	HR	Dummy variable representing high rise development.
7.	Q	Ratio of rent or value of unit to average renter value of comparable units in the county.
8.	SIZE	Number of units in the development.
9.	AGE	Year in which development was completed.
10.	RACE	Binary variable taking a value of "1" for black households and "2" for white households.
11.	REG1	Dummy variable indicating development location in distant metropolitan, rural New Jersey counties.
12.	REG2	Dummy variable indicating development location in high growth, young family suburban New Jersey counties.
13.	REG3	Dummy variable indicating development location in wealthy, established, suburban New Jersey counties.
14.	REG4	Dummy variable indicating development location in resort, retirement New Jersey counties.
15.	REG5	Dummy variable indicating development in rural industrial or service New Jersey counties.
16.	REG6	Dummy variable indicating development in highly developed, poor, core city New Jersey counties.

An additional factor which has received some attention is the social differentiation of developments. Referring to garden apartments a 1964 Rutgers study noted:[16]

> In a variation of Gresham's Law...the prolifer-
> ation of children may well drive out late sleepers
> and childless couples and thus leads to a still
> larger number of children per dwelling unit.

This suggests, at least in part, that a household chooses a dwelling unit on the basis of its neighbors' characteristics, and that this process of self-selection results in some degree of social segregation among residential developments.[17]

Physical design clearly affects the social composition of a development. For example, auxiliary public facilities such as playgrounds may attract families with children, while swimming pools and tennis courts may attract young single persons. Such factors as architectural design or provisions for privacy may also be important.[18] Finally, landlords, via application and interview processes, have some control over the characteristics of tenants in their rental developments.

The following analysis focuses on estimating the joint importance of these factors. The estimation will be done indirectly. Development age and size are physical features available for explicit analysis. No information was collected on other features, or on landlord policies regarding tenant selection in rental units. The fact that the basic unit of observation in this analysis is the individual household makes it possible to introduce "dummy" variables representing specific developments. These dummy variables measure differences among development in their child and population genera- tion not resulting from the effects of other characteristics explicitly included.* They obviously cannot provide precise guides to the importance of individual features of households or develop- ments; but they will provide some indication of the potential for further analysis of these determinants.

We have used single equation multiple regression analysis to isolate important indicators of both school age children and family size of households which reside locally. Only the significance of the variables will be reported here; in the main body of the study actual estimates of school and population load by bedroom type are provided.

---

*Unique development features may pertain to the level or variety of physical amenities provided, landlord or tenant selection policies, type of clientele attracted, etc. It is a variable which states, in effect, that after taking the other several indices into account there is still something unique about a single development or several developments which contributes to either or both of the esti- mates of a housing type's school age children or total household size.

School Age Children

Exhibit 1-3A presents a tabular summary of the determinants of the number of school age children in the four types of housing developments. It is clear *that the commonly used bedroom multiplier technique for estimating the number of school age children has a great deal of authenticity.* Adding auxiliary characteristics of developments and households appears to offer somewhat limited potential for improving our ability to predict the number of school age children, although some small improvement is possible. The race of the household was often significantly related to the number of children of school age in garden apartment units; non-white households tend to be larger and to have more school age children than white households in comparable units. Relative rent or value of units was also occasionally significant, though with disparate affects among the four housing configurations. Development size, age and location, for the most part, appear insignificant.

Social differentiation among developments (unique aspects of the development) was also important for every housing type except townhouses and high rise units. This pattern was true for both owner-occupied units (single family homes) and rental units (garden apartments). As was emphasized above, the reasons for these differences cannot be inferred from the data at hand; but the results suggest that additional research might be useful.

Total Household Size

Exhibit 1-3B presents a similar summary of the results of the analysis of total household size. *Again, the importance of bedroom multipliers is apparent.* However, in several cases other variables also seem useful. Rent levels are important determinants of household size in both garden and high rise apartments, particularly when they represent additional living space not indicated by the bedroom variable. Tenant race was significantly related to household size in garden apartments and possibly in single family homes. Development size appeared to be important in several housing configurations. Development age was not a significant determinant of total household size, though location was often significant.

The overwhelming finding is the continued importance of bedroom count as a determinant of the number of school age children and the total household size. In both cases, there are other determinants of the level and composition of dwelling unit populations. Current research at Rutgers is directed toward expanding the list of auxiliary factors impacting on both of these variables, using information tabulated by the U.S. Census.[19] A subsequent report will summarize the results of these analyses. *At present, however, household size and school attendance data are relatively unaffected*

EXHIBIT 1-3A. BEDROOMS AND AUXILIARY FACTORS AS INDICATORS OF THE NUMBER OF
SCHOOL AGE CHILDREN IN HOUSING UNITS OF THE FOUR TYPES

Basic Factors	Garden Apartments	High Rise Apartments	Single Family Homes	Townhouses
Bedroom Multipliers (BR2-BR4)	More bedrooms; more children	More bedrooms; more children	More bedrooms; more children	More bedrooms; more children
Auxiliary Factors[a]				
Relative Rents (Q)	Higher rents; more children	Higher rents;[b] fewer children	Higher value; fewer children	Not Significant
Tenant Race (RACE)	White households; fewer children	Not Significant	Not Significant	Not Significant
Development Size (SIZE)	Not Significant[b]	Larger Developments; More Children	Not Significant[b]	Not Significant
Development Age (AGE)	Not Significant[b]	Not Not Significant	Not Significant[b]	Not Significant
Unique Development Features	Variable Effects	Not Significant	Variable Effects	Not Significant
Location (REG1-REG6)	Variable Effects	Not Significant	Variable Effects	Not Significant[b]

EXHIBIT 1-3B. BEDROOMS AND AUXILIARY FACTORS AS INDICATORS OF
TOTAL HOUSEHOLD SIZE IN HOUSING UNITS OF THE FOUR TYPES

Basic Factors	Garden Apartments	High Rise Apartments	Single Family Homes	Townhouses
Bedroom Multipliers (BR2-BR4)	More bedrooms; larger households	More bedrooms; larger households	More bedrooms; larger households	More bedrooms; larger households
Auxiliary Factors[a]				
Relative Rents (Q)	Higher Rents; larger households	Higher Rents; larger households	Not Significant	Higher Value; larger households
Tenant Race (RACE)	White Households, smaller households	Not Significant	Not Significant	Not Significant
Development Size (SIZE)	Larger Developments, Larger Households	Larger Developments, Greater Household Size	Not Significant	Larger Developments; Smaller Household Size
Development Age (AGE)	Not Significant[b]	Not Significant	Not Significant	Not Significant
Unique Development Features	Varialbe Effects	Variable Effects	Variable Effects	Variable Effects
Location (REG1-REG6)	Variable Effects	Variable Effects	Variable Effects	Not Significant[b]

Notes: (a) The estimation of these effects is described in detail in Chapter 3.
They take into account the number of bedrooms in a unit, which were
significant in all cases.
(b) See Chapter 3 for additional information.

Source: CUPR Survey 1972-1973.

12

*by development characteristics. Housing type and bedroom count of
the units appear to be the key determinants.*

SOCIAL AND OCCUPATIONAL CHARACTERISTICS OF RESIDENTS

<u>By Household Characteristic</u>

What kinds of people are drawn to these different kinds of housing?
The results of the cross tabulation, supported by regression
analyses, enable us to make certain generalizations (Exhibit 1-4
through 1-7). Professionals are more likely to reside in high rise
and townhouse units; craftsmen, semi-skilled and laborers in single
family homes. Lower middle income persons are more likely to
reside in garden apartments and the modest single family homes
included in our sample; middle to upper income persons are more
likely to reside in townhouses and high rise apartments. Smaller
households tend to live in high rise and townhouse units, larger
families in the other two housing types. Older households reside
in high rise apartments, younger households in garden apartments,*
townhouses and single family units. Female-headed households tend
to reside in rental units, male-headed units in owned configurations.
Out-of-state migrants are more likely to locate in townhouses and
high rise units; and less likely to move into garden apartments
and single family homes. In general, households moving from single
family homes relocate in a garden apartment or in another single
family home (the stage in the life cycle is a major factor in which
type is chosen); former residents of multi-family units are likely
to choose townhouse and to a lesser degree, high rise accommodations
(stage in the life cycle is also important here).

Black households tend to live in garden and high rise apartments
rather than townhouses and single family homes.** Households with

----

*When viewed in comparison with the age distribution of high
rise structures.

**Some attention was paid to ethnic patterns within the sample
developments (not reproduced in exhibits). Usable responses were
secured from 235 black residents of garden apartments (mostly from
three developments) but from only 18 in townhouses. The respective
white respondents numbered 1,499 and 1,063. Black respondents in
high rise developments were again substantially limited to one
development in Newark. Similarly the proportion of black respondents
in single family units was negligible. In no case were there enough
Spanish-speaking respondents to warrant analysis. Hence, it was
impossible to carry out any definitive analysis of either black or
Spanish-speaking households by housing type. Separate analyses were
conducted for the two predominantly black garden apartments (Franklin
Township and Newark, N.J.) and the one black high rise structure

(Continued on next page)

EXHIBIT 1-4. SOCIAL AND OCCUPATIONAL CHARACTERISTICS OF GARDEN APARTMENT RESIDENTS
(Median Rent: 1 Bedroom $169
2 Bedrooms $192)

A. *WHO LIVES THERE (Head of Household)*

1. Occupation

Professional, Managerial, Clerical, Sales	*Craftsmen, Operatives, Service, Laborers*	*Other[1]*	*Total*
60.8	20.0	19.2	100.0

2. Age   *Median - 34.3 years*

3. Sex

Male	*Female*	*Total*
76.1	23.9	100.0

4. Education   *Median - 14.2 years*

5. Income   *Median - $11,871 (Total Household)*

B. *WHERE DO THEY COME FROM (Head of Household)*

1. Previous Place of Residence

Same Town	*State's Major City*	*State's Balance*	*Out of State[2]*	*Total*
21.4	6.1	41.6	30.9	100.0

2. Previous Housing Type

Single Family	*Multi Family*	*Other[3]*	*Total*
45.7	48.7	5.6	100.0

3. Previous Form of Tenure

Owner	*Renter*	*Other[4]*	*Total*
28.2	58.5	13.3	100.0

4. Distance Traveled Commuting   8.5 miles (Median)

Notes: (1) Includes students, retired, housewives, unemployed (1.7%)
  (2) Includes "out of country" (no greater than 2%)
  (3) Includes dormitory and two family
  (4) Includes "lives with family"

Source: CUPR Survey 1972-1973

EXHIBIT 1-5. SOCIAL AND OCCUPATIONAL CHARACTERISTICS OF TOWNHOUSE RESIDENTS
(Median Value: $28,900)

A. *WHO LIVES THERE (Head of Household)*

1. Occupation

Professional, Managerial, Clerical, Sales	Craftsmen, Operatives, Service, Laborers	Other[1]	Total
81.7	10.7	7.6	100.0

2. Age   *Median* - 34.2 years

3. Sex

Male	Female	Total
76.1	23.9	100.0

4. Education   *Median* - 15.5 years

5. Income   *Median* - $18,381 (Total Household)

B. *WHERE DO THEY COME FROM (Head of Household)*

1. Previous Place of Resident

Same Town	State's Major City	State's Balance	Out of State[2]	Total
8.4	3.9	41.4	46.3	100.0

2. Previous Housing Type

Single Family	Multi Family	Other[3]	Total
25.9	68.7	5.3	100.0

3. Previous Form of Tenure

Owner	Renter	Other[4]	Total
21.4	75.3	3.3	100.0

4. Distance Traveled Commuting   25.5 miles (Median)

Notes: (1)   Includes students, retired, housewives, unemployed (0.6%)
         (2)   Includes "out of country" (no greater than 2.0%)
         (3)   Includes dormitory and two family
         (4)   Includes "lives with family"

Source: CUPR Survey 1972-1973

EXHIBIT 1-6. SOCIAL AND OCCUPATIONAL CHARACTERISTICS OF HIGH RISE APARTMENTS
(Median Rent: 1 Bedroom $268
2 Bedrooms $310)

A. *WHO LIVES THERE (Head of Household)*

1. Occupation

Professional, Managerial, Clerical, Sales	Craftsmen, Operatives, Service, Laborers	Other[1]	Total
83.9	2.8	13.3	100.0

2. Age   *Median - 46.4 years*

3. Sex

Male	Female	Total
82.9	17.1	100.0

4. Education   *Median - 15.8 years*

5. Income   *Median - $20,108 (Total Household)*

B. *WHERE DO THEY COME FROM (Head of Household)*

1. Previous Place of Residence

Same Town	State's Major City	State's Balance	Out of State[2]	Total
11.3	4.9	31.4	52.4	100.0

2. Previous Housing Type

Single Family	Multi Family	Other[3]	Total
37.7	59.9	2.4	100.0

3. Previous Form of Tenure

Owner	Renter	Other[4]	Total
29.9	67.1	3.0	100.0

4. Distance Traveled Commuting   9.4 miles (Median)

Notes: (1)   Includes students, retired, housewives, unemployed (1.0%)
(2)   Includes "out of country" (no greater than 2.0%)
(3)   Includes dormitory and two family
(4)   Includes "lives with family"

Source: CUPR Survey 1972-1973

16

EXHIBIT 1-7. SOCIAL AND OCCUPATIONAL CHARACTERISTICS OF SINGLE FAMILY* RESIDENTS
(Median Value: $27,800)

A. *WHO LIVES THERE (Head of Household)*

1. Occupation

Professional, Managerial, Clerical, Sales	Craftsmen, Operatives, Service, Laborers	Other[1]	Total
60.8	35.5	3.7	100.0

2. Age   *Median - 32.0 years*

3. Sex

Male	Female	Total
95.0	5.0	100.0

4. Education   *Median - 12.8 years*

5. Income   *Median - $12,869 (Total Household)*

B. *WHERE DO THEY COME FROM (Head of Household)*

1. Previous Place of Residence

Same Town	State's Major City	State's Balance	Out of[2] State	Total
20.8	2.2	51.2	25.8	100.0

2. Previous Housing Type

Single Family	Multi Family	Other[3]	Total
47.7	47.9	4.4	100.0

3. Previous Form of Tenure

Owner	Renter	Other[4]	Total
33.9	62.6	3.5	100.0

4. Distance Traveled Commuting   15.0 miles (median)

Notes: (1) Includes students, retired, housewives, unemployed (0.5%)
(2) Includes "out of country" (no greater than 2.0%)
(3) Includes dormitory and two family
(4) Includes "lives with family"
(*) Under $30,000 in selling price

Source: CUPR Survey 1972-1973.

17

a secondary worker tend to reside in garden apartments. The higher
the level of education, the less likely are households to live in
garden apartments or single family homes, and the more likely they
are to locate in townhouses and highrises.

By Housing Type

We may further describe brief profiles of the demographic characteristics to be anticipated by housing type. Garden apartment households are likely to be of lower income, larger in size, younger,
and are more commonly headed by females or those not employed.**
Garden apartment residents frequently have moved there from within
the locality or the state in which the development is located; both
adults usually work, and their educational attainments are inferior
to those of residents in the other rental housing type we studied.

Townhouse households are generally characterized by professional
employment and high income; they are also smaller, have migrated
from out-of-state, are of former multi-family occupancy, are
usually white, have only one worker, and have higher educational
attainments.

High rise apartments usually house professionals with higher
incomes, smaller and older households, out-of-state migrants, and
former apartment dwellers; they are less likely to have second
workers, and have high educational attainments.

In modestly priced single family homes, households are generally
blue collar, lower income, larger, younger, headed by a male,
former in-state residents, former home dwellers (though not
necessarily former homeowners), white, rarely have secondary household workers, and have a lower educational attainment.

The Garden Apartment Development Over Time

A major concern of local authorities faced with the possibility
of a new garden apartment development is what will happen to the

----

*(Continued from previous page)

also in Newark. These structures are not included in the results
reported in this summary. An attempt was also made, using multiple
regression analysis, to predict the racial composition of sample
developments. In general, it was found that the racial composition
of the municipality was the primary determinant of development racial
patterns. But the sample of blacks is at best small and its distribution skewed.

**Widows, retired, etc.

the project as it ages.[20] Simply put, the immediate cost-benefit
ratios may be quite attractive, but will they be sustained over
time? There are many elaborations of this question. One of the
most significant is whether the basic maintenance of the structure
will sustain the quality of its rent roll and of its tenantry in
years to come. A second and perhaps even more salient problem is
whether the initial youthfulness of the child population in relatively
new units - a larger study shows approximately half are under kindergarten age - will not eventually result in a very large addition to
the public school register. These important considerations in part
account for some local zoning authorities' reluctance to approve this
type of development.

In order to provide some insight into these concerns, we compared
surveys conducted with occupants of approximately 1,100 dwelling
units in eight garden developments in 1963 and a resurvey in 1972.
What happened to these developments in the nine years between our
two surveys? (See Exhibits 1-8, 1-9).

School Age Children

The most significant finding in viewing the garden apartment over
time is the relative stability of the school-age children multipliers.
In 1963 there were approximately 3.7 children per 100 one bedroom
units; in 1972 the figure is 4.9. An even greater consistency is
noted in the two bedroom units, i.e., 39 per 100 units in 1963
versus 37.5 in 1972.

*For cost revenue purposes the initial number of school-age children
can be expected to hold constant.* If a one hundred unit complex
was built in this area of New Jersey in 1963, in an 80/20 ratio of
one to two bedroom units, approximately 10.76 school children could
be anticipated; in 1972 the figure would be 11.42. The consistency
over time is more than adequate for local planning purposes.

Age and Occupational Characteristics

The garden apartment's availability as a way station in the life
cycle typically attracts relatively young people at an early stage
of their personal domestic relationships, only to graduate them
fairly shortly into more permanent types of housing facilities. This
has become an even more pronounced function of this type of dwelling
unit in recent years.

In 1963 the garden apartment was primarily inhabited by heads of
household aged 26 to 35. Movement out in search of a single family
house was delayed until well into the early thirties. In 1972,
approximately nine years later, a much younger clientele is making
use of the way station; almost one quarter of the heads of household

EXHIBIT 1-8. THE GARDEN APARTMENT OVER TIME: SIMILAR DEVELOPMENTS SURVEYED BOTH IN 1963 AND 1972

County	Municipality	Development	Number of Units Contacted in 1963	Number of[1] Units Contacted in 1972
Middlesex	Highland Park Borough	1. Orchard Gardens	209	201
		2. Montgomery Apartments	192	185
		3. Adelaide Gardens	200	198
		4. Old Queens (Levy Apts.)[2]	30	46
		5. Riverview Apts.[3]	48	45
	Edison Township	6. 311 Division and Greenwood	20	20
		7. Penn and Ovington	20	20
Somerset	Franklin Township	8. Pine Grove Manor	398	369
	TOTALS		1,117	1,084

Notes: 1. Differences in number of units between 1963 and 1972 is due to different field procedures.
2. This development was called Levy Apartments in 1963 but was later renamed Old Queens. It had 46 units in 1963, but only 30 were complete at the time of that survey.
3. Cooperation was refused by the management in 1972 and interviews were conducted using telephone numbers obtained through reverse directories.

Source: CUPR Survey 1972-1973

EXHIBIT 1-9. SCHOOL AGE CHILDREN
IN GARDEN APARTMENT DEVELOPMENTS OVER TIME

	Number of Bedrooms		
Year	*1 Bedroom*	*2 Bedrooms*	*3 Bedrooms*
1963	.037	.390	1.03*
1972	.049	.375	1.31*

*Primarily one development; multipliers not reported in other sections of this article.

Source: CUPR Survey 1972-1973.

are under 25. This change reflects both the growing independence on the part of the more youthful population, who leave the nest at an earlier age and in this community (Highland Park), with a large university nearby, the movement away from the institutional influence of dormitory housing (See Exhibit 1-10).*

A portion of the reshaped household which is sometimes overlooked, however, is the upper end. After children leave for school and retirement approaches, there is a desire for smaller accommodations. The garden apartment is now becoming a repository for the aged. Occupancy over the decade has remained approximately the same for the age group 50 to 65, but the proportion of residents 65 and over in this set of eight garden apartments has almost tripled. This phenomenon is not unusual. Our larger survey of garden apartment developments throughout the state reveals a similarly high proportion of elderly and female headed households; a considerable portion of the latter are widows.

Occupational characteristics have also changed. While the proportion of managers/proprietors (9.4), clerical/sales (14.1), and craftsmen/ foremen (7.1) has remained essentially the same, the percentage of

---

*There have also been slight changes in the age structure of the general population over the period 1960 to 1970 which reflect similar trends.

EXHIBIT 1-10. AGE STRUCTURE AND OCCUPATION OF GARDEN
APARTMENT RESIDENTS OVER TIME

A. AGE OF HEAD OF HOUSEHOLD

	1963	*1972*
Under 25 years	5.2	22.5
26-35	48.4	28.0
36-49	25.7	18.3
50-64	13.9	13.5
65 and over	6.8	17.7
Total Responding	100.0 (n=308) Median 33.2	100.0 (n=622) Median 35.9

B. OCCUPATION OF HEAD OF HOUSEHOLD
(PRIMARY WAGE EARNER)

Professional, Technical and Kindred Workers	48.9	24.0

Managers, Officials and Pro-
    prietors (Except Farm
    Salaried, Self-Employed)
	9.9	9.4

Clerical, Sales and Kindred Workers	14.0	14.4
Craftsmen, Foremen and Kindred Workers	9.5	7.1
Operatives and Kindred Workers	4.6	10.9

Service Workers (Except
    Protective Service,
    Waiters, Bartenders, Cooks)
	2.3	5.4

Laborers (Including Farm)	1.1	2.5

Miscellaneous (Students,
    Retired, Unemployed,
    Armed Forces)
	9.7	26.3

Total Responding	100.0 (n=476)	94.1 (n=631)

Source: CUPR Survey 1972-1973

professional/technical workers (23.5) is barely half what is was a
decade ago. Instead the number of semi-skilled,* service workers
and laborers has doubled (18.5) and the number of non-workers
(students and retired) has more than doubled, with the largest
increase among the retired. The statewide survey also indicates
that garden apartments house the smallest number of professionals
and managers, and the greatest proportion of retired among the
housing types we surveyed.

Journey to Work and Previous Residence

The current journey to work estimates among garden apartment
residents lend some insight into changing resident profiles within
this dwelling type (Exhibit 1-11). There has been an approximate 6
percent increase among people who commute to a place of employment
which is less than 10 miles away. There has also been an increase
among those who do not commute because they no longer are employed.
Together, increases in these percentages have reduced the total
number of residents who travel more than 10 miles to work by almost
one-half. When cross-tabulated by age (not shown) it becomes
obvious that residents have taken a local job at a reduced salary,
a choice available to the young; and there is a growing proportion
of elderly who have left the job market.

Garden apartments now appear to draw a substantial proportion of
residents from local areas. Currently there are barely half as
many out-of-state residents as there were ten years ago. While
there have been some small increases in those coming from large
in-state cities and other in-state suburban areas, by far the
largest increase is among those moving from elsewhere in the same
town. During the ten year period this percentage more than doubled.

These data again reflect our figures for the state as a whole:
garden apartment residents travel fewer miles than residents of
any other dwelling type to their place of employment, and they
have by far the greatest percentage of occupants drawn from the
local area.

Summary

The obvious conclusion to be drawn here is that although the
garden apartment is no longer the domain of a substantial body
of professionals, its new entrants, the young adults and the
elderly, have not altered the unit's municipal cost picture.

----

    *operatives

EXHIBIT 1-11. JOURNEY TO WORK AND PREVIOUS RESIDENCE OF GARDEN
APARTMENT RESIDENT OVER TIME

A. JOURNEY TO WORK OF HEAD OF HOUSEHOLD

Home-to-Work Radius in Miles	1964	1973
0-5	37.1	40.0
5-10	14.2	17.7
10+	38.2	22.8
Not Applicable (Retired, Student Unemployed, Etc.)	10.5	19.5
Total Responding	100.0 (n=513)	100.0 (n=631)

B. PREVIOUS RESIDENCE OF HEAD OF HOUSEHOLD

Same Town	10.0	22.5
State's Major Cities	4.6	5.5
Other Areas of the State	40.8	51.8
Total State	55.4	79.8
Out of State	44.6	20.2
Total Responding	100.0 (n=522)	100.0 (n=631)

Source: CUPR Survey

24

School age children multipliers and the resultant municipal cash flow have remained almost identical for one and two bedroom units in this ten year period.*

The high degree of comparability of garden apartment tenantry regardless of the age of development is particularly noteworthy. The aging units seem to stay abreast of the market.

Bedroom Multipliers in Perspective

High Rise (Exhibit 1-12)

Few studies have reported total household size for high rise structures. Our own findings are 1.82 and 2.48 persons per unit for one and two bedroom units respectively. This clearly is less than those reported for garden apartments and reflects considerable difference in occupant characteristics. While these findings are remarkably consistent for each development surveyed, continuous auditing over time is called for.

Data on public school age children are also difficult to place in perspective. Most of the literature does not count the number of school age children by bedroom type for high rise structures, but provides average figures for all units within a structure, without regard to their size. As we have indicated earlier, .012 and .181 school age children may be found in one and two bedroom high rise units respectively.

If an equal distribution of one and two bedroom units is assumed (a common distribution in our survey) approximately 10 school age children would be found per 100 unit high rise structure. This figure is just slightly lower than that reported by Del Guidice[21] (one school age child for every 7.6 dwelling units) and identical to the conclusions both of Melamed[22] and the Westchester County Planning Board[23] (10 school age children per 100 dwelling units); while only slightly higher than that reported for Fairfax (Va.)[24] and Montgomery (Md.) Counties (0.09).[25]

The high rise structure, with its low number of total household members and of school age children and its high average dwelling unit value, continues to be a very favorable asset in terms of municipal cost revenue.

_____

*There is no discussion of figures obtained for three bedroom garden apartment units. Most were found within a single development which converted over the decade from co-op to rental tenure.

EXHIBIT 1-12. HIGH RISE SCHOOL-AGE CHILDREN MULTIPLIERS: SUMMARY

Originator of Study

Unit Type	Westchester County[1] (1971)	Del Guidice[2] (1963)	Holley[3] Summary (1966)	CUPR Survey[4] (1973)	Fairfax (Va.)[5] Montgomery Counties[6] (Md.) (1965, 1966)
Studio	--	--	--	0.000	--
One Bedroom	--	--	--	0.012	--
Two Bedrooms	--	--	--	0.181	--
Three Bedrooms	--	--	--	--	--
All Units	0.10	0.13	0.08	--	0.09

Sources:
1. Westchester County, N.Y. Planning Board. School Taxes and Residential Development. White Plains, November 1971.

2. Dominic Del Guidice. "Cost-Revenue Implications of High-Rise Apartments." Urban Land, February 1963, pp. 3-5.

3. Paul N. Holley. School Enrollment by Housing Type. Chicago, Ill.: American Society of Planning Officials, Planning Advisory Service Report No. 210, 1966.

4. CUPR Survey 1972-1973.

5. Fairfax County Planning Division. Student Contribution from Apartments and Mobile Homes. Fairfax, Virginia. 1966.

6. Maryland-National Capital Park and Planning Commission. "Dwelling Unit Density, Population and Potential Public School Enrollment Yield by Existing Zoning Classification for Montgomery and Prince Georges Counties." Silver Spring, Maryland. 1965.

Garden Apartment (Exhibit 1-13)

Total household size figures found for garden apartments in this
study (1.90 [1 Bedroom] and 2.8 [2 Bedroom]) are almost identical to
those recently reported in an extensive study completed by the
Monmouth County, New Jersey Planning Board.[26]   In their survey of
726 garden apartment units distributed among five planning areas,
they found 1.85 and 2.83 residents per household respectively.

Garden apartment school age children multipliers reported by our
study are about as large (i.e., approximately .04 [1 Bedroom];
.40 [2 Bedroom]) in 1973 as they were in 1964. This was observed
in a much expanded sample (n≈3,600) as well as in units within
similar developments over time (n≈700).

The figures reported here for one bedroom units (0.046) are higher
than those found by the Monmouth County, New Jersey Planning Board
(.020) and by Robert Burchell in a 1972 study of the Twin Rivers
Planned Unit Development (0.010);[27] the two bedroom figures (.344)
are slightly lower than those of the Monmouth County Planning
Board (0.420) and higher than those of Twin Rivers (0.293). If,
however, an 80/20 ratio of one to two bedroom units is assumed, a
figure of 10.6 children per 100 garden apartment units is very
close to the 13.0 figures reported by Monmouth County and the 11.9
figure observed in the Twin Rivers PUD. It is also identical to
the total obtained by the National Association of Home Builders in
their original 1963 study.[28]

Townhouse (Exhibit 1-14)

There is a paucity of literature that summarizes either the total
household size of townhouses or the number of school age children
by bedrooms. For total household size, the findings of this study
(i.e., 2.68, 3.35 and 3.74 persons per unit for 2, 3 and 4 bedroom
units) must await future verification.

The townhouse is a comparative newcomer to suburban areas and
school age children have been examined only generally in the
Fairfax (Va.) and Montgomery County (Md.) studies.[29] Robert
Burchell, in the Twin Rivers PUD study, provided preliminary
figures (n=603) for 2, 3 and 4 bedroom townhouse units. Figures
found in Burchell's study are roughly comparable to what we have
reported here, as is indicated in Exhibit 15. Carl Norcross has
recently compiled statistics on attitudes and resident profiles
of townhouse residents, but he did not investigate total household size or number of school age children per se.[30]

The multipliers obtained in this study and in Burchell's study are
also quite comparable, although the developments under comparison
differ slightly in their allocation of 2, 3 and 4 bedroom units.

EXHIBIT 1-13. GARDEN APARTMENT SCHOOL AGE CHILDREN MULTIPLIERS: SUMMARY

			Originator of Study				
Unit Type	Burchell[1] (1972)	Monmouth County Planning Board[2] (1973)	Sternlieb[3] (1964)	CUPR Survey[4] (1973)	Holley Summary[5] (1966)	Fairfax County,Va.[6] (1966)	Rolde (NAHB)[7] (1962)
One Bedroom	0.010	0.020	0.037	0.046	--	--	--
Two Bedrooms	0.293	0.420	0.390	0.344	--	--	--
Three Bedrooms	--	--	1.030	--	--	--	--
All Units	0.119	0.130	--	--	0.30	0.21	0.110

1. Robert W. Burchell. Planned Unit Development: New Communities American Style. New Brunswick, N.J.: Rutgers University, Center for Urban Policy Research, 1972.

2. Monmouth County, N.J. Planning Board. Multi-Family Housing in Monmouth County Freehold, January 1973.

3. George Sternlieb. The Garden Apartment Development: A Municipal Cost-Revenue Analysis. New Brunswick, New Jersey: Bureau of Economic Research, Rutgers University, 1964 (Condensed in Urban Land, September 1964).

4. CUPR Survey 1972-1973.

5. Paul N. Holley. School Enrollment by Housing Type. Chicago, Ill.: American Society of Planning Officials, Planning Advisory Service Report No. 210, 1966).

6. Fairfax County Planning Division. Student Contribution from Apartments and Mobile Homes. Fairfax, Virginia. 1966.

7. Rolde (Robert L.) Company. Garden Apartments and School Age Children. Washington, D.C.: National Association of Home Builders, 1962.

EXHIBIT 1-14. TOWNHOUSE SCHOOL AGE CHILDREN MULTIPLIERS:
SUMMARY

	Originator of Study			
Unit Type	*Burchell*[1] *(1972)*	*CUPR Survey*[2] *(1972-1973)*	*Holley Summary*[3] *(1966)*	*Barton-Aschman*[4] *Summary (1970)*
Two Bedrooms	0.258	0.220	--	--
Three Bedrooms	0.440	0.665	--	--
Four Bedrooms	0.896	1.026	--	--
All Units	0.454	--	0.820	1.28

Sources: 1. Robert W. Burchell, Planned Unit Development: New Communities American Style. New Brunswick, N.J.: Rutgers University, Center for Urban Policy Research, 1972.

2. CUPR Survey 1972-1973.

3. Paul N. Holley. School Enrollment by Housing Type. Chicago, Ill.: American Society of Planning Officials, Planning Advisory Service Report No. 210, 1966.

4. Barton-Aschman Associates. The Barrington, Illinois Area: A Cost-Revenue Analysis of Land Alternatives. Chicago, 1970. (Condensed in Stuart, Darwin C. and Teska, Robert B. "Who Pays for What: A Cost Revenue Analysis of Suburban Land Use Alternatives," Urban Land, March, 1971), pp. 3-16.

Burchell found approximately 0.454 school age children per townhouse unit in a PUD whose bedrooms were distributed 30/55/15 for 2, 3 and 4 bedroom units. In our study we found .500 school age children per unit in townhouse developments with an overall ratio of 40/55/5 for 2, 3 and 4 bedroom units. Both of these figures are substantially lower than those summarized by Holley for Fairfax (0.65) and Montgomery Counties (1.00).

Single Family (Exhibit 1-15)

The findings for single family homes pertain to developments with a 1972 advertised price of less than $30,000 for a three bedroom unit. This limit was specified because this type of unit is growing rapidly in New Jersey in the outer reaches of metropolitan areas, frequently in sections formerly devoted to recreation/retirement where second or seasonal homes have been predominant.*

In terms of total household size the figures of 3.31 and 3.72 persons per unit for three and four bedroom units have not been verified by equivalent studies. The findings for school age children do, however, have a basis of comparison. The figure for three bedroom units (0.626 public school age children) is about the same magnitude as the figures reported by Barton-Aschman Associates for both Fox Point (0.50) and Barrington (0.52) Illinois.[31] The figure for four bedroom units (1.293) is somewhat lower, however, than those reported (2.02 and 1.63 respectively) for these two developments.

If we assume a 60/40 ratio of three to four bedroom units in our developments, the combined school-age children figure would be 0.90 for the single family developments observed in this study. This figure is almost identical to that found by Holley (0.94)[32] and certainly within the range of the results reported for all units in Barrington, Illinois (1.03) and in Fairfax County (1.08).

For the Future

The information provided here will hopefully be of use to professional planners whose daily tasks include residential municipal cost-revenue analysis. The data are drawn from a large sample and have been deliberately detailed and annotated to offer the widest range of possible uses.

Certain methodological improvements must be made in the field as a whole if work in this area is to progress. This particularly holds true for estimates of total household size in all dwelling types, and of school age children in high rise and townhouse units. The following are, in our opinion, critical improvements:

———————

*In addition, the choice was made in order to secure as close comparability as possible in basic carrying costs of housing.

30

EXHIBIT 1-15.   SINGLE FAMILY SCHOOL AGE CHILDREN MULTIPLIERS:
SUMMARY

	Originator of Study			
Unit Type	*Barton-Aschman Associates (1970)[1]* *Fox Point, Ill.*	*Barrington, Ill.*	*CUPR Survey[2]* *(1972-1973)**	*Holley Summary[3]* *(1966)*
Two Bedrooms	--	0.20	--	--
Three Bedrooms	0.50	0.52	0.626	--
Four Bedrooms	2.02	1.63	1.293	--
Five Bedrooms	2.28	2.19	--	--
Six Bedrooms	2.60	--	--	--
All Units	2.10	1.03	--	0.94

*New developments of less than $30,000 for a three bedroom single family
unit.

Sources: 1.   Barton-Aschman Associates.   The Barrington, Illinois Area;
A Cost-Revenue Analysis of Land Alternatives. Chicago, 1970.
(Condensed in Stuart, Darwin C. and Teska, Robert B. "Who
Pays for What: A Cost Revenue Analysis of Suburban Land
Use Alternatives," Urban Land, March, 1971), pp. 3-16.

2.   CUPR Survey 1972-1973.

3.   Paul N. Holley.   School Enrollment by Housing Type.   Chicago,
Ill.: American Society of Planning Officials, Planning
Advisory Service Report No. 210, 1966.

1. In reporting results of bedroom multipliers, the size of the sample must always be reported. This is critical for assigning weights, if one wishes to group multiple findings or revise multipliers based on additional or more recent information.

2. Both school age children and total household size must be reported by number of bedrooms. The bedroom variable appears too versatile not to be employed regularly.

3. In reporting figures for housing types within developments or municipalities as a whole, the distribution of bedrooms must be reported. Otherwise the findings for all units of a certain housing type cannot be placed in perspective.

4. Multiple findings by housing type should not be grouped. Those in the planning field will require this base data to predict the municipal cost-revenue impact of proposed developments -- frequently in suburban or exurban areas.

5. Surveys of total household size or school age children for high rise public housing developments or low rise, low income co-ops must not appear within simple averages for suburban housing of similar construction type. The social characteristics of occupants of this housing are too unique to be included in the general findings for garden apartment or high rise units.[33] "Averaging" this type of information detracts from, rather than adding to, the accuracy of the information available by housing type.

NONEDUCATIONAL COSTS

The second section of this investigation focuses on local costs other than education. The object was to view from both macro and micro levels the impact of growth upon municipal expenditure patterns. In most cases, however, *the population base to which growth contributes proved to be a much larger force than the change increment itself*. Thus, while it would have been ideal to say a certain type of development imposed a certain level of cost, if one considers the effects of concurrent development and an existing population base, such isolation and assignment of cost to one development is an impossibility.

The relationships investigated in the previous sections of this study do enable one to equate some level of municipal expenditure to a particular development, however. The characteristics of a development which determine its number of school children also determine its total population. Thus, the bedroom count for dwelling units within developments, as it did in the case of school children, dominates all characteristics in predicting total household size. An estimate of total average household size times the number of units in a development equals the population to be introduced

locally. The population introduced locally times per capita cost
of local municipal services is an indication of municipal costs
introduced by that development.

While to a certain degree this approach ignores costs specifically
related to a type of development, discussions with municipal officials revealed that local cost variation is so slight for low rise
developments (garden apartments, townhouses, and single family
homes) that the per capita figure over time is a more than adequate
assessment of cost. In the case of the high rise structure, except
for equipment increases in the area of fire service, the development
form does not present itself as a unique local cost over and above
the local per capita figure.

In relying on the per capita municipal expenditure figure as an
estimate of assignable cost, based on the number of local residents
a development produces, one must be cognizant of the variation of
this index with growth and its relation to both the direction of
growth and to the population base upon which growth grafts its
effects of change.

In the chapter dealing with municipal services, multiple regression
analysis is used to select and signify the relative importance both
of population change and its direction as a determinant of per
capita municipal expenditures. Since the impact of growth is to a
large degree a function of population size, communities were also
partitioned according to the magnitude of their population base.
Thus established is the importance of size and growth as a future
indicator of municipal expenditure, the separable classes of growth
which exist within a state, and for the communities that fall within
these various groupings, their significantly different expenditure
patterns.

Once population base and both direction and rates of growth have
been isolated as significant determinants of municipal cost, the
expenditure profiles characteristic of a particular size and class
of city (the latter categorized by growth) are analyzed across
basic areas of municipal service (government administration, public
safety, public works, health and welfare, recreation and culture,
and statutory and unclassified). The means and medians of total
per capita, partitioned per capita and percent change in per capita
municipal expenditures are calculated for each grouping of cities
and their variation over the period 1960 to 1970 is analyzed.

The examination of such variation was deliberate, detailed and
tedious - in some instances it approached myopic concern. In this
case, the level of detail was deemed necessary as this study is one
of the few instances that a large number of small communities have
been investigated in terms of municipal costs and revenues and
similarly one of the few times the dual partitioning (both by
growth rate and population base) has been employed. Hopefully,

the variation documented here will prove fruitful to those who proceed in the attempts to model municipal expenditure patterns employing techniques other than "straight line" extrapolation.

Even though growth is an important determinant of municipal expenditures, it is just one of many forces impacting on local costs. While within the field of public finance it may now seem an appropriate time to dissect the impact of growth, still other variables affecting the municipal fisc cannot be ignored.

A following chapter of the study views demographic, social and economic characteristics of communities in an attempt to gauge their effect on per capita expenditures. Again multiple regression analysis was used within a series of partitioned sets of communities to isolate both the significance and relative impact of a community's socio-economic profile on its per capita municipal expenditures.

The final portion of the study concludes with a description of how this work's findings may be used by public officials and thus serves as a bridge between theoretical explorations and practical policy applications.

It must be remembered that the second task of the study was to examine municipal costs and not costs related to education. With such an assumption, the impact of special taxing districts is minimal and effectively can be ignored. Nonschool special taxing districts in New Jersey are found primarily in the public works sector (garbage, sewer, light and water) and to a small degree in the area of public safety in the form of fire protection. Only the latter, as a special district, has increased significantly since 1960 and is found proportionately in cities of 1,000 to 25,000 across all growth rates. Its impact on trend analysis while significant is evenly distributed.

The conclusions of this section fall into two major parts, which will be discussed separately. The first discusses the results of the observed relationship between population growth and municipal expenditures. The second analyzes the relationships between municipal expenditures being impacted upon by variables other than growth.

The Impact of Growth on Municipal Costs

Disregarding both direction of growth and community size, it was found that per capita costs increase as communities alter their population base. Viewing communities via an "averaged" growth rate for both increases and declines, extremely small and large communities cost more to run on a per capita basis than intermediate size communities. Also, it was found that large cities that are slowly growing spend less per capita than large cities that are declining and finally, that small municipalities either growing or declining spend a similar amount per capita.

When, as detailed in the final section, the averaging method is looked at more critically, a much richer texture to the variation of the per capita curve was observed. This caused us to question the explanation of municipal expenditures via a straight line model which heavily biased general findings of expenditure variation by trends which were more characteristic of large, slow growth communities than those of other growth rates. The following results, while in basic agreement with earlier findings, modify them somewhat and provide the detail from which new models of expenditure variation should be specified.

Total Per Capita Variation

We have found that the variation in total per capita municipal expenditure across increasing levels of population base is not a straight line function. Rather, the left hand edge of the curve across all growth rates is hyperbolic in nature expressing a relationship of initially high per capita costs in small cities which decrease as city size increases to a trough at the community size level of approximately 10,000. From here, in declining and slow growth communities, costs begin to increase and continue hyperbolic throughout the size ranges of 10,000 to 25,000, 25,000 to 50,000, and 50,000+ to levels of expenditure that existed at the smaller size ranges of 100 to 1,000 and 1,000 to 5,000.

Again, in moderately growing communities expenditures are initially higher in small communities, yet the trough reached at the 10,000 community size range is maintained and per capita expenditures remain relatively stable throughout the remaining categories of community size. In rapidly growing communities per capita costs continue to be higher for small communities yet decrease significantly as population base increases.

Per Capita Allocation

Per capita allocation according to growth rate and population base also displays characteristic trends. In small declining and slow growth communities, 85 percent of the budget is devoted to the three main service areas, i.e., government administration, public safety, and public works. Over two-thirds of this expenditure allocation in small communities is funneled to government administration and public works. As community size increases, the three areas dominate to a lesser degree (70 percent),* yet public safety grows in importance and in communities in excess of 50,000, soon approaches 40 percent of the local per capita expenditure. To a large extent

---

*The importance of more recreation health/welfare and expenses becomes more visible.

35

the new dominance of public safety is at the expense of the previously dominant public works function.

Similar allocation patterns are in evidence for the three major service areas in moderately growing communities. The decline of the public works function is not so marked, nor is the increase of the local public safety budget as in other groups. In small, moderately growing communities, public safety expenditures are 20 percent less than declining communities and public works 20 percent more.

In rapidly growing communities allocation patterns are less clear than for other growth groupings. In small, rapidly growing communities, the three areas of major service dominate (85 percent of the budget) to the same level that they did in declining and slow growth communities. Yet they are equally important (i.e., approximately 28 percent each) and equal apportionment continues throughout increasing classification of size.

In all communities recreation allocations seem to be more a function of population size than of growth rate. As a percent of the budget they tend to increase from 4 percent to 10 percent as city size approaches 25,000 and then decrease to 7 to 8 percent for communities in excess of 50,000.

Throughout the spectrum of communities, health and welfare expenditures occupy the smallest percent of the budget (2 to 4 percent) and vary slightly within this range, negatively with growth rate and positively with city size. In communities in excess of 50,000 population, the health and welfare allocation increases dramatically to 8 percent of the budget both in declining and slowly growing communities. Finally, statutory contributions also increase with city size and decrease with growth rate in similar fashion as the health and welfare budget allocation, yet are frequently twice (6 to 8 percent) the magnitude of the latter.

One of the most difficult areas of all in which to draw trends is in the area of changes in service emphasis as a function of growth. The patterns of all growth groupings are much more pronounced than those of any individual growth partition utilized here. The most obvious trend observed was a clear increase in the amount of change a budget undergoes with increasing rates of growth. Declining and slowly growing communities maintain fairly similar allocation patterns, whereas rapidly growing communities vary expenditure emphases quite significantly.

A second obvious characteristic of changes in program allocation as a function of growth was the similarity of pattern in terms of emphasis or deemphasis across all growth rates. There has been positive emphasis as a result of the maturing of cities in the program areas of government administration, public safety, recreation and culture, and statutory contributions. There has been general decline in percent allocation in the areas of public works and health and welfare. To a certain degree this latter finding is misleading as it well may be a surrogate for an increasing level of intergovernmental participation in these two areas. With increasing federal and state support of various public works activities and the county government in New Jersey increasing its role in welfare activities, the extent of deemphasis by local communities is difficult to gauge.

The Impact of Variables Other Than Growth on Municipal Costs

The social class characteristic that most strongly affects per capita expenditures is the percentage of families below the poverty level; this factor was found to increase per capita expenditures in growing cities. Two life cycle characteristics were also found to cause a variation in per capita expenditures: (1) young families setting up housekeeping facilities; (2) and the "empty nesters" who no longer face the expenditure requirements of a full family. We have found that, as hypothesized, young families tend to restrict the level of per capita expenditures, whereas the presence of older families tends to increase municipal expenditures.

Fiscal pressures generated through ethnicity-based preference patterns was studied in terms of the presence of minority group families and persons of foreign stock. For cities growing in population, we found that the presence of minority group families increased expenditures. Similarly, foreign stock families elevated the expenditure level for growing cities but lowered the level for cities in decline.

The private economic sector has been found to produce sizable impact upon the municipal fisc. Using the commercial or industrial employee density as the indicator of this characteristic, it was found that both commercial and industrial enterprises increase per capita expenditures. Further, it was found that commercial enterprises generate higher expenditure requirements than do industrial firms.

The residential portion of the private sector's economic base was identified in the study by nine classes of housing. The results showed that the totality of social characteristics surrounding duplex units, structures with five to nine dwelling units, and structures with nineteen to forty-nine dwelling units produced for each housing class significant positive impacts upon the level of per capita expenditures. Independently of structural configuration, the rental form of tenure was found to permit an increase in per capita expenditures.

Several characteristics associated with the local governmental structure have been found to produce significant independent impacts upon municipal expenditures. Most significant was the level of the per capita equalized property tax base. An increase in the level of the per capita equalized property tax base increases, in turn, the level of per capita expenditures. As a major cause of this relationship, the post World War II suburbanization pattern has been found to cluster high value commercial and industrial tax ratables within some municipalities without at the same time driving municipal expenditures to a level requiring as high a tax rate as in industrially-poor municipalities.

Some municipalities within the state have access to large non-property tax revenue sources. Most relevant in this case is the presence of public utility tax revenues. It was found that cities with higher concentrations of public utilities property used the associated revenue to increase per capita expenditures; this analysis was done on a dollar of public utilities revenue producing an additional dollar of expenditure basis.

Governmental form and its impact on local per capita cost were analyzed in terms of the presence or absence of a dependent school district. It was found that municipalities with dependent school districts had on the average a $16 per capita higher municipal expenditure level than municipalities with independent school systems.

MUNICIPAL/SCHOOL COST REVENUE ANALYSIS: A SELECTED EXAMPLE

While to a certain degree the information summarized previously advances the state of the art for the social scientist and academician, of what practical value is this study to the local municipal official or planner? The answer, of course, lies in the figures obtained for school age children and total household size from the first portion of the study and the reliability of the simple unadjusted per capita figures from the study's second half.

The school-age children multiplier is applied to units by number of bedrooms to estimate school costs; total household size is also applied to units by number of bedrooms to estimate municipal, county and deduction costs.

The first task in any municipal cost-revenue investigation is the problem of defining both municipal and school costs and determining the appropriate charging methods. These are subject to a variety of interpretations and approaches, principally revolving around the differences between marginal and average costing. Should the additional residents brought into the municipality be thought of as costing the town just those additional dollars associated with their advent or a proportion of the total based on the town's average costs?

It appears that for the general case, average costing, except in exceptional circumstances, is more useful for long-range planning. An area of growing population which is not planning for eventual expansion of its municipal and school services is living off capital and sooner or later will have to accept further expenditure. Moreover, this necessary cost of expansion should not be blamed on the last straw, but should be attributed as a consequence of long-term growth. Thus, for most situations, average costing is probably most useful as a building block for immediate impact studies.

Another minor issue also arises in regard to school costs. Should the total expenditure per student be employed as the basic cost, regardless of revenue source, or simply that cost which is allocated to the municipality in terms of the property tax mechanism? Again, for immediate impact studies the direct property tax cost implication has probably the most conceptual clarity and is the most useful. This is the cost that directly impacts the local resident.

To generate the basic building blocks of cost, then, an average cost methodology is recommended, where the cost of service is defined as that expenditure which must be financed through the property tax system. The examples which follow employ this property tax approach.

There are, however, certain inherent difficulties in the property tax approach.[34] Despite the number of studies that have been done, municipal cost-revenue analysis appears to involve a number of serious methodological problems. It is at best a complicated procedure to which too little theoretical attention has been given. This lack of theoretical development is not surprising in view of the fact that most studies are carried out for or by local planning agencies and school districts with an eye to immediate zoning decisions. The issue of appropriate cost allocation and measurement is a crucial one, as yet not resolved in favor of a particular methodology.

It is in fact quite difficult to assign educational and municipal service costs to areas or land uses served.

> ...the study of costs and revenues in relation to the way that land is used (either categories of use or patterns of development) is much more involved. Research of this kind which is limited in scope is manageable. Such questions as determining the net costs of residential subdivision development at various densities have been satisfactorily handled by a number of analysts. But if there is to be full understanding of the fiscal impact of existing or proposed policies, comprehensive studies on a citywide or metropolitan area-wide basis are required. And it is here that there are so many variables involved as to defy the means presently in the analyst's hands. Not only are there a variety of uses, with varying

characteristics in many separate locations, but there may
also be several political jurisdictions involved, with
distinct revenue sources, providing different services
at varying levels. The quality of local record-keeping
and its adaptability to cost-revenue analysis will vary
from local unit to local unit, but even within a single
municipality there will be variations from department to
department. Not the least of the handicaps facing the
researcher is the sheer mass of data. Probably because
of these difficulties only a few studies of a comprehensive scope have been attempted. The hope for the
future, if there is one, is in the promise offered by
increased application of machine statistical analysis
to data handling in the political and social sciences.[35]

There are several activities of community-wide benefit (what Mace
calls "services to people" in contrast to "services to property")
whose costs cannot be tied to land or identifiable uses, even
though financed out of property tax revenues (since the property
tax is based on an ability to pay principle, not a benefit principle).
Unfortunately for municipal cost-revenue research, this is applicable to public education, health, welfare, and recreation expenditures. "Even in the case of such services as fire and police
protection, garbage collection and sewage disposal, which are
closely identified with the development of land, there are significant aspects related to the health, safety, and welfare of the
community as a whole which are not properly chargeable to specific
parcels of property."[36]

That "services of community-wide benefit" cannot logically
be charged to particular land uses is most obvious in
connection with public education. While this activity
is patently essential to the welfare and prosperity of
the total community (extending beyond the urban area
to the state and nation as well), many cost-revenue
analysts employ highly questionable criteria and arbi-
trarily assign its costs to particular land uses. School
costs, they say, are attributable to residential land
use, since people who have children to be educated live
in houses. On the other hand, "childless" business
and industry make few or no demands upon the city's
schools. Considerations generally ignored are that (1)
the people who work in the factories, stores, and offices
are the parents of the children who attend the schools,
and (2) business could not function without a literate,
trained labor force. The same reasoning applies, of
course, to such other community-wide benefits as public
health, welfare, and recreation programs. Charging all
(or most) school costs to residential uses has the a
priori effect of making residential uses appear extremely
expensive "to serve." Since educational expenditures

bulk so large in the budgets of cities where schools are a direct municipal responsibility, revenues are rarely adequate to meet school and other costs in all but the highest value residential areas.[37]

The impact of a housing development on educational and municipal service costs depends on a number of factors besides configuration and demographic composition. Hence, the acceptability of a particular development varies by community. If educational and municipal facilities and services are already overutilized (for example, overcrowded classrooms), the costs of adding the residents of a new development will be greater than the average cost. If there is underutilization, costs will be lower than average. Rarely, however, is a new school, police station, or fire station constructed because of a single housing development. Average costs vary among communities for different services. The breakdown between residential, commercial, and industrial land uses affects cost allocation.

Only property tax revenues are considered in the typical study, which ignores significant nonproperty tax revenue sources. Property taxes are generally a shrinking proportion of local revenues, which are also available through nonproperty taxes and use charges, intergovernmental grants and revenue sharing, and utility service charges. (In New Jersey, there is still primary reliance on the property tax. There is no state income tax.) Often, developers are required by subdivision ordinances to bear part or all of the costs of installing new capital facilities. (Planned Unit Developments are becoming increasingly popular in New Jersey.) Hence, the revenue side of the picture may be seriously distorted, resulting in higher net cost than may actually be warranted. Moreover, one would expect substantial effects of community growth and new residential development on the local economy and hence on municipal revenus. Typically, assessed valuation has been used to estimate property tax costs. But assessment procedures vary widely and are probably suspect at best.

The indifference to revenues other than taxes introduces a major error in the analysis. In the long run this error will be compounded since property taxes are a shrinking percent of local revenues. Industry which usually shows up favorably does not provide a sales tax base, while densely settled, low income families may prove a fiscal bonanza to a city with a sales tax. Similarly, subventions from a central government are more frequently a function of population rather than industrial or commercial use. Therefore, a more inclusive definition of the fiscal base of a city may result in a shift in the advantages to the city of the different uses.[38]

Cost-revenue research has been narrowly focused in its concern with the property tax base which probably does not adequately measure the appropriate costs and benefits of community growth. In a sense, cost-revenue analysis manipulates land use to maintain the existing local fiscal structure and its administrative apparatus. The emphasis on balanced or high revenue land use to provide an "adequate" property tax base rests on questionable assumptions. Even on the property tax basis, alone, community growth and new residential development probably means more revenue than in the past. It is widely believed that single family residential development is detrimental to the property tax base. This belief is more often than not the result of questionable cost allocation procedures. A study sponsored by the National Association of Home Builders and the Urban Land Institute demonstrates net revenues for typical housing construction in California, New Jersey, and North Carolina.[39]

Methodology: Educational Costs-Residential Sector

The basic format of constructing modular educational cost units for a municipality involves the comparison of the income which the community derives from the specific residential configuration with the education tax levies required to service it. This approach necessitates, first of all, estimates of the school children generated by each type of dwelling unit. Exhibit 1-2 provides a summary of these basic demographic variables.

The impact variables and demographic characteristics allow us to use an approach which can be summarized as follows:

1. Public School Children Per Dwelling Unit x School Property Taxes Levied Per Student = Local Educational Costs Per Dwelling Unit

2. Market Valuation Per Dwelling Unit x Equalized School Property Tax Rate = Revenue Generated

3. Educational Surplus or Deficit = 1 - 2

Methodology: Noneducational Costs - Residential Sector

In order to calculate the property tax portion of noneducational costs assignable to a development (municipal,* county,** and

---

*taxes imposed for support of the municipal budget including the reserve for uncollected taxes based on tax requirement of the municipality, school(s), and county

**taxes imposed for support of county government including the levy for the county libraries

deductions*) total household size rather than school children becomes the important multiplier. Total household size as a result of various residential and bedroom configurations appears in Exhibit 1-16

Using the total household figure (persons per unit), a similar methodology is employed to calculate noneducational costs as was the case for education expenditures. Once again the income derived from a particular residential configuration is compared to the cost it generates.

The approach may be summarized as follows:

1. Costs

   a. Municipal Costs

      Persons Per Dwelling Unit x Municipal Property Tax Levied Per Capita

   b. County Costs

      Persons Per Dwelling Unit x County Property Tax Levied Per Capita

   c. Deduction Costs

      Persons Per Dwelling Unit x Deduction Property Tax Levied Per Capita

2. Revenues

   Market Valuation Per Dwelling Unit x Equalized Municipal/ County/Deduction Property Tax Rates

The current general parameters provided on the accompanying exhibit may be obtained through the relevant municipal and school officials by telephone. Similar information is also tabulated by the New Jersey Taxpayers Association in a report which is published annually. This information, while over one year old, is, nonetheless, accurate and a very convenient "one shot" source. It is probable that similar information from comparable sources is available in other states.

---

*the levy required to offset $50 veterans (effective 1964) and $80 senior citizens deductions from taxes (effective 1964). The senior citizens deduction increased to $160 from $80, effective in 1972 with the state reimbursing municipalities for one-half of the deduction.

EXHIBIT 1-16.   GENERAL PARAMETERS: MANALAPAN TOWNSHIP, N.J.*
(SELECTED EXAMPLE)

1973 Total Population	16,156
1973 Total Assessed Valuation	$140,616,586
County Equalization Ratio	95.32
1973 Total Equalized Valuation	$147,520,550
1973 Assessed School Tax Rate	3.661
H.S. (Freehold)	1.152
Manalapan-Englishtown RSD	2.509
1973 School Enrollment	5,230
H.S. (Freehold)	1,082
Manapalan-Englishtown RSD	4,148
1973 Municipal Tax Rate (Includes Fire District 1 Rate)	
Assessed	.072
Equalized	.069
1973 County Tax Rate (including library)	
Assessed	.715
Equalized	.682
1973 County Property Tax Levied (Equalized)	$1,006,090
1973 County Property Tax Per Person	$62.27
1973 Deductions	
Assessed	.039
Equalized	.037
1973 Deduction Property Tax Levied (Equalized)	$54,583
1973 Deduction Property Tax Per Person	$3.38
1973 Total Tax Rate	
Assessed	4.487
Equalized	4.277
1973 Total Property Tax Levied (Equalized)	$1,162,462
1973 Total Property Tax Per Person	$71.95

1973 Equalized Valuation $= \dfrac{\$140,616,586}{.9532} =$ $147,520,550

1973 Equalized Valuation/Pupil $= \dfrac{\$147,520,550}{5,230} =$ $28,206.61

1973 School Property Tax Levied/Pupil $= .03489(\$28,206.61) = \$984.12$

*This case is presented here for illustrative purposes only. Assessed values and tax rates, etc. will vary by community.

HIGH RISE COST REVENUE ANALYSIS

General Parameters:

A. 1 Bedroom Unit Rent = $275/monthly
    2 Bedroom Unit Rent = $350/monthly

B. 1 Bedroom Unit Pupils = .012
    2 Bedroom Unit Pupils = .181

C. 1 Bedroom Unit Persons = 1.817
    2 Bedroom Unit Persons = 2.484

D. Market Value Approximately 8 times annual rent roll

    1 Bedroom = $275 x 12 x 8 = $26,400
    2 Bedroom = $350 x 12 x 8 = $33,600

1 Bedroom High Rise

Educational Cost = (.012 pupils) ($984.12/pupil) = $ 11.81
Municipal Cost   = (1.817 persons)($6.30/person) =   11.78
County Cost   = (1.817 persons)($62.27/person) = 113.14
Deductions   = (1.817 persons)($3.38/person) =   6.14

    Total Property Tax Cost   = $142.87

Revenue = (Market Valuation/Dwelling)(Equalized Property Tax)
Revenue = ($26,400)(.04277) = $1,129.13

    Total Revenue = $1,129.13
    Total Surplus = $1,129.13 - $142.87 = $986.26

2 Bedroom High Rise

Educational Cost = (.181 pupils) ($948.12/pupil) = $171.61
Municipal Cost   = (2.484 persons)($6.30/person) =   15.65
County Cost   = (2.484 persons)($62.27/person) = 154.68
Deductions   = (2.484 persons)($3.38/person) =   8.40

    Total Property Tax Cost   = $350.34

Revenue = (Market Valuation/Dwelling)(Equalized Property Tax Rate)
Revenue = (33,600)(.04277) = $1,437.07

    Total Revenue = $1,437.07
    Total Surplus - $1,437.07 - $350.34 = $1,086.73

GARDEN APARTMENT COST REVENUE ANALYSIS

General Parameters:

    A. 1 Bedroom Unit Rent: $225/monthly
          2 Bedroom Unit Rent: $275/monthly

    B. 1 Bedroom Unit Pupils: .046
          2 Bedroom Unit Pupils: .344

    C. 1 Bedroom Unit Persons: 1.902
          2 Bedroom Unit Persons: 2.805

    D. Market Value Approximately 6 times Annual Rent Role
        1 Bedroom: $225 x 12 x 6 = $16,200
        2 Bedroom: $275 x 12 x 6 - $19,800

1 Bedroom Garden Apartment

Educational Cost = (.046 pupils) ($984.12/pupil) = $ 45.27
Municipal Cost = (1.902 persons)($6.30/person) = 11.98
County Cost   = (1.902 persons)($62.27/person) = 118.44
Deductions   = (1.902 persons)($3.38/person) =   6.43

    Total Property Tax Cost   = $182.12

Revenue = (Market Valuation/Dwelling)(Equalized Property Tax)
Revenue = ($16,200)(.04277) = $692.87

    Total Revenue - $692.87
    Total Surplus - $692.87 - $182.12 = $510.75

2 Bedroom Garden Apartment

Educational Cost = (.344 pupils) ($948.12/pupil) = $326.15
Municipal Cost = (2.805 persons)($6.30/person) = 17.67
County Cost   = (2.805 persons)($62.27/person) = 174.67
Deductions   = (2.804 persons)($3.38/person) =   9.48

    Total Property Tax Cost   = $527.97

Revenue = (Market Valuation/Dwelling)(Equalized Property Tax Rate)
Revenue = ($19,800)(.04277) = $846.85

    Total Revenue - $846.85
    Total Surplus - $846.85 - $527.97 = $318.88

TOWNHOUSE COST REVENUE ANALYSIS

General Parameters:

A. 2 Bedroom Unit Pupils: .220
    3 Bedroom Unit Pupils: .655
    4 Bedroom Unit Pupils: 1.026

B. 2 Bedroom Unit Persons: 2.675
    3 Bedroom Unit Persons: 3.349
    4 Bedroom Unit Persons: 3.741

C. 2 Bedroom Unit Market Value: $35,000
    3 Bedroom Unit Market Value: $39,000
    4 Bedroom Unit Market Value: $43,000

2 Bedroom Townhouse

    .220 pupils/unit
   2.675 persons/unit

Educational Cost = (.220 pupils) ($984.12/pupil) = $216.51
Municipal Cost   = (2.675 persons)($6.30/person) = 16.85
County Cost   = (2.675 persons)($62.27/person) = 166.57
Deductions   = (2.675 persons)($3.38/person) =   9.04

   Total Property Tax Cost = $408.97

Revenue = (Market Valuation/Dwelling)(Equalized Property Tax Rate)
Revenue - ($35,000)(.04277) = $1,496.95

   Total Revenue   = $1,496.95 - $408.97
   Revenue Surplus = $1,087.98

3 Bedroom Townhouse

    .655 pupils/unit
   3.349 persons/unit

Educational Cost = (.655 pupils) ($984.12/pupil) = $644.60
Municipal Cost   = (3.349 persons)($6.30/person) = 21.10
County Cost   = (3.349 persons)($62.27/person) = 208.54
Deductions   = (3.349 persons)($3.38/person) = 11.32

   Total Property Tax Cost = $885.56

Revenue = (Market Valuation/Dwelling)(Equalized Property Tax Rate)
Revenue = ($39,000)(.04277) = $1,668.03

   Total Revenue   = $1,668.03
   Revenue Surplus = $1,668.03 - $885.56 = $782.47

4 Bedroom Townhouse

    1.026 pupils/unit
    3.741 persons/unit

Educational Cost = (1.026 pupils) ($984.12/pupil) = $1,009.71
Municipal Cost = (3.741 persons)($6.30/person) =   23.57
County Cost   = (3.741 persons)($62.27/person) =   232.95
Deductions   = (3.741 persons)($3.38/person) =   12.64

Total Property Tax Cost = $1,278.87

Revenue = (Market Valuation/Dwelling)(Equalized Property Tax Rate)
Revenue = ($43,000) (.04277) = $1,839.11

    Total Revenue = $1,839.11
    Revenue Surplus = $1,839.11 - $1,278.87 = $560.24

SINGLE FAMILY COST REVENUE ANALYSIS

General Parameters:

    A. 3 Bedroom Unit Pupils: .626
        4 Bedroom Unit Pupils: 1.293

    B. 3 Bedroom Unit Persons: 3.307
        4 Bedroom Unit Persons: 3.720

    C. 3 Bedroom Unit Market Value: $27,000
        4 Bedroom Unit Market Value: $30,000

1. 3 Bedroom Single Family Unit

    .626 pupils/unit
    3.307 persons/unit

Educational Cost = (.626 pupils) ($984.12/pupil) = $616.06
Municipal Cost = (3.307 persons)($6.30/person) = 20.80
County Cost   = (3.307 persons)($62.27/person) = 205.62
Deductions   = (3.307 persons)($3.38/person) = 11.18

    Total Property Tax Cost = $853.66

Revenue = (Market Valuation/Dwelling)(Equalized Property Tax Rate)
Revenue = ($27,000)(.04277) = $1,154.79

    Total Revenue = $1,154.79
    Revenue Surplus = $1,154.79 - $853.66 = $301.13

2. 4 Bedroom Single Family Unit

    1.293 pupils/unit
    3.720 persons/unit

Educational Cost = (1.293 pupils) ($984.12/pupil) = $1,272.47
Municipal Cost = (3.720 persons)($6.30/person) =   23.44
County Cost   = (3.720 persons)($62.27/person) = 231.64
Deductions   = (3.720 persons)($3.38/person) =   12.58

    Total Property Tax Cost = $1,540.13

Revenue = (Market Valuation/Dwelling)(Equalized Property Tax Rate)
Revenue = ($30,000)(.04277) = $1,283.10

    Total Revenue = $1,283.10
    Revenue Surplus = $1,283.10 - $1,540.13 = -$257.03

THE OVERALL COMMUNITY PROPOSAL

COST REVENUE ANALYSIS

In view of the various price levels attached to each of the residential types, a positive or negative cost revenue picture appears
for each of the residential types according to bedroom count. In
the example which follows the following distribution of residential
units among the four housing types will be hypothesized for a
balanced development in Manalapan Township for illustrative purposes.

SINGLE FAMILY
    3 Bedroom   337
    4 Bedroom   338
  SUBTOTAL (S.F.)   675
TOWNHOUSES
    2 Bedroom   337
    3 Bedroom   338
  SUBTOTAL (T.H.)   675
GARDEN APARTMENTS
    1 Bedroom   200
    2 Bedroom   100
  SUBTOTAL (G.A.)   300
HIGH RISE
    1 Bedroom   150
    2 Bedroom   50
  SUBTOTAL (H.R.)   200

TOTAL   1,850

SINGLE FAMILY UNITS: 675
      337   3 Bedroom
      338   4 Bedroom
  3 Bedroom Units
    Total Property Tax Cost = 337[$853.66]
                        = $287,683.42
    Total Property Tax Revenue = 337 [$1,154.79]
                        = $389,164.23
    Total Surplus = $389,164.23 - $287,683.42
             = $101,480.81
  4 Bedroom Units
    Total Property Tax Cost = 338[1,540.13]
                     =$520,563.94
    Total Property Tax Revenue = 338[$1,283.10]
                       = $443,687.80
    Total Surplus = $443,687.80 - $520,563.94
             = -$76,876.14
  Total Single Family Revenue Surplus = $101,480.81 - $76,876.14
                             = $24,604.67

TOWNHOUSE UNITS: 675
    337   2 Bedroom
    338   3 Bedroom
2 Bedroom Units
    Total Property Tax Cost = 337 [$408.97]
                           = $137,822.89
    Total Property Tax Revenue = 337[$1,496.95]
                           = $504,472.15
    Total Surplus = $504,472.15 - $137,822.89
                  = $366,649.26
3 Bedroom Units
    Total Property Tax Cost = 338[$885.56]
                           = $299,319.28
    Total Property Tax Revenue = 338[$1,668.03]
                           = $563,794.14
    Total Surplus = $563,794.14 - $299,319.28
                  = $264,474.86
Total Townhouse Revenue Surplus = $366,649.26 + $264,474.96
                           = $631,124.12
GARDEN APARTMENT UNITS: 300
    200   1 Bedroom
    100   2 Bedroom
1 Bedroom Units
    Total Property Tax Cost = 200[$182.12]
                           = $36,424
    Total Property Tax Revenue = 200[$692.87]
                           = $138,574
    Total Surplus = $138,574 - $36,424
                  = $102,150
2 Bedroom Units
    Total Property Tax Cost = 100[$527.97]
                           = $52,797
    Total Property Tax Revenue = 100[$846.85]
                           = $84,685
    Total Surplus = $84,685 - $52,797
                  = $31,888
Total Garden Apartment Revenue Surplus = $102,150 + $31,888
                           = $134,038
HIGH RISE UNITS: 200
    150   1 Bedroom
     50   2 Bedroom
1 Bedroom Units
    Total Property Tax Cost = 150[$142.87]
                           = $21,430.50
    Total Property Tax Revenue = 150[$1,129.13]
                           = $169,369.50
    Total Surplus = $169,369.50 - $21,430.50
                  = $147,939
2 Bedroom Units
    Total Property Tax Cost = 50[$350.34]
                           = $17,517
    Total Property Tax Revenue = 50[$1,437.07]
                           = $71,853.50
    Total Surplus = $71,853.50 - $17,517
                  = $54,336.50
Total High Rise Revenue Surplus = $147,939 + $54,336.50
                           = $202,275.50

Summary of the Educational/Noneducational Cost Revenue Statement

From the calculations produced below the specific example chosen
for the Manalapan Township Community would be a sufficiently lucra-
tive one in terms of the hypothetical cost-revenue situation to
produce a one million dollar surplus annually.

RESIDENTIAL TYPE	Surplus(+) or Deficit(-)*
SINGLE FAMILY	
3 Bedroom	+$101,480.81
4 Bedroom	-$ 76,876.14
TOWNHOUSE	
2 Bedroom	+$366,649.26
3 Bedroom	+$264,474.86
GARDEN APARTMENT	
1 Bedroom	+$102,150.00
2 Bedroom	+$ 31,888.00
HIGH RISE	
1 Bedroom	+$147,939.00
2 Bedroom	+$ 54,336.50
TOTAL (SURPLUS)	+$962,042.29

The one-million dollar surplus for Manalapan Township (Monmouth
County) may be contrasted with a $250,000 deficit annually that
would occur in Edison Township (Middlesex County) if exactly the
same dwelling units were constructed. The difference between surplus

RESIDENTIAL TYPE	Surplus(+) or Deficit(-)**
SINGLE FAMILY	
3 Bedroom	-$119,860.79
4 Bedroom	-$384,025.46
TOWNHOUSE	
2 Bedroom	+$139,160.78
3 Bedroom	-$ 26,502.58
GARDEN APARTMENT	
1 Bedroom	+$ 40,102.00
2 Bedroom	-$ 15,293.00
HIGH RISE	
1 Bedroom	+$ 77,901.00
2 Bedroom	+$ 20,886.00
TOTAL (SURPLUS)	-$267,632.05

---

*See previous computations for base. Note this illustration is
inserted strictly as an example. Costs/revenues will vary depending
on price, tax policy, etc. These variables must be inserted in the
matrix shown for each municipality in order to yield specific results.
**The base and computations have not been included for this
illustration.

and deficit is of course a function of the extent of the non-residential base of the community under comparison. Those communities with greater percentages of commercial and industrial uses frequently have lower equalized tax rates and higher per pupil property valuation. Thus, any revenue which also imposes a cost (residential uses) is looked upon much less favorably in terms of the cost-revenue situation than would be the case in the almost-totally residential community where the burden of costs is distributed across only a residential base resulting in a higher tax rate and lower per pupil equalized property valuation. For this latter case, in any residential type which produces some value yet possibly fewer school children, the higher tax rate times the structure value will be looked upon favorably in terms of improving the existing burdensome situation.

Of course, both market demand and value of the various dwelling units are purely speculative. The exercise does, however, provide a local area with a method for gauging reality of local costs which may be used to gauge the relative impact of singular or competing developments. While the situations in these examples are contrived, the anticipation is, nonetheless, real. If a procedure such as this is employed and, once utilized, in any way eases this anticipation, then study in its entirety will have been extremely worthwhile.

CONCLUSION

If planners and policymakers are called upon to make decisions whose consequences have broad impacts on the quality of life of a state's citizens and the efficiency of its economic institutions, they must be provided with an inventory of facts.

Due to the myriad of local political subdivisions in New Jersey as well as in others, we find that an inventory of facts in terms of the impact of housing development on municipal costs needs to be further supplemented. There must be a procedure for assembling and employing these facts that is both logical and consistent. Additionally, it must be capable of being replicated locally with available information at minimal costs.

The last portion of this summary is such a procedure. It is a fast, inexpensive, and relatively simple means of evaluating the cost revenue posture of a housing development.

It may further be refined by information contained in the larger study to reflect, for instance, the weighting ratios sometimes associated with school children multipliers or possibly the variation in total per capita costs as a function of an anticipated growth rate or population base marginally different from the present one.

In this era of increasing "fiscal localism" on the part of the federal government, the decisions made at the municipal level take on a new importance. The days of the "10 percent ante" as a contribution to the funding decision of a higher level, for the foreseeable future, appear to be over. Local officials must be provided with a barrage of information and a mechanism for its use to act in their own behalf. The larger study and this inclusive summary go towards this specific end.

[1] George Sternlieb. The Garden Apartment Development: A Municipal Cost-Revenue Analysis. New Brunswick, N.J.: Bureau of Economic Research, Rutgers University, 1964. (Condensed in Urban Land, September 1964).

[2] Rolde (L. Robert) Company. Garden Apartments and School Age Children. Washington, D.C.: National Association of Home Builders, 1962.

[3] Ruth L. Mace and Warren J. Wicker. Do Single-Family Homes Pay Their Way? A Comparative Analysis of Costs and Revenue for Public Services. Washington, D.C.: Urban Land Institute, 1968.

[4] Barton-Aschman Associates. The Barrington, Illinois Area: A Cost-Revenue Analysis of Land Alternatives. Chicago, 1970. (Condensed in Darwin C. Stuart and Robert B. Teska "Who Pays for What: A Cost Revenue Analysis of Suburban Land Use Alternatives," Urban Land, March 1970, pp. 3-16).

[5] Paul N. Holley. School Enrollment by Housing Type. Chicago, Ill.: American Society of Planning Officials, Planning Advisory Service Report No. 210, 1966.

[6] Dominic Del Guidice. "Cost-Revenue Implications of High-Rise Apartments." Urban Land, February 1963, pp. 3-5.

[7] Anshel Melamed. "High-Rise Apartments in the Suburbs." Urban Land, No. 10 (1961), pp. 3-8.

[8] Carl Norcross. Open Space Communities in the Market Place: A Survey of Public Acceptance (ULI T.B.#57) Washington, D.C.: Urban Land Institute, 1966.

[9] Westchester County, New York Planning Board. School Taxes and Residential Development. White Plains, November 1971.

[10] Arcadia, California, Planning Department. A Statistical Comparison of Multiple-Family Dwelling Units and Elementary School Enrollment. Arcadia, June 1970.

[11] Newton, Massachusetts, Planning Department. Apartment Study, April 1971.

[12] Monmouth County, New Jersey Planning Board. Multi-Family Housing in Monmouth County. Freehold, January 1973.

[13] Stuart and Teska, op. cit.

[14]Carl Norcross. Apartment Communities; the Next Big Market (ULI T.B.#61) Washington, D.C.: Urban Land Institute, 1968.

[15]John F. Kain. "Urban Form and the Cost of Urban Services," Cambridge, Mass.: Program on Regional and Urban Economics, Harvard University (Unpublished), 1967.

[16]Sternlieb, The Garden Apartment Development.

[17]See for instance John B. Lansing, Robert W. Marans, Robert B. Zehner. Planned Residential Environments. Ann Arbor, Michigan Survey Research Center, Institute for Social Research, University of Michigan, 1970.

[18]See for instance Stuart and Teska, "Who Pays for What."

[19]A more extensive analysis employing census variables is being completed by Franklin James and Duane Windsor of the Center for Urban Policy Research.

[20]A typical example would be the concerns of the Fullerton, California study: Fullerton, California Development Services Department, Apartment Survey, Fullerton, 1972.

[21]Del Guidice, "Cost Revenue Implications."

[22]Melamed, "High Rise Apartments in the Suburbs."

[23]Westchester County Planning Board, School Taxes and Residential Development.

[24]Fairfax County Planning Division. Student Contribution from Apartments and Mobile Homes. Fairfax, Virginia. 1966.

[25]Maryland-National Capital Park and Planning Commission. "Dwelling Unit Density, Population and Potential Public School Enrollment Yield by Existing Zoning Classification for Montgomery and Prince George's Counties." Silver Spring, Maryland. 1965.

[26]Monmouth County Planning Board, Multi-Family Housing in Monmouth County.

[27]Robert W. Burchell. Planned Unit Development: New Communities American Style. New Brunswick, N.J.: Rutgers University, Center for Urban Policy Research, 1972.

[28]Rolde, op. cit.

[29]Fairfax County Planning Division. Student Contribution from Apartments and Mobile Homes; Maryland-National Capital Park and Planning Commission. "Dwelling Unit Density, Population and Potential Public School Enrollment Yield by Existing Zoning Classification for Montgomery and Prince Georges Counties."

[30]Carl Norcross, Townhouses and Condominiums: Resident's Likes and Dislikes (ULI Special Report) Washington, D.C.: Urban Land Institute, 1973.

[31]Barton-Aschman, The Barrington, Illinois Area.

[32]Holley, School Enrollment by Housing Type.

[33]See George Sternlieb and James W. Hughes, "A Profile of the High Rent Center City Resident," Real Estate Review (Fall 1973).

[34]Ruth L. Mace, Municipal Cost-Revenue Research in the United States: A Critical Survey of Research to Measure Municipal Costs and Revenues in Relation to Land Uses and Areas, 1933-1960 (Chapel Hill: Institute of Government, University of North Carolina, 1961), chapter 1.

[35]Mace, op. cit., p. 22.

[36]Mace, op. cit., p. 22, n. 11.

[37]Mace, op. cit., pp. 23-24.

[38]Julius Margolis, "On Municipal Land Policy for Fiscal Gains," National Tax Journal, IX (September 1956), p. 250.

[39]Mace and Wicker, op. cit.

CHAPTER 2

WHO LIVES WHERE--AND WHY

CHARACTERISTICS OF RESIDENTS IN VARIOUS FORMS OF HOUSING

In this chapter, analysis is undertaken of a number of significant
characteristics of residents of different housing types. The presentation will turn first to such personal factors as occupation, age,
marital status, education and income. From these characteristics
the focus will turn to previous occupancy status, longevity at
present address, and to commuting patterns. The final section will
be devoted to the expenditure patterns of residents, which, in
turn, may have significant impact upon the municipal costs and
revenues associated with residential growth.

Occupation of Primary and Secondary Workers

Clearly, different housing types vary in appeal to distinct socio-
economic groups. As shown in Exhibit 2-1, 63.8 percent of the
townhouse dwellers have heads of households who are in professional
and managerial capacities. The same holds true for 62.8 percent
of the high rise apartment heads of household. By way of contrast,
the equivalent figures in single family housing and garden apartments are 46.5 and 46.9 percent, respectively. Operators and
craftsmen both bulk particularly large in the single family sample,
with 31.9 percent, as against less than half that proportion in
the other housing types.

Retired heads of household are concentrated in garden apartment
units and are nearly absent from the single family home sample.
(The latter, by design, were built within the last year.) Clearly,
there is a significant variation based on the stage of the life
cycle of the household. The basic carrying costs of the single
family homes and the townhouses were roughly comparable to those
of the rental units.

In general, second workers in the sample are relatively scarce
with only 28.6 percent of the total households having this
composition. The characteristic varied, with approximately 29
percent of the high rises and townhouse units having a second
worker; while 31 percent of the garden apartments were so occupied
in contrast to the single family homes at the 23.7 percent level.
(See Exhibit 2-2).

The bulk of second workers was split between clerical employment
and professional occupations, with operatives sizably represented
only among the single family group. Among the other housing configurations, the second workers, if not professional, tended to be
employed in clerical positions.

EXHIBIT 2.1 OCCUPATION OF HEAD OF HOUSEHOLD BY HOUSING TYPE

Housing Type	Total	Professional	Managerial	Clerical	Craftsman	Operative	Service Worker	Laborer	Retired	Student	Unemployed	Housewife	(NR/DK)
Total	6,638	2,258	1,356	1,083	527	289	203	19	616	122	79	87	(140)
Garden Apartments	2,994	1,001	399	416	306	154	122	14	409	76	52	39	(51)
Townhouses	1,749	656	460	310	87	50	50	1	92	10	11	19	(34)
High Rise Apartments	1,284	445	362	269	17	7	11	1	102	32	13	24	(26)
Single Family Homes	611	150	134	88	117	78	19	3	12	3	3	4	(29)
							Percent Distribution							
Total	100.0	34.0	20.4	16.3	7.9	4.4	3.1	0.3	9.3	1.8	1.2	1.3	
Garden Apartments	100.0	33.6	13.3	13.9	10.2	5.1	4.1	0.5	13.7	2.6	1.7	1.3	
Townhouses	100.0	37.5	26.3	17.7	5.0	2.9	2.9	0.1	5.3	0.6	0.7	1.1	
High Rise Apartments	100.0	34.6	28.2	20.9	1.3	0.6	0.9	0.1	8.0	2.5	1.0	1.9	
Single Family Homes	100.0	24.6	21.9	14.3	19.1	12.8	3.1	0.5	2.0	0.5	0.5	0.7	

Note: Numbers and percents may not add due to rounding.

Source: CUPR Survey 1972-1973.

EXHIBIT 2-2. OCCUPATION OF SECOND WORKER OF HOUSEHOLD BY HOUSING TYPE

Housing Type	Total	Professional	Managerial	Clerical	Craftsman	Operative	Service Workers	Laborers	Retired	Students	Unemployed	Not Employed	(NR/DK)
Total	6,696	737	128	794	29	102	111	4	19	40	10	4,721	(82)
Garden Apartments	3,013	335	35	401	18	37	72	3	16	21	1	2,073	(32)
Townhouses	1,747	233	28	205	2	9	20	0	2	10	3	1,238	(35)
High Rise Apartments	1,301	130	61	150	8	5	4	0	1	7	6	928	(9)
Single Family Homes	634	40	4	38	1	51	16	1	0	2	0	482	(6)

Percent Distribution

Housing Type	Total	Professional	Managerial	Clerical	Craftsman	Operative	Service Workers	Laborers	Retired	Students	Unemployed	Not Employed	(NR/DK)
Total	100.0	11.0	1.9	11.9	0.4	1.5	1.7	0.1	0.3	0.6	0.2	70.5	
Garden Apartments	100.0	11.1	1.2	13.3	0.6	1.2	2.4	0.1	0.5	0.7	0.0	68.8	
Townhouses	100.0	13.3	1.6	11.7	0.1	0.5	1.1	0.0	0.1	0.6	0.2	70.9	
High Rise Apartments	100.0	10.0	4.7	11.5	0.6	0.4	0.3	0.0	0.1	0.5	0.5	71.3	
Single Family Homes	100.0	6.3	0.6	6.0	0.2	8.0	2.5	0.2	0.0	0.3	0.0	76.0	

Note: Numbers and percents may not add due to rounding.

Source: CUPR Survey 1972-1973.

Age of Head of Household

The evidence of variation in resident characteristics by housing
type as a function of stage in the life cycle is corroborated when
analysis is undertaken of age of head of household. In Exhibit 2-3
the proportion of elderly (65 and over) heads of household varies
quite strikingly among the several types surveyed. In garden
apartments, for example, 15.0 percent of the heads of household were
65 or over, with high rise apartments about half of that at the 8.0
percent mark. In the single family homes, by way of contrast, 1.1
percent were in an equivalent category with the townhouses at the
3.9 percent level.

Indeed, the pattern is even more striking in heads of households
aged 50 to 64. Here 34.7 percent of the high rise apartment heads
of household are in this category, with the garden apartment far
behind at 13.1 percent. This latter figure is greater than the
townhouses' 12.3 percent, while the single family homes in the
sample have only 4.4 percent of their number in this category.

When youthful heads of household (those 25 and under) are considered, the pattern is reinforced. More than one out of five of
garden apartment household heads are in this category versus
roughly one in ten of the townhouse and high rise apartment
equivalents. Strikingly enough, in the modest one family homes
represented in the sample, one out of six heads of household are
aged 25 or under with the bulk of the single family home owners
in the 26 to 35 category--no less than 60.2 percent of this group.

It is evident in Exhibit 2-3 that single family home ownership not
infrequently may be almost the first housing for young couples;
however, a rather considerable proportion of these homeowners
previously lived in garden apartments. The high rise development,
on the other hand, is distinctively geared to older heads of
household where, as indicated, 42.7 percent are in the 50 years of
age and over category. The garden apartment development bridges
both ends of the spectrum with about one in four of its residents
at the 50 and over mark. The sample of townhouses is relatively
small, but it should be noted that the equivalent age group in
this type of housing configuration numbers only 16.2 percent.

Analysis was undertaken of the impact of number of bedrooms in the
housing unit on the age distribution of the head of household.
In general, heads of household under 25 as well as 65 and over
tended to be quite heavily represented in the efficiency and one-
bedroom units in garden apartments. The same held true in the more
modest sized townhouses, particularly the two-bedroom configurations.
Typically, as the number of bedrooms increases, the proportion of
both decline in both garden apartments and townhouses.

EXHIBIT 2-3. AGE OF HEAD OF HOUSEHOLD BY HOUSING TYPE

Housing Type	Total				Age			
		Under 21	21-25	26-35	36-49	50-64	65 and Over	(NR/DK)
Total	6,640	59	973	2,685	1,229	1,073	621	(138)
Garden Apartments	2,973	39	638	1,035	426	391	445	(72)
Townhouses	1,773	12	136	959	378	218	69	(10)
High Rise Apartments	1,259	5	96	309	313	437	101	(51)
Single Family Homes	635	2	104	382	112	28	7	(5)
			Percent Distribution					
Total	100.0	0.9	14.7	40.4	18.5	16.2	9.4	
Garden Apartments	100.0	1.3	21.5	34.8	14.3	13.1	15.0	
Townhouses	100.0	0.7	7.7	54.1	21.3	12.3	3.9	
High Rise Apartments	100.0	0.4	7.6	24.5	24.8	34.7	8.0	
Single Family Homes	100.0	0.3	16.3	60.2	17.7	4.4	1.1	

Note: Number and percents may not add due to rounding.

Source: CUPR Survey 1972-1973.

62

The pattern was not particularly clear in the high rise developments sampled here, but became strikingly evident in the division
of occupants in three- and four-bedroom one family houses. In part,
this pattern may be a function of lower income levels among more
youthful owners, since, as would be anticipated, there is a substantial cost differential between the bedroom size categories of
one family houses.

Sex and Marital Status of Head
of Household

Nearly a quarter of the garden apartment and high rise apartment
units have households headed by females: the figures are 23.9 and
17.1 percent, respectively. In contrast, the townhouses and single
family homes are at only 6.7 and 5.0 percent in this category.
Part of this difference may be explained by marital status variation, with 18.9 percent of garden apartment units and 16.1 percent
of the high rise apartments occupied by single unrelated individuals.
The equivalent figure for townhouses and single family homes is
under 3.5 percent.

Widows make up approximately 9.5 percent of the heads of households
of garden apartment and 8.1 percent of high rise units, while they
are only 3.5 percent of the townhouse, and less than 1 percent of
the single family unit heads of household. The bulk of widows in
garden apartments are in efficiency and one-bedroom units and the
balance are in twos and threes. The sample in the other housing
types is much smaller, but in general tends to confirm the anticipated relatively small housing configuration used by such individuals.

Education of Head of Household

When tabulated by the education of head of household, single family
homes are dominated by the less than college educated group with
54.9 percent of their heads of household in this category. (See
Exhibit 2-4.)

In townhouses only 24.2 percent of the heads of household had no
college education at all. The high rise apartment was lowest at
the 22.3 percent level, while the garden apartments were much higher at 41.6 percent. Enhancing this basic pattern, graduate education
was much more common among townhouse dwellers and high rise apartment heads of household than in garden apartments and single family
homes.

Again, it should be noted that the single family homes here were
deliberately limited to those in a moderate price range, roughly
equivalent (or as close to equivalent as could be found) in

EXHIBIT 2-4. EDUCATION OF HEAD OF HOUSEHOLD BY HOUSING TYPE

Housing Type	Total	Education						
		No Diploma	High School	Junior College	College Degree	Master's Degree	Ph.D. or Equivalent	(NR/DK)
Total	6,618	373	1,910	872	2,426	719	318	(160)
Garden Apartments	2,948	212	1,015	399	917	290	114	(97)
Townhouses	1,757	41	385	236	783	230	82	(26)
High Rise Apartments	1,286	56	230	131	583	170	115	(24)
Single Family Homes	626	64	280	105	142	28	7	(14)
				Percent Distribution				
Total	100.0	5.6	28.9	13.2	36.7	10.9	4.8	
Garden Apartments	100.0	7.2	34.4	13.6	31.1	9.8	3.9	
Townhouses	100.0	2.3	21.9	13.5	44.6	13.1	4.7	
High Rise Apartments	100.0	4.4	17.9	10.2	45.4	13.2	8.9	
Single Family Homes	100.0	10.2	44.7	16.8	22.7	4.5	1.1	

Note: Numbers and percents may not add due to rounding.

Source: CUPR Survey 1972-1973.

64

carrying costs to the rents of the higher priced units within the sample and the values of the townhouses.*

When these data are analyzed in light of the age of head of household data shown earlier, there is an indication that it may well be the blue collar worker, or certainly the less than college trained worker, who is able to amass the down payment on a house--or willing to make a long range commitment of this kind perhaps more quickly than his more educated peer.

Variations in Total Household Income

The data presented below are shown with a certain degree of temerity. Many people in all honesty do not have an adequate idea of their real incomes, and still others may well fudge the data. Within those limitations, it is clear that the several housing types attract quite dissimilar income groups which are not necessarily related to the variation in carrying costs of the housing.

Approximately three-quarters of the respondents revealed their total household income. (See Exhibit 2-5.) About 38 percent of the respondents in garden apartments had incomes of under $10,000, with the equivalent figure in townhouses less than 7 percent, and in high rise apartments barely 10 percent. Strikingly enough, in single family homes it was over 29 percent.

There is substantial variation in incomes of $20,000 a year or more. Household incomes of this size are most prevalent in the townhouse and high rise units with the former above the 32 percent and the latter above the 46 percent mark. In contrast, the equivalent incidence, both for the garden apartment and single family homes, is below the 10 percent level.

---

*Most of the one-family respondents gave answers when asked the current market value of their house. These centered at the $25,000 to $34,000 level with about half in this group. An additional three in ten were at the $20,000 to $24,000 range with all but a few of the remainder in the over $34,000 range. Much of this variation was explained by the fact that the size of the house was measured by bedroom configuration and practically all of the more modestly priced houses were limited to two bedrooms.

The townhouse market, which overall had values ranging between $15,000 to slightly under $50,000, was dominated by that half of the entire group who indicated that their units were worth between $25,000 and $34,000. An additional three in ten indicated values between $20,000 and $24,000, with the balance scattered toward higher levels, thus exhibiting a price pattern roughly comparable to that of the one family homes.

EXHIBIT 2-5. TOTAL HOUSEHOLD INCOME BY HOUSING TYPE

Housing Type	Total	Under $5,000	$5,000-9,999	$10,000-14,999	$15,000-19,999	$20,000+	(NR/DK)
Total	4,938	311	867	1,403	1,275	1,083	1,840
Garden Apartments	2,227	261	592	696	482	196	818
Townhouses	1,364	29	64	312	512	447	419
High Rise Apartments	845	11	73	213	153	394	465
Single Family Homes	503	10	137	182	128	46	137

Percent Distribution

Housing Type	Total	Under $5,000	$5,000-9,999	$10,000-14,999	$15,000-19,999	$20,000+
Total	100.0	6.3	17.6	28.4	25.8	21.9
Garden Apartments	100.0	11.7	26.6	31.3	21.6	8.8
Townhouses	100.0	2.1	4.7	22.9	37.5	32.8
High Rise Apartments	100.0	1.3	8.7	25.2	18.1	46.7
Single Family Homes	100.0	1.9	27.3	36.2	25.4	9.2

Note: Numbers and percents may not add due to rounding.

Source: CUPR Survey 1972-1973.

66

It is clear that the townhouse is attracting a market that is quite
dissimilar from the traditional one family house--at least as determined by the units for which there are data.

WHERE DO THE RESIDENTS OF VARIOUS
HOUSING TYPES ORIGINATE?

One of the major questions raised by citizens groups in considering
the approval of various types of housing configuration is the origin
of the tenantry. For example, they question whether a proposed housing project is essential in terms of housing the town's present
residents, or other citizens within the state, or, for that matter,
people from out of state but who may be employed locally.

Previous Place of Residence

Exhibit 2-6 shows the origins of present tenants or owners of the
various types of housing configuration examined in this study.
Nearly one out of five heads of household in high rise and single
family home units (11.3 percent and 20.7 percent, respectively) had
resided just previously in the same community. In garden apartments
the figure is a surprisingly high 21.5 percent; in townhouses it is
much lower at 8.4 percent.

Certainly, the familiar advice given to homeseekers, of "try the
community before you buy" is one that has long been familiar to the
field. In this light, the antecedents of the single family residents
are not surprising. The more significant figure, however, is that
for the rental units as a group. It shows that *somewhere between
one-ninth and one-fourth of the units examined currently provide
housing for tenants who were previously citizens of the respective
communities.*

Relatively few of the occupants of any of the housing configurations
come from New Jersey's major cities. This pattern may result from
the fact that much of the white middle class migration from the
Newarks, the Hobokens, the Jersey Citys of the state has already
occurred. In any case, only 6.1 percent of the garden apartment
dwellers and less than that in the other groups came from any of
the six major cities in the state. (The major cities are given in
the Methodology Appendix.) High rise apartments were next in order
at 4.9 percent level, with townhouses at 3.9 percent, and single
family homes at a very low 2.2 percent.

It is the rest of New Jersey (smaller communities and rural areas)
which make up the great bulk of the previous residence place of the
occupants presently in each configuration. Over half (51.2 percent)
of the single family homeowners have their previous residences in
such locales with approximately 42 percent of the garden apartment

EXHIBIT 2-6.   PREVIOUS PLACE OF RESIDENCE BY HOUSING TYPE

| | | | Previous Place of Residence | | | | |
Housing Type	Total	Same Town	N. J. Major City	N. J. Balance	Out of State	Outside U. S.	(NR/DK)
Total	6,763	1,081	334	2,738	2,474	136	(15)
Garden Apartments	3,040	653	187	1,264	866	70	(5)
Townhouses	1,780	149	70	737	799	24	(3)
High Rise Apartments	1,309	147	64	412	648	38	(1)
Single Family Homes	634	131	14	325	161	3	(6)
			Percent Distribution				
Total	100.0	16.0	4.9	40.5	36.6	2.0	
Garden Apartments	100.0	21.5	6.1	41.6	28.5	2.3	
Townhouses	100.0	8.4	3.9	41.4	44.9	1.4	
High Rise Apartments	100.0	11.3	4.9	31.5	49.5	2.9	
Single Family Homes	100.0	20.7	2.2	51.2	25.4	0.5	

Note: Numbers and percents may not add due to rounding.

Source: CUPR Survey 1972-1973.

and townhouse dwellers from similar origins. Once again the figures for high rise apartments at the 31.5 percent mark are quite different.

This last category shares with townhouses a substantial mixture of out-of-state residents with each of them substantially over the 40 percent mark (49.5 percent in high rise and 44.9 percent in townhouses). The garden apartments and single family houses, both at about the 25 percent level, contrast markedly. Newcomers from outside the United States are typically minimal in proportion, reaching their peak at 2.9 percent for high rise apartments.

In sum, the bulk of this relatively new housing is occupied by New Jerseyans, typically New Jerseyans from the very same communities where the sample units are located or from similar, largely suburban, areas.

Previous Housing Type

In recent years, there has been increased interest in the whole question of housing succession and "filtering down." The classic Lansing study of the chain of moves consequent upon the addition of new rental or private housing units, has shown the surprising multiplier involved in terms of the number of families who trade up in their housing as a function of new unit construction.[1] Where did the various occupants of the several types of housing discussed here live prior to their present residences? (See Exhibit 2-7.)

Garden Apartments

A surprising 46.4 percent of the present residents of garden apartments in the sample came from single family homes. This is much more a function of the formation of new households striking off on their own, emerging from families living in one family residences, than it is of the aged giving up their former single family dwellings. An additional 46.5 percent of garden apartment residents came from another apartment. Clearly, though many of the current garden apartment dwellers are perhaps short term in their present facilities, they are still relatively longer term in apartment units of one type or another. Only 5.7 percent came out of multi-family units--two and three family structures--with a mere 1.4 percent coming out of group quarters. These were typically heads of households coming from dormitories and the like.

Townhouses

The situation is somewhat dissimilar when the townhouse dweller is observed. Here two out of three, 67.5 percent, came out of apartments. The townhouse, in part, is filling the role which the small

EXHIBIT 2-7. PRESENT HOUSING TYPE BY PREVIOUS HOUSING TYPE

Present Housing Type	Total	Previous Housing Type				
		Single Family Home	Multi-Family Home	Apartment	Group Quarters	(NR/DK)
Total	6,674	2,651	325	3,621	76	(104)
Owner						
Townhouses	2,376	767	123	1,470	15	(47)
Single Family Homes	1,755	462	95	1,184	13	(28)
	621	305	28	286	2	(19)
Renter						
Garden Apartments	4,298	1,883	202	2,151	61	(57)
High Rise Apartments	2,995	1,389	171	1,394	41	(50)
	1,303	494	31	757	20	(7)
		Percent Distribution				
Total	100.0	39.7	4.9	54.3	1.0	
Owner						
Townhouses	100.0	32.3	5.2	61.9	0.6	
Single Family Homes	100.0	26.4	5.4	67.5	0.7	
	100.0	49.2	4.5	46.0	0.3	
Renter						
Garden Apartments	100.0	43.8	4.7	50.0	1.4	
High Rise Apartments	100.0	46.4	5.7	46.5	1.4	
	100.0	37.9	2.4	58.1	1.6	

Note: Numbers and percents may not add due to rounding.

Source: CUPR Survey 1972-1973.

unit in the tract development once did. An additional 26.4 percent came out of single family homes, with 5.4 percent having lived in multi-family facilities. The balance, a relatively small proportion, came from group facilities or other such accommodations.

High Rise Apartments

More than half, 58.1 percent, of the high rise apartment dwellers previously lived in other apartments, with 37.9 percent coming from single family occupancies, and 2.4 percent from multi-family structures.

Single Family Homes

The bulk of the single family occupants were split relatively evenly in origin between previous single family residences and apartments at 49.2 percent and 46.0 percent, respectively. An additional 4.5 percent came from multi-family facilities.

Clearly, there is substantial mobility between each of the several forms of housing discussed here, with the townhouse playing a singular role.

Previous Owner/Renter Status

More than one-fourth of garden apartment dwellers owned their previous housing quarters with the bulk, 58.5 percent, coming from rental facilities and 13.3 percent from others, especially group facilities or living with families (Exhibit 2-8). The townhouse profile is skewed even more heavily toward rental origin at 75.3 percent; only 21.4 percent were previously owners. The high rise dwellers match the garden apartments in terms of previous ownership at 29.9 percent, while in single family homes previous owners number fully one in three (34.0 percent). In the context of national or even state owner/renter ratios, it is clear that all of the housing configurations tenantry studied here are definitely skewed in origin toward renters; it is equally evident, however, that there is a substantial mobility in status.

COMMUTER PATTERNS

The linkage between job location and housing has received much attention in recent years as one of the formulas advanced in proposed modification of zoning laws--the concept that communities which take in new job generating facilities should also provide some housing for the resulting work force.

EXHIBIT 2-8. PREVIOUS OCCUPANCY STATUS BY HOUSING TYPE

Housing Type		Previous Occupancy Status			
	Total	Owner	Renter	Other	(NR/DK)
Total	6,737	1,835	4,379	522	(41)
Garden Apartments	3,017	849	1,766	403	(28)
Townhouses	1,782	382	1,343	58	(0)
High Rise Apartments	1,303	390	873	40	(7)
Single Family Homes	634	215	397	22	(6)
		Percent Distribution			
Total	100.0	27.2	65.0	7.8	
Garden Apartments	100.0	28.1	58.5	13.3	
Townhouses	100.0	21.4	75.3	3.3	
High Rise Apartments	100.0	29.9	67.0	3.0	
Single Family Homes	100.0	34.0	62.6	3.5	

Note: Numbers and percents may not add due to rounding.

Source: CUPR Survey 1972-1973.

Unfortunately there are relatively little data available on actual patterns of commuting. Given the great variation in time/distance ratios as a function of highway networks and other means of transportation, these data are not quite as useful as would be anticipated. It may be much more pertinent to think in terms of how long the journey to work takes, rather than the absolute distance. This problem is most evident in New Jersey where 60 mph limited access highways contrast very sharply with local roads, the effective flow of which may be barely a quarter of that figure.

Given these limitations, it is still worthwhile to analyze just how far people travel to work and whether there is a variation in terms of the housing types from which they originate. As shown by Exhibit 2-9, a considerable proportion of the garden apartment and high rise dwellers simply do not travel to work--16.6 percent and 9.8 percent, respectively. The patterns of the principal wage earners, however, reveal that more than a third of all the respondents (37.7 percent), grouping all housing types together, travel more than fifteen miles. However, this figure is distorted by the townhouse representatives, many of whom commute to New York City and who comprise more than half, 50.2 percent, of those traveling more than fifteen miles. The single family homeowners are quite dissimilar with 45.1 traveling equivalent distances and an additional 12.1 percent going eleven to fifteen miles.

It is clear that the garden apartment units tend to be chosen within reasonable range of work since more than half, 51.1 percent, of the heads of households travel under eleven miles to work. By way of contrast the same holds true for only 13.2 percent of the townhouse dwellers. And, while higher, the proportion is still a relatively modest 39.7 percent in one family homes.

Does this indicate that people are willing to travel further to buy a house within their means that meets their interest, and/or is it that despite shifts in jobs and job location availability, they will cling to their homes? Unfortunately, we do not have data on this point and can only guess that the answer may well be a composite of both motivations. In any case, the garden apartment and high rise units have greater proportions of heads of households who have relative proximity to their workplace. The one family house and the townhouse, perhaps because of limited availability and perhaps because of preference, typically are sited much further away.

More than half of the second workers in every housing group travel less than eleven miles to work. Indeed, nearly 40 percent travel less than four miles. Probably the dwelling unit is not chosen for the convenience of the second worker, but rather the job search pattern of the second work is limited to proximate areas.

EXHIBIT 2-9. DISTANCE TRAVELED TO WORK BY HEAD OF HOUSEHOLD BY HOUSING TYPE

Housing Type	Total	Distance Traveled to Work					
		Less Than 5 Miles	5-10 Miles	11-15 Miles	More Than 15 Miles	Does Not Travel	(NR/DK)
Total	6,474	1,261	1,332	705	2,442	734	304
Garden Apartments	2,905	762	723	303	633	483	140
Townhouses	1,717	115	112	152	1,227	110	66
High Rise Apartments	1,248	276	364	176	309	123	62
Single Family Homes	604	107	133	73	272	19	37
			Percent Distribution				
Total	100.0	19.5	20.6	10.9	37.7	11.4	
Garden Apartments	100.0	26.2	24.9	10.4	21.8	16.6	
Townhouses	100.0	6.7	6.5	8.9	71.5	6.4	
High Rise Apartments	100.0	22.1	29.1	14.1	24.8	9.8	
Single Family Homes	100.0	17.7	22.0	12.1	45.1	3.2	

Note: Numbers and percents may not add due to rounding.

Source: CUPR Survey 1972-1973.

CONSUMER EXPENDITURE PATTERNS

One of the classic arguments against current zoning practice is that the former close spatial conjunction of residence and nonresidential ratable has been disrupted. The residence and the municipal costs engendered by it may be in one tax locus, the shopping center in a second, and the workplace in a third. The first community bears the tax burden and the other two locations get most of the tax benefits. Certainly, the rise of the highway oriented shopping center as well as the commutation patterns would tend to confirm, at least in part, this scenario. There is, however, a fair amount of exception to the model, as shown in an analysis of consumer expenditure patterns.

Consumers were asked what proportion of their purchases of food, clothing, house furnishings, and gasoline were made in their residence community. Clearly, the responses must be viewed conservatively; the particular locus of purchasing even though thought of by the respondent as "within the community" may well be over the boundary line. The pattern of proximities, however, is worthy of note; while varying substantially from one type of commodity to another, it still implies that the earlier model may well be an oversimplification.

Food

With relatively small variation there is a clear pattern that bulk food purchases, regardless of housing type, are made in the immediate vicinity of the shopper's dwelling, with 74.6 percent of the total sample answering that 75 to 100 percent of all their food expenditures were made in the town in which their home was located. This went from a high of 85.8 percent in townhouses to a low of 70.1 percent in garden apartment units. An additional 7.3 percent in the latter group said that 50 to 75 percent of their food purchases were made locally.

Clothing

The pattern was quite different for clothing expenditures. Here more than half, 56.9 percent of the sample, bought less than 25 percent of their clothing purchases locally, and only 21.6 percent bought 75 to 100 percent of them in their immediate community. The distribution, however, among housing types was quite dissimilar with the single family home residents clearly more substantial local buyers. In their case 46.8 percent bought upwards of 75 percent of their purchases locally, while only 32.7 percent bought less than 25 percent.

House Furnishings

House furnishing purchases also had a broader geographic spread, with 71.9 percent of respondents indicating that less than 25 percent of their expenditures were local and only 16.3 percent answering that three-fourths of their purchases were made in their community of residence. As before, it is the single family home residents who are the least mobile, with their respective answers 54.5 percent and 35.4 percent. Nearly double the proportion of single family homeowners bought 75 to 100 percent of their home furnishings locally as compared to the occupants of the other housing types.

Gasoline Expenditures

Gasoline taxes are increasingly important, both on state and local levels. Given the peculiarities of the New Jersey tax rebate law, a local gasoline expenditure represents a significant source of income to the community. (Half of the current $0.08 per gallon state tax is rebated to the community in which the purchase is made.) In this light it is useful to know that 57.4 percent of the respondents questioned bought 75 to 100 percent of their gasoline locally, and an additional 12.3 percent bought 50 to 75 percent of it near their homes.

Conclusions

Certainly these observations are very rough and much more detailed analysis of actual buying patterns would be required in order to provide a definitive analysis. Patterns clearly are dependent on the level of local shopping facilities. The data do, however, reveal a significant potential secondary impact on the community's economy.

PREDICTING THE CHOICE OF HOUSING TYPE

In order to determine who lives where, a regression format was used to analyze the choice of housing type. We sought to predict the probability that households of various characteristics would consume housing of a particular configuration. When using such an approach, regression coefficients may be interpreted quite literally as probabilities. The equations estimate the probability that households in the sample will reside in the four housing types: i.e., they attempt to replicate the housing choices of only households in the sampled units. They are not directly applicable to the total population of households, because the sample of households is distinctively biased by design to provide a number of recently constructed units of the four major types, and not a random sample

of all units.   The analysis presented below is intended to introduce
an approach for future research rather than as definitive predictions of future housing occupancy.   Though absolute magnitudes of
relationships are of little importance, patterns of differences in
housing choices are more robust, and representative of overall
patterns.

In Exhibit 2-10 are presented the results of the four equations that
were fitted.   In this case, the observations are the 4,131 fully
completed questionnaires.   Each equation predicts the effect of a
given characteristic on the probability that a household--control-
ling for all other characteristics--will locate in a garden apartment, townhouse, high rise apartment, or single family home.

The variables of particular interest are total household income
(grouped as $5,000-$9,999, $10,000-$14,999, and $15,000 or more,
with under $5,000 excluded from the regression as the dummy variable),
family size (grouped as two persons and three or more persons, with
single person households as the dummy variable), age of head of
household (grouped as 35-49 years old and 50 or more years old,
with under 35 as the dummy variable), sex of head of household (male-
headed households are the dummy variable), migration pattern (out-
of-state migrants, with New Jersey residents as the dummy variable),
previous housing type (grouped as single family and 2, 3 and 4 family
homes, with apartments and group quarters as the dummy variable),
ethnicity, presence of a secondary worker in the household, and
education (grouped as high school graduate, junior college and college, and post-graduate training, with less than high school
graduation as the dummy).

In general, the R^2 of the four equations are quite low: .177 (F =
85.074) for garden apartments (I), .145 (F = 71.582) for townhouses
(II), .142 (F = 69.921) for high rise apartments (III), and .101
(F = 44.423) for single family homes (IV).   Notice that R^2 and the
corresponding F's uniformly decline across housing type from garden
apartments to single family homes.   Garden apartments are the
largest proportion of the field sample, single family homes the
smallest.   However, many of the variables proved to be statistically
significant in their influence upon housing choice.   Most of the
regression coefficients are in expected directions.

Garden Apartments

In general, garden apartments are most attractive to middle-income
households.   Households in both the $5,000-$9,999 income class,
and the $10,000-$14,999 are both more likely to choose a garden
apartment than are those with higher or lower incomes.   This is
hardly surprising.   The high density and utilitarian appointments
of these units are designed to make them accessible to households
in this range of income.

EXHIBIT 2-10.   REGRESSIONS ON CHOICE OF HOUSING TYPE

Variable	I Garden Apartments	II Townhouses	III High Rise Apartments	IV Single Family Homes
Income				
5,000-10,000	.166* (.018)	-.179* (.017)	-.046* (.015)	.058* (.011)
10,000-15,000	.060* (.015)	-.074* (.014)	-.006 (.012)	.019* (.009)
15,000+	-.209* (.017)	.074* (.015)	.147* (.014)	-.012 (.010)
Family Size				
2 Family	-.091* (.020)	.101* (.018)	-.035* (.016)	.025* (.012)
3+ Family	-.284* (.020)	.302* (.018)	-.134* (.016)	.116* (.011)
Age of Head of Household				
35-50 years	-.095* (.016)	a	.126* (.013)	-.032* (.009)
50 or more years	-.116* (.015)	.003 (.013)	.194* (.012)	-.082* (.009)
Sex of Head of Household				
Female	.089* (.019)	-.006 (.017)	-.042* (.015)	-.041* (.011)
Migration				
From Out of State	-.079* (.012)	.019* (.011)	.102* (.010)	-.042* (.007)
Previous Residence				
Single Family	.087* (.012)	-.111* (.011)	a	.024* (.007)
Multi-Family	.076* (.027)	-.003 (.025)	-.065* (.022)	-.007 (.016)
White	-.250* (.037)	.049 (.033)	.096* (.030)	.111* (.021)
Secondary Worker	.073* (.014)	-.023* (.013)	-.017 (.011)	-.033* (.008)
Education of Head of Household				
High School	-.057* (.024)	.039* (.021)	.036* (.019)	-.019 (.014)
Junior College or College	-.121* (.027)	.110* (.024	.073* (.022)	-.062* (.016)
Higher Education	-.139* (.023)	.093* (.021)	.142* (.019)	-.095* (.014)
(Constant)	.9667	.039	-.021	.016
R^2	.177	.145	.142	.101
F	85.074	71.582	69.921	44.423
σ	.452	.407	.370	.263

Notes: (a) This variable failed to attain the significance level required by
the stepwise regression program for entry into the equation.
(*) Significant at the .05 level (one-tail test).

Source: CUPR Survey 1972-1973.

Again not surprisingly, the garden apartment is most attractive to smaller households. Compared to single person households, both two-person and larger households are less likely to locate in garden apartments. The small size and high density of these units makes them fairly unattractive to larger households, and makes larger households fairly unattractive tenants as well.

Compared to the under 35 group, older groups are less likely to locate in garden apartments.* Based on these data, one would expect to find younger households in garden apartments. Moreover, female-headed households are more likely to be located there than in other housing types. Out-of-state migrants are less likely to settle in garden apartments than are New Jersey residents. It appears that families previously living in single and duplex-type homes are more likely to move to garden apartments than are previous apartment dwellers. The most likely explanation of this is initial family formation, i.e., households moving from houses to garden apartments are new households leaving their parent's homes.

Households with a secondary worker are more likely to be found in garden apartments and less likely to be found in all other housing types, compared to single-worker households. This result may be partial corroboration for the "life-cycle" thesis of garden apart-ment dwelling, which states that this housing type often repre-sents a sort of way-station for dwellers at a certain stage in their lives as they seek to improve their living standard and before they have children.

After taking into account other household characteristics, household race powerfully affected residence choice. Non-white households in the sample were fully 25 percent more likely to choose garden apartments than were similar white households. Though the absolute representation of non-white households in these units was quite small (4.8 percent), still it appears that the garden apartment may serve an important housing function for non-white households in suburban areas.

Education showed a clear and consistent pattern. Compared to respondents with less than a complete high school education, a person with more education is less likely to reside in a garden apartment. The negative regression coefficients rise smoothly with educational level.

_____

*All of the following statements are based upon holding factors other than that being generalized constant, i.e., age/choice holding income, size of household constant, etc.

Townhouses

The higher a household's income, the less likely it is to locate in a townhouse until the $15,000 mark, where the regression coefficient becomes positive. Hence, one would expect to find more high income households in such developments. Two-person and larger households are more likely to reside in townhouses.

The age coefficients for townhouses are not significant: no particular pattern is expected in townhouses by age; other variables are probably more influential. Similarly, the sex coefficient is insignificant.

Out-of-state migrants are more likely to locate in townhouses than are New Jersey migrants. This pattern of interstate appeal may result from the increasing rise of Planned Unit Developments which incorporate townhouses. Such developments have been attractive to previous residents of New York City in particular. The townhouse was chosen more often by households moving from apartments, duplexes or other multi-family units.

Though neither race nor the presence of secondary workers in the household was related to the choice of a townhouse, education again showed a clear and consistent pattern: as educational attainment rises, so does the tendency to reside in a townhouse.

The townhouse shares important features with both the regular single-family home, and the apartment. It offers homeownership and the interior space of the one-family home, and some of the social density and economy of the apartment. In addition, thus far it is rare among newly constructed housing units in New Jersey, and like the high rise, undoubtedly offers a style of life and exclusivity which are attractive to many people. As a result, the tenants choosing the townhouse share features with tenants of each of the other unit types. They are attractive to well-educated and higher income households, as are the high rise units examined below, and are attractive to larger households, just as the one-family home, also discussed below. The importance of style may be reflected in the attractiveness of both townhouses and high rise units to immigrants from other states, a group dominated by New York City emigres. To these households, perhaps the townhouse offers a combination of urban style and suburban amenities.

High Rise Apartments

In many respects, the population characteristics of high rise structures are similar to those of townhouses. The picture, with respect to income, is mixed. The coefficient for the $10,000 to $15,000 is insignificant. The $5,000 to $10,000 group is less likely to reside in high rises, the over $15,000 group more likely than the under $5,000 group. Thus, the high rise unit is most attractive to higher income households. The household size co-efficient is insignificant for the two-person category but negative for the larger category. Hence, as in garden apartments, smaller households are to be expected in high rises.

However, unlike the garden apartment, the high rise units were most attractive to older, more mature households, and, rather surprisingly, to male-headed households. Clearly, the high rise apartments provide relative luxury within the spectrum of apartments in New Jersey. This conclusion is buttressed by the appeal of high rise units to well-educated households. The high rise apartment (and the townhouse) is most attractive to households headed by a person with post-graduate training of some sort.

The high rise offers a hermetic analog of an urban environment. This urban style is reflected in the attractiveness of the high rise unit to households immigrating from other states. The sampled high rises are located on the peripheries of New York or Philadelphia, and these households are principally emigres from the two cities.

Thus, the sampled high rise units appear to appeal to a narrow spectrum of small, sophisticated and well-off households with a taste for urban living.

Single Family Homes

The single family homes in the sample largely are priced under $30,000. The sampled units offer minimal housing amenities among new one-family homes in the state. These sampled units were concentrated in the less accessible suburban regions of New Jersey. They are thus quite atypical of new single-family homes in the state. However, their analysis is crucial in assessing the social and fiscal consequences of enabling such units to be constructed in other portions of the state in a program to provide moderate income housing through changes in zoning and other development controls.

Because housing expenditures and household income are closely related, the sampling of one-family homes places distinct limits on the ranges of household income within the sample. These homes were most attractive to families receiving between $5,000 and $10,000 incomes, and were more attractive to households with incomes of less than $5,000 than they were to households earning more than $15,000. Clearly this is not typical of all one-family homes in New Jersey.

The coefficient of household size is insignificant for two-person households. Larger households have, as expected, a higher probability of purchasing homes than single persons. Older groups are less likely to locate in single family homes, compared to the under 35 group. One would expect to find younger households purchasing such homes. Male-headed households are more likely to move into homes than female-headed households.

It is New Jersey residents rather than out-of-state migrants that are more likely to settle in these single family homes. But these low priced single family homes are distant from the cities of New York and Philadelphia. White households are more likely to live in these homes than black households (there were very few black respondents in such developments), but again the comparatively isolated location of the sampled units may be in part responsible.

Households with a secondary worker are not likely to be found in these low priced one family homes. The educational attainment of their owners is likely to be low: these homes appealed most strongly to persons with a high school education.

Conclusions

Based on these regression results, the following conclusions or generalizations may be drawn. Lower income households are more likely to reside in garden apartments and the modest single family homes represented in the sample; higher income households are more likely to reside in townhouses and high rise apartments. Smaller households tend to be found in both high rise and garden apartments, larger families in the other housing types. Younger households are to be expected in garden apartments and modest single family homes, older households in high rises. Female-headed units tend to reside in garden apartments, male-headed units in single family homes. We would expect out-of-state migrants to locate in townhouses and high rises with a greater probability than New Jersey residents, in the other housing types with a smaller probability. In general, we expect households coming from single or multi-family homes to locate much more in garden apartments and single family homes than do households coming from apartments, much less in townhouses and high rises. Black households tend to be attracted most to garden apartments and least to townhouses and single family homes, though they comprised a small portion of households in every housing type. Households with a secondary worker tend to reside in garden apartments. The higher the level of education, the less likely it is that households will locate in garden apartments or low priced single family homes, and the more likely that they will locate in townhouses and high rises.

82

All of these conclusions should be viewed cautiously in light of the fact that the low R^2's imply a very large unexplained variance in housing choice: there are many factors that have not been taken into account and probably cannot be measured. It must be kept in mind that the samples of housing units and households are far from random, so that these patterns may not be exactly representative of overall trends.

Nevertheless, based on these results, brief profiles may be described of the demographic characteristics to be expected in each housing type. In garden apartments, one should expect households that are lower income, smaller, younger, New Jersey residents, with a secondary worker, and lower in educational attainment. In townhouses, households should be characterized by higher income, larger size, out-of-state migration, former apartment occupancy, white race, no secondary worker, and higher educational attainment. In high rise apartments, one should expect higher income, smaller households, older households, out-of-state migrants, former apartment dwellers, no secondary workers, and higher educational attainment. In modest new single family homes, households should be characterized by lower income, larger size, younger age, male heads, New Jersey residents, former home dwellers (though not necessarily former homeowners), white households, no secondary worker, and lower educational attainment.

[1]Lansing, John B., Charles Wade Clifton and James N. Morgan. New Homes and Poor People: A Study of Chains of Moves. (Ann Arbor, Michigan: Survey Research Center, Institute for Social Research, University of Michigan, 1969).

CHAPTER 3

THE IMPACT ON PUBLIC EDUCATION

A dominant theme at any planning board meeting concerned with proposals for additional housing is the impact of the proposed development on the school system. The cost of education may make up as much
as 80 percent of operating costs in some suburban communities.
Even in central cities where education is diluted by the rising
role of other demands--welfare, police, fire, and the like--it is
typically the largest single factor in the operating budget.

Despite the significance of the area, the realities of school load
which can be anticipated from various forms of housing is a subject
which has been surrounded much more by diatribe and folklore than
by fact. For that reason, among the prime objectives set for the
present study was a clarification of this essential variable: what
is the number of children by school category generated by various
forms of housing amenity?

SIZE OF UNIT IN VARIOUS HOUSING CONFIGURATIONS

The accompanying Exhibit 3-1 reveals a substantial variation in the
typical size of units among the several housing types considered in
the study. In garden apartments, for example, fully half of the
units in the total sample had one bedroom, with an additional 3.3
percent efficiencies. Only 3.2 percent were three bedroom units.

The bulk of the newer suburban apartment developments tend to have
75 to 80 percent of their units in one-bedroom or efficiencies with
the balance in two-bedroom configurations. While court decisions
have declared it to be illegal for communities to limit apartment
construction along bedroom count lines, the market has basically
been in accord with this limitation.

High rise developments are equally characterized by small units as
are garden apartments. Fully 12.1 percent of the units in the sample
are efficiencies, and an additional 42.3 percent have one bedroom.
There are no four-bedroom units and only 13.1 percent have three
bedrooms.

Single family houses, as would be anticipated, are sharply skewed
toward larger size dwelling units, with 40.2 percent of the units
in the eight sample tract developments having four bedrooms, and
an additional 56.6 percent have three bedrooms. By way of contrast,
only 3.3 percent have two-bedroom units, and there are no efficiencies
or one-bedroom facilities.

EXHIBIT 3-1. NUMBER OF BEDROOMS BY HOUSING TYPE

Housing Type	Total	Efficiency	One	Two	Three	Four	(NR/DK)
			Bedroom Type				
Total	6,765	258	2,461	2,174	1,504	367	13
Garden Apartments	3,037	100	1,816	1,072	48	0	8
Townhouses	1,781	0	92	657	923	109	2
High Rise Apartments	1,306	158	553	424	171	0	4
Single Family Homes	640	0	0	21	362	257	0
			Percent Distribution				
Total	100.0	100.0	100.0	100.0	100.0	100.0	
Garden Apartments	44.9	38.8	73.8	49.3	3.2	0.0	
Townhouses	26.3	0.0	3.7	30.2	61.4	29.9	
High Rise Apartments	19.3	61.2	22.5	19.5	11.4	0.0	
Single Family Homes	9.5	0.0	0.0	1.0	24.1	70.1	
			Percent Distribution				
Total	100.0	3.8	36.4	32.1	22.2	5.4	
Garden Apartments	100.0	3.3	59.8	35.3	1.6	0.0	
Townhouses	100.0	0.0	5.2	36.9	51.8	6.1	
High Rise Apartments	100.0	12.1	42.3	32.5	13.1	0.0	
Single Family Homes	100.0	0.0	0.0	3.3	56.6	40.2	

Note: Numbers and percents may not add due to rounding.

Source: CUPR Survey 1972-73.

HOUSEHOLD SIZE

It is evident from Exhibit 3-2 that the bulk of garden apartments
and high rise households are quite small. In both cases, less than
13 percent, 12.8 percent, and 12.9 percent, respectively, have four
or more persons with over 87.2 percent of the garden apartment households and nearly 87.1 percent of the high rise apartments having
three or fewer persons. In contrast, the townhouse category has
nearly 40 percent of its households with four or more persons. A
more detailed linkage of household size and housing type by bedroom
want is provided in Exhibit 3-3. Clearly these data are related
to the school load.

CHILDREN

Number of Children Under 18 By Housing Type

It is the single family homes that have the highest number of
children under 18 with an average of 186.6 children who fall into
that category per one hundred units or 1.866 children per unit.
The low point in housing configurations is that for high rise which
is at 32.6 children. Garden apartments are close to this last
figure at 46.9, while townhouses occupy a midpoint of 114.8.

Pre-Kindergarten Age Children

A substantial proportion of the children under 18 in each of the
housing configurations are pre-kindergarten. For example, 83.8
children of that age are to be found in each one hundred units of
single family housing; that is, 45 percent of the total children
under 18 are in this category. In garden apartments, the figure
is 27.1, or 58 percent, while in townhouses there are 52 percent,
with 59.9 out of the 114.8 children per one hundred units at the
pre-kindergarten level. In high rise developments, on the other
hand, there are only 11.1 pre-kindergarten children of the 32.6
total school children per one hundred units, or 34 percent.

Public School Load By Housing Type and Bedroom Count Per One Hundred Housing Units

The figures mentioned above are for occupied units. The realities
of school load, however, are impacted by two other variables. The
first of these is the level of vacancy either in terms of apartments which are not being used because they are not contracted for
(i.e., vacant and available for rent following the census definition),
and secondly the impact of turnover. An apartment may have been
vacated and, coterminous with that occasion, leased by a newcomer.

EXHIBIT 3-2. HOUSEHOLD SIZE BY HOUSING TYPE

Housing Type	Total	Household Size					
		1	2	3	4-6	7 or More	(NR/DK)
Total	6,770	1,138	2,554	1,438	1,566	74	(7)
Garden Apartments	3,038	730	1,326	592	382	7	(7)
Townhouses	1,782	84	489	508	678	24	
High Rise Apartments	1,310	319	626	196	163	6	
Single Family Homes	640	5	114	142	343	37	
			Percent Distribution				
Total	100.0	16.8	37.7	21.2	23.1	1.1	
Garden Apartments	100.0	24.0	43.7	19.5	12.6	0.2	
Townhouses	100.0	4.7	27.4	28.5	38.0	1.3	
High Rise Apartments	100.0	24.4	47.7	15.0	12.4	0.5	
Single Family Homes	100.0	0.8	17.7	22.2	53.5	5.8	

Note: Numbers and percents may not add due to rounding.

Source: CUPR Survey 1972-73.

EXHIBIT 3-3. LINKAGE OF HOUSEHOLD SIZE AND BEDROOM COUNT BY HOUSING TYPE

Household Size	Total	Efficiency	Number of Bedrooms				NR/DK
			One	Two	Three	Four	
Total	6,758	258	2,454	2,174	1,506	365	(20)
Garden Apartments	3,030	100	1,809	1,072	48	0	(15)
1	730	89	574	68	0	0	
2	1,321	2	948	366	5	0	
3	589	0	235	347	8	0	
4-6	382	9	46	292	34	0	
7 or more	7	0	6	0	1	0	
Townhouses	1,781	0	92	657	923	109	(1)
1	84	0	30	42	12	0	
2	489	0	61	260	165	3	
3	507	0	1	228	256	22	
4-6	678	0	0	126	468	84	
7 or more	24	0	0	2	22	0	
High Rise	1,306	158	553	424	171	0	(4)
1	319	139	150	30	1	0	
2	623	15	363	213	32	0	
3	196	4	35	127	30	0	
4-6	162	0	2	54	105	0	
7 or more	6	0	3	0	3	0	
Single Family	641	0	0	21	364	256	(0)
1	5	0	0	0	4	1	
2	114	0	0	7	79	28	
3	141	0	0	10	94	38	
4-6	344	0	0	4	175	165	
7 or more	37	0	0	0	12	25	

(continued)

EXHIBIT 3-3. LINKAGE OF HOUSEHOLD SIZE AND BEDROOM COUNT BY HOUSING TYPE
(Continued)

Household Size	Total	Efficiency	Number of Bedrooms			
			One	Two	Three	Four
			Percent Distribution			
Total	100.0	3.8	36.3	32.2	22.3	5.4
Garden Apartments	100.0	3.3	59.7	35.4	1.6	0.0
1	100.0	12.1	78.6	9.3	0.0	0.0
2	100.0	0.2	71.8	27.7	0.4	0.0
3	100.0	0.0	39.8	58.9	1.3	0.0
4-6	100.0	2.5	12.1	76.5	8.9	0.0
7 or more	100.0	0.9	85.9	0.0	14.1	0.0
Townhouses	100.0	0.0	5.2	36.8	51.8	6.1
1	100.0	0.0	35.9	49.7	14.4	0.0
2	100.0	0.0	12.5	53.1	33.8	0.6
3	100.0	0.0	0.2	44.9	50.3	4.4
4-6	100.0	0.0	0.0	18.5	69.1	12.4
7 or more	100.0	0.0	0.0	7.9	92.1	0.0
High Rise	100.0	12.1	42.3	32.5	13.1	0.0
1	100.0	43.4	46.9	9.4	0.3	0.0
2	100.0	2.4	58.3	34.2	5.1	0.0
3	100.0	2.2	18.0	64.5	15.3	0.0
4-6	100.0	0.0	1.2	33.7	65.1	0.0
7 or more	100.0	0.0	50.3	0.0	49.7	0.0
Single Family	100.0	0.0	0.0	3.3	56.8	39.9
1	100.0	0.0	0.0	0.0	80.6	19.4
2	100.0	0.0	0.0	6.2	69.4	24.4
3	100.0	0.0	0.0	7.1	66.4	26.6
4-6	100.0	0.0	0.0	1.2	50.9	47.9
7 or more	100.0	0.0	0.0	0.0	32.4	67.6

Notes: Numbers and percents may not add due to rounding.
Source: CUPR Survey 1972-73.

Not uncommonly, however, there is an interregnum while the unit is being repainted or while previous commitments of the new occupant are being honored, such as the sale of the previous house or a shift from a distant locale.

This latter consideration is most evident in garden apartment developments which typically have relatively high tenant turnover. If, for example, average length of stay of approximately three years (roughly borne out by our findings) and a two-week "vacancy" on each move are projected, this in itself would present approximately a factor of 0.75 percent "vacancy" rate. At the same time there are always apartment units being held off the market for one or another reasons. Given these factors, after consulting the 1970 census vacancy data figures, we have ascribed a total vacancy of 3 percent for all causes. There may well be argument on this figure either on the high or low side. The basic numbers, however, are relatively little affected by variations within any reasonable scale.

A second variable, whose impact may be substantial in some areas and negligible in others, is utilization of private or parochial schools, which, in New Jersey, absorbs approximately 15 percent of all children under the age of 18 attending school.

Garden Apartment

The bulk of the children to be found in garden apartments, whether one or two bedroom, are pre-kindergarten age. Similarly, of the total of 4.6 children of school age in one hundred one-bedroom units, fully 0.5 are of kindergarten age, or approximately one in ten. The same youthful distribution holds true in the two-bedroom facilities where the total number of children attending public schools is 34.4 with no less than 3.2 of this group in kindergarten.

In another part of this study, comparison is undertaken of developments surveyed in 1964 in terms of the school children load compared with those same developments which are incorporated in the current study. It is of interest to note, however, that the total findings presented in this exhibit compare closely to the total for the earlier sample. There the number of public school attenders per one hundred one-bedroom units in garden apartments was at the 3.7 level; for two-bedroom units, it was 39; while for three-bedrooms, it was 103. The variation in the one-bedroom unit configuration seems to be a function of the fact that one-fourth of the children found there earlier were going to private or parochial school, whereas in the current sample in one bedroom garden apartments there were no children going to parochial school. If this is allowed for, plus a slightly higher vacancy rate secured in the earlier effort, there is a remarkable consistency in the ratios obtained.

EXHIBIT 3-4. PUBLIC SCHOOL ATTENDEES PER DWELLING UNIT
BY NUMBER OF BEDROOMS

Bedroom Type	Grade Level	Pupil Multiplier*
Garden Apartment		
One Bedroom	Kindergarten	.005
	Grammar School	.024
	High School	.017
		.046 (n = 1,816)
Two Bedroom	Kindergarten	.032
	Grammar School	.250
	High School	.062
		.344 (n = 1,072)
Townhouses		
Two Bedroom	Kindergarten	.029
	Grammar School	.134
	High School	.057
		.220 (n = 657)
Three Bedroom	Kindergarten	.097
	Grammar School	.450
	High School	.108
		.655 (n = 923)
Four Bedroom	Kindergarten	.125
	Grammar School	.712
	High School	.189
		1.026 (n = 109)
High Rise		
Studio	Kindergarten	.000
	Grammar School	.000
	High School	.000
		.000 (n = 158)
One Bedroom	Kindergarten	.006
	Grammar School	.006
	High School	.000
		.012 (n = 553)
Two Bedroom	Kindergarten	.021
	Grammar School	.115
	High School	.045
		.181 (n = 424)
Single Family*		
Three Bedroom	Kindergarten	.083
	Grammar School	.408
	High School	.135
		.626 (n = 362)
Four Bedroom	Kindergarten	.152
	Grammar School	.969
	High School	.172
		1.293 (n = 257)

Note: (*) Pupils per sample unit.

Source: CUPR Survey 1972-73.

Townhouses

The townhouse developments examined in the course of this study were limited to two, three, and four bedrooms. In two-bedroom units the number of school age children attending public schools are substantially under the equivalent figure for the two bedroom garden apartment configuration; the explanation for this may lie in the other demographic variables associated with the difference in tenancy of these developments. In three-bedroom units, the number of children per one hundred units attending public schools triples to the 65.5 mark. In four-bedroom developments the townhouses produced essentially one child attending public schools for each unit.

High Rise Apartments

In efficiency units there are no children attending public schools or of pre-kindergarten age. In one-bedroom units there are 1.2 children, approximately one-quarter the number of equivalent size units in garden apartments. In two-bedroom high rise units there are only 18.1 (under the garden apartment or townhouse equivalent).

Single Family Homes

In single family homes, with three bedrooms there are 62.6 children attending public school per one hundred units, quite comparable to the equivalent sized townhouse, while in four-bedroom units there are 129.3.

As is evident from the data presented in Exhibit 3-5, within the several housing configurations there is substantial school child age variation which is of significance when the data are re-evaluated based upon the weighting formula of the New Jersey Educational Association.

Weighting Costs

Based on analysis of actual operating experience, the New Jersey Education Association has adopted a system of weighting average costs of schooling. Weighted enrollments make allowances for the differences in costs of operating kindergarten, elementary, secondary, and other programs, thereby providing reasonably comparable data for use with kindergarten through twelfth grade districts. There is considerable local variation in the weighting factors; however, the general weights shown below come very close to actual experience. The New Jersey Education Association weights are as follows:

EXHIBIT 3-5. WEIGHTED SCHOOL LOAD PER 100 APARTMENTS
BY HOUSING TYPE BY BEDROOM TYPE

| | | Weighted School Load | | |
| | | Number at Grade Level | Student Weight for Grade Level | Weighted Total Student Load |
Bedroom Type	Grade Level			
Garden Apartment				
One Bedroom	Kindergarten	0.5	0.5	0.25
	Grammar School	2.4	1.0	2.40
	High School	1.7	1.3	2.21
		4.6		4.86
			Total	
Two Bedroom	Kindergarten	3.2	0.5	1.60
	Grammar School	25.0	1.0	25.00
	High School	6.2	1.3	8.06
		34.4		34.66
			Total	
Townhouses				
Two Bedroom	Kindergarten	2.9	0.5	1.45
	Grammar School	13.4	1.0	13.40
	High School	5.7	1.3	7.41
		22.0		22.26
			Total	
Three Bedroom	Kindergarten	9.7	0.5	4.85
	Grammar School	45.0	1.0	45.00
	High School	10.8	1.3	14.04
		65.5		63.89
			Total	
Four Bedroom	Kindergarten	12.5	0.5	6.25
	Grammar School	71.2	1.0	71.20
	High School	18.9	1.3	24.57
		102.6		102.02
			Total	
High Rise				
One Bedroom	Kindergarten	0.6	0.5	0.30
	Grammar School	0.6	1.0	0.60
	High School	0.0	1.3	0.00
		1.2		0.90
			Total	
Two Bedroom	Kindergarten	2.1	0.5	1.05
	Grammar School	11.5	1.0	11.50
	High School	4.5	1.3	5.85
		18.1		18.40
			Total	
Single Family				
Three Bedroom	Kindergarten	8.3	0.5	4.15
	Grammar School	40.8	1.0	40.80
	High School	13.5	1.3	17.68
		62.6		62.63
			Total	
Four Bedroom	Kindergarten	15.2	0.5	7.60
	Grammar School	96.9	1.0	96.90
	High School	17.2	1.3	22.36
		129.3		126.86
			Total	

Source: CUPR Survey 1972-73.

Level	Weight
Kindergarten	0.5
Elementary	1.0
Secondary	1.3

Most kindergarten pupils attend double shifts, which account for the low weighting. Conversely, high school students require a larger non-teaching professional staff.

In Exhibit 3-5 the data presented earlier are reevaluated in terms of these weights accorded the several age groups.

THE GARDEN APARTMENT DEVELOPMENT OVER TIME

One of the major concerns of local authorities when faced with the possibilities of a new garden apartment development is the question of what will happen to the project as it ages. Simply put, the immediate cost-benefit ratios may be quite attractive, but will they be sustained over time?

There are many parameters to this concern. One of the most prominent is the question of whether the basic maintenance of the structure will prove adequte to sustain the quality of its rent roll and of its tenantry over time. A second and perhaps even more salient question is whether the initial youthfulness of the child population-- approximately half of them as shown in the larger study are under kindergarten age--in relatively new units will not eventually result in a very large addition to the public school register. These are important considerations which account for some of the hesitancy of local zoning authorities in permitting this type of development.

In order to provide some insight into the concerns mentioned above, we undertook to compare surveys conducted in eight garden developments in both 1963 and 1972. What has happened to these developments in the nine years between the two surveys?

School Age Children

The most significant finding in viewing the garden apartment over time is the relative stability of the school-age children multipliers. In 1963 there were approximately 3.7 children per one hundred one-bedroom units; in 1972 the figure is 4.9. An even greater consistency is noted in the two bedroom units, i.e., 39 per one hundred units in 1963 versus 37.5 in 1972.

For cost revenue purposes the initial number of school-age children can be expected to hold constant. If a one hundred unit complex

95

EXHIBIT 3-6. THE GARDEN APARTMENT OVER TIME: SIMILAR DEVELOPMENTS SURVEYED BOTH IN 1963 AND 1972

County	Municipality	Development	Number of Units Contacted in 1963	Number of Units Contacted in 1972
Middlesex	Highland Park Borough	1. Orchard Gardens	209	201
		2. Montgomery Apartments	192	185
		3. Adelaide Gardens	200	198
		4. Old Queens (Levy Apts.)*	30	46
		5. Riverview Apts.**	48	45
	Edison Township	6. 311 Division and Greenwood	20	20
		7. Penn and Ovington	20	20
Somerset	Franklin Township	8. Pine Grove Manor	398	369
TOTALS			1,117	1,084

Notes: 1. Differences in number of units between 1963 and 1972 is due to different field procedures.
2. (*) This development was called Levy Apartments in 1963 but was later renamed Old Queens. It had 46 units in 1963, but only 30 were complete at the time of that survey.
3. (**) Cooperation was refused by the management in 1972 and interviews were conducted using telephone numbers obtained through reverse directories.

Source: CUPR Survey 1972-73.

EXHIBIT 3-7. SCHOOL AGE CHILDREN IN GARDEN APARTMENT DEVELOPMENTS OVER TIME

	Number of Bedrooms	
Year	1 Bedroom	2 Bedrooms
1964	.037	.390
1973	.049	.375

Source: CUPR Survey 1972-73.

was built in this area of New Jersey in 1963, in an 80/20 ratio of one to two bedroom units, approximately 10.76 school children could be anticipated; in 1972 the figure would be 11.42. The consistency over time is more than adequate for local planning purposes.

Age and Occupational Characteristics

The garden apartment's availability as a way station in the life cycle typically attracts relatively young people at an early stage of their personal domestic relationships, only to graduate them fairly shortly into more permanent types of housing facilities. This has become an even more pronounced function of this type of dwelling unit in recent years.

In 1963 the garden apartment was primarily inhabited by heads of household aged 26 to 35. Movement out in search of a single family house was delayed until well into the early thirties. In 1972, approximately nine years later, a much younger clientele is making use of the way station; almost one-quarter of the heads of household are under 25. This change reflects both the growing independence on the part of the more youthful population, who leave the nest at an earlier age and in this community, (Highland Park), whi has a large university nearby, the movement away from the institutional influence of dormitory housing (See Exhibit 3-8)*.

---

*There have also been changes in the age structure of the general population over the period 1960 to 1970 which reflect similar trends.

Major Age Groups in N.J.: 1960-70**
(numbers in thousands)

Age Group	1960	1970	Abs. Change	Percent Change
0-4	642	589	- 53	- 8%
5-14	1106	1403	+297	+27%
15-24	717	1121	+404	+56%
25-29	362	463	+101	+28%
30-39	907	817	- 90	-10%
40-49	853	943	+ 90	+11%
50-64	918	1134	+215	+23%
65+	560	697	+137	+24%

**derived from General Population Characteristics: N.J. PC(1)-B32, U.S. Dept. of Commerce, Oct. 71.

EXHIBIT 3-8. AGE STRUCTURE AND OCCUPATION OF GARDEN
APARTMENT RESIDENTS OVER TIME

A. AGE OF HEAD OF HOUSEHOLD

	1964	1973
Under 25 years	5.2	22.5
26-35	48.4	28.0
36-49	25.7	18.3
50-64	13.9	13.5
65 and over	6.8	17.7
Total Responding	100.0 (N=308)	100.0 (N=622)
	Median 33.2	Median 35.9

B. OCCUPATION OF HEAD OF HOUSEHOLD (PRIMARY WAGE EARNER)

	1964	1973
Professional, Technical and Kindred Workers	48.9	24.0
Managers, Officials and Proprietors (Except Farm Salaried, Self-Employed)	9.9	9.4
Clerical, Sales and Kindred Workers	14.0	14.4
Craftsmen, Foremen and Kindred Workers	9.5	7.1
Operatives and Kindred Workers	4.6	10.9
Service Workers (Except Protective Service, Waiters, Bartenders, Cooks)	2.3	5.4
Laborers (Including Farm)	1.1	2.5
Miscellaneous (Students, Retired, Unemployed, Armed Forces)	9.7	26.3
Total Responding	100.0 (N=476)	94.1 (N=631)

Source: CUPR Survey 1972-73.

A portion of the reshaped household which is sometimes overlooked, however, is the upper end. After children leave for school and retirement approaches, there is a desire for smaller accommodations. The garden apartment is now becoming a repository for the aged. Occupancy over the decade has remained approximately the same for the age group 50 to 65, but the proportion of residents 65 and over in this set of eight garden apartments has almost tripled. This phenomenon is not unusual. Our larger survey of garden apartment developments throughout the state reveals a similarly high proportion of elderly and female headed households; a considerable portion of the latter are widows.

Occupational characteristics have also changed. While the proportion of managers/proprietors, (9.4) clerical/sales (14.1), and craftsmen/foremen (7.1) has remained essentially the same, the percentage of professional/technical workers (23.5) is barely half what it was a decade ago. Instead the number of semi-skilled (operatives) service workers and laborers has doubled (18.5) and the number of non-workers (students and retired) has more than doubled, with the largest increase among the retired. The state-wide survey also indicates that garden apartments house the smallest number of professionals and managers, and the greatest proportion of retired among the housing types we surveyed.

Journey to Work and Previous Residence

The current journey to work estimates among garden apartment residents lend some insight into changing resident profiles within this dwelling type (Exhibit 3-9). There has been an approximate 6 percent increase among people who commute to a place of employment which is less than 10 miles away. There has also been an increase among those who do not commute because they no longer are employed. Together, increases in these percentages have reduced the total number of residents who travel more than 10 miles to work by almost one-half. When cross-tabulated by age (not shown) it becomes obvious that residents have taken a local job at a reduced salary, a choice available to the young; and there is a growing proportion of elderly who have left the job market.

Garden apartments now appear to draw a substantial proportion of residents from local areas. Currently there are barely half as many immigrants from out-of-state as there were ten years ago. While there have been some small increases in those coming from large in-state cities and other in-state suburban areas, by far the largest increase is among those moving from elsewhere in the same town. During the ten year period this percentage more than doubled.

EXHIBIT 3-9. JOURNEY TO WORK AND PREVIOUS RESIDENCE OF GARDEN APARTMENT
RESIDENT OVER TIME

A. JOURNEY TO WORK OF HEAD OF HOUSEHOLD

Home-to-Work Radius in Miles	*1964*	*1973*
0-5	37.1	40.0
5-10	14.2	17.7
10+	38.2	22.8
Not Applicable (Retired, Student Unemployed, Etc.)	10.5	19.5
Total Responding	100.0 (N=513)	100.0 (N=631)

B. PREVIOUS RESIDENCE OF HEAD OF HOUSEHOLD

Same Town	10.0	22.5
State's Major Cities	4.6	5.5
Other Areas of the State	40.8	51.8
Total State	55.4	79.8
Out of State	44.6	20.2
Total Responding	100.0 (N=522)	100.0 (N=631)

Source: CUPR Survey 1972-73.

These data again reflect our figures for the state as a whole: garden apartment residents travel fewer miles than residents of any other dwelling type to their place of employment, and they have by far the greatest percentage of occupants drawn from the local area.

PREDICTING SCHOOL LOAD AND POPULATION

This section will measure the potential of more sophisticated techniques for improving our ability to plan for the impact of new housing development on municipal population and the number of school age children.

Two basic paths toward this goal will be examined. First, the power of the ad hoc introduction of readily available auxiliary housing and household characteristics into the prediction method will be examined. Second, the promise of basic research into the determinants of the social structure of housing developments will be assessed. This second task will be accomplished by measuring differences in the children and population generation of individual developments which are both sizable and uncorrelated with the known characteristics of the developments.

The household survey described above will be used in this analysis. The variables to be used are listed and defined in Exhibit 3-10. Individual households are the basic observations. The variables measured are of the number of bedrooms in each housing unit, the rent or value of the unit relative to comparable units in the county, the location of the unit, and the race of the household. In addition, two development characteristics are included. These are the age of the development and the number of units in the development. Each of these variables has been suggested to be of importance to the children and population generation of housing development.[2]

Each of the above characteristics of a development can be accurately or crudely forecast by a municipality. An additional factor is the social differentiation of developments. In part, a household chooses a dwelling unit on the basis of the characteristics of its neighbors, and this process of self-selection can accomplish some degree of social segregation among residential developments.[3] For instance, referring to garden apartments, Sternlieb has suggested that "In a variation of Gresham's Law..., the proliferation of children may well drive out late sleepers and childless couples and thus lead to a still larger number of children per dwelling unit."[4]

In addition to this social process, physical design features may be important in determining the social composition of a development. For example, auxiliary public facilities such as playgrounds may

EXHIBIT 3-10. VARIABLE DEFINITIONS

	Variable Name	*Definition*
1.	BR2	Dummy variable indicating two-bedroom units
2.	BR3	Dummy variable indicating three-bedroom units
3.	BR4	Dummy variable indicating four-bedroom units
4.	TH	Dummy variable representing townhouses
5.	GA	Dummy variable representing garden apartments
6.	HR	Dummy variable representing high rise development
7.	Q	Ratio of rent or value of unit to average rentor value of comparable units in the county
8.	SIZE	Number of units in the development
9.	AGE	Last two digits of year in which development was completed
10.	RACE	Binary variable taking a value of "0" for black households and "1" for white households.
11.	REG1	Dummy variable indicating development location in Hunterdon, Sussex or Warren Counties
12.	REG2	Dummy variable indicating development location in Mercer, Middlesex, Monmouth or Passaic Counties
13.	REG3	Dummy variable indicating development location in Bergen, Morris, Somerset and Union Counties
14.	REG4	Dummy variable indicating development location in Atlantic, Cape May and Ocean Counties
15.	REG5	Dummy variable indicating development location in Cumberland or Salem Counties

Source: CUPR Survey 1972-73.

attract families with children, while swimming pools and tennis courts may attract young single persons. Such factors as architectural design, or provision for privacy may be of importance here as well. Finally, landlords have a measure of control over the characteristics of tenants in rental developments.

Development age and size are the only physical features available for explicit analysis. Fortunately, the basic observation in this analysis is the individual household. This circumstance makes it possible to introduce dummy variables representing individual developments. These dummy variables will measure differences among developments in their child and population generation not resulting from the effects of other characteristics explicitly included. These dummy variables will obviously not provide concrete guides to the importance of individual features of households or developments. They will provide some notion of the potential for further analysis into these determinants.

Single-equation multiple regression techniques will be employed in this analysis. A step-wise procedure will be used to assess presently used multiplier techniques and their potential for improvement. An improvement will be assessed only in terms of the increment it offers in predictive power over simpler techniques.

Summary of the Results

Exhibit 3-11 presents a tabular summary of the results of the investigation of the determinants of the number of school-age children in housing developments of the four types. It is immediately clear that the potential for improvement provided by the ad hoc addition of available auxiliary characteristics of developments and households is limited but significant. Household race was significant only for garden apartments. Not surprisingly, non-white households in these rental units tend both to be larger and to have more school age children than white households in comparable units. Relative rent or value of units was also occasionally significant. Levels of housing price represent not only quality and space features of the unit not measured by the bedroom variables, but also suggest the socio-economic characteristics of probable residents. Higher relative rents or values are associated with fewer number of school-age children in sampled high rise units and in single-family homes. In both cases, this presumably represents the impact of socio-economic characteristics, because as will be seen, higher rents and value are also associated with larger total numbers of persons per household. Higher rents in garden apartment units were associated with more school-age children. This may result from greater living space in these units not measured by the bedroom variables.

EXHIBIT 3-11. THE RELATIONSHIP OF AUXILIARY FACTORS TO THE NUMBER OF SCHOOL AGE CHILDREN IN HOUSING UNITS OF THE FOUR TYPES[a]

Auxiliary Factors	Housing Type			
	Garden Apartments	*High Rise Apartments*	*Single Family Homes*	*Townhouses*
Relative Rents (Q)	Higher rents; more children	Higher rents;[b] fewer children	Higher value; fewer children	Not Significant
Tenant Race (RACE)	White households; fewer children	Not Significant	Not Significant	Not Significant
Development Size (SIZE)	Not Significant[b]	Larger Developments; More Children	Not Significant[b]	Not Significant
Development Age (AGE)	Not Significant[b]	Not Significant	Not Significant[b]	Not Significant
Unique Development Features	Variable Effects	Not Significant	Variable Effects	Not Significant
Location (REG1-REG6)	Variable Effects	Not Significant	Variable Effects	Not Significant[b]

Notes: (a) The estimation of these effects is described in detail below. They take into account the number of bedrooms in a unit, which were significant in all cases.

(b) See text and footnotes for additional information.

Source: CUPR Survey 1972-1973.

Though neither development age nor size was a very significant determinant of the numbers of children, social differentiation among
developments was important for every housing type except townhouses; and geographic region was important for garden apartments
and single-family homes. In both cases, effects were variable.
The explanation of these differences cannot be inferred from data
at hand. Nevertheless, the results suggest that additional
research may be useful. However, because bedroom variables were
highly significant in every case, it is apparent that the simple
bedroom multiplier technique has a great deal of authenticity.
Real improvements over it will be difficult.

Exhibit 3-12 presents a similar summary of the results of the
analysis of total household size. Again, the importance of
social differentiation and geographic location is apparent.
These relationships imply the potential value of an in-depth
analysis of the factors producing these differences. In addition,
in several cases ad hoc auxiliary variables also seem to have some
utility. Rent levels are important determinants of household
size in both garden and high rise apartments, and in townhouse
units, where they may represent additional living space not
measured by the bedroom variable. Tenant race was significantly
related to household size in garden apartment units. Development
size appeared to be important in garden apartment developments,
high rise units, and townhouses. Thus, there is a small
inventory of simple changes which might profitably be introduced
in methods for planning the population generation of some types
of residential development.

Garden Apartments

The data available for this analysis are most complete for
garden apartment developments. Over 3,000 households in thirty
developments of this type were contacted. Developments were
located in all regions of the state. The developments varied
considerably in both age and size, and a substantial number of
non-white households were included in the sample. As a result,
the entire range of issues outlined above can be examined for
these apartments more satisfactorily than will be possible for
the other housing types. The examination of garden apartments
will guide the interpretation of the analysis of the other types
of development. The results will be presented in two parts.
First, the determination of the number of school age children
per household will be examined. It will be followed by an
examination of total household size.

School-Age Children. Exhibit 3-13 contains five regression
equations for garden apartment units. In each case, the number
of school age children in a household is the dependent variable.
The first equation includes only dummy variables indicating units

EXHIBIT 3-12. THE RELATIONSHIP OF AUXILIARY FACTORS TO TOTAL HOUSEHOLD SIZE IN HOUSING UNITS OF THE FOUR TYPES[a]

	Housing Type			
Auxiliary Variables	Garden Apartments	High Rise Apartments	Single Family Homes	Townhouses
Relative Rents (Q)	Higher Rents; larger households	Higher Rents; larger households	Not Significant	Higher Value; larger households
Tenant Race (RACE)	White Households, smaller households	Not Significant	Not Significant	Not Significant
Development Size (SIZE)	Larger Developments, Larger Households	Larger Developments, Greater Household Size	Not Significant	Larger Developments; Smaller Household Size
Development Age (AGE)	Not Significant[b]	Not Significant	Not Significant	Not Significant
Unique Development Features	Variable Effects	Variable Effects	Variable Effects	Variable Effects
Location (REG1-REG6)	Variable Effects	Variable Effects	Variable Effects	Not Significant[b]

Notes: (a) The estimation of these effects is described in detail below. They take into account the number of bedrooms in a unit, which were significant in all cases.
(b) See text and footnotes for additional information.

Source: CUPR Survey 1972-1973.

106

Variables	I	II	III	IV	V[b]	Mean	Standard Deviation
Intercept	.0416	.2719	.0952	.6980	.2455		
BR2	.3349* -(.0196)	.3220* (.0196)	.3405* (.0207)	.3394* (.0208)	.3404* (.0226)	.3476	.4763
BR3	1.8630* (.0741)	1.8006* (.0744)	1.8463* (.0776)	1.8465* (.0777)	1.7448* (.0793)	.0162	.1262
BR4	---	---	---	---	---	---	---
Q	---	.0566 (.0823)	.0571 (.0817)	.0571 (.0817)	.3844* (.1265)	1.0000	.1127
RACE	---	-.2923* (.0496)	-.2971* (.0506)	-.2979* (.0507)	-.2160* (.0518)	.9627	.1896
SIZE	---	---	---	-.0002* (.0001)	a	222.59	150.51
AGE	---	---	---	-.0072* (.0022)	-.0064 (.0062)	63.97	5.22
REG1	---	---	.2045* (.0521)	---	.0438 (.1079)	.0516	.2213
REG2	---	---	.1906* (.0360)	.0865* (.0370)	.3281* (.0756)	.3788	.4852
REG3	---	---	.1761* (.0369)	.0506 (.0385)	a	.3371	.4728
REG4	---	---	.2702* (.0461)	.2152* (.0471)	a	.0844	.2780
REG5	---	---	.1258* (.0502)	.0894 (.0571)	a	.0691	.2536
σ(Est)	.4802	.4773	.4742	.4743	.4667		
r^2	.2424	.2522	.2634	.2634	.2920		
F	425.57	224.12	105.38	94.82	36.18		
n	2663	2663	2663	2663	2663		

Notes: (a) This variable failed to attain the significance level required by
the stepwise regression program for entry into the equation.
(b) Additional variables were included. See text.
(*) Significant at the .05 level (one-tail test).

Source: CUPR Survey 1972-1973.

107

with two-bedrooms and with three or more bedrooms. This regression
is comparable to the school load multiplier techniques presently
in use. The other equations represent successively more complex
estimation procedures. The other equations will be compared to the
baseline of equation one.

The interpretation of Equation 1 is quite simple. A dummy variable
takes only one of two values: one, or zero. "BR2" takes the value
of "one" if the garden apartment unit has two bedrooms, and zero
otherwise. "BR3" takes the value of "one" if the unit has three
or more bedrooms, and zero otherwise. There are thus three
possible combinations of values of the two variables: (1) both
zero, which represents a one bedroom or efficiency unit; BR2 "one"
and BR3 "zero," which represents a two bedroom unit; and BR2 "zero"
and BR3 "one," which indicates a unit with three or more bedrooms.

The equation predicts the number of school age children resident in
a housing unit. For a one-bedroom unit, the prediction is:

$$SAC = .0416 + (.3349*0) + (1.8630*0)$$

$$= .0416, \text{ where SAC is the number of school-age children in the unit.}$$

For a two-bedroom unit, the prediction is:

$$SAC = .0416 + (.3349*1) + (1.8630*0)$$

$$= .0416 + .3349$$

$$= .3765$$

For a three-bedroom unit, the prediction is:

$$SAC = .0416 + (.3349*0) + (1.8630*1)$$

$$= .0416 + 1.8630$$

$$= 1.9046*$$

---

*These initial "predictions" are in fact less than they may
appear to be, because in each case they simply equal the mean
number of school age children in apartments of each of the three
sizes. It should be emphasized that their sole purpose is to
allow the measurement of the comparative advantage of incorpora-
ting auxiliary information into the estimation techniques.

Three measures of the explanatory power of the equations are presented. These are the standard deviation of the equation estimate (σ(Est)), the coefficient of determination (r^2), and the "F-statistic" assessing the overall explanatory power of the regression. For planning purposes, perhaps the most important of these is the standard deviation of the estimate. This measure provides a crude estimate of the confidence intervals surrounding actual estimates of the number of school age children resident in a development. The coefficient of determination (r^2) is of less importance. This measures the proportion of the total variation in the number of children per household that the regression explains. Because the regressions are estimated on individual households, r^2 cannot be expected to be extremely large. The important measure of the adequacy of the techniques is their ability to predict the aggregate number of children in a development, and not the number in any particular household.

The F-statistic measures the overall statistical significance of the equation. They are of little importance here because in every case they show enormous significance levels. An F-statistic not presented in the table will be of importance, however, and will be referred to several times in the text. This is the test of the significance of the increment of explanatory power (r^2) provided by the inclusion of a specific group of variables in the regression equation. A significant increment to the explanatory power of the equations can be directly translated into more accurate analyses of the fiscal implication of a development.

In addition to this test, the size of coefficients relating school age children and auxiliary characteristics of the household and the development will be examined. These coefficients offer estimates of the magnitudes of these relations, and of the possible planning errors occasioned by not taking them into account.

In equation two, variables representing the relative rent levels of the unit compared to other comparable units in the same county (Q) and household race (RACE) were added. RACE was significant, with a coefficient suggesting that white households have significantly fewer school age children. Relative rent levels had no significant impact. The size of the coefficient of RACE suggests that in even a garden apartment development containing only two-bedroom units, all non-white tenantry would imply 75 percent more school age children than in a comparable white development. The absolute size of the difference in school children between white and black households was so substantial that despite the small representation of non-white households in the sample, the incorporation of tenant race added a significant increment to overall predictive power.*

---

*$F_{(2,2658)}$ = 17.42

The addition in equation three of five dummy variables representing
the location of the development further enhances the explanatory
power of the equation.* The coefficients are quite large. They
suggest that households in garden apartments located outside the
three-county (Burlington, Camden, and Gloucester) area comprising
the New Jersey portion of the Philadelphia suburbs have substantially
more school age children per household than do those within the
area. Households in shore regions comprising Atlantic, Cape May
and Ocean counties have the greatest number of children, and
households located in Burlington, Camden, and Gloucester counties
have the least. The regression suggests that a development of
one hundred garden apartments of a typical bedroom unit configuration located in the shore region might be expected to have almost
thirty more school age children than it would if located in the
Philadelphia suburbs. This difference between regions is only
slightly smaller in magnitude than the difference between one- and
two-bedroom apartments, which traditionally has been the most
important variable.

The final equation adds two characteristics of the development--
the year in which the development was constructed (AGE) and the
number of units in the development (SIZE). Both are statistically
significant. Their coefficients suggest that both larger and more
recent developments generate fewer school age children. However,
both are reduced to insignificance by the introduction of dummy
variables representing unique characteristics of individual
developments. This suggests that more recent garden apartment units
differ in some unknown respects from their predecessors, and that
age itself is not the operative factor. Once again, the potential
for further research is clear.

Likewise, the apparent power of the geographic variables is somewhat misleading. It results in part from the ability of location
to act as a proxy for other unknown determinants of the characteristics of households resident in a development. First, the physical
design of a development may be important. The only design
features of a development which were available for analysis were
its size and age, neither of which were important. More detailed
analysis might uncover important design factors. The provision
of a playground for children may affect the composition of
residents much differently than does a golf course, for instance.

The features of residents in a development are not determined
entirely by the physical design of the development. The garden
apartment development imposes a substantial degree of communal

---

*The   F-statistic   testing the joint power of these five
variables is F$_{(5,2653)}$ = 8.02.

110

living, and under some circumstances these contacts might be abrasive. As a result, tenants can be presumed to select a development in part on the basis of the characteristics of its tenants. Moreover, because the garden apartment is a rental unit, landlords have a substantial degree of control over tenant characteristics. This control can be used not only to meet landlord desires regarding tenant characteristics (such as the barring of children or pets) but also to avoid abrasive heterogeneity among tenants.

These processes of self-selection by tenants and by landlords creates a great deal of heterogeneity in the tenant characteristics of developments. Its importance for the analysis of the generation of school age children can be demonstrated easily. The final equation (Equation five) introduces individual developments, in addition to their location, size, and age variables. This is possible because individual households are the units of analysis. In this regression equation, the most significant variables (with race, BR2 and BR3) were development dummy variables. Only one location variable was significant. Fifteen of the twenty-seven development variables were statistically significant. Their coefficients were sizable, ranging from (-.40) to (+.32), and were thus on the order of magnitude of the coefficient of BR2 (.34). The relative unimportance of location is dramatically indicated by the fact that three of the developments with significant dummy variables were located in Vineland, New Jersey. One (Vineland Gardens) showed a large positive coefficient (+.32); and two showed large negative coefficients: Thornberry (-.20); and Brentwood, (-.40). Clearly, location is not the dominant factor. The increment of explanatory power was also quite significant.*

It is not possible with the data at hand to examine these inter-development differences; however, some conclusions are apparent. *First, the common approach to estimating school age children in garden apartments has a great deal of authenticity.* Though RACE does have potential value, real improvements will be difficult. However, it is also true that the potential of improved understanding here is substantial.

Total Household Size. The analysis of total household size will exactly parallel that of school age children. Again, beginning from a version of the common bedroom multiplier technique, additional variables will be introduced in a stepwise manner. The results of the analysis are essentially the same as for school age children. Exhibit 3-14 contains five regression equations, each with total household size (SZH) as the dependent

---

*$F_{(20,2632)}$ = 5.31

EXHIBIT 3-14. REGRESSION EQUATIONS EXPLAINING TOTAL HOUSEHOLD SIZE
IN GARDEN APARTMENT UNITS

Variables	I	II	III	IV	V^b	Mean	Standard Deviation
Intercept	1.8596	2.0558	1.4867	4.4709	.4202		
BR2	.9893* (.0364)	.9587* (.0362)	1.0502* (.0373)	1.0156* (.0373)	1.0217* (.0395)	.3476	.4763
BR3	2.5412* (.1373)	2.3938* (.1371)	2.3754* (.1403)	2.3838* (.1391)	2.3872* (.1383)	.0162	.1262
BR4	---	---	---	---	---	---	---
Q	---	.4817* (.1516)	.4707* (.1477)	.4732* (.1464)	1.3481* (.2202)	1.0000	.1127
RACE	---	-.6907* (.0915)	-.5786* (.0915)	-.6045* (.0908)	-.4082* (.0906)	.9627	.1896
SIZE	---	---	a	a	.0018* (.0005)	222.59	150.51
AGE	---	---	---	-.0433* (.0064)	a	63.97	5.22
REG1	---	---	.2930* (.0941)	-.4897* (.1485)	.2072 (.1262)	.0516	.2213
REG2	---	---	.3146* (.0650)	.1403* (.0694)	-.3880* (.1170)	.3788	.4852
REG3	---	---	.5723* (.0667)	.3014* (.0773)	.4086* (.1154)	.3371	.4728
REG4	---	---	.8337* (.0832)	.8650* (.0827)	a	.0844	.2780
REG5	---	---	.6257* (.0907)	.8397* (.0954)	a	.0691	.2536
σ(Est)	.8903	.8800	.8568	.8497	.8145		
r^2	.2725	.2897	.3279	.3394	.3977		
F	498.16	271.06	143.82	136.22	56.03		
n	2663	2663	2663	2663	2663		

Notes: (a) This variable failed to attain the significance level required by
the stepwise regression program for entry into the equation.
(b) Additional variables were included. See text.
(*) Significant at the .05 level (one-tail test).

Source: CUPR Survey 1972-1973.

112

variable. Equation one includes only BR2 and BR3 as independent variables. Interpreted exactly as before, the equation predicts on average that 1.86 persons will reside in a one-bedroom or efficiency unit; 2.85 persons will reside in a two-bedroom unit; and 4.40 persons will reside in a three bedroom unit. The explanatory power of this equation (as measured by the coefficient of determination) exceeds that of the analagous equation for school children, but the total variation of SZH exceeds that of SAC. As a result, the size of confidence intervals surrounding estimates of SZH will exceed those of estimates of SAC, though this latter difference is not extremely important.*

The results of equation two through four differ in three instances from those presented earlier. First, unit rent level (Q) is quite significant for SZH, though it was of little importance for SAC. Consistently, higher relative rent levels are associated with greater household size. This seems reasonable, as the higher rent may reflect additional living space in the unit not measured by the bedroom variable. In addition, as with school age children, RACE is significant, with a coefficient suggesting that white households tend to be considerably smaller than non-white households in comparable units. Development size (SIZE) and age (AGE) shows a mixed pattern of statistical significance, and their effects appear to be unreliable. Households may tend to be somewhat smaller in more recent developments and in smaller developments. These are fugitive effects, however. SIZE and AGE may then be acting as proxies for some more profound development characteristics.

Once again, however, geographic variables are important, both in magnitude and in significance. In equation four the magnitudes of their coefficient approach that of BR2. As before, they apparently are acting largely as proxies for unique development characteristics. When dummy variables were added to equation four representing individual developments, the significance of the geographic variables was decimated. Only three were any longer significant, and the overall explanatory power of the regression was considerably enhanced.**

The conclusions of the analysis of SZH and SAC are similar. *As before, the bedroom multiplier appears to be robust and reliable.*

---

*As a result of these higher significance levels, each embellishment of the basic equation added statistically significant increments in overall explanatory power.

**$F_{(21,2631)}$ = 12.14

High Rise Apartments

The high rise apartment development appeals to a much different market than the garden apartments discussed above. Crudely put, it is the luxury alternative within the rental market. The high rise appeals most strongly to small (one or two members), mature (head of household 35 years of age or more), and high income ($15,000 ore more) households. The garden apartment most strongly attracts small (one member), young (under 35), and low to moderate income household ($5,000-$10,000). Their pupil and population generation ought to be much different.

At the same time, because both are rental units with a high degree of communally shared space and facilities, it again seems reasonable to expect that social segregation and development differentiation ought to be important for high rise developments.

School Age Children. Exhibit 3-15 presents the five basic regressions analyzing the number of school children in high rise units. Equation one presents the typical bedroom multipliers. It suggests that on average a one-bedroom unit can be expected to house .01 children; a two-bedroom unit, .19 children; and a three-bedroom unit, .87 school age children. Not surprisingly, given the age and economic circumstances of residents in high rise units, each of these multipliers lies far below its counterpart for garden apartments.

The addition of "RACE" and "Q" in equation two adds significant explanatory power. Higher relative rent levels are associated with lower numbers of school age children. The higher rents are being used to purchase an ambience in which children play very little part. Unlike garden apartments, household race is unrelated to the number of school age children in high rise units. The number of non-white households in the sampled units was very small, so this finding is not surprising.

The geographic area variables were of no importance, both in terms of statistical significance and in terms of absolute magnitude. However, the addition of dummy variables representing individual developments in equation five did significantly enhance the predictive power of the regression.* Because in two cases there was only a single development in a region, so that the geographic variables already represented individual developments, this degree of improvement is substantial enough to hold out the promise of analysis of the determinants of the social composition of high rise developments. It is clear that consideration of unit rental levels offers the prospect of immediate improvement on the bedroom multiplier technique.

_____

*$F_{(4,937)} = 2.40$

EXHIBIT 3-15. REGRESSION EQUATIONS EXPLAINING SCHOOL AGE CHILDREN
IN HIGH RISE UNITS

Variables	I	II	III	IV	V[b]	Mean	Standard Deviation
Intercept	.0131	.2377	.2448	.2131	.2421		
BR2	.1753* (.0351)	.1762* (.0350)	.1729* (.0355)	.1612* (.0357)	.1333* (.0373)	.3287	.4700
BR3	.8622* (.0504)	.8616* (.0501)	.8703* (.0527)	.8639* (.0526)	.8022* (.0582)	.1218	.3272
BR4	---	---	---	---	---	---	---
Q	---	-.3466* (.1051)	-.3466* (.1051)	-.3473* (.1048)	-.2113* (.1193)	.9999	.1507
RACE	---	.1223 (.2427)	.1225 (.2428)	.0531 (.2436)	.0377 (.2429)	.9957	.0654
SIZE	---	---	---	.0002* (.0001)	.0003* (.0001)	356.4070	240.5296
AGE	---	---	---	---	-.0023 (.0102)	69.4006	2.1139
REG1	---	---	---	---	---	---	---
REG2	---	---	a	a	a	.1400	.4700
REG3	---	---	-.0190 (.0352)	.0501 (.0443)	a	.3913	.4883
REG4	---	---	---	---	---	---	---
REG5	---	---	---	---	---	---	---
σ(Est)	.4896	.4872	.4874	.4860	.4846		
r²	.2369	.2459	.2461	.2513	.2589		
F	146.66	76.86	61.50	52.64	32.73		
n	948	948	948	948	948		

Notes: (a) This variable failed to attain the significance level required by
the stepwise regression program for entry into the equation.
(b) Additional variables were included. See text.
(*) Significant at the .05 level (one-tail test).

Source: CUPR Survey 1972-1973.

115

Total Household Size. Exhibit 3-16 presents the regression results for total household size in high rise housing units. They differ from the results for school age children in several aspects. As before, equation one presents the bedroom multipliers. On average, 1.65 persons reside in a one-bedroom unit; 2.52 in a two-bedroom unit; and 3.73 in a three-bedroom apartment. The size of these multipliers is in large part impervious to the addition of auxiliary variables into the relationship. Neither RACE nor Q contributed significantly to the power of the equation. None of the geographic variables is significantly related to total household size. In striking contrast, the individual development dummy variables were highly significant. Thus, as expected, significant differences do exist among developments in the intensity of their use, and analysis of this differentiation may add much to the ability to plan for the needs of new high rise developments. It appears that no ad hoc changes can be made successfully in the techniques used to estimate the total population of high rise units.

Single Family Homes

Unfortunately, single family homes (typically owner-occupied) are least well represented in the sample of housing units. First, fewer than 600 units in eight developments are available for analysis. Second, for reasons discussed elsewhere, the homes represent only the low end of this housing type, in terms of both price and quality. This bias is illustrated by the characteristics of households owning these homes. By and large, the sampled single family homes appeal to low to moderate income ($5,000 to $10,000), and young (head of household under 35 years of age) households of greater than average size (three or more members). Virtually all homes had either three or four bedrooms--too few smaller or larger units were included to make their analysis possible.

This sample is thus least capable of providing a satisfactory test of the adequacy of the bedroom multiplier technique. Nevertheless, the results of the analysis are somewhat similar to those above.

School Age Children. Exhibit 3-17 shows the five regressions explaining school age children in these homes. Equation one presents the bedroom multiplier estimates which could be made using the sample. A home with three or fewer bedrooms can be expected to house .53 school children; while one with four or more bedrooms can be expected to house 1.32 children. As pointed out elsewhere, these are fairly low estimates, and presumably this reflects the peculiarities of the sampled units.

It is apparent that overall these equations are much more unruly than the corresponding equations for garden apartments or high-rises. The coefficient of BR4 estimates the difference between the number of children in a home with four bedrooms and one with three or fewer.

EXHIBIT 3-16. REGRESSION EQUATIONS EXPLAINING TOTAL HOUSEHOLD SIZE
IN HIGH RISE UNITS

Variables	I	II	III	IV	V^b	Mean	Standard Deviation
Intercept	1.6532	1.9847	1.9693	1.8309	1.5402		
BR2	.8675* (.0560)	.8658* (.0562)	.8731* (.0571)	.8782* (.0576)	.7744* (.0586)	.3287	.4700
BR3	2.0799*	2.0802	2.0615*	2.0643*	1.8934*	.1218	.3272
BR4	---	---	---	---	---	---	---
Q	---	-.1212 (.1689)	-.1213 (.1689)	-.1210 (.1690)	.3467* (.1876)	.9999	.1507
RACE	---	-.2108	-.2113	-.1814	-.2311	.9957	.0654
SIZE	---	---	---	-.0001 ( )	.0005* ( )	356.4070	240.5296
AGE	---	---	---	.0023 (.0147)	a	69.4006	2.1139
REG1	---	---	---	---	---	---	---
REG2	---	---	---	---	a	---	---
REG3	---	---	.0409 (.0566)	a	-.1875* (.0777)	.3913	.4883
REG4	---	---	---	---	---	---	---
REG5	---	---	---	---	---	---	---
σ(Est)	.7823	.7828	.7830	.7832	.7618		
r^2	.4425	.4430	.4433	.4436	.4759		
F	375.07	187.49	150.02	125.02	85.07		
n	948	948	948	948	948		

Notes: (a) This variable failed to attain the significance level required by
the stepwise regression program for entry into the equation.
(b) Additional variables were included. See text.
(*) Significant at the .05 level (one-tail test).

Source: CUPR Survey 1972-1973.

117

EXHIBIT 3-17. REGRESSION EQUATIONS EXPLAINING SCHOOL AGE CHILDREN
IN SINGLE FAMILY HOMES

Variables	I	II	III	IV	V^b	Mean	Standard Deviation
Intercept	.5284	1.8563	1.0265	1.9922	.4390		
BR2	---	---	---	---	---	---	---
BR3	---	---	---	---	---	---	---
BR4	.7878* (.1137)	.7771* (.1126)	1.2691* (.1460)	1.3040* (.1551)	1.2006* (.1612)	.3964	.4896
Q	---	-1.4993* (.3560)	-1.4957* (.3461)	-1.4988* (.3459)	-1.4999* (.3448)	.9995	.1542
RACE	---	.1814 (.2181)	.3509 (.2148)	.3492 (.2147)	.1537 (.2158)	.9645	.2528
SIZE	---	---	---	-.0002 (.0005)	.0030* (.0019)	259.7443	160.6921
AGE	---	---	---	-.0152 (.0162)	.0084 (.0167)	67.9361	6.9759
REG1	---	---	---	---	---	.0700	.2500
REG2	---	---	---	---	---	---	---
REG3	---	---	---	---	---	---	---
REG4	---	---	.4893* (.1591)	.6335* (.2551)	a	.3200	.4669
REG5	---	---	.9669* (.1677)	1.1481* (.2840)	.0471 (.2719)	.3218	.4676
σ(Est)	1.3130	1.2938	1.2577	1.2570	1.2376		
r^2	.0796	.1095	.1615	.1655	.1955		
F	47.9789	22.6743	21.2258	15.5566	13.2668		
n	557	557	557	557	557		

Notes: (a) This variable failed to attain the significance level required by
the stepwise regression program for entry into the equation.
(b) Additional variables were included. See text.
(*) Significant at the .05 level (one-tail test).

Source: CUPR Survey 1972-1973.

For the other housing types, the comparable coefficients had been
very stable as additional variables were entered into the equations.
Here, the addition of geographic and development variables almost
doubles the magnitude of the coefficient of BR4. This doubling
is very difficult to explain, but clearly raises serious questions
about the reliability of bedroom multipliers made using the sample.

Relative values of these homes (Q) is quite significantly related to
the number of school age children. The coefficient of Q implies
that after taking into account number of bedrooms, higher cost and
quality homes typically house fewer school age children. This
finding has clear implications about attempts by local governments
to enhance the quality and price of homes through zoning and other
land use control. It appears that such policies may not only work
to increase the property tax revenue from individual homes, but
also decrease the additional school costs of additional development.
More research is clearly needed here. However, RACE is not a
powerful variable. There is no evidence that RACE offers any
promise for improved forecasting techniques for these single family
homes.

The geographic variables are very powerful.* For single family
homes, it is difficult to distinguish these geographic variables
from the developmental variables of so much importance for previous
housing types. It does appear that as before these geographic
variables are acting as proxies for unique features of the developments. The introduction of development dummy variables significantly
increases explanatory power.** As a matter of fact, as a group the
development dummy variables have greater explanatory power than
does the bedroom multiplier BRR. (Equation one, which includes only
BR4, yields a coefficient of determination of [.08]. The introduction of the development dummy variables increases this to [.20].
This is a natural result of the small degree of variation within
the sample in their bedroom configuration, of course.) Thus, the
findings with regard to school age children are ambiguous. In
this limited sample, it appears that the social ecology of the
developments, however it is determined, dominates the determination
of the number of children.

Total Household Size. The equations explaining total household size
(SZH) in single-family homes are presented in Exhibit 3-18. Equation
one estimates that SZH is 3.54 in homes with three or fewer bedrooms,

---

*Their introduction in equation three yields an F-statistic
of 17.07.

**$F_{(3,546)}$ = 6.78

EXHIBIT 3-18.   REGRESSION EQUATIONS EXPLAINING TOTAL HOUSEHOLD SIZE
IN SINGLE FAMILY HOMES

Variables	I	II	III	IV	V^b	Mean	Standard Deviation
Intercept	3.5415	3.4963	2.4488	1.8775	5.7989		
BR2	---	---	---	---	---	---	---
BR3	---	---	---	---	---	---	---
BR4	.8537* (.1174)	.8452* (.1180)	1.4223* (.1481)	1.4707* (.1576)	1.3174 (.1588)	.3964	.4896
Q	---	-.1145 (.3733)	-.1062 (.3510)	-.1070 (.3514)	-.1140 (.3412)	.9995	.1542
RACE	---	.1690 (.2286)	.4599* (.2178)	.4608* (.2181)	.1703 (.2143)	.9645	.2528
SIZE	---	---	---	-.0005 (.0005)	a	259.7443	160.6921
AGE	---	---	---	.0116 (.0164)	-.0442 (.0345)	67.9361	6.9759
REG1	---	---	---	---	---	.0700	.2500
REG2	---	---	---	---	---	---	---
REG3	---	---	---	---	---	---	---
REG4	---	---	.3421* (.1614)	.1806 (.2592)	.4836 (.3100)	.3200	.4669
REG5	---	---	1.3067* (.1701)	1.1268* (.2885)	.7885* (.3567)	.3218	.4676
σ(Est)	1.3548	1.3564	1.2756	1.2769	1.2288		
r^2	.0870	.0881	.1964	.1978	.2598		
F	52.9148	17.8127	26.9393	19.3331	21.3359		

Notes: (a) This variable failed to attain the significance level required by
the stepwise regression program for entry into the equation.
(b) Additional variables were included. See text.
(*) Significant at the .05 level (one-tail test).

Source: CUPR Survey 1972-1973.

120

and 4.4 when four or more bedrooms are available. As before, the coefficient of BR4 is quite unstable, raising doubts concerning its true value. RACE is significant in equations three and four and suggests that white households have between .4 and .5 more members than do non-white households in comparable units. Though the instability of the coefficient among equations is disquieting, RACE may be an important factor in the determination of SZH in single family homes. Neither development size (SIZE) nor age (AGE) offers any promise of improving production techniques for household size.

Once again, the geographic dummy variables are extremely significant, with large absolute coefficients.* There appears to be true geographic pattern, because geographic variables retained their significance after the introduction of development dummy variables. However, as with school age children, inter-development social differentiation dominates the explanation of variations in household size.

The bedroom multipliers show the same sensitivity to the introduction of the geographic dummy variables. The coefficient of BR4 increases from unity to 1.6 when these variables are introduced. The sensitivity underlines their inter-development variation, and the importance of taking these differences into account. A sample drawn from only a few developments cannot be expected to be applied reliably to any other development. For planning purposes, these multipliers should be estimated from data on a broad variety of units in a large number of developments.

Townhouses

Like the single family home examined in the previous section, townhouses in the sample were almost exclusively owner-occupied. Despite the fact that the costs of these townhouses did not differ a great deal from those of the single family homes, they appealed to a much different household. The purchasers of the townhouses had relatively high incomes, were relatively well educated, and were much more heterogeneous in terms of age.

More contrast may result from the fact that the density of townhouse living is intermediate between that of garden apartments and single family homes. The pressure for social segregation may be somewhat more intense.

---

*$F_{(2,551)} = 37.14$

121

School Age Children. Exhibit 3-19 presents the five basic
regressions explaining the number of school age children resident
in a townhouse. As before, equation one presents the bedroom
multipliers. These multipliers show that on the average, no
children reside in one-bedroom townhouses; .25 live in a two-
bedroom unit; .63 in a three-bedroom home; and 1.06 in a four-
bedroom unit. The introduction of auxiliary variables in equations
two, three, and four yield some striking conclusions: *none of the
additional variables provided any measurable increment to overall
explanatory power*. Neither race, value, age, size, location, or
other unspecified features of the developments represented by the
development dummy variables have any substantial effect on the
number of school age children resident in a townhouse. Social
differentiation among townhouse developments appears to be negligible.
This may be the result of the relative homogeneity of residents in
townhouses and of the basic townhouse physical design.

It is apparent that the simple bedroom multipliers appear to be
quite appropriate for the analysis of the generation of school
children in townhouse developments.

Total Household Size. The results for total size of household
residing in townhouse units are somewhat different. These are
shown in Exhibit 3-20. The bedroom multipliers shown in equation
one estimate that on average 1.68 persons live in a one-bedroom
unit; 2.76 in a two-bedroom unit; 3.58 in a three-bedroom townhouse;
and 4.22 in a four bedroom unit.

These results differ from those regarding school age children in
that relative price, location, and inter-development variation are
each possibly significant determinants of the number of persons in
a household. They were not significantly related to the number of
school age children. As with high rise units, higher value units
generate greater household size. As before, this pattern may
result from greater intensity of use of these higher cost units, or
perhaps from additional space in the unit not reflected in its
number of bedrooms.

Location variables in equations three and four are statistically
significant, and they do add to the overall explanatory power of the
relationship.* As before, however, they may be acting as proxies
for interdevelopment differences, rather than true location variation.**

---

*$F_{(2,1344)}$ = 12.08

**The development dummies add no significant explanatory power
over the geographic variables. Though the effects of geography and
unique development characteristics are impossible to distinguish, the
results for the other housing types suggest that development differentiation is the more powerful variable.

122

EXHIBIT 3-19. REGRESSION EQUATIONS EXPLAINING NUMBER OF SCHOOL AGE CHILDREN IN TOWNHOUSE UNITS

Variables	I	II	III	IV	V^b	Mean	Standard Deviation
Intercept	-.0000	-.2629	-.1756	.7578	-.1013		
BR2	.2475* (.0891)	.2459* (.0894)	.1646 (.1025)	.1716* (.1022)	.1716* (.1022)	.3531	.4781
BR3	.6290* (.0868)	.6273* (.0872)	.5340* (.1042)	.5286* (.1039)	.5286* (.1039)	.5160	.4999
BR4	1.0557* (.1166)	1.0554* (.1166)	.9527* (.1321)	.8954* (.1330)	.8954* (.1330)	.0642	.2453
Q	---	.2301 (.1449)	.2297 (.1449)	.2295 (.1444)	.2295 (.1442)	1.0000	.1457
RACE	---	.0348 (.1651)	.0426 (.1652)	.0473 (.1646)	.0473 (.1646)	.9832	.1287
SIZE	---	---	---	.0007* (.0002)	a	448.1422	165.9075
AGE	---	---	---	-.0193* (.0063)	a	65.4001	5.7140
REG1	---	---	---	---	---	---	---
REG2	---	---	.0166 (.0490)	a	a	.4572	.4983
REG3	---	---	---	---	---	---	---
REG4	---	---	-.0943 (.0688)	.1217 (.0985)	-.1728* (.0699)	.1987	.3991
REG5	---	---	---	---	---	---	---
σ(Est)	.7751	.7750	.7747	.7723	.7723		
r^2	.1008	.1026	.1044	.1107	.1107		
F	50.39	30.77	22.39	20.89	20.89		
n	1352	1352	1352	1352	1352		

Notes: (a) This variable failed to attain the significance level required by the stepwise regression program for entry into the equation.
(b) Additional variables were included. See text.
(*) Significant at the .05 level (one-tail test).

Source: CUPR Survey 1972-1973.

EXHIBIT 3-20. REGRESSION EQUATIONS EXPLAINING TOTAL HOUSEHOLD
SIZE IN TOWNHOUSE UNITS

Variables	I	II	III	IV	V^b	Mean	Standard Deviation
Intercept	1.6770	1.2910	.8464	.6235	1.0575		
BR2	1.0828* (.1224)	1.0841* (.1228)	1.3593* (.1396)	1.3609* (.1397)	1.3609* (.1397)	.3531	.4781
BR3	1.9037* (.1193)	1.9051* (.1197)	2.2101* (.1420)	2.2090* (.1421)	2.2090* (.1421)	.5160	.4999
BR4	2.5361* (.1603)	2.5363* (.1601)	2.7698* (.1800)	2.7573* (.1819)	2.7573* (.1819)	.0642	.2453
Q	---	.4136* (.1991)	.4138* (.1975)	.5795* (.2853)	.4138* (.1975)	1.0000	.1457
RACE	---	-.0293 (.2268)	-.0329 (.2251)	-.0319 (.2252)	-.0319 (.2252)	.9832	.1287
SIZE	---	---	---	.0003 (.0007)	-.0012* (.0003)	448.1422	165.9075
AGE	---	---	---	---	.0080 (.0066)	65.4001	5.7140
REG1	---	---	---	---	---	---	---
REG2	---	---	.1954* (.0668)	.2978 (.2198)	a	.4572	.4983
REG3	---	---	---	---	---	---	---
REG4	---	---	.4477* (.0938)	.5795* (.2853)	a	.1987	.3991
REG5	---	---	---	---	---	---	---
σ(Est)	1.0655	1.0646	1.0560	1.0563	1.0563		
r^2	.2431	.2455	.2588	.2590	.2590		
F	144.32	87.6023	67.0534	58.6684	58.6684		
n	1352	1352	1352	1352	1352		

Notes: (a) This variable failed to attain the significance level required by
the stepwise regression program for entry into the equation.
(b) Additional variables were included. See text.
(*) Significant at the .05 level (one-tail test).

Source: CUPR Survey 1972-1973.

124

Thus, there does appear to be some interdevelopment variation in household size, but none in school age children. Overall, however, the basic bedroom multipliers appear to be extremely powerful for townhouses.

[1]For the earlier study see George Sternlieb, The Garden Apartment Development: A Municipal Cost Revenue Analysis (New Brunswick, N.J.: Bureau of Economic Research, Rutgers University, 1964).

[2]Ibid.

[3]See Thomas Schelling, "On the Ecology of Micromotives," The Public Interest, Fall 1971, pp. 59-98, for an excellent discussion of such a process of segregation.

[4]Sternlieb, op. cit., p. 4.

[5]This F-test is defined in Roger E. Alcaly and Alvin Klevorick, "Food Prices in Relation to Income Levels in New York City," (April 1970), Cowles Foundation Discussion Paper.

CHAPTER 4

THE PUBLIC SECTOR: THE IMPACT OF POPULATION CHANGE ON MUNICIPAL EXPENDITURE LEVELS

The relationships investigated in the early chapters of this study enable one to equate some level of municipal expenditure to a particular development. It was determined that a singular characteristic of a development, i.e., numbers of bedrooms, in large part determines both the number of school age children and total household size of the development unit. An estimate of total average household size times the number of units in a development equals the population to be introduced locally. The population introduced locally times a per capita cost of local municipal operational expenditures is an indication, admittedly crude,* of municipal costs introduced by that development.

While to a certain degree this ignores costs specifically related to development configuration, discussions with municipal officials revealed that local cost variation is so slight for low rise developments, e.g., single family (detached/attached) garden apartments, townhouse/condominiums, etc. that the per capita figure is an adequate one. In the case of the high rise structure, except for equipment increases in the area of fire service, the development form does not present itself as a unique local cost over and above the local per capita figure.

---

*There are at least two strategies for calculating the local cost of new residential development: marginal and average costing. Under the former approach the cost of additional residents brought into a municipality is projected by empirically calculating those additional expenditures associated with their arrival. Under the latter strategy municipal costs of new residents are assumed to be simply a proportion of the total local expenditures based on the town's average costs. We illustrate these two approaches for calculating educational costs below.

Under the marginal cost approach we would determine the net additional expenditures generated by a stated number of new residents. In contrast, if we followed the average cost approach we would calculate the average per person non-school expenditures and then multiply this average by the expected number of residents in the new development.

Both the marginal and average costing techniques have advantages and disadvantages. The former methodology has the limitation of often requiring time consuming and costly interviewing of local officials. It has the advantage of yielding a very accurate short term projection of costs, not only of total costs but of line-item expenditures, e.g., number of new teachers to be hired, new police

Continued

In relying on the per capita municipal expenditure figure as an estimate of assignable cost, based on the number of local residents a
development produces, one must be cognizant of the variation of
this index with growth and its relation to both the direction of
change and to the population base upon which growth grafts the
effect of change.

This chapter employs regression analysis to select and signify the
relative importance both of population change and its direction as
a determinant of per capita municipal expenditures. Since the
impact of growth is in large degree a function of population size,
the chapter partitions communities according to 1) the magnitude
of their established population base and 2) the direction of the
population change over the decade 1960 to 1970.

This will establish both the importance of growth as a future
indicator of municipal expenditures and the separate classes of
growth which exist within a state.

THE ECONOMICS OF THE PUBLIC SECTOR

Although the study of the public economic sector has been pursued
for as long as the analysis of the private sector, it has generally
been dominated by theories designed to minimize the harmful impact
of government's revenue generating process upon the various firms
and households of the private sector. The pioneering study of
local government expenditures by Solomon Fabricant (1952)[1] describes
the considerable growth in local public expenditures during the
first half of the twentieth century as well as its very significant
fraction of the yearly gross national product of the country.
Following this preliminary work, the thrust has been to inquire
as to why local public expenditures occur and how they vary from
one city to the next. The study that follows forms a part of the
more recent theoretical endeavors.

        Footnote * continued --
cars to be purchased, etc. The latter advantage can be invaluable
to local budgeting and purchasing officials who almost invariably
operate on a line-item basis.

The average costing approach has the advantage of not requiring
expensive and time consuming interviewing of local officials.

Previous studies directed toward the area of municipal expenditure patterns concentrated on municipal or state-wide variation in factors such as population size, population density, and income level.[2] In time this list was expanded to include the rate of growth of the municipality and characteristics of the housing stock;[3] the local tax base, intergovernmental revenues, and estimates of daytime population;[4] governmental structure;[5] and finally, estimates of the conditions under which public goods had to be delivered and the personal tastes of the citizenry.[6]

Thus, the twenty-year history of this area of analysis has found urban economists overviewing public expenditure patterns and finally searching both for common characteristics that follow from these expenditure patterns and for urban structural characteristics and processes of change that may contribute to their variation.

Urban Structural Characteristics

Population Size and Per Capita Expenditures

It appears that the use of population size as an explanatory factor can be more vigorously refined to mean the extent of the development of a public goods and services delivery system. Thus, using this interpretation, previous research efforts suggest to us that demographic factors affect municipal operating expenditures in several ways. First, in terms of absolute size, small cities must distribute large initial costs over a small population thus producing elevated levels of per capita expenditures (START-UP) values. Cities ranging through middle size can exploit the previously capitalized public goods capacity thereby decreasing their per capita expenditures (EFFICIENCY). Lastly, large cities reacting to the probability of high human interaction should be increasing their output of public goods and services and in all probability also increasing their expenditure level over that of the middle sized city (URBAN COST EMERGENCE). Exhibit 4-1 displays data, gathered from a set of New Jersey municipalities, that conform to these generalizations.

The index used to represent the degree of development of the delivery system is the municipality's 1960 population. We are assuming that there is a rank-order relationship between population size and the development of the public goods delivery system. It is recognized that this can produce erroneous results. First, a township large in surface area can contain significant numbers of citizens in relatively rural surroundings. Thus, the 1960 population level can overestimate the level of this determinant in areas of low population density. Second, size of city ignores the relative efficiency levels among the various municipalities as well as degree of upkeep required to sustain a given level of public service production. In both of these cases the pressure on the older central cities will be underestimated.

EXHIBIT 4-1. THE CHARACTERISTICS OF THE SIX POPULATION SIZE STRATA CREATED FROM 557 NEW JERSEY MUNICIPALITIES

1960 Population Size Range	Number of Cities	Mean City Size for 1970	1970 Per Capita Municipal Operating Expenditures		
			Mean	Standard Error	Standard Deviation
Less than 1,000	55	970	176.18	28.16	208.83
1-5,000	238	3,811	99.04	5.87	90.59
5-10,000	117	9,307	91.78	3.74	40.55
10,000 to 25,000	102	19,208	100.21	4.37	44.12
25,000 to 50,000	32	40,281	120.39	7.06	39.92
50,000 and over	17	108,423	160.37	16.33	67.30

Source: CUPR Survey 1972-1973

Per Capita Expenditures in Growing Communities

In terms of population change, studies of municipal expenditures have produced three partial and one well developed explanation for the observed impact of growth upon per capita municipal expenditures. The most commonly used explanation was provided in Harvey Brazer's study of city expenditures.

> As a city's population grows, the need for public services increases, but *per capita operating expenditures may be expected to lag as existing facilities are used more intensively,* either because of existing excess capacities or because budgetary allocations commonly do not keep pace with the expansion of service requirements.[7]

Clearly Brazer's hypotheses are restricted to growing cities. Further it is implicitly limited to large established municipalities with preexisting public goods delivery systems.

Brazer clearly isolates (and by some may have been thought to initiate the term) expenditure "lag" but he assigns no behavioral reason for its occurrence. However, if one assumes that a municipality's policy-making apparatus is geared to increase the present wealth and income of its citizens, then the hypothesis is congruent with the economist's income or benefit maximizing

theory of behavior.[8] Taxpayers within the community will tend to
avoid the payment of taxes either for excess operating expenditures
or for debt service to the extent that the benefit is expected to
accrue to newcomers.* A non-fiscal device such as the subdivision
ordinance, which assigns cost directly to expected users, further
protects the existing taxpayers from benefit spillovers to the
newcomers. Thus, while avoiding any subjective reasoning as to
why the phenomenon occurs, the fact remains that Brazer has documented a definite expenditure lag occurring with positive population growth. The start-up cost concept is at the core of the one
well developed model of the impact of growth on public expenditures.

An alternative to the expenditure lag position has also been recognized. L. R. Gabler states:

> If the budget process tends to anticipate growth
> in population, a positive relationship would emerge;
> if it lags, then the association would be inverse.[9]

Gabler accepts the position that if the actors within the local
decision making process are clearly apprised of the best estimates
of future needs, they will find and use the political power requisite for the generation of local revenue necessary to prevent
future problems.

In what is up to now the most detailed theoretical exposition on
the impact of growth upon the public expenditures, Dick Netzer
brings together both the economic conditions and population
indices which lead to fiscal stress under conditions of population
growth.[10] First, to the extent that the municipalities are at the
beginning of the growth phase, the common amenities of urban living
such as sewerage, refuse disposal, parks and fire protection will
be nonexistent or minimal in terms of service level. This will
necessitate the expenditure of public revenue for what are termed
start-up costs. This term must be broadly taken; start-up costs
can literally mean the creation of the human organization and the
physical facilities necessary to deliver public services. In addition and more commonly this term will mean the expansion of the
existing bureaucracy and the leasing or construction of additional
working space or equipment as growth dictates. Similarly, labor
intensive functions such as police, public works and administration
produce requirements for trained personnel such as police or fire
chiefs, water and sewer inspectors, and municipal administrators,
a certain proportion of whom are necessary regardless of the existing population size. Apropos of this point, Spangler argues that:

_____

*Another component of the explanation is that at a certain pop-
ulation base efficiency occurs as a result of both excess capital
and human resources. Expansion of per capita expenditures does not
occur until these excesses are depleted.

The most important determinant of unit cost may be
the _rapidity_ with which the rate of output changes.
Thus the areas having most rapid population growth
have higher per capita government expenditures because of the continual disruption of existing
routines for doing work.[11]

(We must realize that Spangler's statement at this time is an un-
tested hypothesis. In the real world it could well be the case
that a decrease in the _quality_ of service as growth increases
would contribute to a steady or decreasing level of per capita
expenditure).

Second, fiscal pressure is produced by the level of public services
expected to be available for the new suburbanite. That is, new
suburbanites, many of whom were urban residents, expect the same
high level of public services to be produced in their newly
developed municipality as was available in their previous place
of residence. To meet this demand the newly suburbanized municipality must finance the creation of new human and physical
delivery systems. Third, existing trends show that newly arrived
suburbanites have a disproportionately high number of school
children. Indeed many have moved specifically because of this
consideration. This immediately places not only a choice before
local interest groups but potential confrontation as to the funding of municipal versus school functions. The ultimate fiscal
impact of such conflict is difficult to estimate. It has been
suggested, however, that the size of the various effective interest groups and the requirements generated by commercial and industrial concerns will largely determine both the absolute spending levels and the degree of support given to municipal as opposed
to school levies (and by extension, associated expenditure levels).
At any rate, the effect of this conflict, assuming at least partial
recognition of the public schools' revenue absorption competition,
would be to shift downward per capita municipal operating expenditures.

Lastly, the earlier stated conditions will force the rapid development of public facilities as well as an increase in the municipal
and public school staffs. If there is a debt limit based upon
municipal property valuations (such as in New Jersey) this can
prove a barrier to those forms of capital construction that cannot
be financed through revenue bonds.

Again this competition of capital public services, i.e., funding
the construction of schools instead of roads, sewers and public
buildings will influence per capita municipal operating expenditures.

Each of the above factors, as Netzer notes, acts to segregate the
population into oldtimers and newcomers with the probability being high that the old-time population will balk at the passage of

132

larger tax levies--the effect being to lower the public expenditure level of the community.

While Netzer concentrates on different pressure groups impacting on municipal costs, a larger perspective might assign causation to existing population bases and growth rates in communities where these groups come into existence.

Certainly the arguments are equally evident for the case of start-up costs. Netzer's second point, i.e., the urban appetites of new suburbanites, may be explained as an interim stage in communities either delaying economies of consumption or contributing to their demise. Efficiency itself may be explained not by a compilation of public services occasioning decreased municipal expenditures but rather by the excess capital accumulation as a function of the established servicing base mentioned previously.

The work previously reviewed has emphasized the impact of population growth upon this expenditure side of the local budget. Noting that for the most part local expenditures are the "flip side" of the local revenue coin, it will still be useful to look at population growth as a force provoking changes in the ease with which local revenue can be generated. In a study of fifty-seven New York counties, Jesse Burkhead found:

> Increases in population not only increase the property tax base, but tend to occur in counties with high average per capita income. Whether income levels induce population in-movement or vice-versa cannot be determined from this analysis, but it would appear that *population increases bring requirements for property tax revenue that exceed the increases in income.*[12]

Burkhead's study is centered upon a factor economists call the "income elasticity of property tax collections." As derived by him, this is a summary measure of the percent change from 1949 to 1959 of countywide per capita property tax collection divided by the 1950 to 1960 percent change in the per capita countywide personal income. On the average the fifty-seven counties increased their property tax revenues at a rate 50 percent higher than the personal income of their inhabitants.

This suggests to us that rapidly growing areas will generate, over time, elevated general tax rates (expenditures). In turn, however, the high tax rate will act as an effective inhibitor of further expenditure or tax increases. Again this points to the existence of a lag phenomenon, this time from the revenue side of the ledger.

Per Capita Expenditures in Declining Communities

Previous analyses implicitly assumed a set of municipalities that were growing in population. Yet, a significant fraction of cities are experiencing population decline. For example, from 1960 to 1970 fully sixty-seven of New Jersey's 567 municipalities lost population. This phenomenon is not limited to New Jersey. On the national level, cities in many of the older industrial states are experiencing population loss. Exhibit 4-2 shows the percentage of municipalities declining in population in a selected subset of states.

EXHIBIT 4-2. THE NUMBER OF CITIES AND PERCENTAGE OF TOTAL MUNICIPALITIES OF 2,500 OR MORE EXPERIENCING POPULATION LOSS: 1960-1970

State	Number of cities experiencing loss	Percent of state's cities of 2,500 or more experiencing loss
Connecticut	16	9
Illinois	48	13
Indiana	35	23
Massachusetts	39	12
Michigan	58	26
New Jersey	46	19
New York	121	29
Ohio	71	20
Pennsylvania	238	55

Source: U. S. Bureau of the Census, Census of Population: 1970, Vol. 1, Characteristics of the Inhabitants, Table 31, Land Area and Population of Places of 2,500 or more for the United States and Puerto Rico, and of Towns of 2,500 or more for the New England states: 1960-1970.

Despite the extent of this phenomenon, knowledge of the impact of declining population on municipal expenditures is still severely limited; further, the impact of the many forms of decline need investigation.

The problem has been examined in case study form. George Sternlieb and Robert W. Burchell have described in detail the increased municipal expenditures required to service abandoned parcels in Newark, New Jersey.[13] An earlier statement on the same city found that as the city's population declined, municipal expenditure levels increased.[14]

A potential explanation for part of this phenomenon has been offered by William Baumol. It is Baumol's contention that municipal employee wages are tied to the wage level of the private economic sector. Productivity increases in the private sector allow the

134

workers to increase their wage rate; in turn, by demanding wage increases regardless of productivity increases, public sector employees attempt to maintain a comparable level of consumption.[15] This suggests that the level of expenditures necessary to maintain the local public goods delivery system is not linearly responsive to changes in the numerical population base. In conclusion, these works suggest that there are interaction effects between population size and the direction of population change that make the use of a single explanatory model highly unreliable.

The Importance of Population Growth in Prior Studies

Among the first significant studies to examine the determinants of per capita municipal operating expenditures was that by Stanley Scott and Edward Feder (1957).[16] Their study involved 192 California cities of over 2,500 population for the year 1950. Their model explained approximately 59 percent of the change among the cities in per capita municipal expenditures and showed that a 1 percent change in the rate of population growth was associated with a 3.1 percent _decrease_ in per capita expenditures.

This was followed in 1959 by the first detailed national study. In it Harvey Brazer studied the expenditure behavior of 462 cities of over 25,000 population (1950).[17] In Brazer's model 57 percent of the change in per capita expenditures was explained. Further, a single unit rise in the percentage increase in population over the decade was shown to correspond to a 6.3 cent decline in per capita public expenditures. Following this, Brazer subdivided the group of cities and ran separate regression studies on the cities of three states: California, Ohio, and Massachusetts. In California, a state showing rapid population growth, thirty-five cities were included. It was found that a one unit change in percent growth rate corresponded with a decline of 7.5 cents in per capita municipal expenditures.* In Ohio, a state of but moderate growth, only the police function was shown to be affected by population increase. However, in this case police expenditures were shown to rise by 3.9 cents per capita for a one unit change in the percent rate of growth. Massachusetts was chosen both because it had thirty cities in its original sample and because many of its cities had an absolute decline in population. The impact of this decline was noticed for but one function--fire protection. It was found that for a one-unit rise in the percent population change, expenditures for fire protection declined 6.9 cents per capita.

---

*Assume a city of 50,000 persons in 1940 growing to 50,500 in 1950. Based on the conclusions cited above the city will spend $3,787 less on police protection in 1950 than if it had remained at 50,000 over the decade. At 1940-1950 pay scales this translates into approximately one police patrolman less on the force for the growing city ($0.075 x 50,500 = $3,787.50).

135

Translating this into a condition of population loss, it shows that for a one-unit increase in population loss rate, the remaining citizens spend 6.9 cents more per capita for fire protection. These results are summarized in Exhibit 4-3.

Briefly, previous empirical efforts have found that the relative change in a municipality's population, measured in terms of the average percent population growth, has had a significant impact upon the level of per capita expenditures. Growth has been found for the most part to result in a lower level of expenditures when compared to expenditure levels of relatively stable municipalities.*

The results of this study, obtained from a large number of New Jersey municipalities, based on preliminary analyses in which multiple regression techniques were employed, yielded results which appeared to contradict the conclusions of most previous work. These results implied that on the average a municipality which grew in population during the 1960 to 1970 decade spent proportionately more for per capita municipal purposes than the more stable municipality. This is in contradiction to the research of the past twenty years which suggests that a negative net regression coefficient relating per capita municipal operating expenditures to population change should be obtained. In contrast, we derived a positive relationship.

In order to resolve the apparent contradiction, a critical examination of our model ensued. The proper specification of the regression model is essential in order to avoid an erroneously large residual error term and to protect against the effects of a non-randomly distributed and unspecified independent determinant.[18]

When compared with the present state of the art, our model appeared adequate. Thus, the alternative is to hypothesize the presence of certain interaction effects which biased the impact of percent population change upon the dependent variable.

THE MODEL AND METHOD

The model commonly used to test municipal expenditure hypotheses is the multiple regression model. We have chosen a variant of this framework: analysis of covariance. This form of analysis has been used twice in the past to analyze the determinants of per capita expenditures. Elliott Morss et. al., used it, "...to separate...from those due to systematic interactions with specific variables."[19] In a study similar to our own, Bernard Booms used analysis of covariance for the purpose of separating the unspecified

---

*Burkhead worked exclusively with property tax revenues. His findings, while similar to ours, conflict with the existing literature. Burkhead centered on both rural and urban counties but did not stratify for their differences.

EXHIBIT 4-3. SUMMARY OF EMPIRICAL STUDIES DEALING WITH THE IMPACT OF GROWTH ON PER CAPITA EXPENDITURES

Author of Study	Objective Included in Study	Change in Per Capita Expenditure for a 1 Percent Increase in Growth Rate	R^2 Percent of Variation in Per Capita Expenditure Explained by Authors Model
Scott & Feder	192 California cities of over 2500 population in 1950	-0.031* (.013)**	59%
Brazer	462 cities of over 25,000 in 1950	-0.063 (.027)	57%
	35 California cities	-0.075 (.032)	45%
	Police expenditure in 32 Ohio cities	+0.039 (.009)	68%
	Fire expenditure in 30 Massachusetts cities	-0.069 (0.044)	23%
Weicher [20]	Fire expenditure of 206 Central cities in 1960	-2.07 (0.665)	64%
Libera [21]	498 cities of 25,000 or more as of 1950	-11.352	69%
Lind [22]	Total per capita local expenditure of all cities and towns in Rhode Island	38.89 (18.85)	78%
Hiibner [23]	21 Florida municipalities of over 25,000 per capita operating expenditure	-0.02	50%

*Net regression coefficients of these studies (Not a bivariate model. The coefficient for the population variable has been removed from the equation and presented separately. Obviously the net regression coefficient takes into account the effects of other factors; the size of the coefficient as well as its significance as affected by both the number of variables and the types of other variables included in the model.)
**Standard error of the estimate

Source: CUPR Survey 1972-1973.

effects of local governmental form, i.e., mayor or managerial, on per capita common municipal expenditures for cities of 25,000 to 100,000 in population.[24]

The present study uses analysis of covariance to determine if a significant improvement in explanation of per capita municipal operating expenditures occurs when city size and direction of population change are used to stratify the universe of New Jersey cities. Our analysis will proceed through three models:

Model 1 will generate a multiple regression analysis of the pooled set of New Jersey municipalities. In addition to the usual set of net regression coefficients and their standard errors, this exercise will generate the residual sum of squares for the dependent variable; it is this package of error that each of our proposed improvements will attempt to reduce.

In Model 2 the pooled set of cities will be stratified by city size. Six strata will be produced; two multiple regression analyses will be run on each stratum. First, the assumption of common slopes for each independent variable among the six strata is used to generate an error sum of squares value for the dependent variable. This is created by summing each error term over the six strata. An F test is used to determine if the reduction in error sum of squares from Model 1 is significantly different from zero. We then reproduce each regression run under the assumption that the net regression coefficients for each independent variable can vary for each run. Following this, an F test is calculated from the summed residuals; this will allow us to judge if the stratification of cities by size offers a significant improvement over Model 1.

Model 3 reorganizes the set of cities by direction of growth and city size range. Thus, six strata of cities that grew during the 1960 to 1970 decade are formed; similarly, six strata of cities that lost population are formed. The use of the analysis of covariance parallels that described in Model 2.

Empirical Analyses

The objects used for this analysis are 557* of the 567 New Jersey municipalities. The time period over which population change is analyzed is 1960 to 1970. Analysis is limited to one dependent variable; this is the 1970 per capita municipal operating expenditures. The independent variables are clustered into three sets. The first set contains only one variable; this is the percent change in population from 1960 to 1970. It is the only variable

---

*Ten cities were excluded from the analysis because of missing employment data.

138

for which a detailed examination will follow in this chapter. Second,
two independent variables are used to stratify the set of cities;
as a surrogate for the degree of public goods delivery system development, we use the 1960 population. Next, as an indicator of the
direction of population change, a dichotomous variable is constructed
from the sign of the 1960 to 1970 percent change in population.

The third cluster of independent variables is composed of those
determinants most commonly used in previous analyses. They can be
roughly categorized as indices of social class, life cycle, race,
economic base, and fiscal capacity of the municipality.

The first step in the empirical analysis is a description of the
characteristics of the dependent variable (per capita municipal
operating expenditures). We must determine if a characteristic
pattern exists between the dependent variable and city size class
or city size class partitioned by direction of population change.

EXHIBIT 4-4. CHARACTERISTICS OF THE 489 NEW JERSEY CITIES
THAT GAINED IN POPULATION FROM 1960 TO 1970

1960 Population Range	Number of Cities	Mean Per Capita Municipal Opera- ing Expenditures	Mean 1960 Population	Mean 1970 Population
Less than 1,000	52	179.97 (29.61)*	671 (32)	998 (65)
1,000 to 5,000	205	95.56 (4.84)	2,708 (76)	4,093 (174)
5,000 to 10,000	108	92.57 (4.01)	7,154 (137)	9,536 (255)
10,000 to 25,000	86	95.80 (4.68)	14,865 (443)	19,841 (847)
25,000 to 50,000	28	112.79 (6.60)	34,393 (1,229)	41,112 (1,942)
Over 50,000	10	125.21 (10.11)	74,621 (9,569)	79,698 (9,792)

Note: *The numbers in parentheses represent the standard error of the means
for the values above them.

Source: CUPR Survey 1972-1973

Comparison of the per capita expenditure and city size data in Exhibits 4-1, 4-4, 4-5 produce the following generalizations: First, a "U" shaped curve is produced by each set of data when per capita expenditures are compared with population size. *Thus, to the extent that other factors do not bias the results, we find that extremely small and large municipalities cost more to run on a per capita basis than intermediate sized municipalities. Second, we find that large cities that are slowly growing spend less per capita than large cities that are declining, and third, that small municipalities either growing or declining spend a similar amount per capita.* Exhibit 4-6 displays these results graphically.

EXHIBIT 4-5. CHARACTERISTICS OF THE SIXTY-EIGHT NEW JERSEY CITIES THAT LOST POPULATION FROM 1960 TO 1970

1960 Population Range	Number of Cities	Mean Per Capita Municipal Operating Expenditures	Mean 1960 Population	Mean 1970 Population
Less than 1,000	5	181.00 (45.30)	554 (210)	492 (209)
1,000 to 5,000	29	94.30 (19.80)	2,731 (243)	2,490 (218)
5,000 to 10,000	9	82.24 (7.49)	7,011 (407)	6,552 (353)
10,000 to 25,000	16	123.91 (9.55)	16,519 (930)	15,811 (925)
25,000 to 50,000	4	173.59 (18.10)	36,323 (4,603)	34,394 (4,209)
Over 50,000	7	210.58 (28.10)	160,524 (49,242)	149,161 (46,929)

Note: *The numbers in parentheses represent the standard error of the means for the values above them.

Source: CUPR Survey 1972-1973

Model 1: Multiple Regression Analysis on the Pooled Sample of 557 New Jersey Municipalities

As was shown earlier in Exhibit 4-3, studies of municipal expenditures usually find that the per capita expenditures are negatively

140

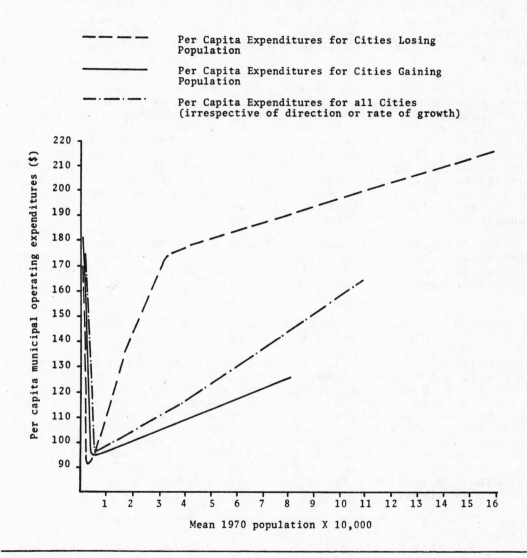

EXHIBIT 4-6. PER CAPITA MUNICIPAL OPERATION EXPENDITURES OF NEW
JERSEY MUNICIPALITIES BY SIZE OF CITY AND DIRECTION
OF POPULATION CHANGE

‒ ‒ ‒ ‒ Per Capita Expenditures for Cities Losing
Population

────── Per Capita Expenditures for Cities Gaining
Population

‒·‒·‒· Per Capita Expenditures for all Cities
(irrespective of direction or rate of growth)

Per capita municipal operating expenditures ($)

Mean 1970 population X 10,000

Source: Tables 1, 4, and 5.

related to percent population change. However, Roger Lind's Rhode Island study[25] is in contradiction with this tradition. Our study of New Jersey coincides with Lind's findings. Exhibit 4-7 shows that when considered as one system, New Jersey cities increase their per capita municipal expenditures by 26 cents for every one percent increase in the level of percent growth. This value is significantly different from zero at the 0.001 level; however, in light of its contradiction of past results its validity must be questioned.

An indicator of the success of the model can be obtained by comparing the size of the band in which approximately 67 percent of the cities' values on the dependent variable are contained prior to regression with the size of the same band after regression. This is done when we compare the standard error of the estimate against the standard deviation of the dependent variable. The standard deviation of the 1970 per capita expenditure is $98.36, the standard error of the estimate is $49.32. We have reduced the size of the band by about $49 (Exhibit 4-7). Thus, it is evident that either some stochastic forces exist in the causation of the variation in expenditures or that our model is somewhat defective.

For those determinants absent from the present model, two sources of improvement can be developed: first, additional causal dimensions can be sought, and second, the potential misspecifications within the pooled model can be corrected.

Model 2: Multiple Regression Analysis on the Sets of Municipalities Stratified by City Size

As indicated above, the existence of a developed public goods delivery system has been suggested as an important factor controlling the level of present expenditures. Using 1960 population as the surrogate of this factor, we find that a strong pattern exists among the coefficients measuring the impact of change from the 1960 to 1970 population level upon 1970 per capita municipal expenditures. Column 2 of Exhibit 4-8 displays these results. Small cities, those under 5,000, show a positive impact of population change upon expenditure levels. As the city size increases, the coefficient becomes negative and increases in magnitude towards the largest size class.

The model generates four regression coefficients significantly different from zero; one coefficient representing the impact of population change on the 5,000 -- 10,000 size range is not noticeably different from zero; this is what we have hypothesized although prior to the study the specific size range obtaining zero impact was not specified. Lastly, the coefficient representing the largest size class is not significantly different from zero; this is the one obvious contradiction with previous research. We have been led to believe that a negative coefficient indicating an expenditure lag

EXHIBIT 4-7.   RESULTS FROM THE REGRESSION OF 1970 PER CAPITA MUNICIPAL
OPERATING EXPENDITURES FOR 522 NEW JERSEY MUNICIPALITIES
ON NINE INDEPENDENT VARIABLES

Variable	*Regression Coefficient*	*Standard Error*
% Population Change	0.14	(0.08)
1970 City Population	-0.0003	(0.0001)
% DU* Built 1969 to 1970	-1.69	(0.99)
% DU Built 1965 to 1968	0.75	(0.59)
% DU Built 1960 to 1964	-1.03	(0.48)
% DU Built before 1939	-0.49	(0.26)
% Single Family Detached	-0.32	(0.26)
% Duplexes	0.85	(0.43)
% of DU in 50+ structures	-1.21	(0.90)
Median House Value	- .0008	(0.0005)
$\frac{\text{Commercial Employment}}{\text{1970 Residential Pop.}}$	-32.83	(23.28)
$\frac{\text{Industrial Employment}}{\text{1970 Residential Pop.}}$	-24.39	(16.44)
% Individuals in families under poverty level	4.01	(0.79)
% of population 22-39 years of age	-3.24	(1.17)
% of population 40-54 years of age	-2.20	(1.18)
% of population over 55 years of age	2.12	(0.69)
High concentrations of professional managerial and absence of craftsman operatives	17.70	(4.45)
Moderate concentrations of professional/managerial and absence of service employees	13.95	(3.47)
High concentration of farm employment and absence of clericals	-19.67	(2.95)
Per Capita Property Value	0.002	(0.0003)
General Tax Rate (equalized)	-0.044	(0.037)
State Aid and Replacement Revenue	0.80	(0.19)
Public Utilities and Miscellaneous Revenues	0.39	(0.09)
Debt Service and Capital Improvements	1.77	(0.12)
Per Capita revenue raised locally for school purposes	0.05	(0.01)

R^2= .87
Standard Error 49.32

Analysis of Variance	Degrees of Freedom	Mean Square	F
Regression	28	137,974	56.71
Residual	496	2,433	

*Dwelling Units

Source: CUPR Survey 1972-1973.

143

EXHIBIT 4-8. REGRESSION COEFFICIENTS FOR THE IMPACT OF POPULATION CHANGE ON 1970 PER CAPITA MUNICIPAL EXPENDITURES ON 6 SETS OF CITY STRATIFICATIONS

1960 Population Size Range	(2) *557 Cities Stratified by Size*	(3)[3] *Cities Gaining in Population*	(4)[3] *Cities Declining in Population*
Less than 1000	0.48[1] (0.26)	0.16 (0.75)	+5.80[1,4] (0.11)
1000 to 5000	0.17[1] (0.08)	0.11 (0.07)	-0.20[1] (0.14)
5000 to 10,000	-0.018 (NIE)[2]	-0.10 (0.16)	.001 (NIE)[2]
10,000 to 25,000	-0.36 (0.09)[1]	-0.08 (6.09)	+.0004 (NIE)[2]
25,000 to 50,000	-0.68[1] (0.14)	-0.31 (0.10)	5.40 (0.94)
50,000 and over	.004 (NIE)[2]	-1.51[1] (0.01)	5.70 (NIE)[2]

Notes: 1. These values are significantly different from zero at the 0.05 level of significance.

2. NIE symbolizes the value of the net regression coefficient if it had been entered into the regression equation at the next step. In no case are they significantly different from zero.

3. The regression equation from which these net regression coefficients were taken are to be found in Chapter 6, Exhibits 6-12 and 6-13.

4. This is interpreted to mean that an increase of 1 percent in the rate of population decline over the decade corresponds to an increased per capita operating expenditure level of $5.80.

Source: CUPR Survey 1972-1973.

should be obtained for cities having a preexisting mature public goods delivery system. Stratification by city size has not shown this to be the case.

This result was anticipated. According to the Sternlieb-Burchell analysis of Newark we can expect declining cities to increase their per capita expenditure whereas cities growing in population will be able to partially fund the growth through previously capitalized delivery system capacity. In order to explore this idea we will repeat the analysis by stratifying both by size and direction of population change; this is done in Model 3. Before proceeding with Model 3's analysis we must indicate the other gains in explanation brought about by city size stratification. As we shall note in the following section, city size as a product of 300 years of urbanization has crystalized many social and economic characteristics in specific size ranges.[26] For example, poor and minority groups cluster in the largest cities, high income recipients and professional and managerial groups reside in intermediate to larger city sizes; lastly, families with large numbers of children concentrate in intermediate to smaller sized municipalities. The interaction as opposed to the independent impact of these factors can be approximated by testing to determine if a significant reduction in the residual sum of squares in the per capita expenditure variable occurs when we move from the pooled cities (Model 1) to the stratified set of cities (Model 2).

After allowing the six equations to act on the variation within the dependent variable, the residual error is found to be 347,704. Compared to the corresponding value derived from Model 1, this amounts to a 71 percent reduction in error. Further, it is shown in Exhibit 4-9 that this increase in explanation is significantly different from zero at the 0.01 level of significance.

The total result, therefore, supports the Netzer argument which suggests that start-up costs inordinately affect expenditure levels of smaller governmental units. However, it also indicates that the often reproduced negative coefficient exists within systems of cities containing municipalities in the upper portion of the rank size spectrum.

Model 3: Multiple Regression Analysis on the Sets of Municipalities Stratified by Both Population Size and Direction of Population Change

Model 2 has shown us that stratification of the system of cities by size can be a meaningful endeavor. Following the Netzer and Sternlieb arguments, we must determine if the direction* of population change offers yet another improvement in our explanation of per capita municipal operating expenditures.

---

*Direction only will be considered here. Levels of population change will be considered in a subsequent section.

EXHIBIT 4-9.   ANALYSIS OF COVARIANCE FOR MUNICIPALITIES STRATIFIED
BY CITY SIZE

Source of Variation	Sum of Squared Residuals	Degrees of Freedom	Mean Square
Residuals from the pooled regression analysis (model 1)	1,206,768	496	2433
Residuals produced after allowing slopes and intercepts of each equation to vary (model 2)*	347,704	386	900
Incremental increase in explanation	858,963	110	7809

$$F_{(110,386)} = 8.67 \qquad F_{(0.01)} = 1.46$$

*Included within each covariance analysis was the test for
homogeneity of slope coefficients. In every case
homogeneity had to be rejected. This preliminary work has
been omitted for the sake of clarity.

Source: CUPR Survey 1972-1973.

Exhibits 4-4 and 4-5 have displayed the distribution of gaining and
declining municipalities over our six population size categories.
Exhibit 4-8, Columns 3 and 4, adds to this the relevant statistics
from multiple regression. Since the number of growing municipalities dominates the system, we should expect to find that their
pattern of coefficients strongly coincide with the pattern produced
by the universe of cities when stratified by city size. (Column 2,
Exhibit 4-8). This is the case. Exhibit 4-8, Column 3, shows that
cities of up to 5,000 population respond to positive growth with a
relatively greater than proportional increase in total expenditures. Moving toward the higher population size strata, a pro-
gressively negative coefficient is found; this parallels the ex-
penditure-lag hypothesis propounded by Brazer and supports our move
toward the more complex Model 3.

Of equal interest is the pattern produced by the municipalities that are declining in population (Exhibit 4-8, Column 4). The coefficients derived are for the most part negative.*

Cities in decline respond to the two size extremes by increasing their per capita expenditures. Small municipalities increase their per capita municipal expenditures by close to $6 for every 1 percent decline in population. This sharply decreases as we move up through the 10,000 to 25,000 size class; here, we find little independent impact from percent population decline on per capita expenditures. However, in the larger size municipalities we find sharp positive response of per capita expenditures relative to a 1 percent loss in population.**

Lastly, we must analyze the value in moving from Model 2 to the more complex Model 3. Model 2 assumed that the direction of change in population did not affect the proposed linear relationship between population change and per capita expenditures. An indication of the strength of that assumption can be gained by comparing the reduction in the error sum of squares from Model 2 with the residual error sustained at the end of Model 3. Exhibit 4-10 is the analysis of co-variance table from which this judgment can be made. It shows that close to 34 percent of the Model 2 residual error can be explained by the addition of the two population change directions. Further, it shows that the increase in explanation is significantly different from zero at the 0.01 level.

TENTATIVE CONCLUSIONS EMERGING FROM THE ANALYSIS

The first hypothesis stated that the level of per capita municipal operating expenditures required to operate local government is affected in different ways by a complex of characteristics summarized by population size. The results derived from Model 2 and displayed in Exhibit 4-8 will not allow us to reject that hypothesis.

———————————

*It must be remembered that the coefficients are being produced in the second quadrant of cartesian coordinate space; all of the previous analyses took place in the last quadrant. Multiplication of each coefficient by (-1) will reverse their signs. This has been done and permits us to describe their pattern in terms of previous analyses.

**A significant net regression coefficient was not found for the largest strata of declining cities. The reason for this is not clear. It may well be that rate of population loss does not influence per capita expenditures; however, the relatively small number of cases within this strata may preclude the detection of its influence.

EXHIBIT 4-10. ANALYSIS OF COVARIANCE FOR MUNICIPALITIES STRATIFIED BY CITY SIZE AND DIRECTION OF PERCENT CHANGE IN POPULATION: 1960 TO 1970

Source of Variation	Sum of Squared Residuals	Degrees of Freedom	Mean Square n
Residuals from the city size stratifica- tion model	347,704	386	900
Residuals from the city size and dir- ection of change Model 3	229,351	319	718
Incremental increase in explanation	118,353	67	1,766

$F(67,319) = 2.45$ $\qquad$ $F(0.01) = 1.65$

Note: Included within each covariance analysis was the test for homogeneity of slope coefficients. In every case homo- geneity had to be rejected. This preliminary work has been omitted for the sake of brevity.

Source: CUPR Survey 1972-1973.

The second and third hypotheses dealt with the direction of popula- tion change: growth and decline. The second hypothesis stated that per capita expenditures will be positive for population growth for small cities but gradually become negative for larger cities. Ex- hibit 4-8, Column 3, shows that this pattern exists.

The third hypothesis stated that the relationship of percent popula- tion loss and per capita expenditures under the condition of popula- tion decline will be positive for small cities and large cities. Exhibit 4-8, Column 4, shows that with the exception of intermediate sized cities (1,000-25,000) this is largely the case.

Lastly, the second and third hypotheses are combined into one hypo- thesis; this states that cities undergoing growth respond to it through different budgetary processes than municipalities that are declining in population. The analysis of covariance dis- played in Exhibit 4-10 shows that a considerable improvement accrues to the explanation of the dependent variable when separate equations are used to describe its relationship to the set of independent deter- minants. Thus, although it is not firm, we cannot reject the new combined hypothesis.

In conclusion the results of our macro-analysis have provided strong encouragement to pursue in greater depth the mechanism by which the rate of population change acts upon the municipal fisc. The limitations of the macro models used above leave us several areas immediately susceptible to a more refined methodology. Each of the models assumed a linear relationship between per capita municipal operating expenditures and the level of population change. We must now see if the relative rate of change over the decade, i.e., slow, moderate, or rapid, operates upon the municipal budget in different ways.

[1]Solomon Fabricant, The Trend of Government Activity in the United States Since 1900, (New York: National Bureau of Economic Research, 1952).

[2]Ibid.

[3]Stanley Scott & Edward L. Feder, Factors Associated with Variation in Municipal Expenditure Levels (Berkeley, California: Bureau of Public Administration, University of California, 1957).

[4]Charles J. Libera, "An Investigation of the Determinants of Municipal Expenditures in the United States," Unpublished Ph.D. dissertation, University of Minnesota, 1969), 32.

[5]Bernard H. Booms, "City Governmental Form and Public Expenditure Levels" National Tax Journal, (Vol. XIX, 1966), p. 187-199.

[6]John C. Weicher, "Determinants of Central City Expenditures: Some Overlooked Factors and Problems," National Tax Journal, (Vol. XXIII, 1970), p. 379-396.

[7]Harvey E. Brazer, City Expenditures in the United States Occasional Paper 66, (New York: National Bureau of Economic Research, 1959), 20.

[8]For an application of the income maximizing model to local government see James L. Barr and Otto A. Davis, "An Elementary Political and Economic Theory of the Expenditures of Local Government The Southern Economic Journal, Vol. XXXIII, Oct. 1966, pp. 149-65. Behavior directed towards present as opposed to future benefits is analyzed by James M. Buchanan, Public Finance in Democratic Processes (Chapel Hill: University of North Carolina Press; 1967).

[9]L. R. Gabler, "Population Size as a Determinant of City Expenditures and Employment - Some Further Evidence," Land Economics (Vol. XLVII #2, May 1971), p. 137.

[10]Dick Netzer "Financing Suburban Development" in Studies of the Nassau-Suffolk Planning Region edited by Dieter K. Zschick (Economic Research Bureau, State University of New York at Stony Brook, 1969), p. 90-94.

[11]Richard Spangler, "The Effect of Population Growth Upon State and Local Government Expenditures," National Tax Journal (July, 1963), p. 195-196.

[12]Jesse Burkhead, State and Local Taxes for Public Education (Syracuse U. Press, Syracuse, N.Y.: 1963), Chapter IV.

[13]George Sternlieb & Robert W. Burchell Residential Abandonment: The Tenement Landlord Revisited (New Brunswick, N.J.: Rutgers University, Center for Urban Policy Research, 1973), Chapter 1.

[14]George Sternlieb The Tenement Landlord (New Brunswick, N.J. Rutgers University, Urban Studies Center, 1966), Chapter 3.

[15]William J. Baumol, "Macroeconomics of Unbalanced Growth: The Anatomy of Urban Crisis" The American Economic Review (Vol. LVII, June 1967), p. 415-426. A recent study of unit costs of goods and services produced through the public sector has lent support to the Baumol hypothesis. This has been reported by: D. F. Bradrod, R. A. Malt, and W. E. Oaks. "The Rising Cost of Local Public Services: Some Evidence and Reflections," National Tax Journal, Vol. XXII #2, 1969.

[16]Scott and Feder, op. cit.

[17]Brazer, op. cit.

[18]J. Johnston, Econometric Methods, (New York: McGraw-Hill, 1972), Chapter 5.

[19]Elliott R. Morss and J. Eric Fredland and Saul H. Hymans, "Flucturations in State Expenditures: An Econometric Analysis," The Southern Economic Journal (April, 1967), p. 504.

[20]Weicher, op. cit.

[21]Libera, op. cit.

[22]Roger Lind, "Determinants of Local Public Expenditures: A Study of Rhode Island's Thirty-Nine Cities and Towns" (Unpublished Ph.D. dissertation, University of Maryland, 1971), 114.

[23]Calvin W. Hiibner, "Determinants of Municipal Policy: A Florida Case Study," (Unpublished Ph.D. dissertation, University of Florida, 1971), 99.

[24]Booms, op. cit.

[25]Lind, op. cit.

[26]James W. Hughes Urban Indicators, Metropolitan Evolution and Public Policy (New Brunswick, N.J., Rutgers University Center for Urban Policy Research, 1973).

CHAPTER 5

MUNICIPAL EXPENDITURES AS A FUNCTION OF
GROWTH RATES

Six basic areas of municipal <u>operational</u> expenditure (government
administration, public safety, public works, health and welfare,
recreation and culture and statutory commitments) will be viewed
in this chapter over the period 1960 to 1970, with specific concentration on total per capita trends, per capita allocations to various
areas of municipal service, and changes in service emphasis over
time.

Five hundred sixty-three* New Jersey communities will be sorted in
accordance with Exhibit 5-1 by both population size and growth
rate groupings. In terms of the former, the population groupings
(1960) will be in intervals similar to those used previously: 100-
1,000, 1,000-5,000, 5,000-10,000, 10,000-25,000, 25,000-50,000 and
over. Growth rate groupings will not only specify direction but will
segregate communities by <u>annual</u> changes of the following order of
magnitude: declining (0-5 percent), slowly increasing (0-2 percent),
moderately increasing (2-5 percent),** moderately to rapidly increasing (5-10 percent),** rapidly increasing (10-20 percent) and explosively increasing (20 percent and over).

TOTAL PER CAPITA EXPENDITURE VARIATION

Exhibit 4-9 displays the relationship between per capita municipal
expenditures, city size, and direction of population change. The
model used to develop it assumes that disaggregation of the pooled
set of cities would not change the overall pattern. However,
Exhibit 5-2 shows that this is not a fully adequate generalization.
Rather, to the extent that the data can be extended, we find a
marked drop in per capita expenditure with increasing growth rate
for the upper half of the cities in the rank size spectrum.

Declining/Moderately/Rapidly Growing Communities

While a well-defined "U" shaped curve relating levels of per capita
expenditure to the established population base is much more pronounced in cities of declining population (Exhibit 5-2), the left

_____

*Four communities have been eliminated from the range of com-
munities due to 1960 populations of less than one hundred.

**Subsequently these growth groupings will be referred to as
Moderate I, Moderate II.

EXHIBIT 5-1. ANNUAL GROWTH RATE BY ESTABLISHED POPULATION BASES
NEW JERSEY MUNICIPALITIES 1960-1970

Population Base (1960)	Average Annual Growth 1960 to 1970						Total
	Declining (-5-0%)	Slow Growth (0-2%)	Moderate Growth I (2-5%)	Moderate Growth II (5-10%)	Rapid Growth (10-20%)	Explosive Growth (20+)	
Less than 1,000	5*	21*	13	13	7	3	62
1,000-5,000	30	88*	49*	41	25*	4*	237
5,000-10,000	7	58*	19	27*	6	0	117
10,000-25,000	13	46*	25*	11	6	1	102
25,000-50,000	5	22	2	2	1	0	32
50,000 and over	7*	9	1	0	0	0	17
Total	67	244	109	94	45	8	567

Note: *Those communities most characteristic of a particular growth rate.

Source: U. S. Census of Population, 1960-1970.

153

DECLINING GROWTH   (A)
   (-5 to 0%)

Cp* $181, $93, $89, $124, $140,
      $211

ΔE 22.4, 11.7, 11.5, 11.0, 11.8,
      9.8

ΔP -1.5, -0.8, -0.8, -0.5, -0.5,
      -0.5

*Cp = 1970 Per Capita Municipal
     Operating Expenditures

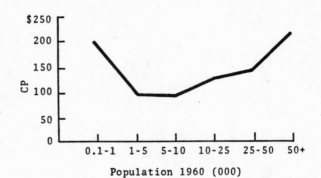

SLOW GROWTH   (B)
   (0 to 2%)

Cp $85, $101, $93, $110, $122,
      $130

ΔE** 15.4, 18.9, 14.0, 13.4,
      19.0, 11.7

ΔP 1.1, 1.3, 1.2, 0.8, 0.9, 0.5

**ΔE = Annual Percent Change In
     Gross Municipal Operating
     Expenditures (1960-1970)

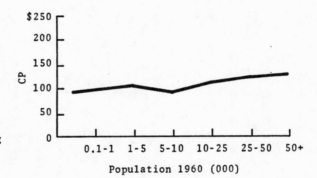

MODERATE GROWTH (I)   (C)
   (2 to 5%)

Cp $215, $111, $109, $87

ΔE 13.9, 20.6, 20.3, 21.3

ΔP*** 3.0, 3.2, 3.3, 3.5

***ΔP = Annual Percent Change
     In Population

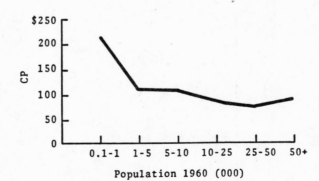

(Continued)

154

MODERATE TO RAPID GROWTH (II) (D)
    (5 to 10%)

Cp* $202, $89, $79, $83

ΔE 20.2, 24.6, 31.1, 25.7

ΔP 6.2, 6.3, 6.0, 6.3

Cp* = 1970 Per Capita Municipal
    Operating Expenditures

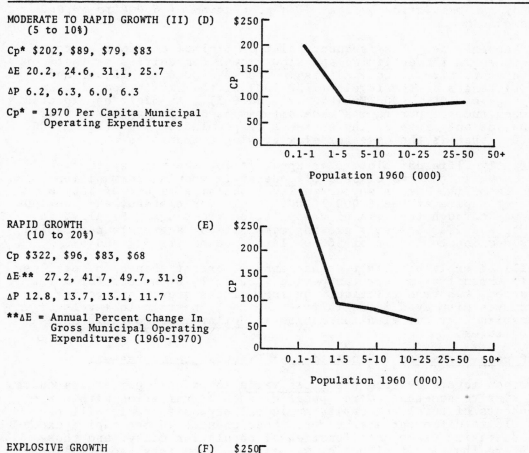

RAPID GROWTH   (E)
    (10 to 20%)

Cp $322, $96, $83, $68

ΔE.** 27.2, 41.7, 49.7, 31.9

ΔP 12.8, 13.7, 13.1, 11.7

**ΔE = Annual Percent Change In
    Gross Municipal Operating
    Expenditures (1960-1970)

EXPLOSIVE GROWTH   (F)
    (20% and Over)

Cp $75.8, $52.5

ΔE 32.7   88.0

ΔP*** 25.9 28.4

***ΔP = Annual Percent Change
    In Population (1960-1970)

**** = Total Municipal Operating
    Expenditures (not indlucing
    Reserves for uncollected
    taxes)

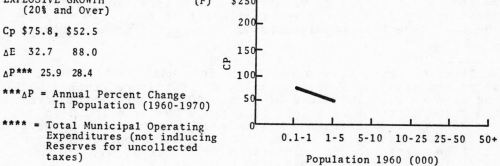

Source: CUPR Survey 1972-1973.

hand edge of this curve is common to all growth groupings. That is, *regardless of rate or direction of growth, per capita municipal costs of smaller cities are initially higher and decline with increasing size of the population base until a population of 5,000 to 10,000 is reached.**

What happens once this frequent point of minimum consumption cost is reached in the declining and slow growth communities is that per capita costs rise in communities in the 10-25,000, 25-50,000 and 50,000+ ranges to the levels ($130-200) of the smaller population groupings of 100-1,000 (Exhibit 5-2 and 5-3). As might be expected, the magnitude of per capita expenditures in declining communities is considerably more at the extremes of population base (100-1,000, 50,000+) than is the case for slow growing communities.

A slightly different picture is apparent for the per capita expenditure curve in the two classes of moderately growing communities. In these cases the curves appear to level out at a figure of $80 to $100 per capita at the 5,000-10,000 population plateau, and continue this way through the remaining population groupings. Finally, in the rapid and explosively growing communities, aggregate per capita costs decline to levels of $60 or less. (Exhibits 5-2 and 5-3.)

As will be explained later, since annual percent change in total per capita expenditures over the period 1960 to 1970, except for a few instances, has been relatively uniform across growth categories, the curves displayed in Exhibit 5-2 not only pertain to levels of per capita cost but also to changes in dollar increments in such expenditures.

Per Capita Variation - Population or Expenditure Increases?

If we now move away from the gross variation of the per capita curve with size to something more specific, such as variation within the components of total per capita municipal expenditure, it will be possible to differentiate between those changes in per capita expenditures taking place as a function of population change and those which are the result of policy variation. From this, some measure of appreciation may be obtained for the impact of increasing expenditures on the respective populations of both declining and growing

---

*The level of per capita expenditures for small communities (100-1,000) is on the order of $200; the point of efficiency reached with increasing size (i.e., 5,000-10,000) is at $80-100 per capita level. The trough found at the 5 to 10,000 size range has been found in the cities of a different state. Masten and Quindry report a regression coefficient relating per capita current general purposes expenditures to 1966 population not significantly different from zero fo Wisconsin cities in the 5,000 to 20,000 city size range. [1]

EXHIBIT 5-3. COMMUNITIES WITH 1960 POPULATIONS OF 5,000-10,000 AND 25,000-50,000: COMPARISON OF 1970 PER CAPITA EXPENDITURES

1960-1970 Change Category	1960 Size Category	Community	Total 1970 Per Capita Municipal Expenditure	Mean of All Other Communities Falling Within Size/Population Groupings
A	5,000-10,000	Bogota Borough Florence Township	$ 96.14 82.06	Increase
Decline/Slow	25,000-50,000	Englewood City Hoboken	215.19 187.48	
B	5,000-10,000	Northfield Park Ridge Borough	80.63 81.59	Level
Moderate I/Moderate II	25,000-50,000	Edison Township Vineland Township	85.76 79.05	
C	5,000-10,000	Jefferson Township West Milford Township	86.06 109.55	Decrease
Rapid/Explosive	25,000-50,000	Parsippany-Troy Hills*	63.41	

Note: *Only community in this subcell.

Source: New Jersey Department of Community Affairs, Division of Local Finance: Thirty-Third Annual Report of the Division of Local Finance. Trenton, N.J. NJDCA, 1970.

157

communities. Prior to discussing these patterns, however, it is necessary to examine the elements of per capita cost and changes in such costs over time.

Per capita cost (C) by definition is the relationship between a level of expenditure (E) and an existing population base (P).

$$C_p = \frac{E}{P}$$

A change in per capita costs (ΔC_p) is a function of either a changing level of expenditure (ΔE), a changing level of population (ΔP) or a combination of the two.

$$\Delta C_p = \frac{\dfrac{E_B}{P_B} - \dfrac{E_A}{P_A}}{\dfrac{E_A}{P_A}}$$

In the case of expenditures, in New Jersey, even applying the consumer price index to obtain steady 1970 dollars from 1960,* there were no cases of decreasing per capita expenditures regardless of observable growth rate. Thus ΔE, while of varying magnitude, in this case is always positive.

The population base, as mentioned previously, has shown negative growth (decline) in sixty-seven New Jersey communities. In these cases per capita costs may have increased not only due to increasing levels of municipal expenditure but also due to an eroding population base over which to allocate these expenditures.

Declining and Slow Growth Communities

Within the growth category of declining and slowly growing communities, smaller (100-1,000) communities experience higher levels of total per capita costs due to excessive start up costs and the

---

* Consumer Price Index for Urban Wage Earners and Clerical Workers. New York - Northeast New Jersey. 1967 Base Year = 100, 1960 = 87.3, 1970 = 119.0 (all items: food, housing, apparel, upkeep, transportation, health and recreation).

inability to reach a servicing threshold wherein economies of consumption may contribute to servicing efficiency.* This may be seen in Exhibit 5-4 in the "total" row for the gross trends of groupings of communities and in Exhibit 5-5 for a single community. This will be the procedure employed for exhibits throughout the remainder of the study. Communities from 1,000-10,000, however, have overcome start up costs and, within this range, reach a point of servicing efficiency which enables their per capita costs to be lower than any of those communities similarly experiencing a declining population. The larger, declining and, to a lesser degree, the larger, slow growth communities, while not having to contend with start up costs, have exceeded the threshhold of servicing efficiency and frequently have encountered a population whose needs are much more expansive in terms of social needs than those encountered in the rural declining situation. In this instance, given a no-growth population base again, per capita costs must rise (Exhibits 5-4 and 5-5).

---

*The use of the term "servicing efficiency" is used in the context of the micro-economic theory of economies of scale. Its aptness in this study is conjectural. Some authors in the field believe that large cities can provide a given service at a lower unit cost than a small city. Based upon this apparent relationship it has been concluded by some that a negative slope in a per capita expenditure versus population size graph represents economies of scale while a positive relationship represents diseconomies. Roy Bahl, writing in Metropolitan City Expenditures, clearly identifies the problem associated with this line of thinking. Using the direction of change in per capita expenditures as the heart of the conceptual problem, the erroneous reasoning process states that the larger the population output by the city for a given level of expenditure the more efficient the operation of the governmental structure of the city of that size range. Clearly what is regarded here is a measure of output for a specific service.[2] Norman Walzer has identified this specifically when he analyzed the cost structure of specific police functions. When comparing his cost per unit product results with that obtained by using per capita expenditures as its surrogate contradictory but statistically insignificant results were obtained. Thus, the use of population as the commodity produced does not identify the economies of scale actually found.[3]

Following Walzer's lead, we prefer the use of the term "economies of consumption" as an indicator of the negative relationship between per capita expenditures and population size. This, however, does not limit theorizing the existence of economies of scale in specific parts of the consumption curve.

EXHIBIT 5-4. 1970 PER CAPITA MUNICIPAL OPERATING EXPENDITURES OF NEW JERSEY MUNICIPALITIES BY ANNUAL GROWTH RATE (1960-1970) AND ESTABLISHED POPULATION BASE (1960)

	Declining (-5 to 0%) (A) Population 1960 (000)							GROWTH RATE — Slow (0 to 2%) (B) Population 1960 (000)							Moderate (I) (2 to 5%) (C) Population 1960 (000)							All New Jersey Communities
Program Area	0.1-1*	1-5	5-10	10-25	25-50	50+	Mean	0.1-1	1-5	5-10	10-25	25-50	50+	Mean	0.1-1	1-5	5-10	10-25	25-50	50+	Mean	Mean
Government Administration	68.4	26.2	17.6	21.3	18.7	32.8	27.0	27.9	25.2	22.4	21.3	17.0	16.5	22.9	50.4	27.5	24.5	16.3			26.8	22.4
Public Safety	26.9	24.2	31.6	44.9	60.1	83.7	38.3	16.6	24.1	30.0	36.1	47.3	54.2	30.5	56.7	27.5	37.7	25.8			32.2	31.2
Public Works	61.6	26.8	27.8	28.5	24.0	22.0	28.6	29.2	33.9	28.1	27.3	26.9	23.0	29.9	52.5	33.1	32.1	24.2			32.9	31.1
Health & Welfare	2.5	2.7	1.9	5.4	5.9	18.3	5.1	1.8	2.0	2.1	3.2	4.1	12.1	2.8	2.7	2.0	2.6	2.2			2.3	2.8
Recreation & Culture	14.2	6.7	3.6	13.1	10.7	17.5	9.5	7.1	10.6	6.8	12.6	12.4	15.1	9.9	33.3	14.6	6.7	14.0			14.1	16.4
Statutory & Unclassified	7.4	5.9	6.8	10.4	20.4	36.2	11.3	3.0	5.6	4.0	1.4	14.9	8.4	7.0	19.7	7.0	6.0	4.8			8.8	4.8
TOTAL	$181.0	$92.5	$89.3	$123.6	$139.8	$210.6	$119.8	$85.5	$101.4	$93.4	$101.9	$122.5	$129.3	$103.0	$215.3	$11.7	$109.5	$87.3			$117.1	$108.7
AC_D ($ annual)	$11.7	$5.0	$5.1	$6.3	$7.5	$11.5	$6.6	$4.3	$5.6	$4.8	$5.8	$5.6	$6.6	$5.4	$8.1	$6.4	$5.7	$4.9			$6.4	$5.0
AC_D (% annual)	31.9	14.2	13.5	12.3	12.8	11.6	14.4	13.2	15.5	11.4	11.6	16.1	10.7	13.5	8.4	15.0	12.8	13.2			12.4	13.1
Sub (n)	n=5	n=30	n=7	n=13	n=5	n=7	n=66	n=21	n=88	n=58	n=46	n=22	n=9	n=240	n=13	n=*	n=19	n=25			n=109	n=563

25-50 and 50+ columns of Moderate (I): NO CASES

	Moderate (II) (5-10%) (D) Population 1960 (000)							Rapid (10-20%) (E) Population 1960 (000)							Explosive (20% and Over) (F) Population 1960 (000)						
Program Area	0.1-1	1-5	5-10	10-25	25-50	50+	Mean	0.1-1	1-5	5-10	10-25	25-50	50+	Mean	0.1-1	1-5	5-10	10-25	25-50	50+	Mean
Government Administration	57.4	23.5	20.1	19.5			26.6	74.8	26.7	19.3	17.8			31.2	23.5	19.8					19.2
Public Safety	36.7	24.4	22.7	25.5			25.9	80.8	30.2	23.9	16.0			34.7	15.2	15.7					15.5
Public Works	65.7	27.7	23.0	22.5			30.8	113.4	28.6	28.5	20.0			39.7	30.4	12.2					17.6
Health & Welfare	3.0	1.9	1.8	2.2			2.1	3.0	2.3	2.3	1.8			2.3	2.8	1.5					1.7
Recreation & Culture	25.8	5.9	5.8	7.5			8.8	39.5	8.8	3.7	8.3			12.6	1.3	1.4					2.2
Statutory & Unclassified	13.6	6.4	5.1	6.2			7.1	23.7	0.2	5.3	4.5			4.7	2.7	1.8					2.2
TOTAL	$202.2	$89.7	$78.5	$83.4			$101.3	$332.2	$96.7	$83.0	$68.4			$125.2	$75.8	$52.5					$58.4
AC_D ($ annual)	$8.2	$4.5	$4.7	$4.4			$5.1	$8.7	$5.0	$4.6	$3.2			$5.3	$1.5	$3.3					$2.6
AC_D (% annual)	8.7	11.3	15.8	11.8			12.3	4.2	12.2	15.0	9.6			11.6	2.0	15.0					10.1
Sub (n)	n=13	n=41	n=27	n=11			n=94	n=7	n=25	n=6	n=6			n=47	n=23	n=4					n=7

25-50 and 50+ columns of Moderate (II) and Rapid: NO CASES; 5-10, 10-25, 25-50 and 50+ columns of Explosive: NO CASES

Note: *Communities of 100 population or less (1960) have been eliminated from this growth categorization (TETERBORO; PAHAQUARRY; PINE VALLEY; TAVISTOCK)

Source: CUPR Survey 1972-1973.

EXHIBIT 5-5A. START-UP - HIGH INITIAL COSTS DUE TO INSUFFICIENT SERVICES OCCASIONING RISING PER CAPITA EXPENDITURES IN A SMALL, SLOWLY GROWING COMMUNITY (FREEHOLD BOROUGH, N.J.)

Year	Population[1]	Total Municipal Expenditures	Total Municipal Per Capita Expenditures	Annual 1960-1970 Percent Increase in Per Capita Expenditures for Indicated Municipality	Mean Annual 1960-1970 Percent Increase in Per Capita Expenditures for All Declining Communities
1960	583.0	$ 19,650	33.71	38.6	14.1
1967	506.4	37,570	62.06		
1968	608.6	75,075	123.36		
1969	611.8	89,307	145.97		
1970	615.0	100,652	163.67		

EXHIBIT 5-5B. EFFICIENCY - LOWER COSTS DUE TO ESTABLISHED SERVICING BASE PRODUCING RELATIVELY STABLE, MODERATE SIZE, SLOWLY GROWING COMMUNITY (EAST RUTHERFORD, N.J.)

Year	Population[1]	Total Municipal Expenditures	Total Municipal Per Capita Expenditures	Annual 1960-1970 Percent Increase in Per Capita Expenditures for Indicated Municipality	Mean Annual 1960-1970 Percent Increase in Per Capita Expenditures for All Declining Communities
1960	7,769.0	$ 517,531	66.61	10.8	14.4
1967	8,305.9	867,434	104.44		
1968	8,382.6	983,797	117.36		
1969	8,459.3	1,057,856	125.05		
1970	8,536.0	1,184,736	138.79		

EXHIBIT 5-5C. URBAN COST EMERGENCE - HIGHER SUBSEQUENT PER CAPITA COSTS DUE TO ERODING POPULATION IN A LARGE SIZE, DECLINING COMMUNITY (ATLANTIC CITY, N.J.)

Year	Population[1]	Total Municipal Expenditures	Total Municipal Per Capita Expenditures	Annual 1960-1970 Percent Increase in Per Capita Expenditures for Indicated Municipality	Mean Annual 1960-1970 Percent Increase in Per Capita Expenditures for All Declining Communities
1960	59,544.0	$ 7,741,534	130.01	17.99	14.4
1967	57,364.5	11,501,747	233.92		
1968	50,196.0	12,937,630	257.74		
1969	49,027.5	14,065,114	286.88		
1970	47,859.0	17,415,589	363.89		

Note: [1]Assumes a linear 1960-1970 Population increase. This assumption is made in subsequent exhibits.

Source: NJDCA Annual Reports for Indicated Years (See Exhibit 5-3 for full citation).

161

The annual change in expenditures (ΔE) has taken place at the rate of 11 to 12 percent for all but the extreme population categories of declining communities while population (ΔP) has decreased annually from 0.5 to 0.8 percent. In the very small communities excessive population decreases have been matched by significant increases in annual expenditures. Rockleigh Borough in Bergen County, New Jersey is such an example. Over the period 1960 to 1970, its population declined 3 percent annually, while its expenditures increased annually at close to 70 percent. In the very large communities both expenditure increase and population decline, as a percent of the base, have been relatively modest. An example is Bayonne City, which had only a 7.7 percent annual increase in operating expenditures and a 0.2 percent annual population loss. An annual per capita increase of from 15 to 30 percent is frequent in smaller declining communities; for the larger communities the annual increase is 12 to 13 percent. The differential in percent increases has occasioned similar annual per capita dollar increases in the extreme size categories of the declining communities, i.e., $11 to $12, whereas members of declining communities of 1,000-5,000 population have suffered $5 to $7 annual per capita increases with only slight variation (Exhibit 5-4). The extreme portions of the "U" shaped curve relating per capita costs to size is newly formed for small declining New Jersey communities whereas for large declining communities it is an extant one (ΔE and ΔP are small).

In slow growth communities where an average annual gross expenditure increase of 15 percent is matched by a 1.1 percent rate of population growth, similar trends in the 1,000 to 50,000 size communities are in evidence. The exceptions to the previous general patterns, of course, are the extreme size communities which are better able to keep up with costs as a result of at least small positive population growth (Exhibit 5-6). Probably the most outstanding difference between declining and slow growth communities is that, holding size of community constant (i.e., 1,000 to 10,000), annual percent increases in total expenditures for slow growth communities are one-third greater than declining communities, yet per capita increases are one-fifth lower.

Moderately Growing Communities

In the moderately growing communities, again those with smaller population bases (100-5,000) experience increased levels of per capita cost ($200-$215) characteristic of their start-up functions.[4] As community size increases to a point approaching 10,000 a condition of servicing efficiency ($80-100 per capita) is reached which remains in evidence throughout the larger categories of size. It is at this point where expansions in the numerator (expenditures) are being met by sufficient increases in the denominator (as a function of population) to occasion relatively slight variance from uniform per capita allocation for size groupings in excess of 10,000 population.

EXHIBIT 5-6. EXAMPLES OF LARGE (50,000+) DECLINING COMMUNITIES
HAVING HIGHER 1960 AND 1970 PER CAPITA EXPENDITURES AS
COMPARED TO LARGE, SLOWLY GROWING COMMUNITIES

Change Category	Community	Total 1960 Per Capita Municipal Expenditures	1970 Total Per Capita Municipal Expenditures
SLOW	Bloomfield Township	$ 56.08	$116.84
	Clifton	50.24	106.31
	Hamilton Township	37.68	80.20
	Paterson	64.98	139.87
DECLINE	Atlantic City	130.01	363.89
	Camden	71.19	169.34
	East Orange	73.61	173.26
	Newark	109.76	211.14

Source: NJDCA 1960 and 1970 Annual Reports (See Exhibit 5-3
for full citation).

In the two classes of moderately growing communities changes in
gross expenditure levels are taking place at the rate of 20 percent
to 25 percent annually while growth is taking place at the rate of
3 percent to 6 percent. The disparity between increasing costs of
government services and the rise in the base upon which to distribute these increases, while unbalanced, is only half as large in
these communities as that found in declining and slow growth communities. In the 100 to 1,000 population grouping of moderately
growing communities the annual per capita expenditure increase is
noticeably less (8 percent versus 13 percent). Yet the annual
dollar increase ($8) is significantly higher than all other cate-
gories of size ($4-6). (Exhibit 5-4. See also Exhibit 5-7,
Columns 1 and 2.) Exhibit 5-4 further indicates that pre-1960
expenditure patterns dominate the very small moderately growing
cities (as demonstrated by the small annual per capita variation,
see also Exhibit 5-7, Column 3) while decade changes have been
more influential in the other size categories.

EXHIBIT 5-7. SMALL (100-1,000) LARGE (1,000+), MODERATELY GROWING COMMUNITIES: COMPARISON OF POPULATION
AND TOTAL PER CAPITA EXPENDITURE INCREASE

Size Category	Municipality	Column I 1960-1970 Annual Percent Population Increase	Column II 1960-1970 Annual Percent Change In Municipal Expenditures	Column III 1960-1970 Annual Percent Change In Per Capita Municipal Expenditures
100-1,000	Hope Township	3.7	5.7	1.4
	Weymouth Township	2.7	8.1	4.2
	Pine Beach Borough	4.2	7.6	2.4
1,000-5,000	Chesterfield Township	2.7	25.3	17.9
	Laurel Springs Borough	2.7	13.5	8.6
	Lawnside Borough	2.8	30.1	21.3
5,000-10,000	Caldwell Borough	2.6	12.4	7.8
	Hopewell Borough	2.8	43.9	32.0
	Mahwah Township	4.3	23.5	13.4
10,000-25,000	Paramus	2.7	21.2	14.6
	Princeton Township	3.1	17.8	11.2
	Wyckoff Township	4.3	22.6	12.7
25,000-50,000	Middletown Township	3.8	17.5	10.0
	Vineland City	2.6	14.8	9.7
50,000+	Woodbridge Township	2.5	14.6	10.0

Source: NJDCA 1960 and 1970 Annual Reports (See Exhibit 5-3 for full citation).

Rapidly and Explosively Growing Communities

The rapidly and explosively growing communities by definition have
rapidly increasing population bases to carry their expanded costs.
Yet even here the per capita burden is initially high before decreasing (Exhibit 5-4). Though this grouping is essentially limited to communities which do not exceed 10,000 population, in the
smallest of these (those from 100 to 1,000) high per capita costs
($300+) characteristic of start-up still dominate. Exhibit 5-8
exemplifies this situation. Barnegat Light Borough, New Jersey,
in 1970, at a per capita cost of $410, must provide significant
start-up services in the area of financial administration, public
works, and recreation which were not even anticipated in 1960.

In the 1,000 to 10,000 population categories, however, there are
dramatic decreases in the levels of per capita expenditure (to the
$55 to $60 level) (Exhibit 5-4). This latter situation again could
well be the result of the lag phenomenon discussed earlier causing
intermittent economies of consumption wherein a servicing level is
attained such that additional population, within some boundary,
does not occasion the common $100 per capita annual municipal expen-
diture.

Rapidly and explosively growing communities exhibit $3 to $5 annual
increases in total per capita expenditures which is approximately
one-half the dollar increase noted by declining communities and two-
thirds that of moderately growing communities (stratifying for size)
(Exhibit 5-4). Since percent per capita increase is approximately
the same as communities in these other two categories of growth,
the existing expenditure base of rapidly growing communities circa
1960 must have been considerably lower.

PER CAPITA EXPENDITURE ALLOCATION

Declining and Slow Growth Communities

As is indicated by Exhibit 5-9, declining and slow growth communities (-5 to 2 percent annually) demonstrate almost identical patterns of internal expenditure distribution within the three areas
of major governmental service: government administration, public
safety, and public works.* In the smaller of these communities
85 percent of municipal expenditures are distributed among these

---

*The frequent expenditure pattern is for small declining or
slow growth communities to spend 40 percent of their budget on
general administration, 15 percent on public safety, and 30 percent on public works; the figures for large communities are respectively 15 percent, 40 percent, and 20 percent.

EXHIBIT 5-8. HIGH START UP EXPENDITURES IN A SMALL (100-1,000), RAPIDLY GROWING COMMUNITY
(BARNEGAT LIGHT BOROUGH, N.J.)

Municipal Expenditure Categories	1960 (Population 287)	1965 (Population 121)	1970 (Population 554)
1. GENERAL GOVERNMENT			
Administrative & Executive	10,359	22,108	44,800
Assessment/Collec. of Taxes	10,420	9,098	8,950
Financial Administration	————	————	10,650
TOTAL	20,779	31,206	64,400
2. PUBLIC SAFETY			
Fire Protection	5,275	2,500	3,500
Police Protection	8,150	10,996	13,750
Civil Defense and Disaster Control	---	300	300
Other Protection	1,105	2,112	539
TOTAL	14,530	15,908	22,941
3. PUBLIC WORKS			
Streets & Roads	24,448	26,616	38,592
Garbage & Trash Removal	5,028	7,500	25,215
Sewers	---	---	12,000
Other	---	---	6,000
TOTAL	29,476	36,732	81,807
4. HEALTH/WELFARE			
Health Services	2,057	3,740	344
Welfare-Public Assistance	100	100	100
Other	---	---	2,300
TOTAL	2,157	3,840	2,744
5. RECREATION/CULTURE			
Beaches and Playgrounds	5,599	34,800	33,000
Parks and Playgrounds	1,724	3,000	8,000
Libraries	100	100	100
Other	---	---	500
TOTAL	7,423	37,900	41,600
6. STATUTORY AND UNCLASSIFIED	636	1,500	5,789
TOTAL (Categories 1 through 6)	$75,001	$127,136	$219,290
Per Capita	$261.33	$301.99	$410.65

Source: NJDCA 1965 and 1970 Annual Report (See Exhibit 5-3 for fuel citation).

EXHIBIT 5-9. PROGRAM AREAS PERCENT OF 1970 OPERATING BUDGET OF NEW JERSEY MUNICIPALITIES BY ANNUAL GROWTH RATE (1960-1970) AND ESTABLISHED POPULATION BASE (1960)

GROWTH RATE

Declining (-5 to 0%) (A) — Population 1960 (000)

Program Area	0.1-1*	5-10	10-25	25-50	50+	Mean
Government Administration	43.2	19.8	17.7	15.5	N	24.6
Public Safety	14.7	25.0	35.8	39.8	O	30.1
Public Works	30.6	31.2	24.0	18.9		27.4
Health & Welfare	2.2	3.4	4.3	4.3	C	4.1
Recreation & Culture	4.4	4.1	9.8	9.2	A	6.0
Statutory & Unclassified	4.9	5.1	8.4	12.3	S/E/S	7.8
TOTAL	100.0	100.0	100.0	100.0	(NO CASES)	100.0
Sub (n)	n=5	n=30	n=7	n=13	n=7	n=66

Slow (0 to 2%) (B) — Population 1960 (000)

Program Area	0.1-1*	1-5	5-10	10-25	25-50	50+	Mean
Government Administration	35.7	28.0	23.9	19.7	14.2	13.1	24.6
Public Safety	17.8	23.3	32.5	33.0	37.6	41.7	30.1
Public Works	33.0	34.2	30.1	26.4	23.0	19.1	27.4
Health & Welfare	2.6	3.4	2.3	2.8	3.3	7.9	4.1
Recreation & Culture	7.2	6.4	6.7	9.1	10.2	6.6	6.0
Statutory & Unclassified	3.7	4.8	4.5	8.4	11.2	11.6	7.8
TOTAL	100.0	100.0	100.0	100.0	100.0	100.0	100.0
Sub (n)	n=21	n=88	n=58	n=46	n=22	n=9	n=240

Moderate (I) (2 to 5%) (C) — Population 1960 (000)

Program Area	0.1-1	1-5	5-10	10-25	25-50	50+	Mean
Government Administration	28.5	27.9	22.2	20.4	N	N	25.0
Public Safety	21.7	22.9	36.9	31.2	O	O	27.2
Public Works	33.3	34.0	30.8	27.4			31.7
Health & Welfare	2.2	2.3	2.6	2.6	C	A	2.5
Recreation & Culture	8.7	7.3	5.6	9.8	A	S	7.9
Statutory & Unclassified	5.7	5.6	1.9	8.6	S/E/S	E/S	5.7
TOTAL	100.0	100.0	100.0	100.0	(NO CASES)	(NO CASES)	100.0
Sub (n)	n=13	n=49	n=19	n=25			n=109

Moderate (II) (5 to 10%) (D) — Population 1960 (000)

Program Area	0.1-1*	5-10	10-25	25-50	50+	Mean
Government Administration	35.3	25.6	23.1	N	N	27.1
Public Safety	16.0	29.2	31.1	O	O	26.5
Public Works	33.8	29.7	27.3			30.8
Health & Welfare	2.3	2.4	2.6	C	A	2.3
Recreation & Culture	7.2	6.8	8.2	A	S	6.5
Statutory & Unclassified	5.4	6.3	7.7	S/E/S	E/S	6.8
TOTAL	100.0	100.0	100.0	(NO CASES)	(NO CASES)	100.0
Sub (n)	n=13	n=27	n=11			n=94

Rapid (10 to 20%) (E) — Population 1960 (000)

Program Area	0.1-1	1-5	5-10	10-25	25-50	50+	Mean
Government Administration	27.1	29.2	23.3	27.0	N	N	27.4
Public Safety	23.6	33.4	29.3	22.1	O	O	29.9
Public Works	33.8	30.4	33.8	30.8			31.2
Health & Welfare	1.3	2.5	2.7	2.7	C	A	2.4
Recreation & Culture	9.3	4.9	4.6	10.6	A	S	7.1
Statutory & Unclassified	4.9	0.0	6.3	6.8	S/E/S	E/S	2.0
TOTAL	100.0	100.0	100.0	100.0	(NO CASES)	(NO CASES)	100.0
Sub (n)	n=7	n=25	n=6	n=6			n=47

Explosive (20% and Over) (F) — Population 1960 (000)

Program Area	0.1-1	1-5	5-10	10-25	25-50	50+
Government Administration	29.0	35.2	N	N	N	N
Public Safety	19.3	26.8	O	O	O	O
Public Works	41.3	30.0				
Health & Welfare	4.4	2.7	C	A	A	A
Recreation & Culture	1.9	2.1	A	S	S	S
Statutory & Unclassified	4.1	3.2	S/E/S	E/S	E/S	E/S
TOTAL	100.0	100.0	(NO CASES)	(NO CASES)	(NO CASES)	(NO CASES)
Sub (n)	n=23	n=4				

All New Jersey Communities

Program Area	Mean
Government Administration	25.4
Public Safety	28.4
Public Works	30.3
Health & Welfare	2.8
Recreation & Culture	7.1
Statutory & Unclassified	6.0
TOTAL	100.0
Sub (n)	n=563

Note: *Communities of 100 population or less (1960) have been eliminated from this growth categorization (TETERBORO; PAHAQUARRY; PINE VALLEY; TAVISTOCK).

Source: CUPR Survey 1972-1973.

three areas, the bulk of which are shared by government administration and public works (Exhibit 5-10). As the population base increases within these communities the previous dominance of these two functions is replaced by a heavy emphasis on public safety (Exhibit 5-10). Moving from smaller to larger communities within this growth grouping, there is also a shift with increased size towards expenditures in the areas of recreation and culture (5 percent to 8 percent). The extra allocation towards these areas comes directly from expenditures previously slotted for the government administration/public safety/public works group. Where this group occupied 85 percent of a small municipality's budget, in larger cities the figure is more frequently 75 percent.

Moderately Growing Communities

In moderate population growth communities (2 percent to 10 percent annually) similar basic trends in the major areas of municipal expenditure are in evidence as was the case for declining and slow growing communities (Exhibit 5-9). Yet areas of per capita expenditure emphasis or de-emphasis are not as accentuated as the population base is varied (Exhibit 5-10). While government administration and public works (again 60 percent to 70 percent of small communities' expenditures) give way to public safety as population base increases, the former still remain significant expenditures (i.e., 20 percent to 27 percent) in the more sophisticated communities of 10 to 25,000 population. Public safety expenditures in larger, moderately growing communities, however, may be one-fifth less than those of declining communities of comparable size (Exhibit 5-10). The cause and effect relationships here certainly should be studied in more detail. (See the section of this work on consumer satisfaction.)

Perhaps the most striking dissimilarity in expenditure allocation between moderately growing and declining/slow growing communities is the maintenance of a minimal allocation towards health and welfare irrespective of city size in the former (Exhibit 5-10). While there is an increasing tendency in declining/slow growth communities to allocate both towards recreation and health/welfare needs, as population base increases, and the same is true for recreation in moderately growing communities, it is definitely not the case for health and welfare. The latter in moderately growing communities is only 2 percent to 3 percent of the per capita budget expenditure in municipalities of 100 to 1,000 as well as those from 10,000 to 25,000. This is only half of the proportion occupied by health and welfare in the budgets of similar size declining communities.

EXHIBIT 5-10. PERCENT OF 1970 BUDGET OF SELECTED NEW JERSEY COMMUNITIES OF VARYING POPULATION BASE AND GROWTH CATEGORIES

Size Category	Change Category	Community		Percent of 1970 Budget for Indicated Municipal Expenditures					
			GA 1	PS 2	PW 3	HW 4	RC 5	SJ 6	Total
I	A. Decline/Slow	Bloomsbury Borough	32.25	21.34	40.32	.41	---	5.68	100.0
100- 1,000		West Wildwood Borough	31.60	22.53	42.25	1.39	---	2.23	100.0
	B. Moderate	Weymouth Township	29.98	18.80	41.51	2.66	---	7.05	100.0
		Frelinghuysen Township	49.71	1.17	44.38	1.70	0.1	3.04	100.0
	C. Rapid/Explosive	Hi-Nella Borough	22.50	20.03	52.19	0.68	3.01	1.59	100.0
		Little Egg Harbor Township	33.55	21.16	38.31	2.75	1.28	2.85	100.0
II	A. Decline/Slow	Moonachie Borough	38.59	32.47	16.01	1.45	2.18	9.30	100.0
1,000- 5,000		Beverly	24.40	34.60	28.90	2.24	---	7.28	100.0
	B. Moderate	Tabernacle Township	51.74	11.37	33.82	2.19	---	0.88	100.0
		North Caldwell Borough	23.59	36.29	30.65	2.310	0.96	6.20	100.0
	C. Rapid/Explosive	Upper Saddle River Borough	19.37	31.84	34.47	2.19	6.74	5.39	100.0
		Evesham Township	28.21	28.11	34.48	1.01	4.66	3.53	100.0
III	A. Decline/Slow	Hammonton Township	20.01	34.52	26.19	4.34	3.92	11.02	100.0
5,000-10,000		Fair Haven Borough	18.96	33.88	27.58	2.30	5.62	11.66	100.0
	B. Moderate	Northfield	20.27	35.00	28.68	0.65	2.78	2.62	100.0
		Carlstadt Borough	20.95	37.62	22.36	2.96	3.56	12.55	100.0
	C. Rapid/Explosive	Cinnaminson	16.47	32.13	34.22	1.06	8.59	7.53	100.0
		Matawan Township	19.49	33.51	33.70	2.34	7.19	13.69	100.0

(Continued)

EXHIBIT 5-10. PERCENT OF 1970 BUDGET OF SELECTED NEW JERSEY COMMUNITIES OF VARYING POPULATION BASE AND GROWTH CATEGORIES (Continued)

Percent of 1970 Budget for Indicated Municipal Expenditures

Size Category	Change Category	Community	GA 1	PS 2	PW 3	HW 4	RC 5	SJ 6	Total
IV 10,000-25,000	A. Decline/Slow	Cliffside Park Borough	19.17	34.36	28.31	2.86	4.69	10.61	100.0
		Ridgefield Park	31.84	27.35	23.02	1.71	6.89	9.19	100.0
	B. Moderate	Wyckoff	30.74	28.59	24.92	1.68	7.90	6.17	100.0
		Piscataway	21.39	35.52	23.44	2.54	9.32	7.78	100.0
	C. Rapid/Explosive	Brick Township	39.82	3.33	38.62	3.25	8.78	6.19	100.0
		Moorestown Township	18.88	27.63	30.13	3.60	15.04	4.72	100.0
V 25,000-50,000	A. Decline/Slow	Englewood	15.11	39.13	16.07	2.54	10.35	16.80	100.0
		Garfield	15.87	31.81	29.93	3.72	6.22	12.45	100.0
	B. Moderate	Vineland	18.68	29.75	27.44	6.86	9.71	7.56	100.0
		Middletown Township	17.07	32.26	26.81	4.59	11.32	8.00	100.0
	C. Rapid/Explosive	Woodbridge Township*	21.55	22.64	27.83	4.4	13.8	9.97	100.0
VI 50,000+	A. Decline/Slow	Newark	9.35	42.04	17.55	13.68	4.27	13.13	100.0
		Paterson	13.36	46.62	16.57	8.13	5.65	9.67	100.0
	B. Moderate	Parsippany Troy Hills*	16.63	34.28	27.47	3.89	12.81	4.92	100.0
	C. Rapid/Explosive	**							

Notes: *Only communities within these subcells.
**No communities in this subcell.

Source: N.J.D.C.A. 1970 Annual Report (See Exhibit 5-3 for full citation).

Rapidly and Explosively Growing Communities

In rapidly and explosively growing communities, expenditure patterns, as indicated by trend lines in proportionate allocation, are
not as clear as for other cells of growth. This is to be expected
due to the considerable change sometimes of an erratic nature such
communities are undergoing. Rapid and explosively growing communities (in excess of 10 percent annually) may be characterized
by a relatively steady proportion of the budget devoted to government administration purposes as city size increases (Exhibit 5-9).
The order of magnitude of this allocation runs from 27 percent
to 31 percent and thus is similar to that found for moderately
growing communities of comparable size. There is no discernible
trend here related to size groupings. The public works function,
as a percent of the budget, varies slightly with city size (33
percent to 27 percent). The percent of the budget devoted to
public works (31 percent) is similar to that allocated in moderately growing communities, whereas the public safety allocation
is 1 percent to 2 percent higher. Again, health and welfare per
capita allocations are small (2.5 percent to 3 percent of the
budget) and for the most part steady.

The recreation expenditure in rapidly growing communities, however,
is significant and fluctuates considerably (Exhibits 5-9 and 5-10).
Typically, explosively growing communities have considerable vacant
land and sufficient recreation can be found in the area of the
home; initially, it may not be a significant municipal concern or
expenditure. In rapidly growing communities, enjoying for the
most part similar density advantages as explosive communities,
apparently recreation was anticipated as a future need. This
may be a function of local recognition of necessity to purchase
land early to minimize acquisition price and having a sufficient
substantial servicing base to do so or perhaps some of the "green
acres" spending of the 1960's showing through.

PER CAPITA SERVICE REDISTRIBUTION AS A
FUNCTION OF GROWTH

The final area which must be broached in any analysis of municipal
expenditures is the changing service emphases which municipalities
undergo as a result of basic program allocation decisions.

In order to gauge this, two measures will be used: the first will
be an analysis of percent of annual program expenditure increases
over the period 1960 to 1970 (Exhibit 5-11); the second will be
a glimpse at the changes in the percent of the per capita allocation that these differing program emphases have had (Exhibit
5-12).

EXHIBIT 5-11. PERCENT ANNUAL INCREASE (1960-1970) IN PROGRAM OPERATING EXPENDITURES OF NEW JERSEY MUNICIPALITIES BY ANNUAL GROWTH RATE (1960-1970) AND ESTABLISHED POPULATION BASE (1960)

GROWTH RATE

Declining (-5 to 0%) (A) — Population 1960 (000)

Program Area	0.1-1*	1-5	5-10	10-25	25-50	50+	Mean
Government Administration	22.7	13.0	13.7	13.0	9.0	15.9	13.7
Public Safety	45.7	12.0	10.0	9.9	20.1	12.5	14.2
Public Works	23.3	11.4	11.0	30.3	8.5	3.8	14.8
Health & Welfare	8.2	25.6	4.3	16.5	7.2	1.0	16.5
Recreation & Culture	48.6	32.6	27.7	24.9	6.9	9.6	25.9
Statutory & Unclassified							
TOTAL	22.4	11.7	11.5	11.0	11.8	9.8	12.0
Sub (n)	n=5	n=30	n=7	n=13	n=13	n=7	n=66

Slow (0 to 2%) (B) — Population 1960 (000)

Program Area	0.1-1*	1-5	5-10	10-25	25-50	50+	Mean
Government Administration	16.8	24.7	20.7	19.1	11.5	14.5	20.5
Public Safety	19.0	16.4	15.7	12.0	17.3	13.3	15.6
Public Works	11.2	14.2	10.6	10.2	15.1	7.9	12.2
Health & Welfare	22.6	5.7	6.3	7.3	8.0	8.9	7.6
Recreation & Culture	246.8	210.3	26.0	25.3	74.2	10.8	100.2
Statutory & Unclassified							
TOTAL	15.4	18.9	14.0	13.4	19.0	11.7	16.2
Sub (n)	n=21	n=88	n=58	n=46	n=22	n=9	n=240

Moderate (I) (2 to 5%) (C) — Population 1960 (000)

Program Area	0.1-1	1-5	5-10	10-25	25-50	50+	Mean
Government Administration	17.3	23.2	20.2	20.0	NO CASES		21.1
Public Safety	20.1	22.5	36.6	23.6			24.9
Public Works	8.1	18.6	10.3	14.4			16.2
Health & Welfare	3.2	8.7	10.3	12.8			9.5
Recreation & Culture	9.3	144.3	25.5	823.9			313.1
Statutory & Unclassified							
TOTAL	13.9	20.6	20.3	21.3			19.8
Sub (n)	n=13	n=49	n=19	n=25			n=109

Moderate (II) (5-10%) (D) — Population 1960 (000)

Program Area	0.1-1	1-5	5-10	10-25	25-50	50+	Mean
Government Administration	27.2	29.2	33.0	34.7	NO CASES		30.6
Public Safety	26.0	37.7	36.4	28.8			34.5
Public Works	13.8	18.4	25.2	15.0			19.3
Health & Welfare	34.3	17.3	16.4	13.9			19.9
Recreation & Culture	25.9	115.6	176.7	65.5			124.2
Statutory & Unclassified							
TOTAL	20.2	24.6	31.3	25.7			26.1
Sub (n)	n=13	n=41	n=27	n=11			n=94

Rapid (10-20%) (E) — Population 1960 (000)

Program Area	0.1-1	1-5	5-10	10-25	25-50	50+	Mean
Government Administration	21.8	47.9	50.9	35.8	NO CASES		42.4
Public Safety	38.8	86.1	59.8	38.0			67.9
Public Works	29.8	29.3	39.6	19.1			30.3
Health & Welfare	26.4	24.8	25.4	18.7			25.6
Recreation & Culture	71.1	209.7	247.9	127.6			184.4
Statutory & Unclassified							
TOTAL	27.2	41.7	49.7	31.9			39.7
Sub (n)	n=7	n=25	n=6	n=6			n=47

Explosive (20% and Over) (F) — Population 1960 (000)

Program Area	0.1-1	1-5	5-10	10-25	25-50	50+	Mean
Government Administration	22.3	126.3	NO CASES				83.5
Public Safety	89.4	159.0					123.9
Public Works	49.0	43.8					44.4
Health & Welfare	10.8	16.7					19.4
Recreation & Culture	8.5	2130.0**					877.8
Statutory & Unclassified							
TOTAL	32.7	88.0					67.1
Sub (n)	n=23	n=4					n=7

Notes: *Communities of 100 population or less (1960) have been eliminated from this growth categorization (TETERBORO; PAHAQUARRY; PINE VALLEY; TAVISTOCK). **Only one case.

Source: CUPR Survey 1972-1973.

EXHIBIT 5-12. 1960-1970 DECADE PERCENT CHANGE IN PERCENT OF THE PER CAPITA ALLOCATION OF NEW JERSEY
MUNICIPALITIES BY ANNUAL GROWTH RATE (1960-1970) AND ESTABLISHED POPULATION BASE (1960)

GROWTH RATE

Declining (-5 to 0%) (A) — Population 1960 (000)

Program Area	0.1-1*	1-5	5-10	10-25	25-50	50+	Mean
Government Administration		0.7	1.9	1.2	-5.3	2.6	0.6
Public Safety		-0.2	-1.8	-1.4	4.8	5.2	0.5
Public Works		-1.7	-1.4	-1.3	-3.9	-4.8	-2.3
Health & Welfare		-1.0	-1.8	-0.1	-2.1	-7.0	-1.6
Recreation & Culture		0.5	-0.1	3.5	1.8	-0.4	1.2
Statutory & Unclassified		1.7	3.0	-1.9	4.7	4.4	1.6
TOTAL		0	0	0	0	0	0
Sub (n)	n=5	n=30	n=7	n=13	n=5	n=7	n=66

Slow (0 to 2%) — Population 1960 (000)

Program Area	0.1-1*	1-5	5-10	10-25	25-50	50+	Mean
Government Administration		5.0	4.2	3.3	5.8	0.0	3.1
Public Safety		0.2	1.1	-1.0	-3.2	2.9	0.0
Public Works		-6.8	-5.4	-4.5	-6.0	-6.0	-6.0
Health & Welfare		-2.1	-1.7	-1.0	-1.7	-0.6	-1.6
Recreation & Culture		3.7	1.4	1.2	0.7	0.5	2.1
Statutory & Unclassified		0.0	.4	1.2	4.4	2.1	2.4
TOTAL		0	0	0	0	0	0
Sub (n)		n=88	n=58	n=46	n=22	n=9	n=240

Moderate (I) (2 to 5%) (C) — Population 1960 (000)

Program Area	0.1-1*	1-5	5-10	10-25	25-50	50+	Mean
Government Administration	2.5	3.9	-0.7	-0.6	NO CASES		1.8
Public Safety	4.2	2.1	7.4	1.0			3.1
Public Works	-10.2	-9.4	-2.6	-8.7			-8.1
Health & Welfare	-1.8	-1.7	-2.2	-1.4			-1.6
Recreation & Culture	2.4	3.9	-0.8	5.0			3.3
Statutory & Unclassified	2.9	1.3	-1.1	4.7			1.5
TOTAL	0	0	0	0			0
Sub (n)	n=13	n=49	n=19	n=25			n=109

All New Jersey Communities

Program Area	Mean
Government Administration	1.7
Public Safety	1.5
Public Works	-7.0
Health & Welfare	-1.6
Recreation & Culture	2.6
Statutory & Unclassified	2.8
TOTAL	0
Sub (n)	n=563

Moderate (II) (5-10%) (D) — Population 1960 (000)

Program Area	0.1-1*	1-5	5-10	10-25	25-50	50+	Mean
Government Administration	5.9	1.7	0.0	3.2	NO CASES		1.9
Public Safety	-0.5	3.0	0.6	1.9			1.6
Public Works	-10.2	9.9	-6.1	-10.7			-9.0
Health & Welfare	-0.1	-1.6	-1.5	-1.6			-1.3
Recreation & Culture	2.0	2.6	3.5	3.9			2.9
Statutory & Unclassified	2.9	4.2	4.0	3.3			3.9
TOTAL	0	0	0	0			0
Sub (n)	n=13	n=41	n=27	n=11			n=94

Rapid (10-20%) (E) — Population 1960 (000)

Program Area	0.1-1*	1-5	5-10	10-25	25-50	50+	Mean
Government Administration	-3.7	0.2	-1.0	3.2	NO CASES		-0.4
Public Safety	0.2	11.3	2.9	3.3			6.8
Public Works	4.3	-10.7	-7.4	-12.3			-8.7
Health & Welfare	-3.2	-2.0	-1.7	-1.5			-1.9
Recreation & Culture	5.7	4.9	3.4	4.8			4.7
Statutory & Unclassified	-3.3	-3.7	3.8	2.5			-0.5
TOTAL	0	0	0	0			0
Sub (n)	n=7	n=25	n=6	n=6			n=47

Explosive (20% and over) (F) — Population 1960 (000)

Program Area	0.1-1*	1-5	5-10	10-25	25-50	50+	Mean
Government Administration	-9.4	9.9	NO CASES				2.1
Public Safety	15.2	10.4					1.6
Public Works	11.9	-16.3					-7.3
Health & Welfare	-7.2	-7.0					-6.0
Recreation & Culture	-0.5	2.1					3.2
Statutory & Unclassified	-0.6	0.9					6.4
TOTAL	0	0					0
Sub (n)	n=23	n=4					n=27

Notes: *Communities of 100 population or less (1960) have been eliminated from this growth categorization (TETERBORO; PAHAQUARRY; PINE VALLEY; TAVISTOCK)

Source: CUPR Survey 1972-1973

New Jersey communities as a whole increased gross program expenditures annually at an average of 20 percent between 1960 and 1970. The range among programs was from 12 percent to 26 percent. At the upper level were government administration and public safety; at significant lower levels, 14 percent to 16 percent, were public works and recreation; finally, health and welfare and statutory expenses increased annually at a rate of 12 percent.

The effect of program expenditure increases may be seen by examining the change in specific program spending as a percent of the per capita allocation over a specified period of time (Exhibit 5-12). Exhibit 5-13 displays changes in percent of the budget for the mean of all size categorizations of a single municipal growth grouping. Exhibit 5-14 repeats this same information for varying growth rates yet the population base of a single set of communities (5,000 to 10,000 range) is held constant.

As may be seen, increases in the percent of the per capita allocation as a result of ten year spending patterns are not too dissimilar for the means of all size communities segregated by growth and a singular size community partitioned by the same variable. *This would indicate that for this particular analysis the population base of community is of only minor import in explaining variation in program emphases over time.* The growth grouping is clearly dominant here.

It is obvious that *as the growth rate of a community increases, the program variation in budget allocation also becomes much greater.*

The direction of change is also important. It is clear for instance that programs such as health and welfare and public works have uniformly decreased across all directions and levels of growth as a percent of the per capita allocation. This is especially true for public works which has decreased an average of 7 percent (i.e., from 30 percent to 23 percent in average local budgets) within New Jersey communities. Also apparent are the steady or positive increases as a percent of the budget of public safety and recreation. This positive emphasis is also true for government administration and statutory expenditures in all growth groupings except for the rapid case.

Declining and Slow Growth Communities

Declining and slow growth communities, irrespective of size, increased their gross program expenditures generally at much smaller rates than other communities falling within the more rapid growth groupings (Exhibit 5-15). Declining communities increased their total expenditures as a percent of the 1960 base at barely half the rate (12 percent) of all New Jersey communities (20.6 percent);

174

EXHIBIT 5-13. 1960-1970 CHANGE IN BUDGET ALLOCATIONS TO SERVICE AREAS BY
VARYING GROWTH RATES OF COMMUNITIES (COMMUNITY SIZE ALLOWED
TO VARY)

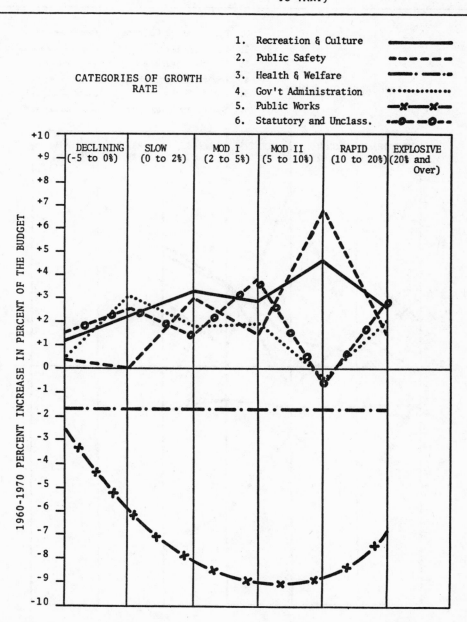

CATEGORIES OF GROWTH
RATE

1. Recreation & Culture
2. Public Safety
3. Health & Welfare
4. Gov't Administration
5. Public Works
6. Statutory and Unclass.

Note: Line Continuity Shown Here is For the Purpose of Visual Aid Only.

Source: CUPR Survey 1972-1973.

EXHIBIT 5-14.   1960-1970 CHANGE IN BUDGET ALLOCATIONS TO SERVICE
AREAS BY VARYING GROWTH RATES OF COMMUNITIES
(COMMUNITY SIZE HELD CONSTANT)*

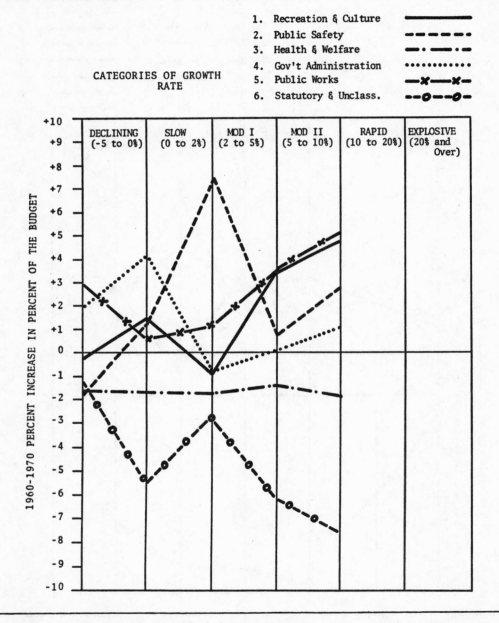

1.   Recreation & Culture
2.   Public Safety
3.   Health & Welfare
4.   Gov't Administration
5.   Public Works
6.   Statutory & Unclass.

CATEGORIES OF GROWTH
RATE

Note: 1.   Line Continuity Shown Here is for the Purpose of Visual Aid Only.
        2.   (*) Communities of 5-10,000 Population.

Source: CUPR Survey 1972-1973.

EXHIBIT 5-15. SELECTED NEW JERSEY COMMUNITIES OF VARYING POPULATION BASE AND GROWTH
CATEGORIES: COMPARISONS OF PERCENT INCREASE IN MUNICIPAL EXPENDITURES

Change Category	Size Category	Community	Annual 1960-1970 Percent Increase in Total Municipal Expenditures	Annual 1960-1970 Percent Increase in Expenditures[1] for Indicated Expenditure Category					
				(2) GA	(3) PS	(4) PW	(5) HW	(6) RC	(7) SJ
Decline/ Slow I	100- 1,000	Roosevelt Borough	32.6	4.5	7.6	-0.05	40.0	8.1	30.0
	1,000- 5,000	Longport Borough	8.5	9.2	11.5	3.4	50.2	4.4	47.5
	5,000-10,000	Palmyra Borough	8.1	16.0	7.5	3.2	11.1	23.0	18.7
	10,000-25,000	Maywood Borough	9.3	7.7	10.5	4.8	6.8	17.1	16.6
	25,000-50,000	Garfield	5.7	0.8	7.8	4.6	3.3	9.0	11.7
	50,000+	Bayonne	7.7	4.6	9.8	5.0	1.3	9.5	10.1
Moderate/ Moderate II	100- 1,000	South Harrison Township	25.4	23.8	18.7	17.2	-5.2	10.0	33.3
	1,000- 5,000	Chesterfield Township	25.3	22.0	49.5	24.7	7.5	10.0	30.4
	5,000-10,000	Readington Township	22.2	29.5	280.4	16.6	1.1	10.0	81.2
	10,000-25,000	Peaquannock Township	20.1	14.7	18.2	11.3	55.5	45.9	81.2
	25,000-50,000	Wayne Township	41.4	39.3	37.7	20.5	89.2	193.4	140.4
	50,000+	Woodbridge Township	14.6	26.2	15.4	4.2	12.8	63.5	29.8
Rapid/ Explosive III	100- 1,000	Hi-Nella Borough	52.8	17.6	101.0	83.3	156.0	10.0	91.3
	1,000- 5,000	Franklin Lakes Borough	145.4	260.4	366.2	6.9	-9.4	10.0	61.8
	5,000-10,000	Jackson Township	105.0	88.7	145.4	89.4	67.5	135.2	457.3
	10,000-25,000	Madison Township	34.6	38.9	44.0	14.3	41.0	73.1	74.0
	25,000-50,000	Parsippany Troy Hills Township	54.3	29.4	55.9	59.0	45.8	223.5	43.9
	50,000+	No Cases							

Notes: 1. An annual 10 percent recreation and culture expenditure increase or a 100 percent increase for
the decade was assigned to these communities not having any 1960 recreation and culture
expenditure but having a 1970 expenditure in this category.

(2) - Government Administration   (5) - Health and Welfare
(3) - Public Safety   (6) - Recreation and Culture
(4) - Public Works   (7) - Statutory and Unclassified

Source: N.J.D.C.A. 1960 and 1970 Annual Reports (See Exhibit 5-3 for full citation).

177

the increase for slow growth communities was three-fourths the general average or approximately 16 percent.*

Contributors to the above trend for declining communities were less than average increases in the areas of government administration, public safety, public works, and recreation, in part counter-balanced by a more average apportionment of expenditure increase in the area of health/welfare (Exhibits 5-12 and 5-15). Slowly growing communities demonstrate a conservative level of spending more proportionate to the New Jersey average of all communities. Yet, here also is the locus of significant annual expenditure increases in the area of public safety, public works, and health and welfare that is noted at other increasing rates of growth.

The expenditure patterns noted in declining communities show slightly positive emphases in terms of percentage increases in per capita allocation to the areas of government administration, recreation/culture, and statutory contributions and declining emphases in the areas of health and welfare and public works. The public safety expenditures as a percent of the budget seems to maintain its prior level. Slow growth communities have shifted their emphases in similar areas yet more forcefully. Changes in percent of the budget allocated to government administration, recreation/culture, statutory contribution and public works, while of similar directions are twice the magnitude.

Moderately Growing Communities

In the two categories of moderately growing communities average annual gross expenditure increases are 75 percent _higher_ than declining and slow growth communities of comparable size (5,000 to 25,000). Since population is increasing at four to six times the rate in this group, actual _per capita_ annual program increases are 1 percent to 3 percent _lower_. This general trend is shown for several communities in Exhibit 5-17.

---

*One must constantly keep in mind the relationship between annual gross expenditure and annual per capita increases. Declining communities, for instance, experiencing a 12 percent annual gross expenditure increase, due to a _dwindling_ base, suffered a 14.4 percent per capita rise; slow growth communities undergoing a 16.2 percent annual program expenditure, as a function of an _expanding_ base, were able to reduce these increases to only 13.5 percent per capita. This gap, displaying the importance of population increase as a given deterrant to per capita expenditure increase (above a given community size servicing level) becomes much more prominent in moderate and rapid slow growth communities (Exhibit 5-16).

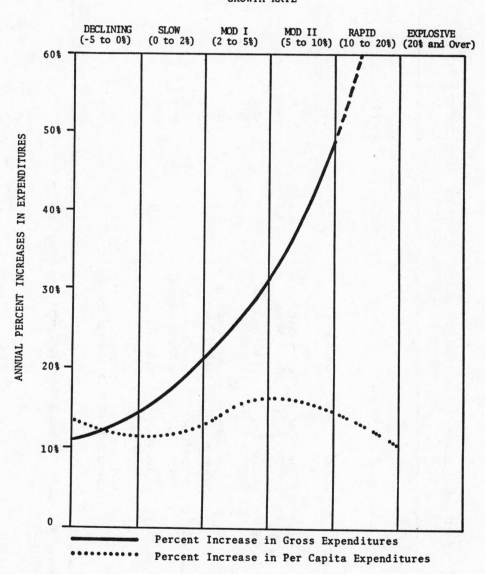

EXHIBIT 5-16. TOTAL EXPENDITURE AND PER CAPITA VARIATION AS A
FUNCTION OF DIFFERING GROWTH RATES

GROWTH RATE

Source: CUPR Survey, spring 1973.

179

EXHIBIT 5-17. DECLINE/SLOW AND MODERATELY GROWING COMMUNITIES: COMPARISONS OF POPULATION AND TOTAL AND PER CAPITA EXPENDITURE CHANGES

Size Category	Change Category	Municipality	1960-1970 Annual Percent Population Change	1960-1970 Annual Percent Increase in Total Expenditures	1960-1970 Annual Percent Increase in Total Per Capita Expenditures
100- 1,000	Decline/Slow	Corbin City	-0.5	6.9	7.7
	Moderate I, II	Alpine Borough	4.6	13.6	6.2
1,000- 5,000	Decline/Slow	Egg Harbor City	-0.3	10.4	11.0
	Moderate I, II	Clinton Town	5.0	17.8	8.5
5,000-10,000	Decline/Slow	Upper Penns Neck Twp.	-0.8	12.5	14.3
	Moderate I, II	Oakland Borough	5.3	21.8	10.8
10,000-25,000	Decline/Slow	Maywood Borough	-0.3	9.3	9.9
	Moderate I, II	Middlesex Borough	4.3	16.6	8.6
25,000-50,000	Decline/Slow	Belleville Town	-0.1	12.1	12.3
	Moderate I, II	Middletown Township	3.8	17.5	10.0
50,000+	Decline/Slow	Paterson	0.1	11.7	11.5
	Moderate I, II	Woodbridge Township	2.5	14.6	9.6

Source: N.J.D.C.A. 1960 and 1970 Annual Reports (See Exhibit 5-3 for full citation).

In the first category of <u>moderately</u> growing communities the areas
of general administration and public safety appear to be emphasized
more so than in the declining and slow growth communities. Again
variation in population base does not appear to alter these allocation patterns (Exhibit 5-18). A continued emphasis on these two
areas of municipal service is apparent in the second category
(5 percent to 10 percent annual population increase) of moderately
growing communities (Exhibit 5-18). For this grouping, gross
increases in general administration expenditures appear to increase
with size while large public safety expenditure increases are much
more prevalent in communities of the 1,000-10,000 population range
(Exhibit 5-18). This expenditure pattern has occasioned positive
growth in the percent of the budget allocated to these functions
(an increase of approximately 2 percent, i.e., from 26 percent
to 28 percent of the budget) within moderately growing communities.

The health and welfare annual gross expenditure increase in the
second category of moderately growing communities is twice the
first and, contrary to the first, is inversely related to population base. The direct relationship of gross expenditure increases
in health/welfare as population base increases appears to reverse
itself at growth rates in excess of 5 percent. Yet, regardless
of specific emphases or variation with size, it is clear that a
portion of the government/administration/public safety positive
gains have come at the expense of the health and welfare functions.
The rate of expansion in this area, although considerable as a
percent of the existing base, is not of sufficient magnitude to
maintain even the function at levels observed in 1960. Health
and welfare decreased 2 percent (from 4 percent to 2 percent)
within the per capita allocations of moderately growing communities.

The public works function had significantly less than average
gross expenditure increases in both categories of moderate growth
groupings experience. More rapid increases were evident in communities of 1,000 to 10,000 and less in smaller communities and
in communities of 10,000 to 25,000. Yet it is in the moderately
growing communities where the public works de-emphasis as a percent of the budget is marked by a decrease of 8 percent to 9
percent. It is in the moderate growth communities that there
begins to be a priority shift away from the public works function
to the areas of general administration and public safety. As
will be demonstrated, the shift to public safety actually occurs
before the trend away from public works.

Rapid and Explosive Growth Communities

Rapid and explosive growth communities' annual expenditure increases
are three to four times the increases noted for declining and slow

1960-1970 Annual Percent Increase in Expenditures for Indicated Program Areas

Population Base	Growth Category	Community	(1) GA	(2) PS	(3) PW	(4) HW	(5) RC	(6) SU
I	A. Slow/Decline	Eagleswood Township	1.4	11.9	9.7	-0.7	10.0[7]	
		Roosevelt Borough	4.5	7.6	-0.05	40.0	8.1	
	B. Moderate I	South Harrison Twp.	23.8	18.7	17.2	-5.2	10.0[7]	
100-1,000	C. Moderate II	Washington Township	9.9	9.2	4.2	2.8	10.0[8]	
		Alpine Borough	17.7	14.0	-1.1	4.2	33.2[8]	
		Ship Bottom Borough	10.2	16.8	12.7	-1.1	17.3	
II	A. Slow/Decline	Bordentown City	10.9	6.5	4.0	7.0	54.2[8]	
		Longport Borough	9.2	11.5	3.4	50.2	4.4	
	B. Moderate I	Absecon City	11.0	22.2	4.4	13.8	7.0[7]	
1,000-5,000	C. Moderate II	Chesterfield Twp.	27.7	25.7	24.7	7.5	10.0[7]	
		Linwood City	13.9	29.6	13.5	-4.8	33.8[8]	
		Sommers Point			14.0	7.8	26.1	
	A. Slow/Decline	Bogota Borough	5.3	8.8	4.4	1.7	11.6	
		Ventnor City	7.2	8.5	3.9	-1.3	4.5	
	B. Moderate I	Carlstadt Borough	15.3	12.1	11.4	-6.3	-6.7	
		Readington Township	29.5	280.4	16.6	1.1	10.0[7]	
	C. Moderate II	Galloway Township	22.3	28.3	11.9	20.2	38.1[8]	
		Northfield City	34.1	37.8	25.3	-5.0	14.4	
	A. Slow/Decline	Dumont Borough	11.5	12.0	302.7	61.8	23.3	
		Maywood Borough	7.7	10.5	4.8	6.8	17.1	
	B. Moderate I	Batontown Borough	26.7	26.0	19.4	-3.4	40.9[8]	
		Middlesex Borough	21.4	17.1	7.1	13.9	109.0[8]	
	C. Moderate II	North Brunswick Twp.	44.2	28.1	12.7	13.7	134.8[8]	

Notes:
1-6 See Exhibit 4-15.
7. A 10 percent annual increase or a 100 percent decade increase was assigned to those communities not having any 1970 recreation and culture expenditures but having a 1970 recreation and culture expenditure.
8. Extremely large percent increase results from the fact that these communities had only extremely small 1960 recreation and culture expenditures.

Source: N.J.D.C.A. 1960 and 1970 Annual Reports (See Exhibit 5-3 for full citation).

EXHIBIT 5-19.   SELECTED MODERATE AND RAPID/EXPLOSIVE GROWTH COMMUNITIES: COMPARISONS OF POPULATION AND TOTAL AND PER CAPITA EXPENDITURE INCREASES

Size Category	Change Category	Municipality	1960-1970 Annual Percent Increase in Total Expenditures	1960-1970 Annual Percent Change in Population	1960-1970 Annual Percent Change in Total Per Capita Expenditures
100- 1,000	Moderate I, II Rapid/Explosive	Alpine Borough Mantoloking Borough	13.6 10.0	4.6 9.9	61.8 56.6
1,000- 5,000	Moderate I, II Rapid/Explosive	Chesterfield Township Edgewater Park Township	25.3 53.5	2.7 15.9	17.9 14.5
5,000-10,000	Moderate I, II Rapid/Explosive	Readington Township Matawan Township	22.2 45.2	2.5 14.0	15.7 13.0
10,000-25,000	Moderate I, II Rapid/Explosive	Neptune Township Dover Township	17.0 32.9	3.0 15.1	10.8 7.1
25,000-50,000	Moderate I, II Rapid/Explosive	Wayne Township Parsippany-Troy Hills Twp.	41.4 54.3	6.7 11.6	20.7 19.8

Source: N.J.D.C.A. 1960 and 1970 Annual Reports (See Exhibit 5-3 for full citation).

growth communities (Exhibit 5-11). Once again, however, when population changes of these communities are taken into account the annual per capita increase of the two growth clusters are slightly lower (Exhibit 5-12).

In terms of program emphases there are marked dissimilarities in the rapid and explosive case from those noted in declining and slow growth communities. In the former groups general administration and public safety, for instance, increased at twice the mean rate of all other program expenditure increases over the decade. In slow and declining growth communities it barely kept pace with the mean expenditure increase for all programs.

The two programs which expanded the least and most, respectively, within the rapid and explosive growth set, were public works and recreation/culture. In the rapidly growing communities emphasis was significantly shifted away from public works and towards recreation. The public works function dropped 7 percent in per capita allocation while the recreation expenditure increased by the same margin. It is redundant, but nonetheless important, to repeat that within the rapid and explosive growth communities, emphases in program expenditures as a percent of the budget have the greatest internal variation.

TENTATIVE CONCLUSIONS ON MUNICIPAL EXPENDITURES AND GROWTH

In the pooled regression with no partitioning by direction of growth or population base (a mode of analysis used in most previous studies) it was found that per capita costs increase as communities grow. By stratifying for the above two indices, it was found that viewing communities via an "averaged" growth rate for both increases and decline, extremely small and large communities cost more to run on a per capita basis than intermediate size communities. Also, it was found that large cities that are slowly growing spend less per capita than large cities that are declining and finally, that small municipalities either growing or declining spend a similar amount per capita.

When, as detailed in the final section, the average slope was dissected by growth rate, a much richer texture to the variation of the per capita curve was observed. This caused us to question the explanation of municipal expenditures via a straight line model which heavily biased the findings of expenditure variation at the upper level of the rank size spectrum by trends which were more characteristic of slow growth communities than those of other growth rates. The following results, while in basic agreement with earlier findings, modify them somewhat and provide the detail from which new models of expenditure variation should be specified.

Total Per Capita Variation

We have found that the variation in total per capita municipal expenditure across increasing levels of population base is not a straight line function. Rather, the left hand edge of the curve across all growth rates is hyperbolic in nature expressing a relationship of initially high per capita costs in small cities which decrease as city size increases to a trough at the community size level of approximately 10,000. From here, in declining and slow growth communities, costs begin to increase and continue hyperbolic throughout the size ranges of 10,000 to 25,000, 25,000 to 50,000, and 50,000+ to levels of expenditure that existed at the smaller size ranges of 100 to 1,000 and 1,000 to 5,000.

Again in moderately growing communities expenditures are initially higher in small communities, yet the trough reached at the 10,000 community size range is maintained and per capita expenditures remain relatively stable throughout the remaining categories of community size. In rapidly growing communities per capita costs continue to be higher for small communities yet decrease significantly as population base increases.

Per Capita Allocation

Per capita allocation according to growth rate and population base also displays characteristic trends. In small declining and slow growth communities, 85 percent of the budget is devoted to the three main services areas, i.e., government administration, public safety, and public works. Over two-thirds of this expenditure allocation in small communities is funneled to government administration and public works. As community size increases, the three areas dominate to a lesser degree (70 percent),* yet public safety grows in importance and in communities in excess of 50,000, soon approaches 40 percent of the local per capita expenditure. To a large extent the new dominance of public safety is at the expense of the previously dominant public works function.

Similar allocation patterns are in evidence for the three major service areas in moderately growing communities. The decline of the public works function is not so marked nor is the increase of the local public safety budget as in other groups. In small moderately growing communities public safety expenditures are 20 percent less than declining communities and public works 20 percent more.

---

*   The importance of more recreation health/welfare and expenses becomes more visible.

In rapidly growing communities allocation patterns are less clear than for other growth groupings. In small rapidly growing communities, the three areas of major service dominate (85 percent of the budget) to the same level that they did in declining/slow growth communities. Yet they are equally important (i.e., approximately 28 percent each) and equal apportionment continues throughout increasing classification of size.

In all communities recreation allocations seem to be more a function of population size than they do of growth rate. As a percent of the budget they tend to increase from 4 percent to 10 percent as city size approaches 25,000 and then decrease to 7-8 percent for communities in excess of 50,000.

Throughout the spectrum of communities, health and welfare expenditures occupy the smallest percent of the budget (2 percent to 4 percent) and vary slightly within this range, negatively with growth rate and positively with city size. In communities in excess of 50,000 population the health and welfare allocation increases dramatically to 8 percent of the budget both in declining and slowly growing communities. Finally, statutory contributions also increases with city size and decreases with growth rate in similar fashion as the health and welfare budget allocation yet is twice (i.e., 6 percent to 8 percent) its magnitude.

Changes in Per Capita Allocation as a Function of Growth

One of the most difficult areas of all in which to draw trends is in the area of changes in service emphasis as a function of growth. The patterns of all growth groupings are much more pronounced than those of any individual growth partition used here. The most obvious trend is a clear increase in the amount of change a budget undergoes with increasing rates of growth. Declining and slowly growing communities maintain fairly similar allocation patterns whereas rapidly growing communities vary expenditure emphases quite significantly.

A second obvious characteristic of changes in program allocation as a function of growth is the similarity of pattern in terms of emphasis or de-emphasis across all growth rates.* There has been positive emphasis as a result of the maturing of cities in the program areas of government administration, public safety, recreation, and culture and statutory contributions. There has been general decline in percent allocation in the areas of public works and health and

---

*Growth rate is the important variable here. Stratification by size produces like trends.

welfare. To a certain degree this latter finding is misleading as it well may be a surrogate for an increasing level of intergovernmental participation in these two areas. With increasing federal support of various public works activities and the county government in New Jersey increasing its role in welfare activities the extent of de-emphasis by local communities is difficult to gauge.

[1]John T. Maslin Jr. & Kenneth E. Quindry, "A Note on City Expenditure Determinants," Land Economics (Vol. XLVI, Feb. 1970) p. 80.

[2]Roy W. Bahl, Metropolitan City Expenditures (Lexington, Ky.: University of Kentucky Press, 1969) pp. 24-26.

[3]Norman Walzer, "Economies of Scale and Metropolitan Police Services: The Illinois Experience," Review of Economics and Statistics (Vol. LIV, Nov. 1972) p. 431-433.

[4]William Miller, Revenue-Cost Ratios of Rural Townships With Changing Land Uses (Trenton, N.J.: New Jersey Department of Agriculture, 1965) pp. 35-36.

[5]Robert W. Burchell, Planned Unit Development: New Communities American Style (New Brunswick, N.J.: Rutgers University, Center for Urban Policy Research, 1972) Chapter 5.

CHAPTER 6

FORCES, OTHER THAN GROWTH, AFFECTING PER
CAPITA COSTS

Earlier chapters isolated the demographic characteristics-popula-
tion and population-change that affect per capita municipal expenditures. Clearly, however, they do not stand alone. The willingness,
necessity, and ability of a city to raise revenue and spend it through
the various municipal departments, to the extent that they are capable of rational identification, must be found within a conjunction
of pressures. It is this multi-textured set of potential determinants
of per capita municipal operating expenditures that is studied within
this chapter.

ANTICIPATED RELATIONSHIPS BETWEEN SELECTED
SOCIO-ECONOMIC VARIABLES AND PER CAPITA COSTS

The approach used in this chapter is a continuation of the linear
multiple regression framework augmented with analysis of covariance
techniques found in the first section of Chapter 4. The complex
nature of our problem necessitates the inclusion in the model of a
large number of characteristics. Out of a possible set of 320 characteristic fields of knowledge on most municipalities in the state,
thirty-six characteristics have been selected as independent variables for final inclusion in the model.

The order of inclusion for each independent variable in the regression equation follows the step-wise method.*

The selection paradigm is grounded in the group of promising hypotheses put forward and tested during the past twenty years of

---

*The stepwise mode of regression permits the ordered selection
of the independent variables that obtain the best prediction of the
dependent variable. Two criteria are used in the process. First,
normalized regression coefficients are constructed for each independent variable and their respective F values calculated. The
higher the F value the greater the chances that the variable will
be entered into the regression equation before the others in the
data set. The second criterion for entering additional variables
into the equation is their relative independence from the variable(s)
already entered; this is termed "tolerance." Greater tolerances
imply that the variable describes a new independent dimension;
thus, it will have a greater chance of being entered into the
equation.

research. We start by identifying the characteristics of the municipality's citizens that in theory determine variation in per capita expenditures. In order to help predict citizen behavior, a modified form of social area analysis will be used.[1] The use of social area analysis will include a composite group of factors clustered under the headings: demographic characteristics, social class, life cycle and ethnicity. In addition to this, indications of the private business sector will be included. Lastly, and of critical importance, is the structure of the local revenue base. This includes the relative strength of the property tax base as well as the presence of favorable statutory revenue sources within some municipalities.

Demographic Factors and Per Capita Costs

In addition to the demographic factors (population and percent of population change) discussed in Chapters Four and Five, two additional demographic characteristics will be analyzed: (1) gross population density, and (2) the movement of households within and into the community.

The gross population density is a municipality's population divided by its area in square miles. Population density has been thought to influence per capita expenditures in two opposing ways. First, increasing density may decrease per capita expenditures by allowing for a concentration of producing units and a reduction of overhead costs. Second and to the contrary, density symbolizes the increased costs due to the presence of human interaction over space. Essentially, density epitomizes the need for public goods. The increased potential for human interaction with density requires a mechanism to organize the interaction; since the interaction depends upon others, the individual citizen cannot by himself ensure a safe form of interaction. Increasing density makes another's action potentially more disruptive to each citizen; thus, increased production of public goods is desirable. This is essentially the problem of externalities.[2]

In addition to this, it is argued by Baumol that as the potential for human interaction increases, the public expenditures necessary to safely organize these interactions increases with the number of possible interactions.[3] That is, service requirements increase exponentially with density. This will be represented in the linear regression model by squaring the value of each municipality's density. It must be recognized that the use of gross density can underestimate the potential interaction effect. In cities with large areas of undeveloped land or non-residential storage areas, the existing residential population will be confined within a smaller effective area. The use of resident population (the numerator of the density term) excludes interaction generating forces such as the presence of central office facilities, commercial enterprises, and industrial firms.

Patterns of Demographic Factors Over
the Twelve Population Strata

Chapter 5 has shown that percent population change and population
size affect municipal expenditures in different ways. Since the
analysis to follow is anchored on the twelve clusters of cities
produced by this finding, the existence of corresponding patterns
in each of the independent variables must also be identified.

Exhibit 6-1 displays the mean values for each of the independent
variables gathered within the demographic cluster. In terms of
population density there is a sharp increase with increasing population size. Further, for the most part, cities losing population
have a higher density than those gaining population. The twelve
regression models minimize influence of density variation in as
much as it is more strongly a property of all 567 municipalities.

Although density is suspected to be a primary factor in many public
expenditure decisions, its translation into a significant determinant of per capita municipal expenditures is fraught with lengthy
problems. A priori, we cannot judge the dominant cause of fiscal
pressure: neighborhood economies or interaction-based diseconomies.

A complicating factor, one that reappears throughout the study, must
be considered; that is, the determinant of primary interest interactions with a second independent variable. In this case, increased
residential density is associated with pre-automobile urban development; furthermore, the centers of residential density are home to
many poor and minority groups. In the multiple regression model these
factors can be accounted for, but only if they are independent of density within the given set of cities being dealt with. Often we will
be unable to separate these factors; in that case, an estimate of
the independent influence, for example, of density on per capita
expenditures, will be lessened and the model's residual error term
increased.

The Impact of Families that Move

Evidence from past research is minimal with respect to the response
of local government to the phenomenon of a highly mobile society.
Indirectly, through the responses received in mobility studies in
which questionnaires were administered to newcomers to various communities, an empirical structure capable of generating testable
hypotheses will be pieced together.

Charles Tiebout has suggested that: "citizens vote with their feet,"
that is, they move to the community which supplies them with the
package of public goods most desired by them.[4] Based upon this and
the questionnaire responses, we will assign an expenditure preference by the new residents towards a specific local government service.

The primary reasons for movement appear to have changed considerably over time. In a 1955 study, Peter H. Rossi stated that "...The major function of mobility (is) the process by which families adjust their housing to housing needs that are generated by the shifts in family composition that accompany life cycle changes."[5] This suggests that, as of 1955, expanding families were moving towards larger quarters and predominantly interested in public school systems. In turn, mature families, those no longer providing shelter for their children, will be expected to have a tendency to move into smaller housing and be relatively more concerned with municipal services that protect their property values.

Addressing himself to the Rossi hypothesis, Wendell Bell asked new-comers to Park Ridge and Des Plaines, Illinois, the reason for their move. He found that, "a familistic orientation... entered into the decision to move to the suburbs in a total of 83 percent of the cases. That the familialism, as it entered into the suburban move, is largely conjugal familialism is indicated by the fact that only a relatively small percentage of the residents move in order to be closer to relatives not living with them, while a much larger per-centage indicated that they moved because of the children."[6] Thus, to the extent that this form of motivation is still in effect, we will expect that the younger newcomers will emphasize expenditures for school purposes possibly even at the expense of municipal expen-ditures.

More recent research into the motivation behind the move has come from the Rutgers Center for Urban Policy Research. In an analysis of newcomers to Princeton it was found that over 50 percent of those questioned moved for reasons of job change.[7] Further, mobility is equally divided between those in the early to middle child rearing stage, that is 26 to 35 years of age, and the later child rearing stage (36 to 49 years of age). In Plainfield, New Jersey, a city of considerably different characteristics, the researchers found that close to 30 percent of the newcomers moved for the same eco-nomic reasons as in the Princeton study.[8] Furthermore, schools pro-duced a limited 2 percent impact on residential relocation. Yet, the structure of the newcomers seems to be different from those in the Princeton case. Of this group close to 50 percent were in the early child rearing years, and only 17 percent were in the latter stages of the child rearing years (37 to 47 years of age). Weak though it is, we suggest that, as the motivation for living in a particular location swings toward the economic sector, members within each stage of the life cycle will be more apt to choose to increase muni-cipal goods and services. This further will be reflected in ele-vated per capita municipal operating expenditures.

The index of family mobility is the census variable: percentage of total families living in a different house in 1970 when compared to their 1965 place of residence. This is displayed in Exhibit 6-1. In every group of cities, well over 30 percent of the families have

EXHIBIT 6-1. THE INDEPENDENT VARIABLE CLUSTER INDICATING DEMOGRAPHIC CHARACTERISTICS

(1) 1960 Population Range	(2) Direction of Population Change 1960-1970	(3) Percent Population Change 1960-1970	(4) 1970 Population	(5) Percent in a Different House in 1970 as compared with 1965 Residences	(6) 1970 Population Density
Less than 1,000	Loss	-12.8	492	34.0	72.0
1,000-5,000	Loss	- 7.85	2,608	31.3	248.5
5,000-10,000	Loss	- 6.11	6,552	31.5	875.0
10,000-25,000	Loss	- 4.25	15,811	31.9	760.2
25,000-50,000	Loss	- 4.87	32,997	38.6	1,329.9
50,000 +	Loss	- 7.99	149,461	35.4	1,438.8
Less than 1,000	Gain	55.7	1,014	38.3	86.4
1,000-5,000	Gain	48.4	4,098	37.4	142.9
5,000-10,000	Gain	35.1	9,605	35.2	330.3
10,000-25,000	Gain	32.1	19,250	35.1	445.2
25,000-50,000	Gain	21.3	40,145	33.7	717.3
50,000 +	Gain	5.2	77,559	30.4	1,470.7

Source: New Jersey Department of Community Affairs, Division of Local Finance: Thirty-Third Annual Report of the Division of Local Finance. Trenton, N.J., NJDCA, 1970; U.S. Census of Population 1960-1970.

changed residence over the last five years. Cities gaining in population will be expected to have a larger value than those losing
population. This is in light of the fact that migration, as it has
been defined here, includes both absolute population gain and family
moves within the municipality. However, we find that the high correlation between growth and mobility is not universally the case.
Cities gaining in population up to the 25,000 bracket do have a
larger migration rate than those losing population. However, the
two larger population classes above the 25,000 level of cities losing
population have, in fact, a higher migration rate than those gaining
population.

The Social Class of Communities and Per Capita Costs: The Occupational Index

Social class has long been characterized as a mix of occupational,
education, and income conditions, which influences the preference
ranking for public goods by the residents of the community. In
previous studies it has been assumed that there is a positive correlation between social class and the level of public services demanded.
Our analysis uses a variant of the Blau and Duncan occupational index
of the municipality as an indicator of its social class.[9] Blau
and Duncan's ordering of seventeen occupational groups into a rank
ordered social class index is based upon the median income and median education obtained by the members of each group and a study
of intergenerational mobility among the occupational groups. The
result ranks self-employed professionals highest, followed by
salaried professionals, managers, salesmen, clerical, craftsmen,
operatives, service, laborers and farm laborers.

The search for an adequate indicator is simplified by the considerable degree of residential segregation of each occupational group.
The pattern of occupational segregation noticed in previous studies
is revealed for New Jersey municipalities in their set of correlation
coefficients. Exhibit 6-2 displays these results. The professional,
managerial, and sales groups tend to reside together in the marked
absence of craftsmen, operatives, and laborers who in turn also
tend to reside together whether by choice or default. Thus, one
index is used to represent this pattern: percent males over 25
working in professional and managerial occupations.

Let us assume that this index is the purest indicator of the aggregate citizen preference ranking for local public goods. This is
contrary to past studies in which education and income were used;
however, it is justifiable for several reasons. First, the median
educational level of a municipality not only indicates the degree
to which parents of past generations struggled to have their children enter a particular status level, but also it is highly indicative of the age mix of the citizens of the municipality.

EXHIBIT 6-2. ZERO ORDER CORRELATION COEFFICIENTS BETWEEN THE PERCENTAGE OF EACH MALE OCCUPATIONAL GROUP'S PRESENCE IN A MUNICIPALITY AND ALL OTHER OCCUPATIONAL GROUPS IN THE MUNICIPALITY FOR 567 NEW JERSEY MUNICIPALITIES 1970.

	Man	Sales	Cler.	Crafts	Oper.	Trans.	Labor	Farm Man.	Farm Labor	Service	Private Household	Not Rept.
Professional	.61	.53	.02	.50	-.50	-.40	-.50	-.20	-.20	-.30	.08	-.10
Managerial		.58	-.09	-.50	-.60	-.50	-.40	-.20	-.20	.03	.10	-.20
Sales			.20	-.40	-.50	-.40	-.40	-.30	-.30	-.20	.05	-.20
Clerical				.02	.02	.03	-.10	-.30	-.20	-.06	-.03	-.11
Craftsmen					.34	.37	.34	.09	.06	-.02	-.10	-.07
Operators						.50	.30	.20	.20	-.009	-.10	-.10
Transport.							.20	.20	.10	-.002	-.03	.10
Laborers									.20	.07	.003	.03
Farm Man.									.70	-.10	.04	.03
Farm Labor										-.10	.02	-.03
Service											-.02	-.003
Private Hh.												-.005
Not Rept.												

Source: U. S. Census of Population 1970 (New Jersey).

Median education level can represent a diverse set of skills and desires; for example, today's twelve-year school curriculum can represent training for a craftsman's trade, preparation for an academic future, or a program of general studies. Finally, the recent rapid growth in advanced technical education at the junior college level further reduces the conceptual purity of education as an indicator of social preference patterns.

Similarly, objections can be voiced in the use of income as an indicator of social class. Income is a rough indicator of the ability to purchase goods and services. However, interwoven in the median income statistic are variation in the length of time on the job (most likely a function of chronological age), and price level changes due to the economic structure of the local labor market or nearness to a metropolitan area.

The use of the occupational index as a scale of social class preferences assumes that as the percentage of male professional and managerial workers increases within the city, the budgetary decision making apparatus will be proportionately responsive with increased municipal expenditures. From this, it follows that the higher the social class ranking the greater will be the demand for clean, well-maintained streets, plentiful recreation facilities, quality fire protection, and so forth.

This does not, unfortunately, deal with the possibility that a threshold level of professional and managerial worker must be present before the assumed fiscal impact is felt. Further, it does not reflect the possibility that higher social class rankings will correspond to a drop in the level of required municipal services; for example, police patrols may be required less frequently in upper-middle class areas than in poorer areas;[10] this will lower the total manpower requirement of the police department and thus

lower the municipal budget requirements. In order to obtain a positive fiscal response with increasing social class rank, one must
assume that the cost associated with the quality and quantity of
the municipal public goods demand will exceed the savings realized
through a decreased need for certain types of municipal services.

Patterns of the Social Class Indices
Over the Twelve Population Strata

The major index of social class has been identified as the percent
of professional and managerial employees within a municipality.
However, since there is extensive use in the literature of other
variables for this category, we will include a secondary set of
indicators of social class. These are: (1) median family income,
(2) median owner-occupied housing value in the community, and (3)
the percent of individuals below the census defined poverty level.

Exhibit 6-3 displays the mean value for the variables clustered
under the social class grouping. It has by far the most distinctive
pattern of the variables so far identified. *The major social class
variable, the percent of male employment in professional managerial
groups, is higher for all cases of gaining municipalities as opposed
to losing municipalities. Further, cities within the 10,000 to
25,000 population range are found to have the largest percent of
professional managerial employment,* with cities below and above
that range decreasing from that point. Median family income and
median house values follows the same general pattern. When considering social class needs in terms of the percent of the families below
the poverty level, the inverse is the case. *Cities losing population
have by far the greater percentage of poverty families.* Moreover,
cities at either extreme of the rank size spectrum have an elevated
percentage of families below the poverty level.

The Life Cycle of Community Residents
and Per Capita Costs

Life cycle encompasses several diverse sets of forces that impinge
upon the local public fisc. Three distinct phases in the human life
cycle are of concern. First, the dual category of school age children and their parents. Second, mature families in the latter stages
of the child-rearing cycle, and third, members of older families
whose children have left home and who must now adjust not only to
a different orientation towards the home but must also be prepared
for the uncertain years of later life. As indicators of the three
stages of life cycle we have chosen three age cohorts. First the
percent of the total population between 22 and 39 years of age;
second, the percent of the total population between 40 and 54 years
of age; and third, 55 and over. The child-rearing phase of the life

EXHIBIT 6-3. THE INDEPENDENT VARIABLE CLUSTER INDICATING THE PRESENCE OF SOCIAL
CLASS PREFERENCE OR NEEDS

(1) 1960 Population Range	(2) Direction of Population Change 1960-1970	(3) Percent Professional and Managerial 1970	(4) Median Family Income 1970	(5) Median Home Value 1970	(6) Percent Poverty 1970
<1,000	Loss	27.8	12,165	21,440	7.3
1,000-5,000	Loss	15.8	9,087	14,019	9.6
5,000-10,000	Loss	20.7	10,858	18,115	6.5
10,000-25,000	Loss	22.5	11,119	21,162	6.0
25,000-50,000	Loss	21.8	10,432	22,716	9.1
50,000 +	Loss	15.3	8,685	14,998	12.2
<1,000	Gain	25.3	10,417	20,806	6.0
1,000-5,000	Gain	27.2	12,010	23,250	4.6
5,000-10,000	Gain	29.0	12,773	25,452	3.7
10,000-25,000	Gain	29.2	12,899	26,374	3.4
25,000-50,000	Gain	27.7	12,599	26,257	4.2
50,000 +	Gain	18.2	10,662	21,874	6.2

Source: U.S. Census of Population 1970 (New Jersey).

cycle produces probably the greatest financial stress for the family.
To the extent that this stage is over-represented within a single
community, it is likely that the family will be simultaneously low
in their income level and facing high carrying charges from recent
acquisitions of durable household goods. Occupancy in multi-family
rental units may tend to lower these burdens; however, after housing
structure is taken into consideration, this cohort is expected to
have a depressing impact upon municipal expenditures.

The preferences of relatively large numbers of families with heads
in the 40 to 54 year old age cohort present a different situation.
First, the initial period containing the essential family start-up
costs will have largely past. Now, in the higher salary or wage
ranges of their occupation, the family can choose to spend more on
personal accoutrements or for public goods. Further, children from
this age cohort will be leaving the public school system at an increasing rate and leaving a fiscal residuum to be used for others.
Thus, depending upon social class preferences, the presence of
families in this stage of the life cycle will ease the budget constraint faced by local government.

Lastly, the 55 and over cohort represents families whose immediate
child-rearing obligations have passed and who must now be concerned
with their own future welfare. This will move the focus of their
attention from the public schools to the maintenance and protection
of their property and person. This should reflect upon the municipal budget in a positive direction.

Patterns of the Life Cycle Indices
Over the Twelve Population Strata

Exhibit 6-4 displays the patterns of the various life cycle variables. The proportion of the total population between five and
seventeen years old representing a part of the first stage in the
life cycle displays a rather consistent drop in percentage of the
total population when we go from very small cities that are losing
population to the extremely large cities that are losing population.
In contrast, cities experiencing gain find a rising percent of the
population in this age group up to a maximum somewhere in the neighborhood of the 10,000 population size followed by a gradual dropoff
to the higher city size range. The percent of the population between
22 and 34 years, the variable chosen to represent this first stage,
shows no clear trend.

Moving to the percent of the population between 40 and 54 years of
age, for those cities losing population there is a peak at the 5,000
to 10,000 range, with a decline as we move toward the larger city
sizes. This pattern is similar to that found in cities gaining in
population except that there is an overall upward trend as we move
toward the higher city size categories.

EXHIBIT 6-4. THE INDEPENDENT VARIABLE CLUSTER INDICATING THE PRESENCE OF LIFE CYCLE NEEDS AND PREFERENCES

(1) 1960 Population Range	(2) Direction of Population Change 1960-1970	(3) Percent of Total Population 5-17 years old	(4) Percent of Total Population 22-34 years old	(5) Percent of Total Population 40-54 years old	(6) Percent of Total Population over 55 years old
<1,000	Loss	30.3	12.7	19.2	27.7
1,000-5,000	Loss	24.5	20.4	17.8	22.3
5,000-10,000	Loss	26.1	20.1	20.0	20.0
10,000-25,000	Loss	22.9	20.1	19.7	24.2
25,000-50,000	Loss	21.4	25.0	14.9	18.1
50,000 +	Loss	22.8	21.1	17.7	24.2
<1,000	Gain	24.7	20.2	17.1	25.9
1,000-5,000	Gain	26.9	21.6	18.9	19.5
5,000-10,000	Gain	26.7	21.7	19.8	18.5
10,000-25,000	Gain	25.7	11.2	4.1	19.4
25,000-50,000	Gain	24.1	21.3	20.8	20.4
50,000 +	Gain	21.9	21.1	20.3	24.5

Source: U.S. Census of Population 1970 (New Jersey).

In the oldest age group the percentage of the total population in
persons 55 years of age and over is at a maximum in both losing and
gaining distributions in both the smallest and the largest city
sizes; the minimums in both cases occur at the 5,000 and 10,000
city size bracket.

The Ethnicity of Residents and
Per Capita Costs

Throughout American history the clustering of identifiable population subgroups has been commonly noted. Two forms of clustering
have been identified as having distinctively different impacts upon
the local public sector. First, the presence of European ethnic
clusters, such as Scandinavian, German, and Italian settlements,
have been showed by Wilson and Banfield to decrease the demand for
public goods and services.[11] At present, the source of this response is unclear. It may, in part, be due to a strong work-ethic
stimulated by visible models of personal success, or it may be seat-
ed in the support derived from participation in strong community
and church groups. In either case, the presence of sizable percentages of foreign stock has been shown to both depress per capita
municipal expenditures,[12] and to be correlated with public capital
facilities bond election defeats.[13]

In contrast, the presence of racial minorities, such as blacks, has
shown a distinctly opposite effect. After correcting for poverty
and life cycle effects, the percentage of black citizens has shown
a strong stimulating effect on per capita municipal expenditures.[14]
The explanation offered in this case revolves about the unique
situation faced by black America. The uniqueness manifest in all
classes of black America is the unequal treatment dealt them by the
majority white society. Several explanations can be offered for
this phenomenon. According to the theory of status inconsistency,
individuals who do not receive the rewards expected of their position in the private sector will turn towards the government for
corrective action.[15] An alternative explanation focuses on the
white portion of the society. In the latter case, increased governmental expenditures are recognized as a cost of keeping racial bar-
riers in place.

Patterns of the Ethnicity Indices
Over the Twelve Population Strata

Fiscal pressures associated with ethnicity will be analyzed in terms
of two variables. First, the percentage of the total population recorded as being of foreign stock, and second, the percentage of the
total population that are black and Spanish children between the
ages five and seventeen. These are displayed in Exhibit 6-5. As
with previous variables, strong patterns over city size and direction of population change exist for both ethnic indicators. For

EXHIBIT 6-5. THE INDEPENDENT VARIABLE CLUSTER INDICATING THE PRESENCE OF ETHNIC FACTORS

(1) 1960 Population Range	(2) Direction of Population Change 1960-1970	(3) Population Percent Foreign Stock 1970	(4) Percents of Black and Spanish Extraction as a Percent of Total Population in 1970
<1,000	Loss	14.0	0.0
1,000-5,000	Loss	17.0	5.1
5,000-10,000	Loss	24.8	5.1
10,000-25,000	Loss	30.2	3.4
25,000-50,000	Loss	35.8	5.9
50,000 +	Loss	26.7	12.1
<1,000	Gain	21.4	1.3
1,000-5,000	Gain	21.4	1.3
5,000-10,000	Gain	27.8	0.9
10,000-25,000	Gain	30.7	1.3
25,000-50,000	Gain	35.2	2.3
50,000 +	Gain	42.9	3.8

Source: U.S. Census of Population 1970 (New Jersey).

cities gaining population there is a distinct increase in the proportion of foreign stock with size of city; whereas in cities losing population, a peak proportion of foreign stock occurs at the 25,000 to 50,000 size range and declines rapidly at the 50,000 and over. This has been shown to have serious impact upon the future viability of the residential property tax base. The flight of older foreign born and first generation foreign stock indicated in this finding has been documented by Sternlieb in reference to its impact upon the structure of the housing market in Newark, New Jersey.[16]

The presence of minority groups as represented by their increasing numbers of school age children is predominantly a phenomenon of cities that are losing population. Further, it is a phenomenon increasing in degree with city size. Cities that are gaining population register a slight increase over the size range; however, in percentage figures, it is far below that experienced by cities in decline.

The Municipal Economic Base
and Per Capita Costs

Broadly viewed, the economic structure of the municipality represents
its present land use. It will be operationally analyzed here in
terms of residential, industrial, commercial, farm, and vacant land
uses. Previous studies have found that the various types of land use
within a municipality generate specific types of needs for public
goods and services. Low density residential developments as opposed
to high density developments generate different types of coordina-
tion problems. With the frequency of interaction being less in low
density areas, citizens can get along with fewer police, fire, and
recreational services. However, as the probability of face to face
confrontation increases, the need to organize these into harmless
interactions is manifested.

Commercial enterprises bring a separate set of needs. Commercial
areas, to the extent that these are oriented toward the automobile
shopper, generate traffic. Thus, they will generate needs for traffic control and street maintenance. Protection of commercial property requires both police and fire services. Similarly, protection
of the buying public requires health and building code inspection
services. The manufacturing sector is similar to the commercial
in the needs it generates. Here, however, a distinction arises.
Manufacturing firms in New Jersey define a continuous band from capital intensive to labor intensive operations. It is argued that the
relative demand of public service differs among plants ranked in
this axis. Weicher notes that many modern plants have internalized
both the police and fire protection within the corporate umbrella.[17]
What remains is, hypothetically, a modest traffic control problem
in the area of the access to the plant.

Older labor intensive plants are expected to rely more heavily upon
publicly provided police and fire protection. In addition, greater
traffic generation problems implicit in our auto oriented labor
force will place increased burdens upon the public fisc. Lastly,
farm and vacant land* will be expected to generate the lowest levels
of per capita expenditures due to the lack of human interaction
generated by their presence. As indicators of the commercial and
industrial aspects of the communities' economic base, three variables
are used.

---

*Vacant land in this context does not include areas generated
by the central city abandonment process. Rather, it supposes land
previously undeveloped or used for farm purposes only.

The first variable is the ratio of commercial employees to the resident population of the municipality. The second is the industrial employment to residents ratio. This is the ratio constructed from the number of persons employed in the industrial sector of the municipality divided by resident population of the city. The third index of commercial-industrial activity is the equalized valuation of commercial-industrial property as a percentage of the total tax base. This measures the degree to which the municipality relies on non-residential property for its tax base.

These are displayed in Exhibit 6-6. Of the three variables, only the last, that is, the percent of total ratables within the municipality in the form of commercial and industrial property, forms a distinctive pattern over both size of city and direction of population change. *In the case of cities losing population, all strata are more reliant on commercial and industrial ratables than cities gaining in population.* Furthermore, a sharply defined U-shaped curve with extreme values of 46.9 percent and 41.2 percent is found

EXHIBIT 6-6.   THE INDEPENDENT VARIABLE CLUSTER INDICATING
COMMERCIAL AND INDUSTRIAL ENTERPRISES
(ECONOMIC BASE)

(1) 1960 Population Range	(2) Direction of Population Change 1960-1970	1966 Employment to Residents Ratios		(5) Value of Commercial and Industrial Property as a Percent of Total Tax Base 1970
		(3) Industrial	(4) Commercial	
<1,000	Loss	.752	.039	46.9
1,000-5,000	Loss	.084	.148	24.4
5,000-10,000	Loss	.072	.312	25.0
10,000-25,000	Loss	.122	.187	26.0
25,000-50,000	Loss	.093	.222	37.7
50,000 +	Loss	.190	.197	41.2
<1,000	Gain	.067	.088	12.0
1,000-5,000	Gain	.056	.102	18.1
5,000-10,000	Gain	.060	.127	18.9
10,000-25,000	Gain	.083	.119	20.2
25,000-50,000	Gain	.090	.166	26.6
50,000 +	Gain	.100	.221	32.1

Source: New Jersey Department of Labor and Industry Covered Employment Trends (Trenton, N.J. NJDLI, 1970); U.S. Census of Population 1970 (New Jersey).

at either extreme of population size spectrum. A minimum occurs at
the 1,000 to 5,000 population range, this value is 24 percent. For
cities gaining in population, the reliance on commercial and industrial ratables increases with city size, from 12 percent in the
smallest to 32 percent in the largest city size.

The Association Between the Commercial
and Industrial Structure and the Presence
of Low Income Families

It has already been seen that the presence of commercial and industrial firms generates demands for elevated levels of per capita
expenditures. Within the context of this argument, the crucial
problem becomes the ability of the municipality to extract sufficient revenues from the commercial and industrial ratables to pay
for the services they require. In a study of fifty-five San
Francisco and Bay Area municipalities, Julius Margolis explores
several aspects of this problem.[18] Of interest is his finding of
an association between relatively high concentrations of commercial
and industrial employment centers, more densely developed residential areas occupied by the families of lower income workers, and
higher tax rates. Morris Beck has similarly found a positive
relationship between gross residential density and the tax effort
required of local taxpayers in 277 northeastern New Jersey municipalities.[19]

When compared with dormitory suburbs of similar family income level
and residential density, Margolis finds that municipalities rich
in commercial and industrial ratables require a higher equalized
tax rate. Margolis' conclusion is that municipalities are mistaken
in pursuing commercial and industrial ratables for fiscal purposes.
This is because the level of local residential amenity correspondingly declined by allowing low income workers to bid successfully
for residential property and thus reduce the overall per capita
real property tax base.

Twenty years have passed since the fiscal year represented in the
Margolis study. This time period corresponds with the twenty-five
years elapsed since the Lionshead Lake versus Wayne Township zoning
case.[20] This case is thought by many to have fathered much of the
restricted zoning situations present in today's municipalities.
It is this latter statutory phenomenon that challenges the appli-
cability of the Margolis' association hypothesis. Specifically,
it must be determined if municipalities have successfully bid for
commercial and industrial ratables and at the same time driven a
wedge between the location of the job and the worker's residence.
In turn, we must find if the presence of commercial-industrial
ratables is associated with lower general tax rates.

The Municipal Residential Sector and Per Capita Costs

Residential land use forms the backbone of most municipalities in terms of acreage and tax base. To most families the purchase of a dwelling unit most probably forms its largest investment; through the processes of price level increase or liquidation at the end of the amortization period, it represents an important source of capital for the retirement nest egg. Thus, the maintenance of the general residential area will be of great interest to local citizenry and can be reflected in the local budget in several ways. First, in light of the housing shortages, those areas that supply desirable yet expensive public goods will encourage and support high real property values. However, in turn, a sizeable tax base will be required to meet and maintain the level of current public spending and public goods production. Thus a strong tax base that provides local citizens with high quality public services will also encourage a strong market value for available housing. This argument assumes that families to a certain extent shop for the community that provides them with the package of public goods most desired by them.[21] Recent scholars have used this hypothesis with some degree of success; Bahl and Firestein report that suburban migration patterns are strongly related to per capita educational expenditures.[22] As an extension of the above argument, a recent study of northeastern New Jersey residential communities by Wallace Oates finds that when the pressure to maintain high levels of public expenditures results in elevated tax rates, the property value of the average owner occupied house declines.*[23]

This suggests the presence of a set of feedback effects. Relatively high property tax base municipalities with low tax rates should obtain increased per capita expenditures with increasing median housing values. As the tax rate is forced up, however, municipalities that must produce municipal services for their commercial and industrial base will do so at the expense of the local revenues generated for school purposes. In turn, Oates argues that the lower expenditure level school districts generate fewer public goods (i.e., amenities) and as a consequence of tax capitalization will produce a lower level of median housing value. However, if the municipality has but minimal municipal functional requirements, its elevated tax rate can be used to support a high expenditure school system, thus retaining its desirability and higher home values.

Our present study is not designed to test the work of Oates and Bahl; rather, we have chosen to analyze the impact of housing age, tenure and housing stock configuration upon per capita expenditure variation.

---

*Or does not increase with the same rate as property value in communities not burdened with an excessive tax rate.

Variables Used to Describe Characteristics
of the Housing Stock

Exhibit 6-7 displays the characteristics of the housing stock in terms
of its age of development over the city size spectrum of losing
and gaining municipalities. Strong characteristic patterns are
displayed throughout each of the four variables. The first variable, the percent of dwelling units built before 1939, as expected,
is dominated by cities that are losing population. Also the characteristic U-shaped curve appears here. Extremely high values are
found for both very small and very large municipalities losing
population. For cities gaining population a similar U-shaped curve
appears, however, the level of percentage dwelling units has declined
by approximately 20 percent for each category of city.

The housing units built during the 1940's display the effect of the
housing industry of World War II. For the most part, the percentage
of dwelling units built during this period are the smallest of the
four time periods studied. For both cities losing and gaining population, there is a gentle increase in the percent of dwelling units
built during this period as we move towards the higher population size
brackets.

The decade of the 1950's displays the results of the move to suburbia.
For both losing and gaining municipalities, maximum construction has
shifted to the 5,000 to 25,000 population size brackets. Further,
both sets of cities show the characteristic inverted U-shaped curve
in which both small and largest cities have the least construction
of dwelling units during the period. In comparing losing and gaining
distributions, little difference is found. The most recent decade
shows the continued emphasis on suburbanization, especially that
occurring in cities that are gaining population. In this set the
greatest development of housing comes in the lower half of the population rank size spectrum. To a certain extent this pattern is reproduced by cities losing population; however, in several of these
groups construction has dropped to its lowest point for the four
time periods analyzed.

Form of Residential Tenure
and Per Capita Costs

Home ownership, as opposed to the rental form of tenure, has been
recently proposed as a key factor producing a significant independent
depressing effect upon the local tax rate, and, therefore, upon per
capita expenditures. The argument revolves about the degree of
awareness on the part of the citizen that he is a taxpayer. Woo
Sik Kee first developed the empirical basis for this argument when
he showed that the increase in the percent of homeowners within the
city brought a decrease in per capita expenditures for general municipal operating expenditures.[24] Public opinion surveys further

EXHIBIT 6-7.   THE INDEPENDENT VARIABLE CLUSTER REPRESENTING THE AGE DISTRIBUTION OF HOUSING STOCK

(1) 1960 Population Range	(2) Direction of Population Change	(3) Percent of Dwelling Units Built before 1939	(4) Percent of Dwelling Units Built between 1940-49	(5) Percent of Dwelling Units Built between 1950-59	(6) Percent of Dwelling Units Built between 1960-70
<1,000	Loss	60.5	7.9	18.4	13.2
1,000-5,000	Loss	57.7	13.0	17.2	12.1
5,000-10,000	Loss	53.8	14.9	20.8	10.5
10,000-25,000	Loss	56.9	15.2	18.1	9.7
25,0-0-50,000	Loss	55.3	12.5	19.5	12.7
50,000 +	Loss	72.3	10.3	8.3	9.7
<1,000	Gain	44.8	8.9	19.4	27.0
1,000-5,000	Gain	39.9	8.6	22.7	28.7
5,000-10,000	Gain	36.9	9.9	26.8	26.3
10,000-25,000	Gain	34.8	12.2	28.5	19.5
25,000-50,000	Gain	45.7	12.5	22.3	19.5
50,000 +	Gain	58.6	13.0	15.5	12.6

Source: U.S. Census of Housing 1970 (New Jersey).

substantiated this argument. Elizabeth Likhert David documents
that apartment renters prefer the property tax over homeowners.[25]
This implies that renters are less aware of the real property tax
burden that they themselves are paying in their rent than the home
owner who personally sends his check to the municipal treasury or
sees his annual carrying charges increase within the tax rate.
*Renters do not directly experience the property tax payment to the
municipal treasury. Thus, to the extent that other factors do not
act to increase the awareness of renters, it is expected that they
will support increases in public services feeling that others will
be responsible for paying them. In their minds this then acts to
increase their real income.*

The income maximization hypothesis can be carried one step further
by differentiating between families renting single family houses and
duplexes, and those renting apartments. If those citizens paying
rent do not notice direct tax payment, then both characteristics
should make it easier for the city council to raise revenue locally.
However, should the increase in per capita expenditures found by
Kee be due in addition to the higher density living and increased
potential for human interaction, then in addition to the positive
influence of taxpayer unawareness, percent apartment renters will
have a stronger positive impact upon the per capita expenditures
than those renting houses in lower density residential areas.

Exhibit 6-8 displays the independent variable cluster representing
housing tenure. Three characteristics are displayed: first, the
percent of the dwelling units that are renter occupied; second,
total dwelling units that are single family or duplex structures
and renter occupied; and third, the percent of the dwelling units
that are in the form of three or more units per structure and renter
occupied.

Renter occupancy is largely a function of the concentration of multiple dwelling units; as is expected, larger structures for the most
part dominate all others in their percent rental occupancy. This
is more clearly seen in the second variable. The percent of the
total dwelling units that are in the form of three or more units
per structure and renter occupied. The general pattern for losing
municipalities shows a rapid increase in the percent renter occupied
apartments, up to the 25,000 to 50,000 size bracket. Hereafter it
falls back slightly. For cities gaining in population the pattern
is roughly the same with the absence of the falloff at the 50,000
size group. Again for the most part, cities that are losing population have a greater concentration of apartment renters than
cities gaining population. The last component of the renter occupancy term is the percent of the total dwelling units that are in
single family and duplex structures and renter occupied. Here
patterns over city size and population change are unclear. However, the importance of rental tenures as a component in the housing structure is indicated. For those cities gaining population

EXHIBIT 6-8. THE INDEPENDENT VARIABLE CLUSTER REPRESENTING HOUSING TENURE

(1) 1960 Population Range	(2) Direction of Population Change 1960-1970	(3) Percent of Total Dwelling Units That are Single Family or Duplex Structures and Renter Occupied 1970	(4) Percent of Total Dwelling Units That are in the Form of Three or More Units Per Structure and Renter Occupied 1970	(5) Percent of Total Dwelling Units Renter Occupied 1970
<1,000	Loss	5.1	1.9	7.0
1,000-5,000	Loss	22.7	9.3	32.0
5,000-10,000	Loss	24.1	8.9	33.0
10,000-25,000	Loss	16.5	24.2	40.7
25,000-50,000	Loss	17.1	50.9	68.0
50,000 +	Loss	18.7	44.9	63.6
<1,000	Gain	16.6	4.7	21.3
1,000-5,000	Gain	14.5	7.1	21.6
5,000-10,000	Gain	12.5	10.7	23.2
10,000-25,000	Gain	13.0	15.8	28.8
25,000-50,000	Gain	12.9	22.7	35.6
50,000 +	Gain	16.2	37.0	53.2

Source: U.S. Census of Housing - 1970 (New Jersey).

on the average fully 15 percent of the housing stock is in the form
of single family and duplex dwelling units that are renter occupied.
For the cities losing in population much the same pattern exists.

Residential Type and Per Capita Costs

The structure of the housing stock of a municipality can be looked
upon as affecting the budget in several ways. First, due to the
physical and locational characteristics of the dwelling units different types of families will be attracted to them. Garden apartments
are a case in point. In the 1964 New Jersey study, Sternlieb finds
that subject to apartment/bedroom mix, on the average, 0.273 students
are generated by each garden apartment unit.[26] A recent New York
study shows similar results. The average garden apartment generates
from 0.2 to 0.3 school children. As opposed to this, single family
structures are found to generate children in the range of 0.7 to
1.8 per household.[27] Thus, we find a less intensive need for public
school services produced by multiple dwelling unit structures.
Sternlieb estimates that municipalities benefit fiscally from apartment developments having one bedroom or less per dwelling unit.
Paralleling the Sternlieb conclusion, a Barrington, Illinois, study
argues that in light of larger numbers of bedrooms found within
single family structures, (three to five), the presence of multiple
dwelling unit structures usually with only one or two bedrooms will
generate a tax benefit to the remainder of the community. This benefit is maintained even after consideration of the real property
value accruing to the municipal tax base by each type of structure.[28]

We have just examined the hypothesis that renters being less aware
of the property tax are less likely to oppose a given property tax
level than are homeowners. Now, a second fiscal pressure can be found
in this category. The presence of various types of multiple dwelling unit structures, built under the conditions imposed by stringent
zoning ordinances, generate fewer children per household than single
family structures. In a recent analysis of the land use controls
in force within the municipalities of four major northeastern New
Jersey counties, Norman Williams and Thomas Norman found that 83
percent of the land zoned which permits multiple dwellings restricts
their number of bedrooms to one or two per unit. Williams and
Norman further found that the ratio of one to two bedroom units
runs from 65 percent/35 percent in one extreme to fully 90 percent/
10 percent for the other.[29]

The impact of recent residential development upon municipal expenditures can take several forms. This will depend upon the source of
effective political pressure upon the budget process as well as the
expenditures requirement generated within the local school district.
As the proportion of multiple dwelling units within the municipality increases, this can lower the demands of the school district
for local revenues. In turn, that part of the tax base that has
been nominally freed can remain unused thus lowering property tax
rates; or it can be claimed by the municipal government thus, in
theory, elevating the level of services provided by it.

Several factors may be judged as forcing a particular expenditure decision. First, if the tax rate presently is low, then in light of the lack of renter taxpayer awareness, little reason exists not to use the apartment dwellers' marginally unutilized tax base to increase the expenditure level. As the tax rate rises, the argument is mitigated by the potential for tax capitalization on the owner-occupied fraction of the dwelling units in the municipality. The second decision-forcing factor is the presence of commercial and industrial activities that municipal services. Depending upon the tax rate, these economic functions will exploit the apartment renters unutilized tax base. The third factor is the presence of social groupings that define the relative stringency of budget constrain within the community. Thus, one would expect that the presence of large numbers of professional persons would elevate the level of school expenditures, the presence of families beyond the child-rearing age would prefer protection of their housing investment, and lastly, the presence of marginal income laborers and operatives would have a constraining influence on the outflow of income for either purpose.

Exhibit 6-9 displays the seven variables that represent structural configuration of the housing stock. Percent of dwelling units in the single family detached configuration dominates the remainder of the structural types. When comparing gaining and losing municipalities, those that are gaining rank higher in percent single family detached than those that are losing. Further, as we move from the smallest to the largest size city, there exists a general decline in the percent single family detached dwelling units.

The remaining six structural variables define the various forms of multiple units. Generally, as city size increases the percent of dwelling units present in the form of some multiple unit structure increases with it.

Governmental Structure and Per Capita Costs

The social, demographic, and economic characteristics just analyzed represent structural givens to the city, making change possible only with a great deal of political effort. Characteristics that more easily lend themselves to policy manipulations are those statutory structures within which aggregates of people govern themselves, tax themselves, and offer specific types of public goods and services. Two groups of statutory structures will be investigated for their impact upon municipal expenditures and their effect upon the tax effort of the local governmental units. These are: (1) the local revenue structure, and (2) local governmental form. For the purpose of the study it will be most meaningful for us to analyze

EXHIBIT 6-9. THE INDEPENDENT VARIABLE CLUSTER REPRESENTING THE STRUCTURAL CONFIGURATION OF THE HOUSING STOCK

(1) 1960 Population Range	(2) Direction of Population Change 1960-1970	(3) Percent of Total Dwelling Units in Single Family Detached Structures	(4) Percent of Total Dwelling Units in Duplix Structures	(5) Percent of Units in 3 to 4 Unit Structures	(6) Percent of Units in 5 to 10 Unit Structures	(7) Percent of Units in 10 to 19 Unit Structures	(8) Percent of Units in 29 to 49 Unit Structures	(9) Percent of Units in 50 or more Unit Structures
<1,000	Loss	86.1	6.4	1.3	1.1	0.0	0.0	0.0
1,000-5,000	Loss	70.9	9.2	4.2	2.9	1.8	0.9	0.4
5,000-10,000	Loss	63.0	19.6	5.5	2.7	0.4	0.7	0.5
10,000-25,000	Loss	49.9	14.8	9.3	3.9	4.3	4.1	4.3
25,000-50,000	Loss	26.9	14.4	17.1	12.2	10.6	7.2	6.7
50,000 +	Loss	11.7	18.5	13.4	10.1	7.9	7.4	10.1
<1,000	Gain	83.1	7.6	2.3	1.4	1.2	0.5	0.1
1,000-5,000	Gain	81.3	7.0	3.0	1.7	1.7	0.9	0.7
5,000-10,000	Gain	76.7	9.6	3.1	1.9	1.9	1.9	1.3
10,000-25,000	Gain	68.0	12.6	9.8	2.0	2.0	3.9	3.8
25,000-50,000	Gain	58.9	15.2	5.9	3.5	3.5	4.7	4.6
50,000 +	Gain	33.8	24.1	13.3	7.7	7.7	5.8	6.5

Source: U.S. Census of Housing 1970 (New Jersey).

the revenue structure of New Jersey communities in terms of three
components: first, the property tax structure; second, the presence of intergovernmental aid, including replacement tax revenue;
and third, the public utility and miscellaneous tax revenues.

Revenues: The Property Tax

The revenues achieved through the property tax depend upon three
interdependent factors: first, the size of the real property tax
base; second, the size of the general tax rate (this is the sum
of the equalized tax rates for school, county, and municipal purposes); and third, the ability of the municipality to collect the
taxes actually levied. Measures of the strength of the tax base
can take several forms. When concerned with municipal functions,
total dollars of equalized real property value per citizen is usually used. Margolis used this in his San Francisco study refer
earlier. When concern swings to the capacity to fund education,
the measure becomes the total dollars of equalized real property
evaluation per public school pupil residing within the district.
This measure is used by Justice Botter in the recent New Jersey
school finance decision: Robinson vs. Cahill.[30] In order to
judge the extent to which municipalities may have successfully
exported their tax base, we will take the percentage of the total
real property tax base that is in the form of commercial and industrial ratables and use it as a separate index of this aspect of the
property tax structure.

The extent to which the tax base is used is measured by the equalized
general tax rate. For the most part, the composite general tax rate
will be used as a common indicator of tax effort. However, as the
occasion arises, we will be interested in the competitive position
of the municipal revenue generating power with respect to that of
the local school district; in order to identify this, we will use the
school purpose equalized tax rate as an independent determinant of per capita municipal expenditures. Since New Jersey does not have a limit on its
property tax rates for operating purposes, we will be interested to
find the extent to which variations in the tax rate ffect the ability of local government to raise revenue and spend it.

The variables used to identify fiscal pressures associated with the
local property tax are displayed in Exhibit 6-10. The general tax
rate shows a consistently higher value in cities losing than for
those gaining population; further, a general rise in tax rate occurs
as city size increases. The equalized property value per capita
follows the opposite pattern. Higher values are found in cities
gaining population. Likewise, the per capita value drops as city
size increases. Lastly, school revenues per pupil show an inverted
U-shaped pattern for both sets of strata--the exceptions to this
pattern are the extremely small cities which fund their schools

214

EXHIBIT 6-10. THE INDEPENDENT VARIABLE CLUSTER INDICATING
THE PROPERTY STRUCTURES OF THE MUNICIPALITY

(1) 1960 Population Range	(2) Direction of Population Change 1960-1970	(3) Mean Equalized Tax Rate	(4) Equalized Property Value Per Capita	(5) School Revenues Raised Locally Per Pupil
<1,000	Loss	2.48	26,437	778
1,000-5,000	Loss	3.61	6,841	613
5,000-10,000	Loss	3.92	5,966	621
10,000-25,000	Loss	3.66	6,987	790
25,000-50,000	Loss	4.61	5,296	773
Over 50,000	Loss	6.20	4,377	589
<1,000	Gain	2.79	20,954	959
1,000-5,000	Gain	3.19	10,475	792
5,000-10,000	Gain	3.35	8,868	834
10,000-25,000	Gain	3.33	8,384	855
25,000-50,000	Gain	3.61	8,004	861
Over 50,000	Gain	4.08	6,384	706

Source: NJDCA Annual Report 1970 (See Exhibit 6-1 for full
citation).

at the highest rates; this is understandable in light of their extremely high real property tax base.

Revenues: Intergovernmental Aid

The intergovernmental revenues that reach the local governmental
unit come from several sources. Some municipal governments receive
limited federal grants; most commonly, however, cities receive state
grants. These are directed towards road, health, and welfare services. For the fiscal year study, 1970, state aid for roads was
distributed on the basis of road mileage population.[31] In addition
to this, modest amounts are distributed to the municipalities in
the form of health and public assistance grants. Urban aid in block
grant form was, as of 1970, limited to the six municipalities of

over 100,000 in population.* Also included under the state aid
budget line item are revenues received from the state treasury in
lieu of local administration of the property tax on Class 2 Rail-
roads. The effective year for the removal of Class 2 Railroad property from local administration was 1966. Following the state take-
over of this tax base, municipalities containing Class 2 Railroad
property received aid amounting to the difference between Class 2
Railroad property taxes for 1965 prior to the change, and taxes
received in 1966. This aid is subsequently reduced by 10 percent
annually during a ten-year transition period.

The year 1966 provided another statutory change which affected the
local tax base. Business personality was removed from local administration. To make up this loss, a package of state administered taxes
was created to return to the municipalities no less than the largest
amount it received from the tax during the years 1964, 1965, and 1966.
Additional revenue generated by the new state packages also is returned to the municipalities. This, however, is apportioned among the
taxing districts on the basis of real estate taxes resting upon commercial, industrial and farm properties. For the purpose of this
analysis, we have grouped together those intergovernmental revenues
budgeted to state aid with those categorized as replacement taxes.

Revenues: Public Utility

The third source of revenue is the combined category of public utility taxes and miscellaneous revenues. Miscellaneous revenues consist
of locally originated fees, fines, parking charges, and the like.
Their basic design limits their power to generate significant amounts
of local revenue. Contrary to this is the revenue received by some
municipalities from the state treasury by means of the public utilities, franchise tax and gross receipts tax. The public utility
gross receipts tax was created in 1964 in lieu of local administration of the tangible personal property tax. It is imposed at a rate
of 7.5 percent of the gross receipts of street, railway, sewer, water,
trash, gas and electric light, heat and power companies from their
business over, on, in, through or from their lines, mains, etc. in
the state. The inequitable nature of these revenue sources is evident. The Commission on State Tax Policy, stated:

---

*Chapter 64 of the Laws of 1971 have broadened the area to in-
clude all cities of over 15,000 and satisfying formal requirements
based upon: 1)   number of ADC children residing in the community;
2)   the existence of public housing in the community; 3)   an
above average tax rate; and 4)   an equalized evaluation of real
property less than the average per capita basis.

Heavy gross receipts tax collections occur in municipalities because large public utility installations are located there, principally, electric generating stations and other large units in the distribution system. Since the apportionment of gross receipts taxes is on the basis of unit values of scheduled property, on private property as well as on public rights of way, and since the unit values of these large generating and substation installations are high in proportion to the unit values of other scheduled property, mostly on public rights of way, it necessarily follows that those districts who are generating and substation units receive a high percentage of the total gross receipts tax. [32]

The essential question is: Do municipalities use this source of revenue to increase local expenditures over what they would be in the absence of public utilities revenues, or do they use it to reduce their own property tax burden?

The variables used to analyze this situation are displayed in Exhibit 6-11. The first is the per capita expenditures for debt service and current capital improvements; neither of these items was included in the dependent variable. In each case, cities losing population carry a higher burden than gaining cities. Cities on either end of the rank size spectrum carry a larger per capita burden than intermediate sized cities.

Moving to the indices of the two non-property tax revenue structures, there are the familiar U-shaped curves with those cities losing population receiving more per capita revenues than cities gaining population. Several reasons explain this pattern. First, railroad property removed from the local tax rolls is concentrated in the older cities of Hudson and Essex counties, counties rich in cities losing population. Second, the state aid block grants were limited to the six largest cities in the state; most of them are found to be declining in population. Lastly, public utility tax revenues are found to be elevated in both extremes of the declining set of cities; beyond that, the pattern is not clearly defined.

Local Government Form

Our analysis of the impact of local governmental form upon expenditure levels is limited to the type of school district found within the municipality. New Jersey statutes permit two types of school districts vis a vis the budget enactment process: the dependent and the independent. In the dependent school district, a board of school estimate appointed by the city's mayor or chief executive must approve the tax levy to support the school budget.[33] In the independent school district both functions are performed by the voters of the district.[34] This study seeks to determine if the

EXHIBIT 6-11.   THE CLUSTER OF INDEPENDENT VARIABLES REPRESENTING
OTHER BUDGETARY CONSIDERATIONS FOR THE MUNICIPALITY

(1) 1960 Population Range	(2) Direction of Population Change 1960-1970	*Per Capita Expenditures and Receipts (dollars)*		(5) Public Utility and Miscellaneous Revenues
		(3) Debt Service and Current Capital Improvements	(4) State Aid	
<1,000	Loss	29.90	43.68	49.46
1,000-5,000	Loss	15.27	21.37	18.23
5,000-10,000	Loss	14.63	23.96	13.69
10,000-25,000	Loss	20.84	26.73	24.72
25,000-50,000	Loss	21.95	28.57	12.46
50,000 +	Loss	29.74	50.23	30.62
<1,000	Gain	22.39	19.17	27.64
1,000-5,000	Gain	14.25	16.44	25.69
5,000-10,000	Gain	13.98	15.87	17.09
10,000-25,000	Gain	12.64	14.57	19.68
25,000-50,000	Gain	20.64	20.99	20.64
50,000 +	Gain	23.60	28.52	18.61

Source: NJDCA Annual Report - 1970 (See Exhibit 6-1 for full citation).

mayor's influence affects the trade-off between municipal purpose
and local school purpose tax revenues. Margolis[35] argues that single
function governments, such as the independent school districts, are
more susceptible to the activities of a marginal but critical voter
coalition. Under the multi-functional government structure, such as
the dependent form of school district, a package of services, represented by the budget, is directed at many local interest groups.
Thus, the argument goes, the interest groups unfavorable to educational spending must still vote for the budget or suffer the loss
of its own programs. As an indication of the plausibility of this
argument, Margolis shows with 1953 data that when size of city is
held constant, dependent New Jersey school systems spend more per
pupil in average daily attendance than do independent systems.

In order to update the study of the potential impact of governmental form on local purpose expenditures, we will use a dummy variable to specify the type of school district organization. In this case a zero will stand for the presence of an independent school system and a one will represent the dependent school system.

EMPIRICAL RELATIONSHIPS BETWEEN SELECTED
SOCIO-ECONOMIC VARIABLES AND PER CAPITA COSTS:
RESULTS FROM THE REGRESSION ANALYSIS OF THE
TWELVE SUBSETS OF NEW JERSEY MUNICIPALITIES

The regression equation constructed for the purpose of explaining variation in per capita municipal operating expenditures within each size and direction of population change partition are displayed in Exhibits 6-12 and 6-13. Only those coefficients found to be significantly different from zero at the 0.05 level of significance are included within these exhibits.

Demographic Factors and Per Capita Costs

Two demographic variables remain: mobility and population density.* In the description of the model it was suggested that people are moving today for economic rather than school purposes. From this it was suggested that a positive impact on municipal expenditures should be found. In two cases, this was found. The remaining ten strata cities did not produce significant coefficients. For cities over 50,000 and gaining population, an increase of $7.80 was found for each 1 percent increase in families living in a different house in 1970 when compared with their 1965 place of residence. A standard deviation of 3 percent for the mobility variable translates into a range of $23 of per capita expenditures for up to two-thirds of the cities over 50,000 in population. This result was duplicated in the 10,000 to 25,000 strata for cities in decline. Here, however, based upon a standard deviation of 5 percent, the net regression coefficient of $1.60 defines a range of $8 of per capita expenditures for a similar two-thirds of the sixteen cities in this category.

Population density presents a less clear pattern. Again two out of twelve coefficients are significantly different from 0 at the 0.05 level of significance. Both are in the 1,000 to 5,000 size strata. However, the direction of the impact is contradictory. For two-thirds of the 201 cities growing in size, an increase in per capita expenditures of up to plus or minus $6.09 occurs for every plus or minus one standard deviation change in population density. Cities in decline act in the opposite direction. In this case two-thirds

---

*The impact of population size and rate of population change was analyzed in Chapter 4.

EXHIBIT 6-12. RESULTS FROM THE REGRESSION OF 1970 PER CAPITA MUNICIPAL OPERATING EXPENDITURES FOR NEW JERSEY MUNICIPALITIES LOSING POPULATION FROM 1960 TO 1970

Independent Variable Symbol	1960 Population Strata					
	Less Than 1,000	1,000 to 5,000	5,000 to 10,000	10,000 to 25,000	25,000 to 50,000	Over 50,000
Percent Population Loss	5.80	0.20		1.60	5.40	5.70*
Mobility						
Population Density		-.01				
Percent Professional			-3.10		-25.90	
Percent Population Aged 22 to 39 yrs.		-.29				
Percent Population Aged 40 to 54 yrs.			4.30			
Percent Population Aged Over 55 yrs.		3.50		14.50		9.30
Percent Foreign Stock			-.60			
Percent DU Built Prior to 1939			-.70			
Percent DU Built During 50-59		1.40	.70			
Percent DU Built During 60-70		-2.30				
Percent Structures Single Family		.40				
Percent Structures 5 to 9 DU		5.60		-3.60		
Percent Structures 20 to 49 DU				5.90		
Percent Structures Over 50 DU				-3.00		
Percent Structures-House Rentals		1.50				
Percent Apartment Rentals			.80	-.90		
Debt Service		3.00				
School Tax		-.02				
General Tax Rate		.12				
Property Value		.01				
Public Utility				1.07		
R^2	.99	.99	.99	.98	.99	.89
Standard Error	2.16	2.74	7.42	8.39	5.60	46.40
Cases	3	26	9	16	5	7
F	2,633	2,068	10	28	425	14

Note: All coefficients entered in exhibit are significantly different from zero at the 0.05 level of significance with the exception of those marked with an *.

Source: CUPR Survey 1972-1973.

EXHIBIT 6-13. RESULTS FROM THE REGRESSION OF 1970 PER CAPITA MUNICIPAL OPERATING EXPENDITURES FOR NEW JERSEY MUNICIPALITIES GAINING POPULATION FROM 1960 TO 1970

Independent Variable Symbol	1960 Population Strata					
	Less Than 1,000	1,000 to 5,000	5,000 to 10,000	10,000 to 25,000	25,000 to 50,000	Over 50,000
Percent Population Gain	.16*	.11	-.10*	-.08	-.31	-1.51
Mobility						7.80
Population Density		.03				
Percent Professional		2.10				
Median Income	-.03			.005		
House Value	.009					
Percent Below Poverty Level		3.10			-2.10	
Percent Population Aged 5 to 17 yrs.			-3.40	-4.20		
Percent Population Aged 22 to 39 yrs.	10.40			-4.00		
Percent Population Aged 40 to 54 yrs.		2.20		-1.60		
Percent Population Aged Over 55 yrs.				.80		
Percent Foreign Stock						
Percent Minority	4.40			2.30		
Commercial and Industrial Ratables	.01					
Percent DU Built Prior to 1939	9.00	2.30		.30		
Percent Structures Duplexes						
Percent Structures 5 to 9 DU			14.50			
Percent Structures 20 to 49 DU			15.60			
Percent Structures-House Rentals	-2.50					
Percent Apartment Rentals						-.70
Debt Service	4.00	1.20	.41	.56		
School Tax	-.05	.04		.73	.06	
General Tax Rate		-.06	.23		.12	
Property Value	.001	.001	.01	.002		
State Aid		.73				
Public Utility	2.60	.59	1.10	.83	.80	
R²	.97	.94	.95	.95	.89	.98
Standard Error	53.99	31.13	16.16	14.75	17.93	9.13
Cases	49	201	102	73	28	99
F	53	78	15	42	13	15

Note: All coefficients entered in exhibit are significantly different from zero at the 0.05 level of significance with the exception of those marked with an *.

Source: CUPR Survey 1972-1973.

of the twenty-six cities in 1,000 to 5,000 strata decrease per capita expenditures through a range of $3.45 for every plus or minus one standard deviation change in population density.

The Social Class of Communities and Per Capita Costs

The results of four independent determinants clustered under the term social class are described here. First, the percent of professional and managerial employees residing in the city shows a significant fiscal impact in two strata. Cities gaining population in the 1,000 to 5,000 range show a positive response to the presence of professional and managerial residents; a 1 percent increase in professional and managerial residents is associated with an increase in per capita expenditures of $2.10. However, on the contrary, cities in decline within the 1,000 to 5,000 strata decrease their per capita expenditures by $.29 for every 1 percent increase in professional and managerial residents. The reason for the contradictory pattern is not clear from the model. However, as noted in the text, alternative patterns are recognized as possible. To the extent that higher social class families require fewer police services, a lower expenditure level can result. On the other hand, when a municipality is not under a severe property tax base constraint, social class preference patterns may well be effectively exhibited. This form of logic can be applied here. The nine cities declining in population have a considerably higher tax rate and lower per capita tax base than the corresponding averages for the 201 cities gaining population. This suggests that cities with a higher tax burden and per capita expenditure level will use their revenues for basic municipal needs and some of the social class preference services will not be offered.

The remaining social class type indices are not found to be significant determinants. This, however, may be due to the construction of the model. The small number of cities in the strata that are declining in population leave us less sure of the regression coefficients and also limit us to a smaller number of independent variables. For this reason, absence of a coefficient does not imply the lack of potential significance relationships given a larger number of cases.

The Life Cycle of Community Residents and Per Capita Costs

Contrasted with the social class variables, the life cycle cluster is far more successful in explaining per capita expenditures. For families in the early stages of the child-rearing cycle, four of the twelve strata show significant fiscal impacts. Furthermore, the predicted negative coefficient due to an increase in the percentage of families with heads of households from 22 to 39 is found in all cases.

222

The presence of families with heads of households over 55 years of age was suggested to produce a positive impact on the municipal fisc. In four of the five cases a significant positive impact on per capita expenditures was found for this life cycle group. This is particularly noticeable in the lower tax base, high tax rate, declining cities. For example, 66 percent of the seven cities over 50,000 and in decline increase their expenditures at the rate of $9.30 for each 1 percent increase in those over 55 years of age. This translates into a range of $50 per capita for a plus or minus one standard deviation from the mean of those 55 years and older. This result must be viewed with caution. The fact is that judged from an analysis of the residuals from this regression, the percent over 55 variable is correlated with the error term. This means that an unspecified determinant is still present and that its influence is in part being felt through our life cycle variable. Correction of this through a combined case study analysis and introduction of new information into the model must be made in order to gauge more fully the importance of older families to a municipality's budget process.

The Ethnicity of Residents and
Per Capita Costs

Based upon bond election results and regression analysis on a national sample of central cities, we had hypothesized a negative fiscal impact produced by the presence of increasing numbers of families of foreign stock. For the most part, this was not found to be the case. In two sets of cities gaining in population, the presence of foreign stock was found to increase the municipal expenditure effort. In only one set of cities was the hypothesized negative relationship found. This was in the 5,000 to 10,000 population strata.

The fiscal impact of minority groups is shown by the percent of the total population that are black and Spanish children of ages 5 to 17 years old. In only two of twelve cases was this an independently significant factor. In cities gaining population and in the size range of less than 1,000 and 10,000 and 25,000, marked positive responses were found. However, in light of the segregated residential patterns and its obvious non-normal distribution, the development of a different set of cities may well provide a more meaningful field to assess the fiscal impact of minority groups.

The Municipal Economic Base
and Per Capita Costs

Three variables have been included for the estimation of the commercial and industrial economic base. The results of each appear to be largely inconclusive. Large standard errors for each of the regression coefficients, and their instability when changes are made in the set of cities used, leave us unwilling to report any of the

coefficients. In general, however, it appears that the presence of
commercial employment in the city corresponds to an increased per
capita expenditure, while industrial employment appears to act to
reduce the level of per capita expenditures.

The Municipal Residential Sector/Form of
Housing Tenure and Per Capita Costs

The uncertainty dominating the discussion of the commercial and industrial ratables largely holds for the present analysis of the residential economic base and tenure relationship. Further study will be
necessary to establish theoretically sound and empirically significant
relationships.

Governmental Structure and Per Capita Costs

The last set of variables to be analyzed in this preliminary work
deals with the property tax, non-property tax revenues, and non-
operating budget commitments. Perhaps the strongest determinant
brought out by the size and direction of growth partitions is the
impact of phenomena associated with debt service and current capital
improvements on per capita expenditures. The results show that the
smaller the city the larger the positive impact upon per capita
expenditures. The impact is reasonable in that the recent acquisition of physical plant parallels the provisions of a greater quantity
of public goods when compared to the city that has not undergone such
a change. We have theorized that as a city increases in size the
purchase of capital facilities more often than not is for replacement
purposes; thus, the creation of new services and the associated costs
does not necessarily follow the upward movement on the rank size
spectrum. Further, as was previously noted, larger New Jersey cities
face an increasingly stringent budget constraint due to their limited
and excessively utilized property tax base. This will make it more
difficult to raise funds for anything more than the most essential
services. This logic appears to hold in our empirical study for as
we move to the larger city size ranges negative per capita debt
service and capital improvement coefficients are found.

Lastly, two indicators of the impact of the statutory revenue structure merit analysis. The value of the per capita property tax base
has been shown to strongly influence per pupil school expenditures.
The same is the case for its independent influence on per capita
municipal operating expenditures. In an analysis of the 12 strata
(the product of a stratification process that reduces the impact of
the secular decline in property values over size) we find significant
positive impacts upon expenditures. As an example, cities gaining
population in the 5,000 to 10,000 range increase their per capita
municipal expenditures by $10 for each increase of $1,000 in property
value. In light of the fact that the standard deviation of per capita

property value is $3,400, two-thirds of the 102 cities described a range of expenditure accountable to property value of close to $70 per capita. Although this is an extremely high case, it shows that the property value bears considerably more attention in relation to the municipal services provided to citizens than it is presently receiving.

The final revenue structure that provides a strong consistent pattern over the twelve strata is the impact of public utility tax revenue sources upon expenditures. In that these are revenues received from the state (assume that per capita miscellaneous revenues are not causing biasing distributions in this variable) we are interested to find if a dollar of such revenue generates a full dollar of municipal expenditures. In the six cases of which significant coefficients are found, the issue is split. In three cases, coefficients greater than one dollar are obtained. This indicates that public utility revenues were not used as a substitute for local revenue generation. For the other three cases, all of the cities growing in population, the coefficient is positive and less than one. It would appear that the local budgetary process has eased up on the local tax effort. This, however, does not show that the actual tax effort as measured by the general tax rate is less than average or that this revenue service is being properly exploited.

SPECIAL STUDIES INTO PER CAPITA COST VARIATION

The Margolis Association Hypothesis and Per Capita Costs

It was Margolis' suggestion, based upon fiscal and residential patterns present during the early 1950's, that those cities which encouraged "good" industrial ratables would as a consequence grow in their residential concentration of lower income workers. This, in turn, would feed back on the municipal fisc in the form of higher residential densities and, therefore, lower property values. However, post-World War II urbanization in New Jersey has taken place within a radically different set of zoning controls not extant prior to that time. Residential density has been sharply constrained and encouragement has been given for the suburban development of industrial and commercial sites. *Thus, the pervasive use of exclusionary land use controls may have inserted a wedge between the location of industrial firms and residential location of their workers.* It is our hypothesis that population growth has been channeled into structurally different patterns from that occurring in the Margolis study.

Margolis identifies the industrial economic base of a municipality by its employment to resident labor force ratio. A city with a ratio of less than 0.75 is categorized as a dormitory city. This is interpreted to mean that there are 75 percent or fewer job positions in the city as there are households. Cities with an employment ratio greater than 1.25 were discarded from the study under the assumption that they were largely cities containing industrial enclaves and not important contributors to the region's housing stock.

The classification of cities in this study has followed a similar form with slight variation in the particulars. The employment data used are those which have been derived from the New Jersey covered employment rolls. This undercounts actual employment by excluding firms of fewer than four employees. In comparison with the Margolis study, distribution of the employment to residence ratio for the 567 municipalities shows that a slight drop in the boundary values must be in order. Thus, for New Jersey a dormitory city is defined as one with an employment-to-residents ratio of less than 0.65. A balanced city is defined as one with an employment-to-residents ratio greater than 0.65 but less than 1.25.

This study differs from Margolis' in that it is concerned with the impact that change in residential growth patterns has on municipal wealth; to show this affect, both dormitory and balanced cities have been partitioned into four subsets. First, cities with over 25 percent of their 1970 housing stock built prior to 1939; second, cities in which 25 percent of their housing stock was built during 1940 to 1949; third, cities in which greater than 25 percent of their housing stock was built during 1950 to 1959. And fourth, those cities in which greater than 25 percent of their housing stock was built during 1960 to 1970.

The essence of the Margolis' association hypothesis hinges upon two measurable characteristics. First, as a measure of the strength of the local tax base, Margolis uses dollar value of the per capita equalized real tax base; fiscal zoning, it is proposed, operates to maximize this characteristic. The presence of lower income workers is measured by the municipality's median family income. The association hypothesis suggests that median family income will drop with increasing commercial/industrial ratables. Margolis' verification of the association hypothesis can be simplified by the comparison of the two sets of data he generated. First, he found that the equalized real property value per capita for dormitory cities was higher ($5,598) than that for balanced cities ($4,688). Second, it was found that the average household income of dormitory cities ($4,864) exceeded that of balanced cities ($3,800).

If exclusionary zoning has effectively altered the structure of the residential housing market, the Margolis pattern will be reversed. Exhibit 6-14 shows that this is the case. A comparison of columns 1 and 2 shows that the present real property value per capita of balanced cities exceeds the dormitory cities in each of the four time periods. Further, it shows that the more recent the growth, the larger will be the difference in dollars of per capita property value separating balanced from dormitory cities. However, in order to affirm the association hypothesis, one must determine if the median income in the dormitory city is greater than that of the balanced

EXHIBIT 6-14. THE CHARACTERISTICS OF THE SUBSET OF BALANCED AND DORMITORY NEW JERSEY CITIES THAT EXPERIENCED THE CONSTRUCTION OF OVER 25% OF ITS PRESENT HOUSING STOCK (1970) DURING ONE OF FOUR TIME PERIODS

Time Period	1970 Per Capita Real Property Value		1970 Median Family Income	
	Balanced[1] Cities	Dormitory[2] Cities	Balanced[1] Cities	Dormitory[2] Cities
Before 1939	12,987	10,251	10,971	11,815
1940 - 1949	8,155	6,357	11,978	11,069
1950 - 1959	17,066	10,126	14,596	12,832
1960 - 1970	20,172	10,984	13,252	12,422

Notes: 1. Balanced cities are operationally defined as those obtaining a 1966 covered employment-to-resident population ratio between 0.65 and 1.25.
  2. Dormitory cities are defined as those obtaining a 1966 covered employment-to-resident population ratio of less than 0.65.

Source: CUPR Survey 1972-1973.

city. Exhibit 6-14 shows that this is not the case. *In the three recent time periods the present median income in balanced cities exceeds that in dormitory cities. Thus, when the San Francisco experience of Margolis is compared with the New Jersey study, the balanced cities have fiscally benefitted from the growth that has taken place in the last two decades. In turn, this suggests that the association hypothesis has been broken; that is, the ability of laborers and operatives to move the location of their places of work has been reduced. As a result, the housing stock has tended to remain in the hands of higher income families who maintain the property value of the residential areas which in turn raise the total per capita tax base of the municipality.*

The Impact of Rental Occupancy Upon
Municipal Expenditures

The recent trend toward multiple dwelling unit rental tenure occupancy patterns creates a special interest in the identification of these phenomena and the assessment of their influence upon municipal expenditures. Specifically, this study seeks to determine the change in dollar cost to the municipality associated with an increase in the percentage of its citizens who rent their dwelling unit.

The theory explored earlier in this chapter states that per capita municipal expenditures should increase with an increase in the number of renters within the city. The regression equations displayed in Exhibits 6-12 and 6-13 confirm this pattern in three cases while contradicting it in one case. As a result of the uncertainty associated with these findings, a separate study is performed.

The sample of cities used to study this phenomenon are those cities which grew in population during the previous decade, obtain at least 25 percent of the present housing stock from construction after 1950 and have a present population ranging from 5,000 to 90,000.

In effect, the sample selection process limits our consideration to cities that have developed under the post World War II land use patterns and zoning laws. In order to further reduce the presence of extraneous fiscal forces an additional two fold cross classification of the sample set is performed. That is, cities are simultaneously partitioned by an economic typology and an index of relative wealth of the community. The economic typology is that used in the previous section; this is the classification of cities as dormitory and balanced depending upon their value on the employment-to-resident population ratio. The wealth dimension is specified by the general equalized tax rate of the municipality. This measures the relative price paid by local property owners for the package of public services produced for them. It is commonly the case that wealthy municipalities when measured in terms of tax base have a low tax rate.

In order to assay the fiscal importance in the growth of rental occupancy, we must separate the influence of the structural configuration
of the dwelling units from the form of tenure. This has been done by
partitioning rental occupancy into two types: first, the rental occupancy of single family and duplex type structures and second, rental
occupancy in all other forms of multiple dwelling units. When partitioned in this fashion the average municipality used in our sample
has 13 percent of its dwelling units in each structural form of rental occupancy. Exhibit 6-15 displays this result.

If evidence in the form of net regression coefficients is found showing that the rental form of occupancy as distinct from structural configuration does increase per capita expenditures, then it must be
determined if municipalities which are forced to pay a higher price
for their public services capitalize on the presence of renters by
obtaining a larger expenditure level with their presence.

The characteristics of each of the four subsets of cities in terms of
means and standard deviations of fifteen social, economic, and fiscal
indices are displayed in Exhibit 6-15. While the four clusters average approximately the same 1970 population (12,000), the dormitory
cities are growing at approximately twice the rate found for balanced
cities. Family income and percent of the population below the poverty
level are quite similar, with a slight drop in the percent within the
level occurring in the balanced cities. In terms of life cycle, older
families (percent over 55) are found in a range of from 19.7 percent
to 16 percent respectively with balanced cities obtaining 1 percent
less than primarily residential cities and higher tax rate cities having 2 percent less than those with lower tax rates. Young families (persons 22-34) are equally distributed across the four subsets at 22
percent of the total population.

In terms of the business sector, dormitory cities obtain on the average forty to fifty commercial jobs per 1,000 residents, while industrial positions range from fifty to seventy jobs per 1,000 residents.
As expected, per capita property values respond accordingly: dormitory cities obtain on the average $8,500 and balanced cities $13,000.
In terms of revenue generation, balanced cities spend on the average
of $200 per pupil more for schools than the dormitory city; they also
spend on the average of $40 per citizen more on municipal operating
expenditures. Within this variation in characteristics, apartment
and housing rentals average 13 percent each of the total occupied
dwelling units.

Although the four clusters appear to be reasonably matched, there are
significant patterns of variation within each cluster that may influence the interpretation of the two independent rental variables.
This can be seen in the zero order correlation coefficient relating housing and apartment rental occupancy with the remaining fourteen characteristics. These are displayed in Exhibits 6-16 and 6-17. The most
common characteristic associated with housing rentals is the percent

EXHIBIT 6-15. THE MEANS AND STANDARD DEVIATION OF THE VARIABLES USED TO IDENTIFY
THE IMPACT OF HOUSING TENURE UPON PER CAPITA MUNICIPAL EXPENDITURES

| | Type of City | | | |
| | Dormitory | | Balanced | |
	General Tax Rate Less Than 3.00	General Tax Rate Greater Than 3.00	General Tax Rate Less Than 3.00	General Tax Rate Greater Than 3.00
1970 Population	13425 (7673)	16471 (13401)	16351 (13299)	10697 (2980)
Percent Population Change	52.8 (55.3)	50.8 (51.4)	29.3 (34.2)	35.1 (48.2)
Percent Persons Over 55	19.7 (8.9)	17.4 (5.9)	18.8 (3.9)	16.0 (5.0)
Percent Persons from 22-39 Years	22.7 (4.7)	22.3 (3.4)	21.4 (2.8)	22.5 (1.3)
Median Family Income	13361 (3581)	13037 (3012)	13729 (2429)	13237 (2914)
Percent Foreign Stock	31.1 (10.1)	26.4 (8.8)	37.2 (7.9)	35.4 (7.5)
Percent Below Poverty Level	3.4 (2.5)	3.6 (2.2)	2.7 (1.2)	3.1 (2.2)
Commercial Employment-to-Residents Ratio	0.04 (0.03)	.05 (.03)	.24 (.19)	.19 (.13)
Industrial Employment-to-Residents Ratio	0.07 (0.05)	.05 (.05)	.51 (.21)	.62 (.58)
Percent Commercial and Industrial Ratables	17.6 (10.4)	15.26 (8.34)	46.7 (13.3)	36.6 (24.6)
Percent of Dwelling Units That Are Rented - Single Family and Duplex	13.0 (6.7)	10.6 (4.7)	13.7 (7.1)	15.6 (10.0)

(Continued)

EXHIBIT 6-15. THE MEANS AND STANDARD DEVIATION OF THE VARIABLES USED TO IDENTIFY THE IMPACT OF HOUSING TENURE UPON PER CAPITA MUNICIPAL EXPENDITURES (Cont'd)

	Type of City			
	Dormitory		*Balanced*	
	General Tax Rate		General Tax Rate	
	Less Than 3.00	Greater Than 3.00	Less Than 3.00	Greater Than 3.00
Percent of Dwelling Units That Are Rented - Multiple Dwelling Units	12.2 (12.7)	12.4 (13.1)	13.4 (14.4)	18.8 (16.2)
Per Capita Property Tax Base	9987 (4560)	7761 (2640)	15369 (4851)	11207 (5374)
Per Pupil School Revenues Raised Locally	862 (261)	813 (241)	1076 (240)	972 (207)
Per Capita Municipal Operating Expenditures	94.03 (53.78)	85.73 (30.93)	135.02 (29.10)	153.57 (85.84)

Source: CUPR Survey, 1972-1973.

EXHIBIT 6-16. ZERO ORDER CORRELATION COEFFICIENTS BETWEEN THE PERCENT OF DWELLING UNITS IN A MUNICIPALITY THAT ARE RENTER OCCUPIED, MULTIPLE DWELLING UNIT STRUCTURES (EXCLUSIVE OF DUPLEXES) AND A SET OF SOCIAL, ECONOMIC, AND FISCAL CHARACTERISTICS

	Type of City			
	Dormitory		Balanced	
	General Tax Rate Less Than 3.00	General Tax Rate Greater Than 3.00	General Tax Rate Less Than 3.00	General Tax Rate Greater Than 3.00
1970 Population	.33	.32	.61	.50
Percent Population Change	-.02	-.22	-.40	-.91
Percent Persons Over 55	-.02	.39	.73	.96
Percent Persons from 22-39 Years	.48	.21	.79	-.75
Median Family Income	-.18	-.32	-.63	-.73
Percent Foreign Stock	.43	.43	.35	.83
Percent Below Poverty Level	.07	.22	.73	.84
Commercial Employment-to-Residents Ratio	.20	.26	-.34	-.19
Industrial Employment-to-Residents Ratio	.16	.30	-.04	.76
Percent Commercial and Industrial Ratables	.13	.36	.08	.33
Percent of Dwelling Units That Are Rented - Single Family and Duplex	.28	.25	.59	.93
P. C. Property Tax Base	-.26	-.34	-.57	-.87
P. P. School Revenue	-.15	-.10	-.28	-.85
P. C. Municipal Expenditures	-.13	.22	.30	.61

Source: CUPR Survey, 1972-1973.

EXHIBIT 6-17. ZERO ORDER CORRELATION COEFFICIENTS BETWEEN THE PERCENT OF DWELLING UNITS IN A MUNICIPALITY THAT ARE SINGLE FAMILY OR DUPLEXES AND RENTER OCCUPIED AND A SET OF SOCIAL, ECONOMIC, AND FISCAL CHARACTERISTICS

	Type of City			
	Dormitory		Balanced	
	General Tax Rate		General Tax Rate	
	Less Than 3.00	Greater Than 3.00	Less Than 3.00	Greater Than 3.00
1970 Population	.09	-.09	.23	.15
Percent Population Change	-.09	-.26	-.47	-.72
Percent Persons Over 55	.06	.35	.70	.94
Percent Persons from 22-39 Years	.35	.04	.44	-.54
Median Family Income	-.51	-.52	-.75	-.93
Percent Foreign Stock	.14	.02	.39	.98
Percent Below Poverty Level	.42	.50	.48	.98
Commercial Employment-to-Residents Ratio	.08	.09	-.53	-.53
Industrial Employment-to-Residents Ratio	.30	.39	.60	.89
Percent Commercial and Industrial Ratables	.06	.42	.51	.55
Percent of Dwelling Units That Are Rented - Multiple Dwelling Units	.28	.25	.59	.93
P. C. Property Tax Base	-.30	-.32	-.37	-.69
P. P. School Revenue	-.41	-.26	-.59	-.64
P. C. Municipal Expenditures	-.06	-.03	.12	.73

Source: CUPR Survey, 1972-1973.

of the population below the poverty level and the industrial employment-to-residents ratio. Both of these factors increase their positive association from dormitory to balanced cities and from low to
high tax rate cities. On the negative side, median income and per
pupil school revenues raised locally decrease with an increase in
housing rentors.

Apartment rentals are positively associated with both size of city
and percent foreign stock and in dormitory cities are only slightly
correlated with percent poverty. As in the case of housing rentals,
young families (22-39) are more often found to be associated with
percent apartment rentals in the low tax rate city while mature families are associated with the proportion of apartment rentals in the
high tax rate cities. In balanced cities the associations are considerably different and far stronger than in dormitories. For the
balanced cities, low income, old age, lower property tax base, and
housing and apartment rentals are highly associated.

The regression equations displayed in Exhibit 6-18 show that rental
occupancy independent of structure increases the expenditures made by
the municipality. In low tax rate dormitory cities where median family
income and rental occupants have the lowest correlation coefficient,
a 1 percent increase in apartment rentals corresponds to an increase
in per capita expenditures of $1.71. The presence of houses and
duplexes under the rental form of tenure produces a $1.61 per capita
expenditure effect.

Low tax rate balanced cities behave in a similar fashion. Apartment
rentals increase municipal expenditures independently of house rentals
at a rate of $1.65 per 1 percent increase in rental units; however,
house rentals do not exhibit an independent fiscal effect.

The impact of rental occupancy upon the municipal expenditure patterns
of poorer-high tax rate cities is not that proposed in the capitalization hypothesis. In the one case where a significant coefficient is
found, an increase in apartment rentals increased municipal expenditures but at a rate less than half that obtained in the more wealthy
set of cities.

In conclusion we find that there exists a high probability for increased levels of municipal expenditures in those cities growing in
rental occupancy. However, we do not know if this represents the
demand for additional services on the part of renters or a greater
ease in the generation of local revenues due to the passive stance
of local renters towards the budget process.

Residential Development and
Municipal Costs

The continued growth in the number of residential developments consisting of multiple dwelling unit structures appears probable. In

EXHIBIT 6-18. REGRESSION COEFFICIENTS FOR CITIES WITH A 1970 POPULATION OF 5,000 TO 90,000, AND GAINING OVER THE DECADE, AND SUBDIVIDED BOTH BY EMPLOYMENT-TO-RESIDENT RATIO INTO DORMITORY AND BALANCED ECONOMIC BASE CITIES AND BY GENERAL TAX RATE WITH LOW AND HIGH CATEGORIES. DEPENDENT VARIABLE IN 1970 PER CAPITA MUNICIPAL OPERATING EXPENDITURES.

	Type of City			
	Dormitory		Balanced	
	General Tax Rate		General Tax Rate	
	Less Than 3.00	Greater Than 3.00	Less Than 3.00	Greater Than 3.00*
1970 Population			.002	
Percent Population Change	1.99			
Percent Persons Over 55		-2.12		
Percent Persons from 22-39 Years	-4.85			
Median Family Income				
Percent Foreign Stock	-3.42	.70	-21.89	
Percent Below Poverty Level				
Commercial Employment-to-Residents Ratio			38.7	
Industrial Employment-to-Residents Ratio			65.2	
Percent Commercial and Industrial Ratables		-.006		
Percent of Dwelling Units That Are Rented - Single Family and Duplex	1.61			
Percent of Dwelling Units That Are Rented - Multiple Dwelling Units	1.71	.81	1.65	
P. C. Property Tax Base	.008	.007	.004	
Per Pupil School Revenue				
Degrees of Freedom	(9,36)	(8,138)	(6,7)	
Std Error	32.01	18.60	9.58	
F	10.1	33.2	18.8	
R2	.71	.66	.94	

*Insufficient cases to perform a regression analysis.

Source: CUPR Survey, 1972-1973.

the preceding section the fiscal pressure derived from this form of development was studied in terms of rental tenure. This section concludes the analytical studies of Chapter 6 with an analysis of the fiscal pressure present within the structure of the city's housing stock.

The 1970 census of housing identified nine types of residential configuration ranging from single family detached housing to mobile homes. We wish to determine the types of housing configuration that impose additional costs upon the municipality as well as the extent of its fiscal pressure.

The model designed to explore this package of fiscal pressures is composed of a relatively limited set of independent variables. These represent the physical, economic, fiscal, tenure and demographic characteristics assumed to be essential for the purpose of identifying the model.

To the extent that future development of multiple dwellings attracts the same mix of occupants as is presently the case, we can ascribe to the regression coefficients, linking structural type to per capita expenditures, the package of fiscal pressures evolving out of the social conditions surrounding the particular type of development.

The set of cities to be included will be limited to those that are gaining population and ranging in size from 4,000 to 90,000 population as of 1970. The means and standard deviation describing each of the variables used to identify the model are displayed in Exhibit 6-19. As expected, single family detached dwellings obtain the largest share of the housing stock in the average New Jersey municipality within the sample; duplexes follow with an average of 10.0 percent of the municipality's housing stock, three-to-four dwelling unit structures and ten-to-nineteen dwelling unit structures round out those configurations that produce sizeable local housing contributions.

Within the set of structural types only one strong correlation persists; single family detached is negatively correlated with all forms or multi-family development; however, at no time does the zero order correlation coefficient exceed -0.74.

The observed fiscal impact of structural configuration upon per capita municipal operating expenditures is shown in Exhibit 6-20. Four types of multiple dwelling unit types show a significant position fiscal impact; these are the single family attached, duplex, three and four dwelling unit structures and the twenty-to-forty-nine dwelling unit structures. The largest impact is felt from the twenty-to-forty-nine dwelling unit structure; this is $1.97 in per capita municipal operating expenditure for each 1 percent increase in this form of housing configuration.

236

EXHIBIT 6-19. THE MEANS AND STANDARD DEVIATION OF THE SIXTEEN VARIABLES USED TO IDENTIFY
THE IMPACT OF MUNICIPAL HOUSING CONFIGURATION UPON PER CAPITA MUNICIPAL OPERATING
EXPENDITURE OF 292 NEW JERSEY MUNICIPALITIES GAINING POPULATION AND
RANGING IN SIZE FROM 5,000 TO 90,000 IN 1970 POPULATION

Variable Name	Mean	Standard Deviation
Type of Residential Structure		
% Single Family Detached	69.8	23.6
% Single Family Attached	2.4	5.3
% Duplexes	10.9	10.7
% 3 and 4 DU per structure	4.7	5.6
% 5 through 9 DU per structure	2.7	3.9
% 10 through 19 DU per structure	3.7	4.8
% 20 through 49 DU per structure	2.7	3.6
% 50+ DU per structure	2.4	4.1
% Mobile Homes	0.8	2.5
% Rental Tenure	25.8	12.7
Non-Residential Structure Characteristics		
Commercial Employment Density*	38.5	57.5
Industrial Employment Density*	76.6	185.8
Per Capita Real Property Value	8489	3763
General Equalized Tax Rate	76.6	.85
1970 Population	16741	13973
% Change Population 1960-1970	39.1	53.0
Per Capita Municipal Operating Expenditure	97.65	44.64

*covered employment per square mile

Source: CUPR Survey, 1972-1973.

237

EXHIBIT 6-20. REGRESSION EQUATION SHOWING THE IMPACT OF HOUSING STRUCTURE CONFIGURATION
UPON PER CAPITA MUNICIPAL OPERATING EXPENDITURES FOR 292 NEW JERSEY CITIES
GAINING POPULATION AND OBTAINING A 1970 POPULATION OF FROM 5,000 TO 90,000

Independent Variables	Regression Coefficient	Standard Error
% Single Family Attached	1.2	0.38
% Duplexes	0.42	0.20
% 3 and 4 DU per structure	0.95	0.45
% 20 to 49 DU per structure	1.97	0.85
P.C. Property Tax Base	.008	.0007
General Tax Rate	.13	.02
1970 Population	.0003	.0001
% Population Change	-.16	.04

R^2 = .51
Std. Error = 31.89
F = 20.91*

*All regression coefficients and equations have reduced the variation in the dependent
variable significantly above what would be found in a random system at the 0.05 level
of significance.

Source: CUPR Survey, 1972-1973.

238

For that group of structural types representing garden apartment development, that is, developments ranging from five to nineteen dwelling units per structure, no significant fiscal effect is found to exist upon municipal government.

Summary of Findings: Forces Other Than Growth and Per Capita Cost

This section has been an elaboration of the findings and methodology developed previously. Initially, we projected a theory of the fiscal impact of municipal growth and produced evidence showing its relevance for the projection of the current per capita municipal expenditures in a contemporary New Jersey setting.

It has been clear from the beginning that population change and its associated demographic characteristics are not sufficient for an adequate explanation of the different per capita expenditure levels found among the 567 cities of the state. For this reason, we have found it necessary to extract the fiscal effects of population change from the simultaneous activities of ten categories of the municipal activities judged capable of causing change in the level of local per capita expenditures.

The result of this enterprise can now be summarized. Each of the ten categories of physical forces will be outlined and the significant impacts of the independent variables included within each category described. Following this we will conclude our efforts with a statement relating our research to current policy and future research.

Demographic Factors and Per Capita Costs

Four characteristics are grouped under the title, demographic variables: 1970 municipal population, 1960-1970 percent population change, a mobility index, i.e., the percent living in a different house in 1970 when compared to 1965, and finally, population density. Initial research results showed that population size and population change are significant determinants of municipal per capita operational expenditures. Further, it showed that we must consider the set of growing cities as separate and distinct from the cities in decline in terms of the reasons for different levels of per capita expenditures.

This set of findings has formed the foundation for the efforts that followed. The finding that declining cities act significantly different from growing ones forced us to observe the impact of each of the other independent variables under the conditions of a similar direction in population change. Further, our finding that population size formed a significant non-linear causal impact upon per capita expenditures forced us to limit our set of cities to a size range within which a linear relationship can be assumed to exist. The influence of these findings is found in the choice of each of the sets of cities used to analyze the impacts of the other independent variables. For the most part, we chose cities that ranged in 1970 population from 5,000 to 90,000. From this group two subsets were formed, one containing cities in decline, the other containing growing cities.

From the two new subsets of cities, we finalized and completed our comprehensive study of the remaining independent variables. Within the demographic cluster, we found that the five-year range of residential mobility affected per capita expenditures differently according to the direction of the population change; for growing cities it increased municipal expenditures while for declining cities it decreased expenditures. Both of these impacts act counter to the effect of the percent population change upon the municipal budget. An increasing growth rate acts to lower the expenditure level whereas increasing loss rates elevate expenditures. Increased population size acts to produce a slight overall increase in expenditures.

Social Class and Per Capita Costs

Social class is used to define the increasing desire for public goods and services by persons of higher occupational, education, and income levels. However, imbedded within this fiscal pressure is the equally important concept of needs. Cities with large groups of high social class individuals require fewer protection services; this reduces the budgetary requirements of the municipality. The result is to bring together two conflicting fiscal pressures into one index. Not surprisingly, this model did not produce a significant fiscal pressure for this category.

Social class included a second variable: percent of the family population below the poverty level. Its impact upon municipal operating expenditures was found to have a marginal positive influence upon one stratum of cities growing in population.

Life Cycle and Per Capita Costs

The life cycle cluster determinant was used to group persons into various categories according to the extent of their family obligations. We found, as hypothesized, that young families tend to restrict the level of per capita expenditures whereas the presence of older families tend to increase local municipal expenditures.

Ethnicity and Per Capita Costs

The ethnicity cluster was designed to pick up the effectively translated public goods demands made by persons coming from minority cul-
tures. To do this, we used two indices, percent foreign stock and
percent of the total population who are black and Spanish-speaking
children of 5 to 17 years of age. To the extent that percent black
and Spanish-speaking children is independent of the percent below
the poverty level, the presence of minority groups increases per
capita expenditures in cities growing in population.

The percent foreign stock was used to indicate the preference pattern
of persons of European descent. As the research proceeded, however,
it became evident that we were not measuring a constant fiscal pressure; we found rather that the persons of foreign stock decrease
expenditures for cities in decline whereas they are related to increased expenditures for growing cities.

Economic Base and Per Capita Costs

Two sets of variables were used in an attempt to find strong significant indicators of the impact of commercial and industrial firms
upon local per capita expenditures. Initially, we used the employment-to-residents ratios for commercial and industrial activities.
When used in the model their net regression coefficients showed a
sizable fiscal impact, however, we must be chary of the results
due to the rather large standard errors associated with each of
the coefficients.

The most successful indicator of the business sector's fiscal impact
was found to be an employee density measure, i.e., the commercial
and industrial employees per square mile. Using this indicator,
both commercial and industrial concentrations increase per capita
expenditures of the municipality. Further, commercial enterprises
generate higher expenditure requirements than do industrial firms.

The Residential Sector and Per Capita Costs

The residential economic base is identified within the model by
means of nine classes of housing configuration; they range from the
percent of the city's total dwelling units in the form of single
family detached units to the other extreme of the percent of the
dwelling units in structures of fifty or more units. Each of the
housing structure variables was used to explore the impact of the
housing stock upon per capita expenditures; controls were limited
to employment density and fiscal factors. The result showed that
the totality of social characteristics surrounding duplexes, structures with five-to-nine dwelling units, and structures with nineteen-
to-forty-nine dwelling units, each produced significant positive
impact upon the level of per capita expenditures.

241

As a final element tied to residential economic base, we constructed two variables to identify the impact of rental tenure upon municipal expenditures. Based upon the hypothesis that persons renting are less likely to recognize the level of the tax bill, we suggested that this would tend to increase the level of per capita expenditures. This was found to be the case, i.e., cities with larger numbers of single family rental units exhibited higher levels of per capita expenditures. The same result was found for concentrations of apartment rentals.

Governmental Structure and Per Capita Costs

Three separate sets of variables are placed within this cluster. This first group contains indicators of the locally administered property tax, the second, non-property tax revenue, and the third, the type of local governmental form.

The determinants originating within the property tax system all showed consistent, strong and significant per capita expenditure impacts. The per capita equalized real property tax base shows itself to be a strong positive influence on expenditure level. *Further, we found evidence to suggest that post-World War II suburbanization has acted in such a way as to successfully cluster high property value commercial and industrial variables in cities without the concomitant presence of lower income workers and their lower home values. As a result, new dormitory cities obtain lower property values, lower income levels, higher density, and higher than average general tax rates as compared with the more balanced new suburbs.*

The non-property tax revenue index which we chose to use is the per capita public utilities tax. These revenues are returned to the municipality by the state in proportion to the utility's property present within the municipality. As was expected, cities with higher concentrations of public utilities' property used the associated revenue to increase per capita expenditures; this was done on the basis of a dollar revenue for a dollar expenditure.

Out last research result focuses upon the different forms of government present in dependent as opposed to independent school districts. Previous work and theoretical contributions suggest that municipalities with dependent school systems should be more capable of generating voter support for tax levies than those municipalities associated with independent school systems. In terms of per capita municipal expenditures, we found that this was consistently the case. Municipalities coupled with dependent school districts had on the average a $16 per capita higher municipal expenditure level than municipalities with independent school districts.

[1]Eshref Shevky and Wendell Bell, "Social Area Analysis" in The Studies of Human Ecology, edited by George A. Theodorsen, Harper and Row, Evanston, 1961) pp. 226-235.

[2]Richard A. Musgrave, The Theory of Public Finance (New York: McGraw-Hill, 1957) p. 7.

[3]William J. Baumol, "Urban Services,Interactions of Public and Private Decision," in Public Expenditure Decisions in the Urban Community, edited by Howard G. Schaller (Washington, D.C.: RFF, 1963).

[4]Charles M. Tiebout, "A Pure Theory of Local Expenditures," Journal of Public Economy, (Vol. LXIV, 1956) p. 422.

[5]Peter H. Rossi, Why Families Move (New York: Glencoe Free Press, 1955) p. 9.

[6]Wendell Bell, "Social Choice, Life Styles and Suburban Residents" in Suburban Community, edited by William F. Dobriner (New York: Putnam's, 1958) p. 239.

[7]George S. Sternlieb, Robert W. Burchell and Lynne Beyer Sagalyn, The Affluent Suburb (New Brunswick, N.J.: Transaction Press, 1971) Exhibit 4-7.

[8]George S. Sternlieb and W. Patrick Beaton, The Zone of Emergence: A Case Study of Plainfield, New Jersey (New Brunswick, N.J.: Transaction Press, 1972) p. 7.

[9]Peter M. Blau and Otis Dudley Duncan, The American Occupational Structure (New York: Wiley, 1967) p. 27.

[10]John C. Weicher, "The Allocation of Police Protection by Income Class," Urban Studies (October, 1971) p. 207, 220.

[11]James Q. Wilson and Edward C. Banfield, "Voting Behavior on Municipal Public Expenditures; A Study in Rationality and Self-Interest," in The Public Economy of the Urban Community, edited by Julius Margolis (Washington, D.C.: RFF, 1965).

[12]John C. Weicher, "Determinants of Central City Expenditures: Some Overlooked Factors and Problems," National Tax Journal (Vol. 1970) p. 379-396.

[13]William C. Birdsell, "A Study of the Demand for Public Goods," in Essays in Fiscal Federalism, edited by Richard A. Musgrave (Washington, D.C.: Brookings Institution, 1965).

[14]Weicher, "Determinants of Central City Expenditures," op. cit. p. 384.

[15]Gerhard E. Lenski, "Status Crystallization: A Non-vertical Dimension of Social Status," American Sociological Review (Vol. 19, 1954).

[16]George Sternlieb, The Tenement Landlord (New Brunswick, N.J.: Rutgers University Press, 1966 [2ed]) p. 137.

[17]John C. Weicher, "Determinants of City Expenditures," op. cit., p. 385.

[18]Julius Margolis, "Municipal Fiscal Structure in a Metropolitan Region," Journal of Political Economy (Vol. LXV, June 1957).

[19]Morris Beck, "Determinants of the Property Tax Level: A Case Study of Northeastern New Jersey," National Tax Journal, (Vol. 18, March 1965) p. 77.

[20]Lionshead Lake, Wayne Township 8 N.J. Super 468, 73 A.2d 287.

[21]Charles M. Tiebout, op. cit., p. 416-24.

[22]Roy W. Bahl and Robert E. Firestein, Occasional Paper #8, "Urban-Suburban Migration Patterns and Metropolitan Fiscal Structures," Maxwell School of Citizenship and Public Affairs, Syracuse University, 1972.

[23]Wallace E. Oates, "The Effects of Property Taxes and Local Public Spending on Property Values: An Empirical Study of Tax Capitalization and the Tiebout Hypothesis," Journal of Political Economy (Vol. 77, 1969) pp. 957-971.

[24]Woo Sik Kee, "City Expenditures and Metropolitan Areas: Analysis of Intergovernmental Fiscal Systems" (Unpublished Ph.D. Dissertation, Syracuse University, 1964) pp. 76-85.

[25]Elizabeth Likhert David, "Public Preferences and State and Local Taxes," in Essays in State and Local Finance, edited by Harvey E. Brazer (Ann Arbor, Michigan: Institute of Public Administration, University of Michigan, 1967) pp. 85-90.

[26]George Sternlieb, "The Garden Apartment Development, A Municipal Cost-Revenue Analysis," (New Brunswick, N.J.: Bureau of Economic Research, Rutgers, 1964) p. 5.

[27]School Taxes and Residential Development, West Chester County Department of Planning (White Plains, N.Y., November 1971).

[28]The Barrington, Illinois Area - A Cost Revenue Analysis of Land Use Alternatives (Chicago, Ill., February 1970).

[29]Norman Williams and Thomas Norman, "Exclusionary Land Use Controls, The Case Study of Northeastern New Jersey," Syracuse Law Revue, Vol. 22, No. 2, pp. 485-488, 1971.

[30]Robinson V. Cahill, 118 N.J. Super., (1972) 236-257.

[31]Service Levels and State Aid, Part II Report to the New Jersey Tax Policy Commission (Trenton, N.J., 1972) p. 14.

[32]The Tenth Report of the Commission on State Tax Policy: "Increased State Aid to Public Schools and Distribution of the Costs of Expanding Public Services," page 119).

[33]N.J.S.A. Title 18A: 9-2.

[34]N.J.S.A. Title 18A: 9-3.

[35]Julius Margolis, "Metropolitan Finance Problems: Territories, Functions and Growth," Public Finances: Needs, Resources and Utilization (Princeton, N.J.: National Bureau of Economic Research, 1961) pp. 261-262.

CHAPTER 7

CONSUMER SATISFACTION WITH MUNICIPAL
SERVICES: PART I

In a pioneering 1943 study of the factors affecting municipal expenditure patterns, Herbert Simon, after analyzing the expenditures
of the Bay Area communities surrounding San Francisco, concluded
that the real problem in evaluating municipal services was the
nature of the measuring sticks involved.[1] In Simon's work as well
as in some earlier efforts the public expenditure of dollars
was explained as a function of a number of variables. Simon suggested that perhaps the satisfaction produced was a better measuring stick than dollars spent. From his point of view -- as well
as from our own observations -- satisfaction is not always synony-
mous with the flow of funds. In this part of the study we focus
on satisfaction; what the consumer feels he receives in service.

Keeping that goal in mind, while surveying the characteristics of
residents of various types of housing configurations, we tried
to determine their satisfaction with a variety of municipal
services as well as with the overall housing situation. Each
respondent was asked to rate seven major municipal services as
very good, good, neutral, poor, and very poor. The seven services
were police protection, fire protection, sanitation and street
cleaning, recreation, public health and emergency services,
libraries, and public education. The individual responses were
weighted on a 5, 4, 3, 2, 1 basis, running from very good to very
poor, respectively.

In general, there was little difficulty in securing responses to
this set of questions. One problem area was that of the recent
mover or people who had had little experience with the service in
question, such as those who had no children with regard to education.

In the first section of this chapter the overall profile of attitudes towards municipal services is evaluated. How well, for example, does the perception of local public education match that of
the police, of recreation, and so on? From this broad sweep, the
variations in response to the several services is examined as a
function of housing type, municipality, and other pertinent variables. Then, we consider how these same respondents -- having
evaluated the major municipal services -- rank municipal services
in terms of specific improvement. Which one, in their own estimation, should be given priority? In the last part of this section
housing satisfaction is evaluated.

We found considerable variation in the level of consumer satisfaction by municipality for each local government function examined
in the field survey. This is a complex issue and the reasons for
this variation are not easy to determine. Factors probably include

the quantity, quality, and range of services provided, the demand
for services, the cost of providing them, and the respondents'
perceptions of their provision.

Though many of these factors defy analysis, data are available on
the level and rate of change of expenditures by function as well
as the population size and growth rate for the twenty municipalities
sampled. Such data are used in a preliminary fashion as surrogates
for the supply or provision of municipal services on the one hand,
and the demand for such services on the other hand. Even so, the
relative crudeness of such measures should not be overlooked.

INDEX OF SATISFACTION WITH GENERAL GOVERNMENTAL SERVICES

When the ratings given each of the seven services are pooled and
divided by their number, an unweighted index of general governmental service satisfaction is secured. (See Exhibit 7-1) In
general, the respondents view the level and quality of services
that they received quite favorably, with an overall average of
3.91. Within this overall rating, however, there are some significant deviations.

Fire protection has the highest satisfaction index at the 4.29
level. Also over the 4 mark are public health and emergency
services at 4.15, with police protection slightly lower at the 4.08
level. A significant step below, libraries and sanitation and
street cleaning facilities are at the 3.82 and 3.74 levels, respectively, with recreation facilities receiving the lowest rating at 3.39. Education at 3.90 is quite high. While housing
satisfaction will be considered separately, it is noteworthy that
it received an overall evaluation of 3.91, at the higher end of the
spectrum compared to individual municipal services.

For ease in evaluating the patterns underlying the individual
satisfaction ratings, "very good" and "good" were grouped together
as were "very poor" and "poor." Exhibit 7-2 presents the grouped
responses. For each of the municipal service areas, the data
typically are discussed by municipality, housing type, longevity
at address, and age of head of household; other variables are discussed where pertinent.

POLICE PROTECTION

There are few topics more controversial than the need for police
protection and the perceived provision of this vital service.
Police protection secured a positive rating, roughly midway in the
list of services shown, with a substantial deviation between whites
and blacks. Are there other variations?

EXHIBIT 7-1. MEAN RESPONDENT RATINGS OF MUNICIPAL SERVICES

Municipal Service	Population	Number of Observations
Fire Protection	4.285	4,872
Public Health and Emergency Services	4.151	4,363
Police Protection	4.082	5,289
Public Education	3.898	3,511
Libraries	3.822	4,710
Sanitation and Street Cleaning	3.742	5,943
Recreation	3.386	4,946
Housing Satisfaction	3.908	6,714
Index of General Government Services	3.913	1,901

Notes: (1) Respondents classified public service levels in their communities into five quality categories, ranging from very good to very poor. Their ratings were assigned numeric scores, with "very good" valued at five, and very poor at 1. The service quality indices are the average values of these scores.

(2) Differences in the number of observations is attributable to the removal of a varying number of non-respondents from the rating of each municipal service and housing satisfaction. All non-respondents on any rating were removed from the index of general government services, a simple average of the seven municipal services.

Source: CUPR Survey 1972-1973.

EXHIBIT 7-2. RESPONDENT RATING OF MUNICIPAL SERVICES BY MUNICIPALITY

Municipality	Police Protection		Fire Protection		Sanitation and Street Cleaning		Recreation		Public Health and Emergency Services		Libraries		Public Education		Housing Satisfaction	
	Good	Poor	Good	Poor	Good	Poor	Good	Poor	Good	Poor	Good	Poor	Good	Poor	Good	Poor
Brick Twp.	--	--	--	--	--	--	--	--	--	--	--	--	--	--	--	--
Cherry Hill Twp.	354 86.2	11 2.6	383 94.2	3 0.7	326 71.5	19 4.2	136 40.5	107 31.8	248 85.6	14 4.9	329 90.4	20 5.6	201 89.1	2 0.9	317 62.1	82 16.1
Collingswood Boro.	--	--	--	--	--	--	--	--	--	--	--	--	--	--	--	--
Dover Twp.	269 90.1	3 1.0	261 94.3	0 0.0	227 77.9	8 2.6	183 72.5	19 7.5	209 85.8	25 10.1	190 84.6	16 7.0	189 96.5	0 0.0	171 54.2	58 18.5
East Windsor Twp.	723 88.4	13 1.6	701 92.2	12 1.6	563 60.4	168 18.1	388 44.8	264 30.4	543 78.0	72 10.4	415 54.9	184 24.3	523 83.2	42 6.7	738 73.9	81 8.2
Edison Twp.	--	--	--	--	--	--	--	--	--	--	--	--	--	--	--	--
Flemington Boro.	128 88.9	1 0.7	132 94.3	0 0.0	139 84.9	11 6.8	51 38.1	61 45.4	141 97.2	2 1.4	151 97.4	1 0.6	106 96.1	0 0.0	115 67.5	16 9.6
Fort Lee Boro.	303 83.0	25 6.9	342 94.9	2 0.6	351 80.9	23 5.4	246 73.9	29 8.7	213 90.7	12 4.9	280 84.2	21 6.2	119 55.7	27 12.7	356 73.7	35 7.2
Freehold Boro.	123 82.5	11 7.1	141 96.1	2 1.3	122 76.8	8 4.9	62 46.2	38 27.8	105 80.5	4 2.9	108 74.8	26 17.9	44 42.0	26 25.4	144 90.4	7 4.1
Gloucester Twp.	95 95.0	0 0.0	73 89.5	5 5.8	69 63.5	15 13.5	19 22.2	56 64.7	61 92.7	1 1.5	40 58.6	18 26.1	57 72.2	9 10.9	92 85.5	6 5.3
Haddon Twp.	195 87.9	4 1.7	194 91.0	1 0.5	206 82.3	11 4.2	104 59.8	13 7.6	144 86.8	1 0.6	132 75.3	13 7.7	120 81.2	7 4.5	221 83.2	4 1.5
Highland Park Boro.	455 88.2	9 1.7	465 95.6	0 0.0	511 86.9	17 3.0	308 71.5	50 11.6	432 92.2	10 2.2	369 82.6	16 3.5	330 91.3	6 1.8	434 67.6	75 11.7

Continued

EXHIBIT 7-2. RESPONDENT RATING OF MUNICIPAL SERVICES BY MUNICIPALITY (Continued)

Municipality	Police Protection		Fire Protection		Sanitation and Street Cleaning		Recreation		Public Health and Emergency Services		Libraries		Public Education		Housing Satisfaction	
	Good	Poor	Good	Poor	Good	Poor	Good	Poor	Good	Poor	Good	Poor	Good	Poor	Good	Poor
Lakewood Twp.	225 92.1	12 5.1	163 97.6	0 0.0	190 85.0	19 8.5	148 81.9	19 10.8	172 93.3	3 1.6	147 90.1	6 3.7	37 29.6	66 53.1	289 89.6	20 6.1
Lopatcong Twp.	---	---	---	---	---	---	---	---	---	---	---	---	---	---	---	---
Monroe Twp.	---	---	---	---	---	---	---	---	---	---	---	---	---	---	---	---
New Brunswick City	113 61.4	31 17.2	148 87.6	6 3.6	135 58.8	30 13.3	134 62.7	38 17.6	115 73.7	9 5.9	149 71.7	42 20.4	29 23.0	71 56.6	185 59.5	53 17.0
Northfield City	37 49.3	21 27.9	66 94.2	0 0.0	62 72.9	13 15.3	12 14.9	58 74.7	62 87.2	8 11.3	15 23.6	48 76.4	19 44.8	15 37.0	82 83.4	13 13.0
Parsippany-Troy Hills Twp.	519 77.5	35 5.2	537 88.4	2 0.3	507 60.5	183 21.9	233 37.9	217 35.3	477 84.3	34 6.0	339 61.2	69 12.5	263 70.1	44 11.8	662 67.2	134 13.6
Vineland City	274 74.5	25 6.8	249 84.2	6 2.2	255 64.6	74 18.9	121 32.0	173 45.9	256 82.8	26 8.5	268 75.0	43 11.9	193 68.6	39 13.9	329 73.8	49 11.0
Willingboro Twp.	459 92.0	1 0.2	476 96.9	1 0.2	433 81.8	25 4.8	424 78.8	36 6.6	417 94.3	3 0.6	436 88.1	23 5.7	262 72.4	34 9.3	554 89.3	16 2.7

Note: Rating of "good" includes both "good" and "very good" ratings. "Poor" includes both "poor" and "very poor." The first row figures for each municipality lists the number of respondents rating the municipal service as good or poor. Persons reporting the service as average are not listed. The second row of figures presents these good and poor ratings as percents of total reports.

Source: CUPR Survey 1972-1973.

Municipality

There is a striking variation in the profile of responses concerning police protection, according to municipality. (See Exhibit 7-2) If, for the sake of simplicity, we telescope the responses into good, including very good, and poor, including very poor, we run the gamut from a low in Northfield where 49.3 percent of the respondents indicated good, with nearly that proportion, 27.9 percent, indicating poor (the balance, 22.8 percent was neutral), to a high in Gloucester Township where 95 percent of the respondents indicated approval. In that suburban community none signified disapproval.

In general, the more suburban the community the more positive the response. The bulk of such communities hovered around the 85 and 90 percent positive level, with under 5 percent on the negative side. The deviants from this pattern are usually older suburbs and smaller central cities -- New Brunswick and Vineland for example.

The variation clearly indicates a level of evaluation which is not perfunctory and casual. But certainly the data shown in the exhibit ought to be viewed cautiously since the sample was not designed to secure statistically reliable estimates for this particular variable for the entire citizenry of any town.

Housing Type

There are surprising variations when attitudes toward police protection are analyzed by housing type. While in all four housing types the levels of response were very positive, the dissimilarities are significant. In general, it is the low-rise, high-density units' occupants -- those in garden apartments and townhouses -- that feel the most positive about the provision of police protection. The ratios of good to poor ratings (combining very good with good and very poor with poor) are fifteen to one in the garden apartments and fifty to one in the townhouses.

The high rise apartment respondents and the single family home respondents were not nearly so sanguine. Here the response was on the order of nine or ten to one. Much of this difference is explained by the variation of response by municipality when the variation in location of various types of housing configurations is considered. Allowing for the distribution of various housing types between older communities and newer suburbs, the variation in respondent attitudes toward police protection by housing type may not be significant.

Other Variables

There is a significant variation in attitudes toward police protection as the age of head of household increases. Generally, the
older the individual, the more positive is his feeling toward
police protection. Among respondents aged 65 and over, 90.3 percent
felt that their police protection was good. Among those aged 21
to 25, there was only a 72.7 percent positive response, with the
26 to 35 group at 83.6 percent and increasing with the age of
the head of household. Our data on household income levels are
relatively crude, but there seems to be trivial variation. Similarly, when cross tabulations were run by sex and education of
head of household, there was little significant linkage. There
is no particular pattern by longevity at present address with the
exception of the more than ten years group. Here satisfaction was
expressed by 97.1 percent of the respondents.

FIRE PROTECTION

As noted earlier, fire protection was accorded the highest overall
rating among the several services surveyed. Analysis by community
again indicates this pattern with considerable consistency. (See
Exhibit 7-2) The one variant is Vineland where only 84.2 percent
of the respondents were positive and even here the balance was
neutral. As shown in the exhibit, this figure contrasts with much
higher levels of positive response for all those municipalities
for which we have a substantial sample.

In this context, the response rates are not closely related
to the expenditure patterns for the various services. (The
subject of costs and benefits is discussed at the conclusion of
this section.)

Housing Type

There was little variation in attitudes toward fire protection as
a function of housing type. However, single family homes lagged
slightly behind the other types of housing. The latter hovered
in the low 90's, while single family homeowners had only an 85.6
percent positive response. The differences are small but still
statistically significant.

Other Variables

The longer someone has lived at his present address, the more
positive he is about fire protection. For persons living less
than one year at their present address, the figure was 89.2 percent
good; for more than ten years, it was at the 97.3 percent level,
with the one-to-four and five-to-ten year longevities intermediate

252

at 92.4 and 94 percent, respectively. Of course, this conclusion may well be stating the obvious; that is, the more discontented someone is with the level of municipal services, the higher the probability that he will move to another community.

This response pattern seems highly correlated with age of head of household. In general, the older the head of household, the more positive his feelings. (And, the older he is, the more likely it is that he is a long-term resident.) There is no variation of any great importance by sex, education, or the other variables used in the study.

SANITATION AND STREET CLEANING

The consumers' view of sanitation, when first tabulated by municipality, is a controversial one. (See Exhibit 7-2) However, these analyses by municipality are only rough indications -- areas for more research -- not definitive praise or blame for the service in the communities discussed. Keeping this in mind, it is evident that negative attitudes towards sanitation seem to be distributed without relevance to suburban or urban locales. Certainly New Brunswick, an older core city, with a 58.8 percent positive rating is very low, but is matched by East Windsor Township, a relatively suburban setting with only a 60.4 percent positive response. Even a classic suburb like Cherry Hill, near Philadelphia, secured only a 71.5 percent figure.

Housing Type

The variation by housing type is not quite so pronounced as that between municipalities, but even allowing for the latter, there is a significant variation. As shown in Exhibit 7-3, the single family homes have the lowest level of positive response at only 60.9 percent in contrast with the other three groups of housing, all of which are over the 70 percent mark.

Other Variables

Again, there is some increase in positive response by length of residence at present address. There is a much more positive attitude on the part of females than of males, with the former at the 80.3 percent positive level and the latter at only 70.2 percent. This is a significant gap, unlike the narrow sex-related variation in ratios for other services. It may indicate a difference in the types of services grouped under the label sanitation and street cleaning by housewives and male heads of household. The pattern of increased positive attitude as a function of age of head of household is continued here with a reasonably clearcut gradient of under 70 percent at the 21 to 25 age rising to nearly 80 percent at 65 and over.

EXHIBIT 7-3. RESPONDENT RATING OF SANITATION AND STREET CLEANING BY HOUSING TYPE

Respondent Rating	Total	Housing Type			
		Garden Apartments	Townhouses	High Rise Apartments	Single Family Homes
Total	5,944	2,730	1,526	1,114	574
Good	4,264	2,010	1,094	811	350
Neutral	984	410	253	230	91
Poor	695	310	179	73	133
(NA/DK)	(833)	(315)	(257)	(196)	(66)
		Percent Distribution			
Total	100.0	100.0	100.0	100.0	100.0
Good	71.7	73.6	71.7	72.8	60.9
Neutral	16.6	15.0	16.6	20.7	15.9
Poor	11.7	11.4	11.7	6.5	19.1

Note: Numbers and percents may not add due to rounding.

Source: CUPR Survey 1972-1973.

There was no statistically significant variation by income level
or education. Again, this result should be viewed within the limitations of the number of responses.

RECREATION

Recreation received the least positive rating from respondents.
The listing by municipality indicates that there are few communities in which this overall negative attitude will be controverted.
Of the twenty communities considered here, only six had more than
half of their respondents giving recreation positive ratings.

Housing Type

There was significant variation by housing type in response to
recreation facilities. In general, townhouse residents (limited
to a relatively small number of municipalities) were most positive
at 64.1 percent. Single family homeowners, interestingly, were
most negative at 31.1 percent. The high rise apartments were second
most positive at 58.8 percent, with garden apartments lagging substantially at 49.9 percent.

Other Variables

In general, the longer people lived at their present address the
more positive they were about most of the facilities discussed
here, except for recreation. While those people who had lived
more than ten years at their present address -- a relatively small
group were quite positive -- the response levels for all other
categories of tenure length seemed indifferent. Regardless of
variations in education or sex the pattern was fairly consistent.

When age of head of household was considered, there was, however,
a change. Only 40.9 percent of heads of household aged 21 to 25
responded positively, while for the 65's and over it was 75.6
percent. The equivalent figure for the 50 to 64 group was 64.3
percent; for those aged 36 to 49 it was 56 percent with the 26 to
35 age group at 49.3 percent. This pattern perhaps indicates the
varying needs for recreation as a function of age of head of
household, certainly however regardless of the variation. This is
a need which is unfulfilled.

This judgment is supported when the responses are analyzed by
total household income. The lower the income, the lower the
positive rating given to recreational facilities, except for the
under $5,000 category. In this case, the positive rating was 70.1
percent, while for the $5,000 to $9,999 group it was only 52.3
percent. The gradient continues up roughly in proportion to income
level.

PUBLIC HEALTH AND EMERGENCY SERVICES

In general these services (Exhibit 7-2), were given consistently
high ratings in most of the municipalities. The major exception
was New Brunswick with only 73.7 percent giving these facilities a
positive rating, compared with close to 90 percent in the other
cases. New Brunswick is an extreme, but a number of other municipalities also were rated poorly showing significant variation
in perceived service delivery.

Housing Type

Garden apartment, townhouse, and high rise occupants were consistently above the 85 percent positive level. The one deviation was
single family dwellers at 82.5 percent.

Other Variables

There was a slight level of gradient according to length of residence at present address with once again the long-term dwellers
the most positive. The deviation from the average, however, was
relatively small. There was little variation to be observed by
sex, age, or education in this important area, nor was there any
significant gradient by income level.

LIBRARIES

As indicated earlier, libraries and library services had an intermediate to low rating in the overall service evaluation. When considered by municipality, there are significant variations. The
classic high growth township of East Windsor is again at the lower
end of the spectrum with a 54.4 percent positive rating, while,
with the exception of Northfield from which there were very small
samples, every other town was well over the 50 percent mark.

Housing Type

A significant variation exists when attitudes towards libraries
were cross tabulated by housing type (Exhibit 7-4). The single
family homes, which were largely concentrated in areas having relatively poor access to the library facilities, were at the low
point with only 57 percent of their respondents giving a positive
rating. High rise apartment dwellers, by contrast largely sited
close to the traditionally core-oriented main libraries, are at
84.2 percent.

EXHIBIT 7-4. RESPONDENT RATING OF LIBRARIES BY HOUSING TYPE

Respondent Rating	Total	Garden Apartments	Townhouses	High Rise Apartments	Single Family Homes
			Housing Type		
Total	4,710	2,020	1,354	900	435
Good	3,489	1,519	965	758	248
Neutral	619	332	159	63	65
Poor	602	170	230	79	122
(NA/DK)	(2,067)	(1,025)	(429)	(410)	(205)
		Percent Distribution			
Total	100.0	100.0	100.0	100.0	100.0
Good	74.1	75.2	71.2	84.2	57.0
Neutral	13.2	16.4	11.8	7.0	14.9
Poor	12.8	8.4	17.0	8.8	28.0

Note: Numbers and percents may not add due to rounding.

Source: CUPR Survey 1972-1973.

257

Longevity at Present Address

The longer the respondent has lived at his present address, the more positive the rating. The variation is great, going from 67 percent good for less than one year residents, to over 90 percent for the more than ten. The other responses vary in terms of positive rating in direct proportion to longevity.

Other Variables

An interesting negative relationship appears when education and respondent rating of libraries are cross tabulated. The higher the level of education, the lower the rating of the library facility. Among those with less than twelve years of schooling, 84.6 percent felt positive about their library facilities. For high school graduates the figure was 81.6 percent, while for those with college degrees, it was 69.8 percent. The positive response dropped to just over 68 percent for those with training beyond a regular B.A. or B.S.

Age seems to be positively related to attitudes towards library services, but there is no substantial variation by income.

PUBLIC EDUCATION

No area of municipal service generated the level of public sensitivity that public education did. In part this is attributed to the expense involved. However, in addition to the felt level of services secured, both the visions and the reality of variations in those services across municipal boundaries are lively topics of discussion. The impact of the educational system on real estate values and on the "sorting out" of families -- those with children and an interest in education moving to "good" education towns -- needs little description.

Overall, education was intermediate in the ratings given to the services discussed here. However, this moderate rating cloaks a substantial variation when tabulated by municipality. As shown in Exhibit 7-2 some communities such as Dover Township and Flemington received nearly perfect positive ratings of 96.5 percent and 96.1 percent, respectively. At the other end of the scale some older city and troubled suburban areas got only in the 20 to 40 percent category. These communities include Freehold at 42.0 percent, Lakewood at 29.6 percent, and New Brunswick, currently experiencing turbulence in the schools, at a meager 23 percent positive rating.

Precise data were not developed on population self-segregation based on perceived vision of educational establishments. There is some evidence that people with children consider education very important and tend to move to towns which they believe provide better services. It is hoped that a more sophisticated reanalysis of the data will indicate some measure of this self-segregation phenomenon.

Some of the family characteristics which may influence attitudes toward public education are considered below.

Housing Type

The response levels by housing type indicate the skew of family characteristics resulting in varying utilization and, therefore, knowledge of the school systems. For example, in high rise apartments 42.8 percent of those interviewed gave a rating for public education. This rating was nearly matched by the relatively low 49.6 percent of the garden apartment dwellers. By way of contrast, 61.1 percent of the single family home and 58.8 percent of the townhouse residents provided answers in this category.

The data presented include only those who did give responses. The variations are significant with the high rise apartment dwellers least positive at the 62.3 percent level, while garden apartment dwellers at the 81.9 point represented the other extreme. Townhouses and single family home dwellers were intermediate at 70.1 and 72.5, respectively.

Longevity at Present Address

There was a significant gradient based on this factor; the longer one had lived at the same address, the more positive the attitude toward the school system. This pattern may be another example of the self-selection phenomenon. People who have a negative feeling toward a school system may tolerate it until they have an immediate need for its services and then may move to better areas. Similarly, long-term residency in an area may be attributed to positive feelings towards the local schools. In any case, 71.4 percent of the less-than-one-year dwellers who gave responses, had positive feelings toward their school system; while for the more-than-ten-year dweller, the equivalent response was 90.7 percent with a clear gradient for the intermediate groups.

Other Variables

In general, women were much more positive than men in their evaluation of school systems, with 83.2 percent of the former group versus 72.6 of the latter group on the positive side.

There seem to be three distinct step functions when age is considered as a variable. The 21 to 25 age group, those very close to school themselves, gave only a 66.4 percent positive rating. Among those aged 26 to 35, 36 to 49, and 50 to 64 the positive response hovered in the low 70s while for those 65 and over, it moved up to slightly over 82 percent. Interestingly, there was no significant gradient by level of education. This may be the result of the self-selection procedure. The same neutral finding held true for household income.

Number of Children Under 18

There is surprisingly little variation in attitudes toward public education as a function of the number of children under 18. (See Exhibit 7-5) For example, the lowest ratings ever secured from those who had no children with a positive rating was 71.7 percent. The high point was among families with two or three children. Among such respondents, 78.5 percent were positive.

To define further the data presented above, a tabulation was made of those people with no children, those whose families were limited to pre-school children, those with public school children, respondents having both public school and pre-school age children, and households with children in parochial school. (This last group is presented with some trepidation given the small size of useful sample.) In any case, *people who presently have children in public school feel most positive about the offerings there, with more than three-quarters of them giving positive responses* (Exhibit 7-6). Those with no children or who have pre-school age children only, are less positive at 72.0 percent, and 67.3 percent, respectively. Lowest of all in evaluation of public education -- based on a very small sample -- is the 49.4 percent positive response of the heads of households who send their children to parochial school.

In part, this pattern may represent a kind of self-fulfilling prophecy with parents who are negative toward public education offerings having a greater tendency to send their children to parochial schools. The situation is further complicated because there is some indication that white home buyers in areas with reputations for, or the reality of declining school systems tend to be either childless or people who send their children to non-public facilities.[2] However, based on this observation, the bulk of the respondents who had experience with public schools were satisfied with them. This conclusion should not understate the significance of the poor responses which comprise approximately 11 percent of the total -- 11 percent who had children in public school and were not satisfied with them.

WHICH MUNICIPAL SERVICE IS MOST IN NEED OF IMPROVEMENT?

The evaluation of the several municipal services is not necessarily an adequate measure of the felt need for improvement in the services. A taxpayer may feel that a particular municipal service is very poor, but it may be low on his order of priority for additional inputs. Conversely, a service may be seen as adequate but, on the consumer's order of priority, deserving of more inputs. This question of potency as against evaluation was approached by asking each

EXHIBIT 7-5. RESPONDENT RATING OF PUBLIC EDUCATION BY NUMBER OF CHILDREN UNDER 18

Respondent Rating	Total	Number of Children Under 18			
		0	1	2-3	4 or More
Total	3,511	1,573	786	1,050	102
Good	2,604	1,133	572	822	77
Neutral	510	264	115	116	15
Poor	396	76	99	112	9
(NA/DK)	(3,267)	(2,393)	(514)	(346)	(14)
	Percent Distribution				
Total	100.0	100.0	100.0	100.0	100.0
Good	74.2	71.7	72.7	78.5	77.9
Neutral	14.5	17.2	14.7	10.8	12.4
Poor	11.3	11.1	12.6	10.7	9.7

Note: Numbers and percents may not add due to rounding.

Source: CUPR Survey 1972-1973.

261

EXHIBIT 7-6.　RESPONDENT RATING OF PUBLIC EDUCATION BY SCHOOL AGE CHILDREN

Respondent Rating	Total	None	Pre-School Age Children	Public School Children	Public School and Pre-School Age Children	Parochial School Children	Excluded Cases
Total	6,778	3,966	1,364	797	518	112	(21)
Good	2,604	1,133	418	605	398	41	(10)
Neutral	510	264	105	76	51	12	(2)
Poor	396	176	98	57	31	30	(4)
(NA/DK)	(3,267)	(2,393)	(744)	(60)	(37)	(28)	(6)

Percent Distribution

	Total	None	Pre-School Age Children	Public School Children	Public School and Pre-School Age Children	Parochial School Children	
Total	100.0	100.0	100.0	100.0	100.0	100.0	
Good	74.2	72.0	67.3	82.0	82.9	49.4	
Neutral	14.5	16.8	16.9	10.3	10.6	14.5	
Poor	11.3	11.2	15.8	7.7	6.5	36.1	

Note: Numbers and percents may not add due to rounding.

Source: CUPR Survey 1972-1973.

262

respondent at the conclusion of the evaluation section to indicate the municipal service in his own locale for which improvements were most pressingly needed.

Transportation was first. More than two out of five respondents gave this service first priority. It is nearly three times as important as the second most common response, which was recreation at the 13.3 percent mark. This was nearly matched by public education at the 12.8 percent level.

Despite all comments to the contrary, this rank ordering of priorities for education, coupled with the evaluative data presented, indicates that most respondents are reasonably satisifed with schools. Transportation which was not even listed under the municipal service topics has by far the highest priority.

Of the other five areas offered on the list, sanitation secured an 8.6 percent rating while library, public health, and police achieved approximately half that at 4.4 percent, 3.9 percent, and 3.5 percent, respectively. Fire protection, which had received an outstanding overall evaluation earlier, was felt to be the prime target for additional inputs by only 1.4 percent of the respondents. *Despite the enormous public media interest and the problems of crime and police protection, the response in this category was barely a tenth of that in transportation.*

For ease of presentation, the following discussion of variables attached to choice of service most in need of improvement will be limited to the three that received the highest rating: transportation, public education, and recreation.

Variation by Municipality

In nearly all twenty municipalities, transportation secured the highest level of priority. Where this was not the case, the group lumped under "other" secured dominance. This group typically involved either police or fire protection as most important with sanitation or recreation joining the basic trio. Noteworthy is Lakewood where transportation secured 40.6 percent, while public education secured 44 percent. This order of priority with education being more important than or as important as transportation also existed in Freehold and Northfield.

Housing Type

Regardless of housing type, there was surprising unanimity in order of priority for each housing configuration discussed here. The greatest variation was in the single family home group where transportation secured only 28.9 percent of the top priority listings, while recreation was very close at 22.0 percent. The other three groups were substantially consistent, with a somewhat higher public education figure in the townhouse.

Longevity at Present Address

The longer the respondent had lived at his present address, the more forceful was the demand for transportation. It went from 40.4 percent for residents of less than one year to more than three in five in the more than ten year group; the others rose proportionately to longevity of stay. More recently arrived residents may have optimized their transportation problem, at least as it concerns ease of access to work. Conversely, long-term residents may have been impacted by changes in employment locus or increasing congestion which made the journey to work more difficult.

Other Variables

Female respondents feel the transportation problem more keenly than men as evidenced by 51.8 percent of the women giving it top priority versus 42.2 percent of the men. It is interesting that there does not seem to be any clear association between transportation priority and education of head of household. Men chose public education proportionately more frequently than did women, at 13.4 percent and 9.8 percent, respectively. This imbalance occurred also with recreation facilities.

When age was considered as the chief variable, it was evident that there was a basic step function. Heads of household under the age of 50 hovered under the 40 percent response rate for transportation as the prime municipal service needing improvement, while for householders over the age of 50 the response bounced up to 60 percent.

Public education dominated the concerns of 11 to 16 percent of the age group from 21 to 49, while it was less than one-third of that for those over 50. They clearly did not feel the need as strongly, perhaps because they no longer had children in school. Recreation needs also followed the age pattern running approximately one out of seven responses for each of the heads of household from 21 to 50, but barely half that in older age groups.

In general, the demand for public education improvement is associated with higher educational attainment by the head of the household. The reverse is true for recreation facilities. Respondents having no diploma or only a high school education gave this top priority at a ratio of approximately one in six. Graduate degree holders, on the other hand, were down at the one in twelve level.

There was no great variation by income level for transportation, but higher income levels and demand for improvements in public education were clearly related. There was no significant variation in recreational demand except among those with very high incomes (over $30,000 a year) where there was a drop in the number giving recreation top priority.

Reasons for the Priority of Transportation Need

The intuitive response would be to link the level of priority given transportation to the length of journey to work. As indicated in Exhibit 7-7, however, this is not the case. People who do not commute give the improvement of transportation top priority. Over 60 percent of them gave it first rank. Many of these were retired and/or elderly people for whom private transportation may be too costly or trying. In fact, when the distance traveled to work by heads of households who commute are analyzed (see Exhibit 7-7), there is no obvious relationship between the distance commuted and the priority given transportation.

HOUSING SATISFACTION

Determining the quality of housing is a problem that has frustrated even the census bureau. Certainly, one of the prime considerations in this evaluation should be consumer satisfaction. The dissatisfied resident is not going to be a happy member of the community or housing development in which he is uncomfortably situated. In turn, given the high level of governmental influence in the housing market, it is appropriate to consider the various configurations of housing as measured by the peope who must use them -- their occupants. Therefore, the survey included a question asking the respondent to rate his or her housing satisfaction.

An analysis was made by municipality of the responses which, as indicated earlier, were generally positive. The level of variations is evident in Exhibit 7-2. On inspection, however, this pattern tended to relate to the configuration of the housing (garden apartment, single family home, etc.). When separately tabulated a rather substantial variation in positive response appeared. As a result, several of the communities, for which there were respondents only in garden apartments, had the poorest rating. However, they were limited to merely one standard deviation from the overall levels of satisfaction (i.e., the chances are merely two in three that this is not a chance relationship). Even in communities that had respondents in a variety of housing, and had ranked municipal services relatively low, the housing satisfaction responses were basically positive.

Housing Type

It is difficult to distinguish differences in varying levels of housing satisfaction when tabulated by housing types (Exhibit 7-8)

EXHIBIT 7-7. MUNICIPAL SERVICE MOST IN NEED OF IMPROVEMENT BY DISTANCE TRAVELED TO WORK BY HEAD OF HOUSEHOLD

Service Most In Need of Improvement	Total	Less Than 5 Miles	5-10 Miles	11-15 Miles	More Than 15 Miles	Does Not Travel	(NA/DK)
Total	4,366	835	908	487	1,739	396	(304)
Transportation	1,923	367	378	201	728	248	(56)
Public Education	562	80	114	48	301	20	(20)
Recreation	577	148	143	78	187	21	(24)
Subtotal	3,062	595	635	327	1,216	289	(100)
Other Services*	1,304	240	273	160	523	107	(67)
(NA/DK)	(2,411)	(426)	(423)	(217)	(703)	(339)	(137)
Percent Distribution							
Total	100.0	100.0	100.0	100.0	100.0	100.0	
Transportation	44.0	44.0	41.6	41.2	41.9	62.7	
Public Education	12.9	9.5	12.5	9.8	17.3	5.0	
Recreation	13.2	17.7	15.7	15.9	10.7	5.4	
Subtotal	70.1	71.2	69.8	66.9	69.9	73.1	
Other Services*	29.9	28.8	30.2	33.1	30.1	26.9	

Notes: 1 Numbers and percents may not add due to rounding.
2 (*)Other: Police Protection, Fire Protection, Sanitiation and Street Cleaning, Libraries, Public
   Health and Emergency Services, Other, None Needed.

Source: CUPR Survey 1972-1973.

EXHIBIT 7-8. HOUSING SATISFACTION BY HOUSING TYPE

Respondent Rating	Total	Garden Apartments	Townhouses	High Rise Apartments	Single Family Homes
				Housing Type	
Total	6,715	3,008	1,772	1,300	634
Good	4,898	1,981	1,548	854	516
Neutral	1,153	654	145	277	77
Poor	664	374	79	170	41
(NA/DK)	(62)	(37)	(11)	(10)	(6)
		Percent Distribution			
Total	100.0	100.0	100.0	100.0	100.0
Good	72.9	65.8	87.4	65.7	81.3
Neutral	17.2	21.7	8.2	21.3	12.2
Poor	9.9	12.3	4.5	13.0	6.5

Note: Numbers and percents may not add due to rounding.

Source: CUPR Survey 1972-1973.

as the results of differing physical configurations or forms of tenure. Would co-op owners be more positive than renters of equivalent units? Unfortunately, comparable data were not available on cooperatively owned garden apartments or high rise apartments under a condominium configuration, so the results shown here may not be the response to configuration per se but to ownership versus renting.

In any case, it is clear that the townhouse resident and the single family homeowner (no single family homes which were rented were in the sample) were the most satisfied at 87.5 percent, and 81.3 percent, respectively.* By way of contrast, the garden apartment and high rise apartments were appraised by their inhabitants at 65.8 percent and 65.7 percent good, respectively.

Note that these levels of housing satisfaction do not correlate particularly with attitudes towards municipal services. This fact is particularly evident among single family homeowners who rate housing satisfaction very high, but were the group most disgruntled with the available municipal amenities.

In general, the causes of positive or negative attitudes towards housing satisfaction were quite specific. Later in the interview respondents were asked whether there was a defect in their housing unit. It was evident that the answers tended to correlate with housing satisfaction; only 18.3 percent of those who rated their housing as good indicated some level of defect whereas 81.7 percent could cite no defect. The variation is marked when the negative housing raters are considered. In this group 57.1 percent indicated some specific defect in their own units versus 42.9 percent who cited none.

The variation continues when the equivalent questions were asked of housing development defects: two-thirds of those who rated their specific housing as poor cited some housing development defect, in contrast to only half of those who had rated their dwelling unit positively.

Other Variables

There is no apparent relationship between longevity at present address and housing satisfaction. Nor is the variation in response by sex of respondent, education, or age of head of household significant. There was some slight gradient by income level with

---

*There was a minor input of townhouse rentals in the sample. It was too small, however, to permit adequate examination of this variable; that is, whether renters feel differently from owners, given equivalent housing configurations.

minor association of higher income level with improved housing satisfaction, except for the very uppermost income levels, above $40,000. The number of respondents in this group is relatively small, however, and the basic lack of ascertainable relationship seems to hold.

Housing satisfaction, generally, was distributed without reference to size of apartment in garden apartments, with the exception of efficiencies. Here, only 58.7 percent of the 146 respondents rated their apartments very good or good as compared with a typical two-thirds or better in all the other configurations, for which data were gathered. Conversely, 22.1 percent in the former case rated their apartments very poor compared with approximately 10 percent in the other configurations. While the variations were not statistically significant in the other types of housing, such as the townhouse, high rise, and single family home, there was an indication that the smaller the dwelling unit -- estimated by number of bedrooms -- the more negative the response. The overwhelming positive reaction, however, held for the groups as a whole. Similarly, there did not seem to be any striking dissimilarity in the overall evaluation of the housing unit defects, when gauged by the scale of the several housing developments.

CONSUMER SATISFACTION WITH MUNICIPAL SERVICES: PART II

CONSUMER SATISFACTION AS A FUNCTION OF COMMUNITY SIZE AND GROWTH RATE

Is there an optimim size/growth pattern of community in terms of consumer satisfaction? The question has bedevilled philosophers and planners throughout history. The material which follows at best can make only a modest contribution. It is advanced in the hope that it may inspire more definitive efforts.

This section continues our discussion of the factors influencing consumer satisfaction with municipal services by examining the impact of community size and growth rate. Initially we focus on the impact of both of these factors acting together. Then we examine the separate influence of these two variables.

Consumer Satisfaction as a Function of Both Community Size and Growth Rate

To examine whether particular combinations of community size and growth rates demonstrate distinct patterns of consumer satisfaction, the communities that were interviewed were classified into eight groups (See Exhibit 7-9). This grouping reveals consumer satisfaction differences, but the exact trends are unclear (See Exhibit 7-10).

EXHIBIT 7-9.   INTERVIEW COMUNITIES POPULATION-GROWTH GROUPINGS

Group Number	N	1960 Population	1960-1970 Growth Rate (See Page)	Communities
1	2	1-1,500	Slow-Moderate	Flemington Borough Lopatcong Township
2	1	1-1,500	Explosive	East Windsor Township
3	1	5-10,000	Slow	Freehold Borough
4	2	5-10,000	Moderate	Monroe Township Northfield Borough
5	4	10-25,000	Slow-Moderate	Collingswood Township Fort Lee Borough Haddon Township Highland Park Borough
6	3	10-25,000	Moderate-Rapid	Brick Township Gloucester Township Lakewood Township
7	2	25-50,000	Slow-Moderate	New Brunswick City Vineland Township
8	3	25-50,000	Moderate-Rapid	Cherry Hill Township Edison Township Parsippany Troy-Hills Township

Note: Willingboro has been eliminated because it did not fit in any of the above size-growth rate groupings.

270

Municipal Service Rating for Indicated Function	*Percent of Respondents Rating Indicated Service - Good, Neutral or Poor in the Following Population-Growth Rate Community Groupings*							
	1	*2*	*3*	*4*	*5*	*6*	*7*	*8*
Public Education								
Good	92.6	83.2	42.0	63.3	78.5	71.9	27.5	77.9
Neutral	6.7	10.1	32.6	12.5	15.7	10.4	18.4	14.8
Poor	0.7	6.7	25.4	24.2	5.8	17.7	27.0	7.3
Total	100.0	100.0	100.0	100.0	100.0	100.0	100.0	100.0
Police								
Good	90.2	88.4	82.6	64.6	85.7	90.4	70.1	81.0
Neutral	8.7	9.9	10.4	17.1	11.0	5.9	19.6	14.9
Poor	1.0	1.6	7.1	18.2	2.3	3.8	10.2	4.1
Total	100.0	100.0	100.0	100.0	100.0	100.0	100.0	100.0
Fire								
Good	91.8	92.2	96.1	92.6	93.3	93.5	85.5	91.0
Neutral	8.1	6.3	2.6	5.6	6.3	4.9	11.8	8.5
Poor	0.0	1.5	1.3	1.9	0.4	1.5	2.7	0.5
Total	100.0	100.0	100.0	100.0	100.0	100.0	100.0	100.0
Recreation								
Good	42.6	30.4	46.1	18.7	69.3	67.2	43.1	39.0
Neutral	22.8	24.8	26.0	10.3	19.7	15.0	21.0	27.3
Poor	34.6	44.8	27.9	71.0	10.9	17.9	35.7	33.8
Total	100.0	100.0	100.0	100.0	100.0	100.0	100.0	100.0
Sanitation								
Good	83.0	60.5	76.8	61.0	82.7	78.1	62.5	64.7
Neutral	9.3	21.5	18.2	13.0	11.8	14.7	20.7	19.6
Poor	7.7	18.1	4.9	26.1	5.5	7.2	16.8	15.7
Total	100.0	100.0	100.0	100.0	100.0	100.0	100.0	100.0
Library								
Good	88.7	54.9	74.7	42.0	79.5	81.8	73.8	73.3
Neutral	3.6	20.8	7.3	3.5	13.7	9.8	11.2	17.1
Poor	7.7	24.3	17.9	54.6	6.7	8.4	15.0	9.6
Total	100.0	100.0	100.0	100.0	100.0	100.0	100.0	100.0
Public Health and Emergency Service								
Good	91.9	78.0	80.5	85.2	89.6	89.2	79.8	85.3
Neutral	6.5	11.6	16.6	3.5	7.9	5.3	12.6	9.4
Poor	1.7	10.4	3.0	11.3	2.5	5.5	7.7	5.4
Total	100.0	100.0	100.0	100.0	100.0	100.0	100.0	100.0

Note: Totals may not equal 100% because of rounding.

Source: CUPR Survey 1972-1973.

Specifically, respondents in population-growth groupings 1 and 6 generally rated their local services comparatively highly, while respondents in groupings 3, 4 and 7 frequently had an opposite view of local services. For respondents in the other groupings there was no distinct pattern of consumer satisfaction; some of the local services were rated comparatively highly while others were not. As an illustration, respondents in group Number 2 had a comparatively high opinion of their local police, fire and education services and a low opinion of local recreation services.

These trends are hard to decipher, not only because services are not uniformly rated, but also because the various groupings that sometimes had the highest (or lowest) consumer satisfaction levels are composed of communities of various populations and growth rates. To illustrate this point the respondents in groupings 1 and 8 that rated their municipal public health services highly, lived in communities ranging from a 1,000 to a 50,000 population size grouping and experienced growth rates ranging from a slow to a rapid pace (See Exhibit 7-9). To gain a clearer picture of the distinct impacts of community size and growth rate on consumer satisfaction, these two variables are analyzed separately.

Consumer Satisfaction as a Function of Community Size

This section examines whether or not there are significant differences in the level of satisfaction with municipal services in communities of different sizes. Communities are classified, by size, into three groups: small (1960 populations up to 10,000), middle range (1960 populations between 10,000 and 25,000), and large (1960 populations over 25,000). Each group contains roughly equal number of communities (Exhibit 7-11). Consumer satisfaction ratings by respondents in small, middle range and large communities are listed in Exhibit 7-12 and are discussed below.

When consumer satisfaction ratings were stratified by community size, respondents in middle range size communities generally rate their municipality's governmental services more favorably than respondents in small and large cities.

For example, when respondents in middle range size communities were asked about their local recreation, sanitation, and library services, 69, 81, and 80 percent, respectively, gave them a good rating. However, only 42, 66, and 62 percent of the respondents in small cities ranked these three services as good. There were similar low rankings of these services by respondents living in large cities (Exhibit 7-12).

Why should residents in both small and large cities generally have a comparatively low opinion of their community's municipal services? One possible explanation is that small communities often may provide

272

EXHIBIT 7-11.   INTERVIEW COMMUNITY GROUPINGS BY POPULATION SIZE

Community Population Category	N	1960 Population	Communities
Small	6	Up to 10,000	East Windsor Township Flemington Borough Freehold Borough Lopatcong Township Monroe Township Northfield Borough
Middle Range	7	10-25,000	Brick Township Collingswood Township Fort Lee Borough Gloucester Township Haddon Township Highland Park Borough Lakewood Township
Large	5	25,000+	Cherry Hill Township Edison Township New Brunswick City Parsippany Troy-Hills Township Vineland Township

EXHIBIT 7-12. EVALUATION OF MUNICIPAL SERVICES BY RESPONDENTS* FROM DIFFERENT SIZE COMMUNITIES

% of Respondents* Rating Indicated Governmental Function Good, Neutral or Poor

Community Size	Respondents' Rating of Indicated Municipal Services	Education	Police Protection	Fire Protection	Recreation	Sanitation	Libraries	Public Health and Emergency Services
1. Small	Good	78.4	85.4	92.6	42.1	65.5	61.6	81.3
	Neutral	12.2	10.6	6.0	23.3	18.4	14.7	10.5
	Poor	9.3	4.0	1.3	34.6	16.0	23.7	8.2
	Total	100.0	100.0	100.0	100.0	100.0	100.0	100.0
2. Middle Range	Good	76.1	87.4	93.4	68.6	81.2	80.3	89.5
	Neutral	13.8	9.1	5.9	18.0	12.7	12.4	6.9
	Poor	10.2	3.4	0.8	13.4	6.1	7.3	3.6
	Total	100.0	100.0	100.0	100.0	100.0	100.0	100.0
3. Large	Good	68.8	77.4	89.4	40.5	64.0	73.5	83.4
	Neutral	16.2	16.4	9.5	25.0	19.9	14.9	10.5
	Poor	15.0	6.1	1.2	34.5	16.1	11.6	6.2
	Total	100.0	100.0	100.0	100.0	100.0	100.0	100.0

Note: (*)Respondents were from our interview communities (See Exhibit 7-13).

Source: CUPR Survey 1972-1973.

only limited "essential services" such as police protection (they may have a handful of paid part-time patrolmen), and not provide "non-essential services" such as a recreation program. Because of the small community's parsimony in providing services, residents in these municipalities may rate municipal services as inadequate. This seems reasonable as the areas in which small communities rate worst are sanitation, recreation, and libraries.

On the other hand, large communities, though they often provide a full range of services, may be faced with tremendous demands on these services. They might have large, well-equipped police forces, but may also have high crime rates. Consequently, citizens in such municipalities may give municipal services a low rating because they feel that much more has to be done. These large communities rated poorly in the sensitive areas of police and education, as well as in sanitation. The evaluation therefore may not be of size as such, but rather of how our society has allocated functions -- and problems -- among various communities. And this latter is re-lated to scale.

Consumer Satisfaction as a Function of Community Growth Rate

So far we have discovered consumer satisfaction rating differences when we stratified by community size. Will we discover similar differences when we stratify by community growth rate? To effect such an analysis we establish three growth rate categories: decline/slow (from any percent population decline to a 2.5 percent annual 1960-1970 population increase), moderate (from a 2.5 to a 10.0 annual 1960-1970 percent increase in population), and rapid/explosive (10.0 percent plus annual 1960-1970 percent increase in population). (See Exhibit 7-13) The interview results from this stratification are listed in Exhibit 7-14 and are discussed below:

In general, respondents in moderately growing communities had a higher evaluation of municipal services than respondents in either slower or faster growing communities. But, there is only a slight disparity in the rating by respondents in the former as opposed to the latter municipalities. (See Exhibit 7-14) As an illustration 90 percent of the respondents in the moderately growing communities rated their local public health and emergency services as good as compared to 81 percent of those in decline/slow growing communities and 83 percent in rapid/explosive growing localities (See Exhibit 7-14).

Why should respondents in moderately growing communities have a comparatively high opinion of local services? One possible ex-planation is as follows: Rapidly growing localities may not be able to keep up with the expanding demand for local services. Con-sequently, respondents in such communities may have a comparatively low opinion of local services. In contrast, in slow growing com-munities local officials may either not feel strongly compelled to

EXHIBIT 7-13. GROWTH RATE GROUPINGS
THE INTERVIEW COMMUNITIES

Community 1960-1970 Population Growth Rate Grouping	N	1960-1970 Annual Population Growth Rate (in percent)	Communities
Decline/Slow	6	-% to +2.5%	Collingswood Township Flemington Township Freehold Borough Haddon Township Lopatcong Township New Brunswick City
Moderate	8	+2.5% to +10.0%	Edison Township Fort Lee Borough Gloucester Township Highland Park Borough Lakewood Township Monroe Township Northfield Township Vineland Township
Rapid/Explosive	4	+10.0%+	Brick Township Cherry Hill Township East Windsor Township Parsippany Troy Hills Township

EXHIBIT 7-14. EVALUATION OF MUNICIPAL SERVICES BY RESPONDENTS* FROM DIFFERENT GROWTH RATE COMMUNITIES

Community Growth	Respondents'[1] Rating of Indicated Municipal Services	% of Respondents* Rating Indicated Service Good, Neutral or Poor						
		Education	Police Protection	Fire Protection	Recreation	Sanitation	Libraries	Public Health and Emergency Services
Decline/Slow	Good	62.4	80.3	90.0	53.3	73.9	75.2	81.3
	Neutral	17.3	13.7	8.7	24.3	16.5	10.0	10.5
	Poor	20.3	6.0	1.3	22.4	9.6	14.8	8.2
	Total	100.0	100.0	100.0	100.0	100.0	100.0	100.0
Moderate	Good	69.6	83.3	93.0	56.1	77.2	77.9	89.5
	Neutral	16.2	11.2	6.0	16.7	12.7	11.1	6.9
	Poor	14.3	5.5	1.0	27.2	10.2	11.0	3.6
	Total	100.0	100.0	100.0	100.0	100.0	100.0	100.0
Rapid/Explosive	Good	82.6	84.6	91.5	45.7	64.7	67.0	83.4
	Neutral	11.3	12.2	7.5	25.3	20.2	17.9	10.5
	Poor	6.1	3.2	1.0	29.0	15.0	15.1	6.2
	Total	100.0	100.0	100.0	100.0	100.0	100.0	100.0

Note: (*) Respondents were from our interview communities.

Source: CUPR Survey 1972-1973.

expand local services or simply lack the resources given parallel slow growth in resources. As a result, residents in such localities may not rate local services highly. In moderately growing communities there is often sufficient growth to spur local officials to expand or improve local services. Because growth is moderate, such expansion or improvement can often keep pace with the rising demand for local services. These two factors may explain the comparatively high regard for local services by residents in moderately growing communities.

So far we have shown that there are differences in consumer satisfaction with local services both when we stratify by community size as well as by growth rate. But which variable yields larger differences in such satisfaction ratings; are there bigger differences in evaluations of local services in communities of different sizes or growth rates? Comparing Exhibit 7-12 to 7-14 indicates that *in general, size stratification yields greater differences in consumer satisfaction ratings than growth rate stratification.*

Why should this occur? One possible explanation is that community size, as opposed to growth rate, has a *greater impact on establishing the parameters of the range of services that are needed as well as that can be provided.* For example, if a community is small it often does not have to formally provide certain services (recreation and culture) and cannot afford to support many services. On the other hand, large communities, due to social forces characteristic of their size, will often need to provide services such as public safety. And, large communities with their broader tax base, can often provide services like a wide ranging recreation program that are financially impossible for the small municipality.

Community growth rate also affects the provision of services. For example, services may be severely disrupted in the rapidly growing community. Nevertheless, it appears that community size is the basic determinant of what services are needed as well as whether services can be provided.

IS CONSUMER SATISFACTION RELATED TO MUNICIPAL EXPENDITURES?

As described earlier, there was considerable variation in the level of consumer satisfaction by municipality for each local government function examined in the field survey. This is a complex issue and reasons for this variation are not easy to determine. Included as factors are the quantity, quality, and range of services provided; the demand for services; the cost of providing them, and the respondents' perceptions of their provision.

Though many of these factors defy analysis, data are available on the level and rate of change of expenditures by function, the population size, and growth rate for the twenty municipalities sampled. Such data may be used in a preliminary fashion as surrogates for the supply or provision of municipal services on the one hand, and the demand for such services on the other hand. Even so, the relative crudeness of such measures should not be overlooked.

The Level and Rate of Change of Municipal Expenditures

To examine the supply side of municipal services, data were obtained on the 1970 per capita expenditure and the 1960-1970 percent change in per capita expenditures for each of the public services whose quality was evaluated by respondents in the sample. This was done for each of the twenty municipalities. Respondent ratings may be a function of both the level and the rate of change of municipal expenditures. Municipalities were classified into high, medium, and low expenditure categories, roughly by thirds; according to the 1970 data and the 1960-1970 change. For example, the lowest one-third of municipalities, in terms of 1970 expenditures and 1960-1970 change, were grouped together for each of the functions considered. A caveat is necessary here; the expenditure categories varied by function; the expenditure categories were varied somewhat from the one-third rule when the data seemed to warrant. Nonetheless the categories are essentially empirical and not analytical.

These categories were cross-tabulated for each function against respondent ratings of the function in each municipality. The weighted sample was employed. Ratings were, as before, collapsed into good, including very good; neutral; and poor, including very poor, categories.

Level of Municipal Expenditures

The 1970 per capita municipal expenditures by function, rounded to the nearest dollar, appear in Exhibit 7-15. Zero means less than one dollar per capita. In addition, for public education, per capita local school revenue is given as a measure of direct cost to the consumer. School taxes are collected separately, but all municipal taxes are lumped together, complicating the interpretation of taxpayer attitudes on the provision of services. For each function, the municipalities and mean per capita expenditures in each expenditure category are presented in Exhibit 7-16.

Police Protection

Surprisingly, there is little or no variation in consumer satisfaction by expenditure level with police protection. Respondent ratings hovered around the 80 to 85 percent positive mark across expenditure categories. Yet there is considerable variation in expenditures from a low of $1 per capita in Brick Township to a high of $33 per capita in Freehold. The mean per capita expenditure was $12 for low, $19 for medium, and $27 for high communities. The overall mean was $19 for the twenty suburban communities.

EXHIBIT 7-15. FISCAL YEAR 1970 PER CAPITA EXPENDITURES FOR MUNICIPAL SERVICES BY MUNICIPALITY

Municipality	Police Protection	Fire Protection	Sanitation and Street Cleaning	Recreation	Public Health and Emergency Services	Libraries	Total School Expenditures*	Local School Revenue
Brick Twp.	1	0	23	5	2	0	1,499	200
Cherry Hill Twp.	19	0	20	3	2	4	1,237	217
Collingswood Boro.	16	5	13	2	0	3	881	108
Dover Twp.	27	0	25	9	2	1	1,047	218
East Windsor Twp.	25	2	14	2	2	0	1,511	215
Edison Twp.	19	12	18	2	3	2	941	201
Flemington Boro.	21	6	24	2	0	8	1,038	250
Fort Lee Boro.	27	5	16	5	2	2	1,084	117
Freehold Boro.	33	3	32	4	3	2	799	155
Gloucester Twp.	12	0	16	1	1	0	747	113
Haddon Twp.	22	5	16	4	1	7	1,033	185
Highland Park Boro.	21	4	22	3	1	3	1,097	189
Lakewood Twp.	26	5	22	5	2	3	1,968	143
Lopatcong Twp.	8	3	16	3	0	0	961	137
Monroe Twp.	14	3	18	0	1	0	980	104
New Brunswick City	31	22	18	8	4	4	1,020	70
Northfield City	18	9	20	1	0	1	516	105
Parsippany-Troy Hills Twp.	18	0	17	6	2	2	1,076	170
Vineland City	17	4	22	5	5	3	768	112
Willingboro Twp.	13	70	13	3	0	4	833	161

Notes: 1. Numbers were rounded to the nearest dollar.
2. *Total School Expenditures are per pupil based on average enrollment.

Source: 1. Data on all expenditure functions except education were taken from: Department of the Treasury, Division of Local Government, Thirty-Third Annual Report of the Division of Local Government, State of New Jersey 1970: Statements of Financial Condition of Counties and Municipalities (Trenton, 1970).
2. Data on educational expenditures and local school revenue were taken from: Department of Education, Division of Business and Finance, Nineteenth Annual Report of the Commission of Education: Financial Statistics of School Districts, School Year 1969-1970 (Trenton, 1970).

280

EXHIBIT 7-16. FISCAL YEAR 1970 MEAN PER CAPITA EXPENDITURES BY CATEGORY

Municipal Service	Expenditure Category	Mean Per Capita Expenditure	Range of Per Capita Expenditure	Number of Municipalities
Police Protection	Low	11.57	1-17	7
	Medium	19.33	18-21	6
	High	27.29	22-33	7
	Overall	19.40	1-33	20
Fire Protection	Low	0.33	0- 2	6
	Medium	4.11	3- 5	9
	High	23.80*	6-70	5
	Overall	7.90*	0-70	20
Sanitation and Street Cleaning	Low	14.86	13-16	7
	Medium	18.50	17-20	6
	High	24.29	22-32	7
	Overall	19.25	13-32	20
Recreation	Low	1.43	0- 2	7
	Medium	3.33	3- 4	6
	High	6.14	5- 9	7
	Overall	3.25	0- 9	20
Public Health and Emergency Services	Low	0.0	0	5
	Medium	1.63	1- 2	11
	High	3.75	3- 5	4
	Overall	1.65	0- 5	20
Libraries	Low	0.29	0- 1	7
	Medium	2.50	2- 3	8
	High	5.40	4- 8	5
	Overall	2.45	0- 8	20
Total School Expenditures	Low	757.33	516-881	6
	Medium	1,002.86	941-1,047	7
	High	13,053.14	1,076-1,968	7
	Overall	1,051.80	516-1,968	20
Local School Revenue	Low	102.00	70-117	6
	Medium	156.57	137-185	7
	High	212.86	187-250	7
	Overall	158.50	70-250	20

Notes: 1. (*)Inflated by a single community with very high per capita expenditure.
2. Total school expenditures are expressed per pupil. Local school revenue is expressed per capita.

Source: See Exhibit 7-15.

Fire Protection

As in the case of police protection, there was virtually no variation in consumer satisfaction by expenditure level. Respondent ratings hovered in the low 90 percent good range. As reported earlier, fire protection had received the highest overall rating of any municipal service. There was a slight gradient with expenditures, from 91.4 to 94.7 percent. There was considerable variation in expenditures from a low of $0 (i.e., less than $1) in five communities to a high of $70 in Willingboro (a figure which may reflect new facilities or equipment). The mean per capita expenditure was $0.33 for low, $4 for medium, and $24 for high communities. The overall mean was $8. Although the last two figures are inflated by one unusual municipality, the overall respondent ratings are relatively unaffected. [Note that a number of communities has volunteer fire departments.]

Sanitation and Street Cleaning

No real pattern emerges here by expenditure category. One possible explanation is the faulty nature of the expenditure data used. Sanitation and street cleaning proved to be a difficult budget item to define. Several categories of expenditure were combined under this rubric, and an accurate picture of expenditure categories is difficult to establish. Similarly, the respondents may have had widely differing concepts of such service. Garbage removal is often not a municipal service at all but provided by private contractors. Expenditures, as defined in this study, did not vary as much as for police and fire protection. The low was $13 per capita in Willingboro and Collingswood, the high $32 per capita in Freehold. The mean per capita expenditure was $15 for low, $18 for medium, and $24 for high communities, with the overall mean at the $19 mark.

Public Health and Emergency Services

This is another ill-defined municipal service. Public health measures may be supplied by higher-level governments, emergency services by private contractors or fire and police departments. Nonetheless, a clear but paradoxical pattern emerges by expenditure level. The higher the expenditure, the lower consumer satisfaction. The gradient fell from 91.4 percent for low to 85.7 and 80.9 percent positive for medium and high municipalities, respectively. What may be involved, of course, is a lag in municipal provision behind consumer demand, combined with a "rising expectations" phenomenon. The high expenditure communities may tend to be growing areas: East Windsor at $2, Edison at $3, Vineland at $5, and New Brunswick at $4. Perhaps respondents were expressing dissatisfaction with medical and health services -- both private and public -- in general. However, these hypotheses are not fully demonstrated in these data.

Expenditures ranged from a low of $0 in five communities to a
high of $5 in Vineland. New Brunswick ranked second at $4. The
mean per capita expenditure was $0 for low, $2 for medium, $4 for
high communities, and $2 overall.

Recreation

Again, no clear pattern was discernible, although low communities
do fall considerably below medium and high communities in consumer
satisfaction at 40 percent to 63.9 and 54.1 percent good, respectively. Although expenditures are fairly well defined here,
there may be complications arising from the fact that federal,
state, and county governments also supply recreational facilities.
Hence, expenditures perceived by consumers are difficult to define.
As in the case of sanitation and street cleaning, consumers may
have widely differing concepts of what is meant by locally provided
recreation. Police and fire protection in direct contrast are
well-defined municipal services. Where services are not well defined, there may be considerable "noise" in the expenditure and
satisfaction data employed here. Per capita expenditures ranged
from a low of $0 in Monroe to a high of $9 in Dover. There is a
fairly narrow range involved here. The mean per capita expenditure was $1 for low, $3 for medium, $6 for high communities,
and $3 overall.

Libraries

*This function is well-defined and showed a clear pattern, one which
stands in direct contrast to recreation. The higher the expenditure, the higher consumer satisfaction.* In low expenditure municipalities the positive response was 59.6 percent, rising to
74.9 percent for medium, and 85.7 percent for high expenditure
municipalities. The per capita expenditure ranged from $0 in five
communities to $8 in Flemington. The range is fairly narrow (al-
most the same range as for recreation). Mean per capita expenditure
was $0.29 for low, $2 for medium, $5 for high communities, and $2
overall.

Public Education

Since school taxes are collected separately, it was possible to investigate directly the impact of cost as well as expenditure on
consumer satisfaction. Municipal expenditures for other specific
functions are rarely as clearly linked to tax impact. Here, expenditures are defined per pupil rather than per capita, as a more
meaningful measure, though local school revenue is on a per capita
base.

First, total school expenditures per pupil are examined. There is
no definitive pattern, although consumer satisfaction rises in
general across expenditure categories. The positive response was
65.5 percent in low expenditure communities, 77.2 percent in medium,
and 76.5 percent in high. The reason for this is uncertain. Public
education is a well-defined function even though state and federal
funding is involved. Shifting from a per capita to a per pupil
basis may have some effect on the results. But per capita expenditure seems a meaningless concept for public education compared
to other municipal services. Perhaps satisfaction is a bell-shaped
function rising with expenditures and then plateauing or even declining past a certain point as tax costs rise. There may be a
diminishing returns effect in public expenditures in terms of satisfaction. However, the difference between medium and high communities is not very large.

Per pupil expenditures ranged from a low of $516 in Northfield to
a high of $1,968 in Lakewood. Mean per pupil expenditure was
$757 for low, $1,003 for medium, $1,353 for high communities and
$1,052 overall.

Tax costs can be studied directly by using local school revenue
data. (Local school revenues are almost entirely produced by local
property taxes collected by school districts.) An interesting contrast to the results by expenditure pattern emerges. *As school
costs rise, so does consumer satisfaction* -- from 57.6 percent good
for low expenditure municipalities to 65.6 and 88.7 percent good
for medium and high expenditure municipalities, respectively.
These results do not invalidate the diminishing returns hypothesis
presented above because expenditures and taxes may have different
turning points.

Local school revenue ranged from a low of $70 per capita in New
Brunswick (which had fairly high per pupil expenditure) to a high
of $250 per capita in Flemington. Mean per capita revenue was $102
for low, $157 for medium, $213 for high communities, and $158 over-
all.

The phenomenon may be circular. *Communities willing and able to
tax themselves most heavily for schools are those most satisfied
with the product.*

RATE OF CHANGE OF MUNICIPAL EXPENDITURES AND SATISFACTION

The 1960-1970 percent changes in per capita municipal expenditures
by function rounded to the nearest percent are presented in Exhibit
7-17. Zero means less than 1 percent change. The municipalities
and mean percent change by category for each function are presented
in Exhibit 7-18.

EXHIBIT 7-17. 1960-1970 PERCENT CHANGES IN PER CAPITA EXPENDITURES FOR MUNICIPAL SERVICES BY MUNICIPALITY

Municipality	Police Protection	Fire Protection	Sanitation and Street Cleaning	Public Health and Emergency Services	Recreation	Libraries	Total School Expenditures
Brick Twp.	50	Missing	62	49	270	179	229
Cherry Hill Twp.	140	-42	203	468	315	848	Missing
Collingswood Boro.	67	50	76	32	240	133	113
Dover Twp.	155	-91	29	-43	196	-27	24
East Windsor Twp.	1,045	-6	31	202	Missing	Missing	205
Edison Twp.	95	105	114	240	87	223	157
Flemington Boro.	1,212	56	108	-20	416	82	60
Fort Lee Boro.	85	57	173	101	302	271	90
Freehold Boro.	200	117	91	-13	154	114	68
Gloucester Twp.	116	54	149	38	123	1,227	34
Haddon Twp.	65	76	70	69	565	127	45
Highland Park Boro.	69	29	90	13	143	97	85
Lakewood Twp.	96	36	53	30	129	101	71
Lopatcong Twp.	202	182	38	-94	704	Missing	-16
Monroe Twp.	146	87	187	107	32	-47	116
New Brunswick City	99	87	53	52	66	51	54
Northfield City	317	125	149	-69	7	811	51
Parsippany-Troy Hills Twp.	200	-42	217	492	822	2,992	31
Vineland City	159	29	117	403	206	282	112
Willingboro Twp.	72	-21	66	-4	3,439	803	Missing

Source: See Exhibit 7-15.

EXHIBIT 7-18. MEAN 1960-1970 PERCENT CHANGES IN PER CAPITA EXPENDITURES BY CATEGORY

Municipal Service	Change Category	Mean Percent Change	Range of Percent Change	Number of Municipalities
Police Protection	Low	77.6	50- 99	9
	Medium	143.2	116- 159	5
	High	529.3	200-1,045	6
	Overall	229.5	50-1,045	20
Fire Protection	Low	-40.4	-91- -6	5
	Medium	56.1	29- 87	10
	High	132.3	104- 182	4
	Overall	46.7	-91- 182	19
Sanitation and Street Cleaning	Low	59.8	31- 76	8
	Medium	104.0	90- 117	5
	High	154.0	149- 203	7
	Overall	103.8	31- 203	20
Public Health and Emergency Services	Low	-40.5	-94- -4	6
	Medium	54.6	13- 107	9
	High	361.0	202- 492	5
	Overall	102.65	-94- 492	20
Recreation	Low	74.0	7- 129	6
	Medium	228.3	143- 315	8
	High	1,189.2	416-3,439	5
	Overall	432.4	7-3,439	19
Libraries	Low	42.8	-100- 101	6
	Medium	189.9	114- 282	7
	High	1,336.2	803-2,992	5
	Overall	459.3	-100-2,992	18
Total School Expenditures	Low	23.6	-16- 45	5
	Medium	68.4	51- 90	7
	High	155.3	112- 229	6
	Overall	84.9	-16- 229	18

Source: See Exhibit 7-15.

Police Protection

As in the case of 1970 per capita expenditure, little variation existed in consumer satisfaction by rate of change in per capita expenditure over the decade 1960-1970. There was a slight downward gradient; respondents in low change communities rated police protection 85.8 percent good compared to 83.9 percent in medium and 82.2 percent in high change communities. This gradient may indicate that increases in expenditure are geared to felt inadequacy. There was considerable difference in the rate of change, from a low of 50 percent in Brick to highs of 1,045 percent in East Windsor and 1,212 percent in Flemington, which inflated the means. The mean percent change was 77.6 for low, 143.2 for medium, 529.3 for high communities, and 229.5 overall.

Fire Protection

There was virtually no variation as respondent ratings continued to hover in the low 90s; no marked gradient was evident. A fairly large variation in percent change secured from -91 percent in Dover to 182 percent in Lopatcong. The mean change was -40.4 in low communities, 56.1 in medium, and 132.3 in high, with 46.7 the overall mean. Evidently a number of communities have expenditure patterns which are lagging behind population growth.

Sanitation and Street Cleaning

There was no real pattern by rate of change category although medium communities had a somewhat higher positive rating. The same explanations as before -- faulty expenditure data and different definitions of service -- are probably responsible. The lowest rate of change was 31 percent in East Windsor; the highest 203 percent in Cherry Hill. The means were 59.8 in low, 104.0 in medium, and 154.0 in high, with 103.8 the overall.

Public Health and Emergency Services

As in 1970 per capita expenditures for public health, an overall pattern emerges. The higher the growth in expenditures over the decade, the lower the good rating, dropping from 89.8 percent in low expenditure growth communities to 82.2 in high communities. The previous argument regarding public health is thus reinforced. A substantial number of communities (the low category with the highest good rating) actually showed declines in public health expenditures per capita. The lowest rate was -94 percent in Lopatcong, the highest 492 percent in Parsippany. Six communities experienced declines in per capita expenditure. The mean for low communities was -40.5, for medium 54.6, for high 361.0, the overall means being 102.65 percent.

Recreation

The same results did not hold for change over the decade as for
1970 expenditures. Low growth communities did not fall considerably below medium and high communities in consumer satisfaction.
Low and medium communities were both at 52.9 percent, with high
communities rising to 55.6 percent.

The variation in individual municipalities was quite large, from
a 7 percent change in Northfield to a whopping 3,439 percent change
in Willingboro, which inflates the high and overall means. The
mean change was 74.0 percent in low communities, 228.3 in medium,
1,189.2 in high, and 432.4 overall. Even eliminating an unusually
large change, as in Willingboro, did not alter the relationship of
consumer satisfaction and rate of change.

Libraries

Unlike the results of 1970 per capita expenditures for 1960-1970
expenditure change, the higher the change in expenditures, the
lower in general was consumer satisfaction. Respondent ratings
were 83.2 percent good in low, 67.6 percent in medium, and 75.1
percent in high communities. The means were 42.8 percent for
low communities (two municipalities showed declines), 189.9 for
medium, 1,336.2 for high, and 459.3 overall.

Public Education

As before, there is no clear pattern in consumer satisfaction,
which was at the 78.9 mark in low communities, fell to 63.2 in
medium communities, and rose to 79.3 percent in high communities.
Change in per pupil expenditures varied from 16 percent in Lopatcong to 229 percent in Brick. The overall mean was 84.9 percent,
with 23.6 in low, 68.4 in medium, and 155.3 in high communities.

NOTES FOR CHAPTER 7

[1]Herbert A. Simon, Fiscal Aspects of Metropolitan Consolidation (Berkeley, California: University of California, Bureau of Public Administration, 1943).

[2]George Sternlieb and Patrick Beaton, The Zone of Emergence (New Brunswick, N.J.: Center for Urban Policy Research, Rutgers University, 1972), Chapter 4.

CHAPTER 8

SUMMARY AND IMPLICATIONS FOR POLICY

The introduction of new residential growth in a community generates
major concerns to both planners and policymakers. Principal among
these are the characteristics of the future inhabitants of the new
residences and their consequent impact on educational and municipal
service expenditures. Regardless of particular ideological orienta-
tions, the capability to answer these questions is required. Certain types of residential development imply a generalizable set of
occupants and a calculable fiscal impact. Whether planning for a
pre-set social mix or for a minimum fiscal impact, the same baseline
parameters are required. This study attempts to isolate these basic
blocks of necessary information.

This summary will review first the substantive and policy implications
of the cost revenue allocation procedure, summarizing the critical
variables affecting the methodology, the basic underlying parameters,
and the socio-demographic characteristics of the inhabitants of alternative residential types. Second, the implications of changing municipal costs as a function of residential growth, both from theoretical
and practical perspectives, are examined.

COST REVENUE IMPLICATIONS

Conventional municipal cost-revenue techniques are in practice based
on a breakeven analysis. Given the appropriate cost allocation procedures, the financial analyst calculates the costs and revenues of
a particular housing proposal employing the applicable household size
and school load multipliers, taxable valuation of the property, property tax rates, and per capita or per pupil costs of municipal
services and public education. An example of such calculations is
presented in Chapter 1.

The following rules are generally applied to the results of the calculations. If revenues minus costs are zero or positive (costs are
equal to or less than revenues), the housing proposal essentially
pays its way; if negative (costs are greater than revenues), additional ratables are required to lessen the proposal's impact. Among
various competing proposals which are admissible, the one with the
highest surplus value would be favored, other things being equal.
Establishing this ranking is one main purpose of municipal cost-
revenue analysis. In this fashion, the municipality would be able
to maximize the net revenue. This net revenue could be used either
to improve municipal services and public education at the current
property tax rate or to reduce the tax rate while maintaining the
same level of services.

Conversely for any of a variety of reasons a less than fiscally optimum development may be chosen. But certainly public policy should evolve with an appropriate knowledge of the costs of foregone revenues involved.

The demand for broader housing opportunities for the poor and moderate incomed have yet to be coupled with an equivalent fiscal support package. The latter may well develop as revenue sharing becomes more sophisticated. Again, for this purpose reasonable municipal cost data are essential.

Cost Allocation Procedure

In Chapter 1, we argued that the appropriate cost allocation procedure was generally to use average costing rather than marginal costing. Expansion of municipal facilities and services is a function largely of long-term community growth rather than of any specific housing development. The same holds true for school costs. In New Jersey, the property tax is the basic source of local revenue. Hence, that expenditure which must be financed through the property tax is the cost of service that directly affects the local resident.

In reality, the problem is considerably more complicated, especially outside the states like New Jersey which rely heavily on the local property tax (covering municipal, county, and school expenditures) and which provide relatively little state financial aid. The property tax is not really intended to be a measure of benefit to each resident but an index of ability to pay. (The income tax is undoubtedly a better measure of ability to pay, but it is substantially monopolized by the federal and state governments.) Most of the municipal and school budget is not actually chargeable to property or particular land uses as such. In New Jersey, the property tax is applied to all property (residential, industrial, and commercial) equally according to assessed value. Direct property tax revenues are quite often insufficient to meet school and municipal costs in all but the highest value (and hence generally lower household size and school load multipliers) residential areas. The effect of this situation is a reluctance to admit lower cost housing in a great many municipalities. (In the example shown in Chapter 1, all single family homes below $30,000, three-bedroom townhouses, two-bedroom garden apartments, and the overall housing proposal resulted in deficits.)

The emphasis on property tax costs and revenues ignores these other important financial considerations, which have added weight outside of states like New Jersey. First, property taxes are a shrinking proportion of local revenues. Many of the other elements available from other sources vary with number of persons. Intergovernmental grants in particular generally rise with population and local tax effort, possibly offsetting the costs of providing municipal services and public education to new residents. Non-property tax revenues may or may not vary with the income of such residents, depending on the tax. Second, the costs themselves will vary according to the breakdown of a development's population between old and new residents of the community. The relocation of extant residents adds nothing to costs (since they are merely shifting location within the municipality) but may add new revenues (to the degree that they transfer from less valuable older residential property to more valuable new residential property). Therefore, the example in Chapter 1 may overstate the cost of proposed housing. Third, new residents (and perhaps old residents as well when they move to a new location) have an impact on the local economy through consumer spending in the municipality. Even in the absence of local sales taxes gross municipal income may be raised with consequent increases in non-property tax revenues.

Critical Variables

Chapter 1 presented the equations for calculating the cost-revenues balance for municipal services and public education:

1. Overall Educational Surplus or Deficit = (Revenue - Cost) x Number of Dwelling Units

    a. Revenue Per Dwelling Unit = Market Valuation Per Dwelling Unit x Equalized School Property Tax Rate

    b. Cost Per Dwelling Unit = Public School Children Per Dwelling Unit x School Property Tax Levied Per Pupil

2. Overall Municipal Surplus or Deficit = (Revenue - Cost) x Number of Dwelling Units

    a. Revenue Per Dwelling Unit = Market Valuation Per Dwelling Unit x Equalized Property Tax Rate

    b. Cost Per Dwelling Unit = Number of Persons Per Dwelling Unit x Property Tax Levied Per Person

If we dissect these equations, we shall see that there are five determinants of variation in the cost-revenue balance for the property tax. Cost per dwelling unit varies according to the household size or school load multiplier and the property tax levied per capita or per person. Revenue per dwelling unit varies according to market value and the equalized property tax rate. Both the property tax cost and equalized property tax rate depend upon the proportions of residential, commercial, and industrial land uses in the community. The total surplus or deficit then depends on the total number of dwelling units (which is related to the density of dwelling units per acre), as well as the cost-revenue balance per unit.

The first factor to be considered is <u>market value per dwelling unit</u>. Total taxable valuation is given by market value per unit times number of units. On a per acre basis, it depends on density. The density of development is an independent variable to be considered by the local zoning agency in its decisions affecting community growth and new residential development. Townhouses have the highest market value per unit in our sample, followed closely by high rise apartments and then single family homes (see Exhibit 8-1).* Garden apartments fall considerably behind the other three housing types. Given the same equalized property tax rate, these housing types yield revenue in the order just given. Because of higher densities, however, high rise developments exceed all other housing types in taxable valuation per acre, and the position of garden apartments is substantially improved. The data given in Exhibit 8-1 are the average values of the dwelling units of our sample.

EXHIBIT 8-1. MARKET VALUE BY HOUSING TYPE

Townhouses	2 Bedrooms	$35,000
	3 Bedrooms	$39,000
High Rise Apartments	1 Bedroom	$26,400
	2 Bedrooms	$33,600
Single Family Homes	3 Bedrooms	$27,000
	4 Bedrooms	$30,000
Garden Apartments	1 Bedroom	$16,200
	2 Bedrooms	$19,800

The second factor is *the number of persons and public school children per dwelling unit*. These data were reported in Exhibits 1-1 and 1-2. These multipliers are related to the number of bedrooms per dwelling unit. Generally, garden apartments and high rises involve one and two-bedroom units. Townhouses typically have a modular mix of two, three, and four bedrooms, while single family homes are larger, with three and four bedrooms. In smaller dwelling units, high rises have the lowest household size and school

---

*The single family unit sample is not representative of new statewide construction. New units of this type more generally exceed $45,000 in price and thus have the highest value per dwelling unit.

load multipliers. Garden apartments have one-tenth more persons and four times more school children in one-bedrooms, three-tenths more persons and two times more school children in two-bedrooms. These multipliers are also related to considerable differences in occupant characteristics by housing type. Total number of persons and school children depends on number and density of dwelling units constructed. In three and four bedroom units, townhouses actually contain more persons but fewer school children than single family homes.

The third and fourth factors, property tax cost and equalized property tax rate, both depend upon the mix of land uses and the level of municipal services per capita and public education per pupil provided. Assuming constant absolute value of the residential stock, the larger the proportion of industrial and commercial properties, the lower the property tax rate to raise the same revenue because total assessed valuation per capita is higher. On the other hand, the larger the proportion of residential properties, the higher the property tax rate because total assessed valuation per capita is lower.*

The final factor is the number of dwelling units (and its density per acre) actually constructed. The more units per acre, the greater the total taxable valuation of residential property. Density itself, however, is a policy variable to be manipulated by the community. Density of development is a highly relevant consideration. High rise apartments have the highest density, single family homes the lowest. Garden apartments and townhouses have roughly comparable intermediate densities.

An Example

Looking at these determinants, we may draw certain general conclusions about cost-revenue analysis. The example of Chapter 1, structured to yield a particular result regarding balanced housing development, is somewhat misleading for this purpose. We should look instead at the cost-revenue picture per dwelling unit (Exhibit 8-2). High rise developments have the highest density and the second highest market value per dwelling unit (market value per acre is probably the highest). At the same time, they have the lowest household size and school load multipliers. If we examine Exhibit 8-2, we find that high rise apartments are about equivalent to townhouses for two bedrooms and far ahead of garden apartments for one bedrooms in both of the two communities used for illustrative purposes, Manalapan and Edison.

---

*Obviously, certain exclusive residential communities would be an exception to this statement.

EXHIBIT 8-2. REVENUE SURPLUS PER DWELLING UNIT

Housing Type	Manalapan	Edison
Single Family Home		
3 Bedroom	$391.13	$355.67
4 Bedroom	-$227.44	-$1,136.17
Townhouse		
2 Bedroom	$1,087.98	$412.94
3 Bedroom	$782.47	-$78.41
High Rise Apartment		
1 Bedroom	$986.25	$779.01
2 Bedroom	$1,086.73	$417.72
Garden Apartment		
1 Bedroom	$510.75	$200.51
2 Bedroom	$318.88	-$152.93

Townhouses have an intermediate density and approximately the same market value. They have the highest number of persons and school children in larger dwelling units. In the exhibit, three-bedroom townhouses produce a slight deficit per dwelling unit in Edison (due to a lower tax rate). In general, high rises and townhouses are equivalent cost-revenue choices for one and two bedrooms.

Garden apartments also have an intermediate density but the lowest market value per dwelling unit. Density probably makes their market value per acre equal to or greater than that for single family homes. For smaller dwelling units, garden apartments have the highest household size and school load multipliers. In the exhibit, this housing type produced moderate surplus in Manalapan but a deficit in Edison for two-bedroom units.

Single family homes under $30,000 present the poorest cost-revenue picture. They have the lowest density but have market values per dwelling unit approximately equivalent to that of high rises and townhouses. Their household size and school load multipliers are lower than those for equivalent townhouse units. But market value is enough lower to counter this difference. In Edison, single family homes produced moderate to large deficits per dwelling unit. Even in Manalapan, four-bedroom single family homes showed a moderate deficit. However, three bedrooms yielded a moderate surplus.

In Manalapan, a deficit occurs only in single family four bedrooms. In Edison, deficits occur for all single family homes, three-bedroom townhouses, and two-bedroom garden apartments. The overall surplus in Manalapan is $4,847, in Edison $87. If four-bedroom single family homes are eliminated in Edison, the surplus rises to $1,223. Clearly then, the cost-revenue example in Chapter 1 can be changed to cause either a surplus or deficit depending on unit mix. The outcome depends on the breakdown of the proposal by housing type and number of bedrooms.

We may hypothesize a different example which permits a more direct comparison of the four housing types. Let us make the reasonable assumption that more smaller bedroom units will be constructed. The example is given in Exhibit 8-3. In Manalapan, the overall surplus is $337,627, in Edison $79,935. If four-bedroom single family homes are dropped in the latter, the surplus is $108,339. In the Chapter 1 example, Manalapan had a $100,000 surplus, Edison a $250,000 deficit.

EXHIBIT 8-3.   SELECTED COST-REVENUE EXAMPLE

			Net Revenue or Deficit	
Housing Type			*Manalapan*	*Edison*
Single Family Home				
3 Bedroom	100		$30,113	-$35,567
4 Bedroom	25		-$5,696	-$28,404
			$24,427	-$63,971
Townhouse				
2 Bedroom	100		$108,798	$41,294
3 Bedroom	25		$19,562	-$1,960
			$128,360	$39,334
Garden Apartment				
1 Bedroom	100		$51,075	$20,051
2 Bedroom	25		$7,972	-$3,823
			$59,047	$16,228
High Rise Apartment				
1 Bedroom	100		$98,625	$77,901
2 Bedroom	25		$27,168	$10,443
			$125,793	$88,344

Manalapan is a completely residential community. As a result, the property tax rate is higher. Edison on the other hand, has a strong commercial and industrial base, producing a lower tax rate. Therefore, almost any housing proposal appears attractive in Manalapan because the ratables per capita are unusually low. Many proposals appear unattractive in Edison because the existing ratables per capita are so high that only the most expensive development can approximate them. Thus Edison can in fact better afford community growth and new residential development because it has higher assessed valuation per capita. As non-residential ratables grow in Manalapan, assuming constant housing values, its tax rate will drop and housing proposals will appear unattractive. Yet the community has become wealthier and better able to support balanced development.

Socio-Demographic Profiles

It is also of importance to planners and public policymakers to know the characteristics of the occupants of new forms of residential growth as well as their fiscal impact. Whether planning for a pre-determined residential mix or for minimal fiscal impact, the same baseline information is required.

The social and occupational characteristics of residents obviously affect the approval of housing proposals, whatever the context. The median household income in the surveyed high rise and townhouse units is $20,108 and $18,381, respectively. Median education is very high (15.8 and 15.5 years, respectively). Over 80 percent of the residents are in white collar occupations (especially professional and managerial positions). In high rises, only 2.8 percent are in blue collar occupations while 10.7 percent of the townhouse heads of household are in the same status.

On the other hand, single family homes under $30,000 and garden apartments are oriented much more toward the lower middle and working classes. The median household income is $12,869 in single family homes and $11,871 in garden apartments. Median education is lower (12.8 and 14.2 years, respectively). In both housing types, there are considerably more blue collar workers: 35.5 percent in single family homes, 20 percent in garden apartments.

Previous Place of Residence

If we look at the previous place of residence, we find an interesting pattern. Garden apartments of all the housing configurations studied draw to the largest extent from the same municipality (21.4 percent). An additional 47.7 percent come from the rest of the state. Single family homes draw almost as much from the same municipality (20.8 percent) and somewhat more from the rest of the state (53.4 percent). Only 30.9 percent and 25.8 percent come from out of state, respectively. High rises and townhouses draw much more heavily on out of

297

state migrants: 52.4 percent and 46.3 percent, respectively. Very
few come from the same community: 11.3 percent and 8.4 percent,
respectively. Clearly, the marginal costs of garden apartments and
single family homes may be somewhat lower than those calculated, and
the costs of high rises and townhouses higher, depending upon the
nature of the facilities vacated in the same municipality.

Spending Patterns

As mentioned above, there are differential impacts on the local economy by housing type, in terms of consumer expenditure patterns. It
is often argued that because of the rise of highway-oriented suburban
living, residence, shopping, and workplace have been separated. The
residential community bears the tax burden and the other two locations reap most of the tax benefits. Our sample indicates that 74.6
percent of respondents made 75 to 100 percent of all food purchases
in their community: 85.8 percent in townhouses, 71.6 percent in
high rises, 70.8 percent in single family homes, 70.1 percent in
garden apartments. The patttern was quite different for clothing
expenditures. Of single family homes residents, 46.8 percent purchases 75 percent or more in the same community. Townhouses were
next highest at 21.5 percent (over half the entire sample, 56.9 percent purchased less than 25 percent locally). Only 16.3 percent of
our respondents purchased over 75 percent of house furnishings locally. Again, single family homes topped the list at 35.4 percent (over
twice the rate for other housing types).

Gasoline taxes are an important source of local revenue in New Jersey
because of the tax rebate law. Some 57.4 percent of our respondents
bought over 75 percent and 12.3 percent bought at least 50 percent
locally. Townhouses headed the list at 66.2 percent followed closely
by single family homes at 65.2 percent. The overall implication is
that residential development is good for the local economy, especially for food, clothing, and gasoline retailers. The attractiveness
of townhouses and single family homes is improved by their greater
local spending compared to other housing types.

Demographic Changes Over Time

There is often concern that attractive cost-revenue results may dete-
riorate over time. Our data indicate otherwise, at least for garden
apartments in the Highland Park-Edison Township-Franklin Township
area (Middlesex and Somerset Counties) where we compared some 1,100
households in developments surveyed in both 1963 and 1972. Aging
did substantially affect the social and occupation characteristics
of the resident population but not the household size and school load
multipliers. The school load multipliers rose a little for one-
bedroom units (.037 in 1963 versus .049 in 1972) but declined slightly for two-bedroom units (.390 in 1963 versus .375 in 1972). Similar

data are not available for other housing types but their higher market value and resident characteristics would tend to indicate even greater stability than in garden apartments.

There was a significant shift in the distribution of age of head of household and occupation (see Exhibit 1-10). The head was typically younger in 1972 at the middle age brackets (22.5 percent under 25 years versus 5.2 percent), while those over 65 rose from 6.8 percent to 17.7 percent. The rise in household size and school load in younger households was largely counterbalanced by the higher proportion of older families. Occupation shifted from a focus on professional and technical workers (48.9 percent in 1963 versus 24 percent in 1972) toward operatives (4.6 percent versus 10.9 percent) and students and retired persons (9.7 percent versus 26.3 percent).

Resident Satisfaction

In Chapter 7, we discussed consumer satisfaction with municipal services. This is a factor which a zoning agency or planning consultant may well find advisable to take into account. Generally, respondent evaluations were favorable toward all municipal services. The overall index of general government services over 3.9 was on a five-point scale from very poor (1) to very good (5). Fire protection was highest at 4.3 followed closely by public health and police protection both above 3.9 (as was housing satisfaction). Public education, libraries, and sanitation were reasonably high (well above 3.5). Only recreation lagged badly at 3.4 although still positive.

Long-term residents usually gave more favorable evaluations than did new residents. The same pattern often held for older heads of household. There was typically little significant variation by income, sex, education, or occupation. Attitude toward public education had little relationship to number of children under 18. Households with children in public school (closely related to the school load multipliers) felt most positive about public education. On the other hand, households with children in parochial or private schools felt least positive.

We are, of course, most interested in variation by housing type. Some definite patterns occurred in respondent ratings. But it is difficult to interpret these ratings by housing type. The municipality itself is clearly an important source of variation in respondent evaluation of local public services (see Exhibit 7-2). But the housing types are most unevenly distributed across municipality. It is possible that controlling housing type by municipality might well vitiate the patterns discussed in Chapter 7. The survey sample was not drawn in a manner to permit final determination of this issue. It was designed to function by sampling area and housing type. Conclusions can be drawn for both housing type and municipality separately, but it is difficult to evaluate the ratings jointly.

Respondents regarded transportation as the service most in need of improvement, followed by recreation and public education. Transportation is largely the responsibility of state and county government (except for municipal bus service and taxi licensing, etc.) As one might expect, transportation improvements are probably lagging considerably behind community growth. In turn, local government probably has little control over the situation at best.

In terms of housing satisfaction, townhouse and single-family home residents (both homeowners) as one would be expected are most satisfied at 87.5 percent and 81.3 percent, respectively. Garden apartments and high-rise residents (both renters) were considerably less satisfied at 65.8 percent and 65.7 percent, respectively. *Housing satisfaction did not correlate with attitudes toward municipal services*. Single family homeowners rated their housing satisfaction very highly but gave municipal services the lowest rating. (It should be pointed out that our sample of such homes newly built under $30,000 lie largely in less developed townships providing lower levels and qualities of local public services. Their satisfaction might be different in more developed communities where such housing typically does not exist). Dissatisfaction toward housing was largely due to some specific defect in the dwelling unit or the housing development.

It appears from our investigation that there is little general linkage between consumer satisfaction and the 1970 level or the 1960-1970 rate of change of expenditures for municipal services. Some variations in this generalization appeared, however, depending on the particular service. There was minor variation for police protection, fire protection, sanitation and public education for both level and rate of change of expenditures. All these services were rated quite favorably as shown in Exhibit 7-1. They are also fairly well defined local services, except for sanitation. Satisfaction with public education did rise significantly with school costs, from 57.6 percent in low communities to 88.7 percent in high communities.

Public health and libraries were also rated favorably in general; public health is a poorly defined function, libraries a well defined one. The higher the expenditure for public health the lower consumer satisfaction (but dropping only from 91.4 percent in low expenditure communities to 80.9 percent in high ones). The same pattern held for rate of change, dropping from 89.8 percent in low communities to 82.2 percent in high ones. Libraries showed an opposite pattern for expenditures: the higher the expenditure, the higher consumer satisfaction, rising from 59.6 percent to 85.7 percent. However, satisfaction again fell, though erratically, with rate of change, from 83.2 percent in low communities to 67.6 percent in medium and 75.1 percent in high communities.

Recreation was the most poorly rated service. It is also poorly defined. In terms of 1970 expenditures, evaluation rose from only 40 percent favorable in low communities to 63.9 and 54.1 percent in medium and high communities respectively. This result did not hold for change over the decade 1960-1970. Low and medium municipalities were both at 52.9 percent, with high communities rising to 55.6 percent.

Clearly in some cases high expenditures or increases therein reflect felt dissatisfaction which, if not appeased by the time of our survey would account for some of the lack of expressed satisfaction. In other cases the pre sort mechanism, of consumers choosing communities with a pattern of services and expenditures compatible with their wants, clearly plays a role. Much more work in this area clearly needs to be done.

THE COSTS OF MUNICIPAL SERVICES

Theoretical Applications

The results of this research can be viewed from several perspectives: that of the individual municipality, that of the state, and possibly as a vehicle for the definition of further research explorations.

From the point of view of the individual municipality, the parameters isolated provide an estimate of the costs involved in the consumption of municipal goods and services under the conditions of population change. Further, if growth or decline generates greater concentrations of specific age or ethnic groups, the research suggests specific fiscal outcomes as a result of the population variation. A similar statement can be made for the change in the economic base of the municipality.

From the point of view of the state, this effort represents an effort to bring into the hands of policymakers the tools by which to describe the fiscal conditions surrounding the state's 567 municipalities. Further, there is a foundation for a model that estimates the type of functions within which future state aid and general revenue sharing monies could be expended. Still further, it is the basis for a model that could estimate the tax effort by the different types of municipalities under the presence of expanded intergovernmental aid.

From the point of view of future research, the model presented here is one of a small but growing number that recognizes the necessity to incorporate the interaction effects of the several independent variables upon municipal expenditures (in this case, population size and percent change in population). Moreover, our capacity to use a large data base covering two decades and three census periods demands that efforts be made for the construction of more rigorous models that will build in explicitly the impact of social and economic changes over time; the neighborhood effects of surrounding municipalities upon a core municipality; and the interaction of local school finance upon municipal expenditure patterns.

Last, yet perhaps most basic to the study of the state and local public sector, this work forms a foundation for a reasoned analysis of the quantity and quality of public goods and services offered to citizens of the state's municipalities. Today, practically every work in this field, including this one, has studied the economics of consumption; however, there has not been linkage of expenditures with specific services or their level of production. This research and cognate studies to follow serve to generate operational questions. For example, per capita expenditures are found to decline to a minimum near the 10,000 population base level. Is this due to an efficient size of government, a decrease in either the level or number of services offered, or to some other set of factors?

In the end, the policy analyst is concerned with the output of services. The desire is to maximize public service levels but not at the cost of maximizing expenditures; however, once an instrument with which to monitor expenditure levels is obtained, the construction of the links to the output of public goods service can be commenced.

Practical Applications

While the more theoretical aspects of a study of this type must be judged over a considerable period of time, the same is not true for its practical application. The local municipality now has within its grasp a tool to improve the municipal cost/impact analysis of new residential development. Typically, a municipal impact statement, composed within the state of the art, will project municipal costs by applying the current level of per capita costs to an expected population occurring from development. Thus, if a development is to occasion a population growth of 10,000 over a five-year period and current costs of municipal operating expenses are $125 per capita, the assignable municipal cost of the development would probably be projected at $1,250,000 annually, at 100 percent development.

Variations on this most frequently sought technique might be a distribution of this cost to program areas by estimating current levels of proportionate allocation, or a slight escalation of per capita costs into the future based upon brief historical trends of past per capita variation. This procedure, while "cheap and fast," depending upon the type of community, may be subject to considerable error. It does not take into account, for instance, the size of the community and its expenditure patterns before growth or the new size categorization and resulting expenditure patterns after growth; to say nothing about various changes in spending as a function of level of growth.

This study provides three basic modifications for municipal cost prediction: *the per capita expenditures of various size and growth rate categories of communities, the percent of the operating budget which various programs occupy, and the percent change in the budget by program area for similar categories of communities* (Exhibits 8-4, 8-5, 8-6).

EXHIBIT 8-4. 1970 PER CAPITA MUNICIPAL OPERATING EXPENDITURES OF NEW JERSEY MUNICIPALITIES
BY ANNUAL GROWTH RATE (1960-1970) AND ESTABLISHED POPULATION BASE (1960)

GROWTH RATE

Declining (-5 to 0%) (A), Population 1960 (000)

Program Area	0.1-1*	1-5	5-10	10-25	25-50	50+	Mean
Government Administration	68.4	26.2	17.6	21.3	18.7	32.8	27.0
Public Safety	26.9	24.2	31.6	44.9	60.1	83.7	38.3
Public Works	61.6	26.8	27.8	28.5	24.0	22.0	28.6
Health & Welfare	2.5	2.7	1.9	5.4	5.9	18.3	5.1
Recreation & Culture	14.2	6.7	3.6	13.1	10.7	17.5	9.5
Statutory & Unclassified	7.4	5.9	6.8	10.4	20.4	36.2	11.3
TOTAL	$181.0	$92.5	$89.3	$123.6	$139.8	$210.6	$119.8
ΔC_p ($ annual)	$11.7	$5.0	$5.1	$6.3	$7.5	$11.6	$6.6
ΔC_{sub} ($ annual)	31.9	14.2	13.5	12.3	12.8	11.6	14.4
Sub (n)	n=5	n=30	n=7	n=13	n=5	n=7	n=66

Slow (0 to 2%) (B), Population 1960 (000)

Program Area	0.1-1*	1-5	5-10	10-25	25-50	50+	Mean
Government Administration	27.9	25.2	22.4	21.3	17.0	16.5	22.9
Public Safety	16.6	24.1	30.0	36.1	47.3	54.2	30.5
Public Works	29.2	33.9	28.1	27.3	26.9	23.0	29.9
Health & Welfare	2.0	2.1	2.1	3.2	4.1	12.1	2.8
Recreation & Culture	7.1	10.6	6.8	12.6	12.4	8.4	9.9
Statutory & Unclassified	2.7	5.5	4.0	9.4	14.9	15.1	7.0
TOTAL	$85.5	$101.4	$93.4	$109.9	$122.5	$129.3	$103.0
ΔC_p ($ annual)	$4.3	$5.8	$4.8	$5.6	$6.6		$5.4
ΔC_{sub} ($ annual)	13.2	15.5	11.4	11.6	16.1	10.7	13.5
Sub (n)	n=21	n=88	n=58	n=46	n=22	n=9	n=240

Moderate (I) (2 to 5%) (C), Population 1960 (000)

Program Area	0.1-1	1-5	5-10	10-25	25-50	50+	Mean
Government Administration	50.4	27.5	24.5	16.3	N O	C A S E S	26.8
Public Safety	56.7	27.5	37.7	25.8			32.2
Public Works	52.5	33.1	32.1	24.2			32.9
Health & Welfare	2.7	2.0	2.6	2.2			2.3
Recreation & Culture	33.3	14.6	6.7	14.0			14.1
Statutory & Unclassified	19.7	7.0	6.0	4.8			6.8
TOTAL	$215.3	$111.7	$109.5	$87.3			$117.1
ΔC_p ($ annual)		$6.4	$5.7	$4.9			$6.4
ΔC_{sub} ($ annual)	8.4	13.0	12.8	13.2			12.4
Sub (n)	n=13	n=n*	n=19	n=25			n=109

Moderate (II) (5-10%) (D), Population 1960 (000)

Program Area	0.1-1	1-5	5-10	10-25	25-50	50+	Mean
Government Administration	57.4	23.5	20.1	19.5	N O	C A S E S	26.6
Public Safety	36.7	24.4	22.7	25.5			25.9
Public Works	65.5	27.7	23.0	22.5			30.8
Health & Welfare	3.0	1.9	1.8	2.2			2.1
Recreation & Culture	25.8	5.9	5.8	7.5			8.8
Statutory & Unclassified	13.6	6.4	5.1	6.2			7.1
TOTAL	$202.2	$89.7	$78.5	$83.4			$101.3
ΔC_p ($ annual)	$8.2	$4.5	$4.7	$4.4			$5.1
ΔC_{sub} ($ annual)	8.7	11.3	15.8	11.8			12.3
Sub (n)	n=13	n=41	n=27	n=11			n=94

Rapid (10-20%) (E), Population 1960 (000)

Program Area	0.1-1	1-5	5-10	10-25	25-50	50+	Mean
Government Administration	74.8	26.7	19.3	17.8	N O	C A S E S	31.2
Public Safety	80.8	30.2	23.9	16.0			34.7
Public Works	113.4	28.6	28.5	20.0			39.7
Health & Welfare	3.0	2.3	2.3	1.8			2.3
Recreation & Culture	39.5	8.8	3.7	8.3			12.6
Statutory & Unclassified	23.7	0.2	5.3	4.5			4.7
TOTAL	$332.2	$96.7	$83.0	$68.4			$125.2
ΔC_p ($ annual)	$8.7	$5.2	$4.6	$3.2			$5.3
ΔC_{sub} ($ annual)	4.2	12.2	15.0	9.6			11.6
Sub (n)	n=7	n=25	n=6	n=6			n=47

Explosive (20% and Over) (F), Population 1960 (000) — and All New Jersey Communities

Program Area	0.1-1	1-5	5-10	10-25	25-50	50+	Mean	All New Jersey Communities
Government Administration	23.5	19.8	N O			C A S E S	19.2	22.4
Public Safety	15.2	15.7					15.5	31.2
Public Works	30.4	12.3					17.6	31.1
Health & Welfare	2.8	1.5					1.7	2.8
Recreation & Culture	1.3	1.4					2.2	16.4
Statutory & Unclassified	2.7	1.8					2.2	4.8
TOTAL	$75.8	$52.5					$58.4	$108.7
ΔC_p ($ annual)	$1.5	$3.3					$2.6	$5.0
ΔC_{sub} ($ annual)	2.0	15.0					10.1	13.1
Sub (n)	n=3	n=4					n=7	n=563

Notes: *Communities of 100 population or less (1960) have been eliminated from this growth categorization (TETERBORO; PAHAQUARRY; PINE VALLEY; TAVISTOCK)

Source: (UPR Survey 1972-1973.)

EXHIBIT 8-5. PROGRAM AREAS PERCENT OF 1970 OPERATING BUDGET OF NEW JERSEY MUNICIPALITIES
BY ANNUAL GROWTH RATE (1960-1970) AND ESTABLISHED POPULATION BASE (1960)

GROWTH RATE

Declining (-5 to 0%) (A) — Population 1960 (000)

Program Areas	0.1-1	1-5	5-10	10-25	25-50	50+	Mean
Government Administration	43.2	29.7	19.8	17.7	15.5	14.9	24.6
Public Safety	14.7	25.0	35.5	35.8	39.8	40.8	30.1
Public Works	30.6	32.7	31.2	24.0	18.9	11.2	27.4
Health & Welfare	2.2	3.4	2.2	4.3	4.3	8.6	4.1
Recreation & Culture	4.4	4.1	4.1	9.8	9.2	8.4	6.0
Statutory & Unclassified	4.9	5.1	7.2	8.4	12.3	16.1	7.8
TOTAL	100.0	100.0	100.0	100.0	100.0	100.0	100.0
Sub (n)	n=5	n=30	n=7	n=13	n=5	n=7	n=66

Slow (0 to 2%) (B) — Population 1960 (000)

Program Areas	0.1-1	1-5	5-10	10-25	25-50	50+	Mean
Government Administration	35.7	28.0	23.9	19.7	14.2	13.1	24.6
Public Safety	17.8	23.3	32.5	33.0	37.6	41.7	29.0
Public Works	33.0	34.2	30.1	26.4	23.0	19.1	30.1
Health & Welfare	2.6	2.4	2.3	2.8	3.3	7.9	2.7
Recreation & Culture	7.2	6.4	6.7	9.7	10.2	6.6	7.4
Statutory & Unclassified	3.7	4.8	4.5	8.4	11.2	11.6	6.2
TOTAL	100.0	100.0	100.0	100.0	100.0	100.0	100.0
Sub (n)	n=21	n=88	n=58	n=46	n=22	n=9	n=240

Moderate (I) (2 to 5%) (C) — Population 1960 (000)

Program Areas	0.1-1	1-5	5-10	10-25	25-50	50+	Mean
Government Administration	28.5	27.9	22.2	20.4	NO	NO	25.0
Public Safety	21.7	22.9	36.9	31.2	CASES	CASES	27.2
Public Works	33.3	34.0	30.8	27.4			31.7
Health & Welfare	2.1	2.3	2.6	2.6			2.5
Recreation & Culture	8.7	7.3	5.6	9.8			7.9
Statutory & Unclassified	5.7	5.6	1.9	8.6			5.7
TOTAL	100.0	100.0	100.0	100.0			100.0
Sub (n)	n=13	n=49	n=19	n=25			n=109

All New Jersey Communities

Program Areas	Mean
Government Administration	25.4
Public Safety	28.4
Public Works	30.3
Health & Welfare	2.8
Recreation & Culture	7.1
Statutory & Unclassified	6.0
TOTAL	100.0
Sub (n)	n=563

Moderate (II) (5 to 10%) (D) — Population 1960 (000)

Program Area	0.1-1	1-5	5-10	10-25	25-50	50+	Mean
Government Administration	35.3	27.0	25.6	23.1	NO	NO	27.1
Public Safety	16.0	26.3	29.2	31.1	CASES	CASES	26.5
Public Works	33.8	32.1	29.7	27.3			30.8
Health & Welfare	2.3	2.1	2.4	2.6			2.3
Recreation & Culture	7.2	5.6	6.8	8.2			6.5
Statutory & Unclassified	5.4	6.9	6.3	7.7			6.8
TOTAL	100.0	100.0	100.0	100.0			100.0
Sub (n)	n=13	n=41	n=27	n=11			n=94

Rapid (10 to 20%) (E) — Population 1960 (000)

Program Area	0.1-1	1-5	5-10	10-25	25-50	50+	Mean
Government Administration	27.1	29.2	23.3	27.0	NO	NO	27.4
Public Safety	23.6	33.4	29.3	22.1	CASES	CASES	29.9
Public Works	35.8	30.4	33.8	30.8			31.2
Health & Welfare	1.3	2.5	2.7	2.7			2.4
Recreation & Culture	9.3	4.5	4.6	10.6			7.1
Statutory & Unclassified	4.9	0.0	6.3	6.8			2.0
TOTAL	100.0	100.0	100.0	100.0			100.0
Sub (n)	n=7	n=25	n=6	n=6			n=47

Explosive (20% and Over) (F) — Population 1960 (000)

Program Area	0.1-1	1-5	5-10	10-25	25-50	50+	Mean
Government Administration	29.0	35.2	NO	NO	NO	NO	31.0
Public Safety	19.3	26.8	CASES	CASES	CASES	CASES	25.4
Public Works	41.3	30.0					33.1
Health & Welfare	4.4	2.7					3.0
Recreation & Culture	1.9	2.1					4.0
Statutory & Unclassified	4.1	3.2					3.5
TOTAL	100.0	100.0					100.0
Sub (n)	n=3	n=4					n=7

Notes: *Communities of 100 population or less (1960) have been eliminated from this growth categorization (TETERBORO; PAHAQUARRY; PINE VALLEY; TAVISTOCK)

Sources: CUER Survey 1972-1973.

EXHIBIT 8-6. 1960-1970 DECADE PERCENT CHANGE IN PERCENT OF THE PER CAPITA ALLOCATION OF NEW JERSEY
MUNICIPALITIES BY ANNUAL GROWTH RATE (1960-1970) AND ESTABLISHED POPULATION BASE (1960)

GROWTH RATE

Slow (0 to 2%), Population 1960 (000)

Program Area	0.1-1*	1-5	5-10	10-25	25-50	50+	Mean
Government Administration		5.0	4.2	3.3	5.8	0.0	3.1
Public Safety		0.2	1.1	-1.0	-3.2	2.9	0.0
Public Works		-6.8	-5.4	-4.5	-6.0	-3.9	-6.0
Health & Welfare		-2.1	-1.7	-1.0	-1.7	-0.6	-1.6
Recreation & Culture		3.7	1.4	2.0	0.7	0.5	2.1
Statutory & Unclassified		0.0	.4	1.2	4.4	2.1	2.4
TOTAL		0	0	0	0	0	0
Sub (n)		n=88	n=58	n=46	n=22	n=9	n=240

Moderate (I) (2 to 5%) (C), Population 1960 (000)

Program Area	0.1-1	1-5	5-10	10-25	25-50	50+	Mean
Government Administration	2.5	3.9	-0.7	-0.6	NO	CASES	1.8
Public Safety	4.2	2.1	7.4	1.0			3.1
Public Works	-10.2	-9.4	-2.6	-8.7			-8.1
Health & Welfare	-1.8	-1.7	-2.2	-1.4			-1.6
Recreation & Culture	2.4	3.9	-0.8	5.0			3.3
Statutory & Unclassified	2.9	1.3	-1.1	4.7			1.5
TOTAL	0	0	0	0			0
Sub (n)	n=13	n=49	n=19	n=25			n=109

All New Jersey Communities

Program Area	Mean
Government Administration	1.7
Public Safety	1.5
Public Works	-7.0
Health & Welfare	-1.6
Recreation & Culture	2.6
Statutory & Unclassified	2.8
TOTAL	0
Sub (n)	n=563

Declining (-5 to 0%) (A), Population 1960 (000)

Program Area	0.1-1*	1-5	5-10	10-25	25-50	50+	Mean
Government Administration		0.7	1.9	1.2	-5.3	2.6	0.6
Public Safety		-0.2	-1.8	-1.4	4.8	5.2	0.5
Public Works		-1.7	-1.4	-1.3	-3.9	-4.8	-2.3
Health & Welfare		-1.0	-1.8	-0.1	-2.1	-7.0	-1.6
Recreation & Culture		0.5	-0.1	3.5	1.8	-0.4	1.2
Statutory & Unclassified		1.7	3.0	-1.9	4.7	4.4	1.6
TOTAL		0	0	0	0	0	0
Sub (n)	n=5	n=30	n=7	n=13	n=13	n=7	n=66

Moderate (II) (5-10%) (D), Population 1960 (000)

Program Area	0.1-1	1-5	5-10	10-25	25-50	50+	Mean
Government Administration	5.9	1.7	0.0	3.2		NO	1.9
Public Safety	-0.5	3.9	0.6	1.9		CASES	1.6
Public Works	-10.2	9.9	-6.1	-10.7			-9.0
Health & Welfare	-0.1	-1.6	-1.5	-1.6			-1.3
Recreation & Culture	2.0	2.6	3.5	3.9			2.9
Statutory & Unclassified	2.9	4.2	4.0	3.3			3.9
TOTAL	0	0	0	0			0
Sub (n)	n=13	n=41	n=27	n=11			n=94

Rapid (10-20%) (E), Population 1960 (000)

Program Area	0.1-1	1-5	5-10	10-25	25-50	50+	Mean
Government Administration	-3.7	0.2	-1.0	3.2	NO	CASES	-0.4
Public Safety	0.2	11.3	2.9	3.3			6.8
Public Works	4.3	-10.7	-7.4	-12.3			-8.7
Health & Welfare	-3.2	-2.0	-1.7	-1.5			-1.9
Recreation & Culture	5.7	4.9	3.4	4.8			4.7
Statutory & Unclassified	-3.3	-3.7	3.8	2.5			-0.5
TOTAL	0	0	0	0			0
Sub (n)	n=7	n=25	n=6	n=6			n=47

Explosive (20% and Over) (F), Population 1960 (000)

Program Area	0.1-1	1-5	5-10	10-25	25-50	50+	Mean
Government Administration	-9.4	9.9	NO	CASES			2.1
Public Safety	15.2	10.4					1.6
Public Works	11.9	-16.3					-7.3
Health & Welfare	-7.2	-7.0					-6.0
Recreation & Culture	-0.5	2.1					3.2
Statutory & Unclassified	-0.6	0.9					6.4
TOTAL	0	0					0
Sub (n)	n=23	n=4					n=7

Note: *Communities of 100 population or less (1960) have been eliminated from this growth categorization (TETERBORO; PAHAQUARRY; PINE VALLEY; TAVISTOCK).

Source: CUPR Survey 1972-1973

How then can these tools be used most effectively? East Windsor, New Jersey, an explosively growing, exurban community of 12,000 population is an example. Let us assume for the moment that one wanted to predict 1973 per capita costs and specific program changes via conventional and newly developed means. In East Windsor, the first community to enact a PUD ordinance (1967), the assumption will be that the community had a planned unit development on-going and has since been besieged by other developers seeking PUD's, so much so that they have imposed a building moratorium on all other residential developments, with the exception of the single PUD in progress.

The PUD, according to pro forma statistical analyses, will add 10,000 people over the period 1969 through 1973. East Windsor's 1970 population was approximately 12,000, thus the PUD will increase the municipality's population by 80 percent over a five-year period, or 16 percent annually.

Based on 1969-1970 expenditure allocations to program areas according to the following percentage distribution and a 1969-1970 per capita cost of $83.22, we would expect the impact statement to assign a municipal cost to the development of $832,220 distributed as indicated in the following Exhibit.

EXHIBIT 8-7. COMMON IMPACT STATEMENT FOR A DEVELOPMENT
CAUSING A 10,000 POPULATION INCREASE -
EAST WINDSOR, NEW JERSEY

Program Area	Percent of the Budget	Dollar Allocation Based on $83.22 Per Capita
Government Administration	33.0	$275,000
Public Safety	41.3	344,100
Public Works	16.4	136,400
Health and Welfare	2.6	21,520
Recreation and Culture	2.5	20,600
Statutory and Unclassified	4.2	34,600
Total	100.0	$832,220*

Note: (*) Population Increase 10,000.

Source: CUPR Survey 1972-1973.

If a limited amount of additional effort is invested, perhaps this estimate can be refined somewhat. As a result of anticipated population growth and existing population base, one would place East Windsor in the category of rapid growth (10-20 percent annually) communities, of 10-20,000 population (Exhibit 8-4).

One would further expect as a result of the categorization an expenditure emphasis on general administration, public safety, recreation/culture and statutory expenses and somewhat less concern with health and welfare and public works. We know also that this community is experiencing a unique combination of spending lag/lead and has passed a point of relying upon a previously established servicing infrastructure. It can no longer continue to draw upon this base and must increase its per capita municipal costs in the future.

Thus, employing the same distribution, modifying this by half a decade's change in percent change in percent of budget (reflecting expenditure allocation patterns of rapid growth, 10,000-25,000 population communities) a figure of $990,000 distributed somewhat differently may be expected (Exhibit 8-8).*

If the revised prediction is compared with the actual budgetary change, over the period 1969 to 1973, it is at least 50 percent more accurate than the original prediction. While the internal level of consistency is somewhat less important than the accuracy of the total per capita figure, it should be noted that East Windsor had just previously expended considerable funds to expand its public safety and public works functions, thus occasioning the over-estimation in these areas. It must be admitted that while not ideal, the revised estimates, both partitioned and in total, are much more accurate than the original projections.

Future Program Allocation

Municipalities, like many private corporations, often erroneously estimate future personnel needs. They at times overhire; more frequently they do not hire enough and are then faced with the task

_____

*The figure from the growth cell for total per capita costs is not taken directly from Exhibit 8-4. Rather a current per capita figure for the specific community is taken by dividing the most current budget by the estimated population for that year. Once the initial figure is arrived at (1970 East Windsor-$83.22) the percent change in per capita expenditures observed from moving from one growth cell/population base (i.e., $52.50 per capita at population base 1-5,000/growth rate 20 percent + annually) to another (i.e., $68.40 at population base 10-25,000/growth rate 10 to 20 percent annually) is applied to the current figure. In this case it would be a 31 percent increase; this same ratio applied to the existing expenditure level would increase it to $99.00 per capita.

EXHIBIT 8-8. REVISED IMPACT STATEMENT FOR A DEVELOPMENT CAUSING A 10,000
POPULATION INCREASE - EAST WINDSOR, NEW JERSEY

Program Area	Original Percent of the Budget	Percent Change in Percent of the Budget	Revised Percent of the Budget	Dollar Allocation Based on $99.00 Per Capita
Government Administration	33.0	1.6	34.6	$342,540
Public Safety	41.2	1.7	43.0	425,700
Public Works	16.4	-6.2	10.2	100,980
Health and Welfare	2.6	-0.8	1.8	17,820
Recreation and Culture	2.5	2.4	4.9	48,570
Statutory and Unclassified	4.2	1.3	5.5	54,450
Total	100.0	0.0	100.0	$990,000*

Note: (*) Population Increase 10,000

Source: CUPR Survey 1972-1973.

308

EXHIBIT 8-9. COMPARISON OF ESTIMATED DEVELOPMENT IMPACT WITH
ACTUAL BUDGETARY INCREASES FOR THE PERIOD 1969-1973

Program Area	Estimated	Actual
General Administration	343.0	359.0
Public Safety	426.0	296.0
Public Works	101.0	77.0
Health and Welfare	18.0	47.0
Recreation and Culture	49.0	18.0
Statutory and Unclassified	54.0	138.0
Total	$990,000	$935,000

Source: CUPR Survey 1972-1973.

of quickly finding and hiring additional personnel. Similarly,
municipalities may either over or underestimate the need for future
capital resources, e.g., motor vehicles and physical plant.

Frequently a municipality is faced with a need to provide services
in a particular area and is then forced to effect a crash program
of personnel hiring and equipment purchases. For example, an urban
municipality that is faced with the possibility of racial confront-
ations may attempt to "cool" the city by expanding recreation
programs and will search frantically to hire qualified park super-
visors or recreation directors; this is a difficult task in the
light of the current heightened competition for such personnel.
Another example might be a small municipality anticipating a large
PUD development; rapid expansion is frequently necessary in the
inspections department (planning, housing, sanitation) and in the
area of government administration. Similar situations prevail
when a municipality attempts to bolster quickly its ranks of other
skilled personnel, e.g., police, firemen, public health officials,
and budget officers.

In contrast, some municipalities are confronted with the problem
of retaining personnel in one governmental area after this service
area has reached its high point and begins to decline. A municipality, for example, may continue to hire public works officials
long after public works as the dominant local municipal expenditure
has peaked and the current public works staffing is more than adequate. Or a municipality, after a period of rapid growth, may
still continue to hire police officials even though their hiring
is not warranted by the city's observable growth rate.

Similar problems arise in attempting to estimate future equipment
and other resource needs. Thus, a municipality may continue to
replace expensive sanitation and road repair equipment long after
the demand for such public works articles has lessened. In contrast,
a municipality may have underestimated the need for recreation
equipment, due to the variation in use by differing populations and
may then have to embark on an expensive crash purchase program to
acquire necessary playground equipment.

The most direct way for alleviating the municipal resource estimation problem would be for municipalities to be able to predict the
future areas of their expenditure emphasis based on similar communities reaching such a point and reacting analogously. Previously
this was easier said than done, for it is precisely the vagueness
and uncertainty concerning the emphasis on certain program areas
and deemphasis of others which contributes to the difficulty of
correctly anticipating future resource needs.

This study's analysis of the percent of the per capita allocation
to various service areas and specific emphasis on communities of
varying population base and growth rates may help to alleviate

both the problem of estimating future expenditure emphases and that of projecting necessary resources allocation.

With a knowledge of trends in these areas municipal officials may then be better able to forecast future personnel and other resource needs. For example, municipal officials in slowly growing communities of moderate size might anticipate the recruitment of public safety, health and welfare, and recreation and culture officials. As has been indicated, these communities as they increase to larger size begin to increase the proportion of their per capita allocation devoted to these program areas. As municipal officials in these communities potentially plan recruitment and equipment purchases, they might also anticipate the deemphasis of the public works function. Our study has revealed that as slower growing communities increase in size, the public work's percent of municipal budget most probably will decline.

Municipal officials in moderately growing communities could follow similar strategies, but with more moderation. In other words, they might begin to think about potential increased needs in the areas of public safety, health and welfare, and recreation and culture, and to begin to look critically into department heads requests that would further emphasize public works recruitment or equipment purchase. This is true for moderately growing communities because their budget emphases among the various expenditure categories resemble slow and declining communities yet are not as accentuated.

Finally, municipal officials in rapidly and explosively growing communities should plan for continued recruitment and equipment purchases in the general administration area for it is precisely this program area that feels the brunt of rapid expansion.

Attitudes Towards Growth

Very small communities (0-5,000 population) are often apprehensive about allowing housing development and consequent population growth. There are a number of reasons for their reluctance, including fears that increasing size will result in possible aesthetic blight, environmental damage, and social problems. But certainly in most cases a major reason for the small community's reluctance to allow development is apprehension that population growth will dramatically increase both educational and municipal expenditure burdens.

This study indicates that as far as municipal expenditures are concerned, small communities (0-5,000 population) are better off encouraging growth; across all growth categories ranging from declining to explosive it is the small community that has the highest per capita expenditure. Consequently, from a per capita municipal expenditure perspective in an area destined for growth it might be definitely advantageous for municipal officials in small communities

311

*to encourage types of planned growth that would allow development
to take place at a moderate rate and thereby take advantage of the
decreased per capita costs this type of growth would allow.*

Attitudes Towards Population Size

To say that small communities of up to five thousand population
should encourage a type of planned growth begs the question of how
long should growth be encouraged. At what point should these communities begin to discourage further population increase? Furthermore, the strategy outlined in the above paragraph was directed at
the comparatively small numbers of communities having very small
populations (0-5,000) but has left undiscussed what strategy larger
communities should follow.

In a recent publication, Nongrowth as a Planning Alternative: A
Preliminary Examination of an Emerging Issue,[1] Earl Finkler,
described the wide interest in attempting to ascertain what is the
optimal municipal size. Such varied groups as the Advisory Council
on Intergovernmental Relations, the American Society of Planning
Officials, the Commission on Population Growth and the American
Future, and individuals such as urban historian Lewis Mumford,
University of Michigan sociologist Otis Duncan, and economist Wilbur
Thompson have all wrestled with this question.[2]

This interest has not been merely academic; in practice numerous
communities have decided on the maximum size they wish to achieve
and have attempted to discourage or even prohibit growth beyond
these maximum sizes. In 1971, Boulder, Colorado, for example,
sought to stabilize its population at the 100,000 mark. (This
specific resolution was defeated, but a less stringent growth limit
proposal was passed.) In the fall of 1972, Boca Raton, Florida,
imposed a legal limit on the city's population of approximately
100,000.[3] And other communities and levels of government, including
Orange County, California; Wilamette Valley, Oregon; Sacramento
County, California; Dade County, Florida; Petaluma, California;
Martha's Vineyard, Massachusetts, have all either studied,
attempted or actually established growth limits.[4]

Numerous criteria have been employed in setting maximum municipal
size, including environmental, social and political factors. The
Douglass Commission, for example, recommended that communities should
be large enough to provide a manageable number of authorities within
which federal and state agencies can deal. Frequently, however,
the major criterion for establishing growth limits has been economic;
the objective function has been that cities should expand to the
point at which their per capita municipal expenditures are lowered
as a result of economies of scale and other factors.

Boca Raton, for example, established a 100,000 population growth limit because in the words of this municipality's city manager: "We estimate that the cost of providing municipal services increases sharply over 100,000 (population). That's the breaking point when everything starts to cost a lot more.'[6] Even where municipal officials agree that growth limit should be established at the point where economic servicing efficiency is met, there is a problem of determining <u>when</u> such servicing efficiency is reached. Finkler noted that "...no one seems to know how to establish and interpret economic criteria related to an efficient and optimum city."[6] It is our hope that the findings on variations in per capita costs presented here can help public officials evaluate the stages of growth at least on economic criteria.

To review briefly, we concluded that communities of varying growth rates reached servicing efficiency at the following population levels: declining and slow growing at the 10,000 population mark, moderately growing communities at the 10,000 to 25,000 population level, and finally, rapidly and explosively growing communities had continuously declining per capita costs as their population increased.

Knowledge of these trends can help clear some of the uncertainty when growth or non-growth might be employed temporarily to achieve an interim operating efficiency. To give a specific example, municipal officials in moderately growing communities looking to reduce per capita costs may try to hold population at the 10,000-25,000 mark since it is at this population level that per capita costs are lowest. Municipal officials in slow growing communities also seeking to hold down per capita costs would do best by attempting to stabilize growth at the 5,000 to 10,000 population level since this is their particular per capita nadir.

<u>Future Levels of Government Expenditure</u>

A frequently reiterated strategy to reduce or at least to stabilize the cost of municipal expenditures is to curtail the total municipal salaries and wages expenditure. Some of this study's findings shed considerable doubt on the efficacy of such a strategy. Specifically, this action may have little effect, depending on the size and growth pattern of the community in question.

In many smaller communities (1,000 to 10,000 population), non-salary expenditures often constitute a higher percent of total expenditures than do salaries and wages. In the moderate size communities about half or slightly more than half of the total expenditures are devoted to salaries and wages and the rest to other expenditures. It is only when larger communities are considered, e.g., Passaic, Newark, etc. that salaries and wages constitute an extremely large percentage of total expenditures.

The implications of the above trends are obvious. In the small
community a strategy of reducing or attempting to stabilize the total
salaries and wages cost may have little impact on reducing total
expenditures since the former is generally only a fairly small
component of the latter. In contrast, reducing or stabilizing
salaries and wages expenditures in large communities will often
have a dramatic effect, since in these communities the salaries and
wages expenditure constitutes a much larger percentage of the total
expenditure.

We have thus far spoken of either reducing or stabilizing personnel
expenditures as if there were little question that this could be
done but rather that the only question was where such a reduction
or stabilization could have the biggest impact. Such an approach
ignores reality, however, for it is extremely difficult to dampen
total salaries and wages expenditures as will be indicated below.

Many municipalities are faced with growing demands for services by
community residents. Better police protection and recreation
activities, for example, are two services that have increasingly
been demanded by local taxpayers. The more frequent case of
providing new services and/or expanding old ones has meant that
communities have been forced to hire additional employees with a
concomitant increase in their total salaries and wage expenditures.
A related factor has been that the very services that have been
most in demand have often been the most labor intensive. The fact
that there has been an increased demand for governmental services
is a factor precipitating both added governmental hiring and competition within the salaries and wages allocation, thereby escalating
costs.

Other factors also shed some doubt on the ability of governmental
officials to reduce or stabilize the municipal salaries and wages
cost. In the past decade there has been a tremendous inflation
in the individual salaries and wages paid by private industry.
Municipal governments often require similar personnel to those
needed by the private sector and have been forced to match the
salaries offered by the latter. Additionally, the growing union-
ization of municipal employees has led to growing salary demands
by the latter - demands which often must be met to avoid the inter-
ruption of essential services. Whether this balance of forces
will be altered is open to question. Certainly, however, the cost
push forces shown in this work must be slowed.

Population pressures and changes in the standard and ways of life
are creating great expansionary pressures on developing communities. As yet the national government has contributed more to increasing these stresses than to supporting their burden. Certainly
to cite just two examples, the national highway program and the
maintenance of vigorous housing production mechanisms outweigh
the redistributive aid given operating costs. A first step toward
a more equitable relationship must be to quantify the latter.

[1]Earl Finkler, _Nongrowth as a Planning Alternative: A Preliminary Examination of an Emerging Issue_, ASPO Report No. 283 September 1972.

[2]_Ibid._, Chapter III.

[3]_The New York Times_, February 9, 1973.

[4]Finkler, _op. cit._, Chapter IV: William McGivern, "Putting a Speed Limit on Growth," and Earl Finkler, "Can a Trust Turn the Tide on the Islands," _Planning - The ASPO Magazine_ November 1972, p. 263-274.

[5]_The New York Times_, February 9, 1973.

[6]Finkler, _op. cit._, p. 21.

APPENDIX A

SURVEY METHODOLOGY

The material which follows describes the New Jersey survey. Comments and suggestions, however, are given for particular municipalities and for other states that may wish to embark on similar ventures. The presentation first concerns the problems of sampling: How do we obtain a reasonable representation of the universe of housing units, municipalities, or areas of the state? Do various types of housing configurations require particular approaches? Second, how do we put together a questionnaire which will obtain the information desired? What difficulties may be anticipated, either in this initial step, or in administering the questionnaire and weighting the results?

SAMPLING DESIGN

Sampling design in this project is concerned with how to determine and sample the universe of housing developments in a state without compiling an exhaustive list of all dwelling units. The purpose of this survey and the units of observation and analysis largely decided the approach. In the New Jersey municipal cost-revenue study, a statewide household survey of housing developments was undertaken to collect demographic information to use in calculating household size and school load multipliers by housing type and by bedroom count. (Additional data were collected for other purposes, but the multipliers constituted the essential purpose of the survey.) It was intended that any municipality in New Jersey should be able to use such multipliers for cost-revenue analysis of alternative housing proposals.

The bedroom count, the housing type, the housing development, the municipality and the region of the state are potential units of analysis in a municipal cost-revenue study, but the individual household is the unit of observation for most of the data. One must interview a sufficient proportion of the households in each development to permit the development to be included in data analysis - hence the use of housing type and of sample municipalities. The sample of developments must, in turn, permit one to generalize to the sample universe of New Jersey housing for each housing type and all municipalities.

These requirements shape the definition of the sample universe and the procedure employed to select developments from it. In this case, the sample universe must be defined by housing configuration (garden apartments, townhouses, high rise apartments and single family homes), municipality, and county type or region. For reasons that will be explained later, the State of New Jersey was divided into sampling areas which were based on county aggregations defined by a multi-dimensional scaling procedure. Within these sampling areas an effort was made to sample various municipalities. The basic problem was to insure representativeness by housing type and sampling area, so that survey results would be applicable to all municipalities and housing developments not sampled.

Given the limitations of time, money and effort that confront any statewide household survey, it will usually not be feasible to compile an exhaustive list of all housing developments in a state. A truly random sample is prohibitive unless such a list already exists, though clearly if it does, it should be used for random sampling. Given this qualification, the sample universe permits a reasonably representative or typical sample using known developments in the sampling areas delineated by multidimensional scaling.

Selection of Sampling Areas

As a first step in selecting communities from which to draw samples of residential configurations, the state was divided into regions composed of counties. The basic assumption underlying this approach is that if several counties form a homogeneous region or category, then one county may be a representative surrogate for the region as a whole. Instead of having to make selections from all the counties (twenty-one in New Jersey) to insure an adequate state-wide representation, we can choose from a smaller number of regions or types (six in New Jersey). By using observations drawn from counties from each of these six regional groupings, we hoped to achieve a sampling pattern covering the main types of areas in the state in the most economical fashion.

The preferred approach would have been to classify the 567 municipalities of the state into municipal types, and then select observations on the basis of these types. However, at the time the municipal sampling had to be made, crucial variables measuring the 1970 income, education and occupation characteristics of municipal populations had not yet been made public by the U.S. Census Bureau. In order to begin the field work in the summer of 1972, the selection criteria were initially based on a county typology, for which appropriate data were available.

Since the 1970 census data are now available, those initiating current studies may find it preferable to deal directly with the municipal unit. The following methodological procedure is directly applicable.

The General Regionalization Procedure

The basic regionalization (classification or grouping) procedure is to establish the relevant properties of the objects (areas) to

317

be classified and then, to use these properties to assign the objects (areas) into classes. More specifically, classification, in the sense used here, is undertaken in reference to measurements made on the property rather than by reference to the existence or nonexistence of the property per se. Thus we are not grouping, for example, on the basis of a yes-no presence of a non-white population, but on the percent of the total population which is non-white. In general, then, to group objects on a quantitative base we require:

1. A set of objects, k_1, k_2, ... k_n, to be grouped.

2. A set of relevant attributes or properties, p_1, p_2, ... p_m.

3. A set of measures, x_{ij}, on the properties of the objects.[1]

We then have an n by m matrix, X, made up the x_{ij}'s:

$$
\begin{array}{cccccccc}
 & p & p & \cdot & \cdot & \cdot & \cdot & p_m \\
k_1 & x_{11} & x_{12} & \cdot & \cdot & \cdot & \cdot & x_{1m} \\
k_2 & x_{21} & \cdot & \cdot & \cdot & \cdot & \cdot & \cdot \\
 & \cdot & \cdot & \cdot & \cdot & \cdot & \cdot & \cdot \\
\text{Objects} \quad \cdot & \cdot & \cdot & \cdot & \cdot & \cdot & \cdot \\
 & \cdot & \cdot & \cdot & \cdot & \cdot & \cdot & \cdot \\
 & \cdot & \cdot & \cdot & \cdot & \cdot & \cdot & \cdot \\
k_n & x_{n1} & \cdot & \cdot & \cdot & \cdot & \cdot & \cdot
\end{array}
$$

The basic problem of quantitative classification involves searching this matrix for measures of appropriate groupings. The procedure most commonly employed is the minimization of within-group variance on the measures and the maximization of between-group variance.

In order to follow this procedure, it is necessary to estimate the distance - often termed the taxonomic distance - between two objects as they are measured on the m variables. Conceptually, the m variables we are using to classify form an m dimensional space in which each object is located. What is required, then, for classification is a measure of the distance between the objects as they are located in that m dimensional space. This is a problem of multidimensional scaling.[2]

The specific grouping algorithm employed in this study uses a generalized distance function based on within-group variance. For each possible pairing of objects, the means for each of the attributes are calculated and the sum of the squared deviations from the means computed. The pairing of objects which has the minimum value on this latter calculation is assumed to form a class. If, for example, we have the following situation of four objects (k) with measures on each of three properties (p)

Properties

		p_1	p_2	p_3
	k_1	2	3	4
	k_2	3	4	3
Objects	k_3	4	3	3
	k_4	4	3	2

a first step would involve pairing objects k_1 and k_2 and computing the means and squared deviations for each of the properties.

Properties

		p_1	p_2	p_3
$k_1 - k_2$	mean value	2.5	3.5	3.5
$k_1 - k_2$	squared deviation	.25(.5)	.25(.5)	.25(.5) $\Sigma = .75$

This procedure is repeated for all possible pairings (groups).

pairing	sum of squared deviations
$k_1 - k_2$	.75
$k_2 - k_3$	.50
$k_3 - k_4$	.25
$k_2 - k_4$	.75
$k_1 - k_4$	2.00
$k_1 - k_3$	1.25

In this sample, k_3 and k_4 have the most similar variable profiles as measured by the sum of squared deviations and therefore are clustered together to form a homogeneous group, defined by the mean values of

319

the pairing. The procedure is then repeated with K-1 objects using this new pairing as a new object, and the procedure is repeated until only one object or group remains.

A Caveat. In general, the regionalization procedure is a large area comprising n smaller areas which are the units of observation. For each of these n areas, m variables are recorded, describing the relevant properties. In certain cases, particularly when $n > 2m$, it is possible to refine the procedure to offset the possibility that the patterns of covariation in the m variables will overlap. Thus "when several variables display a single pattern of concomitant variation it is desirable to eliminate the redundancies, isolate this pattern and use it in the analysis instead of the several variables. m variables may contain several such patterns, say r, and the analysis is greatly simplified by reducing the dimensions of variation of the n areas from m variables to the more fundamental r basic patterns."[3] This can be accomplished through the use of a principal component factor analysis with rotation according to the varimax criterion. The varimax rotation does not affect the hierarchy of groups, which will be yielded from the grouping algorithm. However, in our analysis, the number of observations is not sufficient to undertake this procedure, and we consequently must accept the possibility that the variables have overlapping patterns of variation.

In other states, if the individual municipalities are chosen as the basic areas of observation, then the alternative methodology discussed above should be employed. This is represented in Exhibit A-1 as data flow option 3a, while the New Jersey procedure uses data flow 3 only.

New Jersey Grouping Analysis

New Jersey counties were clustered into types via a taxonomic grouping procedure entitled HGROUP.[4] Fifteen census variables were used, a number limited by the advanced census material then available. The list can and should be expanded in any replication of this study, particularly if the factor analysis option is employed (Exhibit A-2). On the basis of these variables and the grouping algorithm, the county aggregates presented in Exhibit A-3 were delineated as the major sampling areas.

Group I: Hunterdon, Sussex and Warren Counties

This group comprises three contiguous rural, low-density counties in northwest New Jersey, each just beyond commuting distance from New York City. The taxable ratables are principally concentrated in vacant land, and there are few minority group residents and

EXHIBIT A-1.   NEW JERSEY COUNTY ANALYSIS
ANALYTICAL SCHEME

Data Flow	Printed Output	Summary: Computational Procedure
1. Data Sources		m socio-economic attributes of n spatial units formed into n x m raw data matrix.[a]
2. Coded Raw Data	Raw Data List	n x m raw data matrix reproduced (punched) on computer cards.
3. Transgeneration Program	Transgenerated Data List	BMD-09S[b]: Transgeneration program: converts raw data to standardized scores. Output both printed and entered on tape (for HGROUP input).
3a. Option[c] Transgeneration Program		BMD-09s: Transgeneration program: converts size data to percentages. Output both printed and entered on tape (for BMD-03M input).
Principal Components Factor Analysis Program	Means and Standard Deviations Correlation Matrix Eigenvalues and Eigenvectors Factor Matrix Orthogonal-Rotated Factor Matrix Factor Scores	BMD-03M[d]: Factor Analysis Program Data input via tape of transgenerated data: The means and standard deviations are a by-product of the computation of the correlation matrix. From this m x m matrix, the program performs a principal component solution. The resulting m x r factor matrix is rotated via the varimax criterion so that each factor is stated in terms of those few variables with which it is most highly correlated. The measure of each factor on each spatial area is computed and presented as an n x r factor score matrix, which is printed and punched out on cards.
4. Hierarchical Grouping Analysis Program	Successive Groupings of Spatial Units. From n groups to 1 group	Program HGROUP: Given a set of n spatial areas measured on r or m different characteristics this grouping procedure, on the basis of profile similarity, utilizes the total within-groups variation as the function to be minimized.[e]

Notes: [a]U.S. Census of the Population 1970.
[b]W.J. Dixon, ed., BMD Biomedical Computer Programs (Los Angeles: University of California, 1968), pp. 421-430.
[c]This option not employed in the county analysis. It is essentially a means of reducing the number of variables to a more parsimonious set. One prerequisite to choosing this option is that $n \geq 2m$, a condition not met in the county analysis.
[d]Dixon, op. cit., pp. 169-185.
[e]Donald J. Veldman, Fortran Programming for the Behavioral Scientist (New York: Holt, Reinhart, and Winston, 1967), Chapter 12, especially pp. 308-317.

EXHIBIT A-2. NEW JERSEY COUNTY ANALYSIS VARIABLE SET
1970

1. Percent of the Population: Urban
2. Percent of the Population: Negro
3. Percent of the Population: Spanish
3. Percent of the Population: Employed in Manufacturing
5. Median Family Income
6. Percent of the Families: on Public Assistance
7. Percent of the Families: in Poverty
8. Percent of the Families: on Social Security
9. Density: People per Square Mile
10. Percent of the Population: <5 Years of Age
11. Percent of the Families: Income < $3,000
12. Percent of the Families: Income $15,000+
13. Percent Ratables: Residential and Apartment
14. Percent Ratables: Commercial and Industrial
15. Percent Ratables: Vacant Land

Notes: All variables are normalized (divided by standard
deviation).

EXHIBIT A-3. SAMPLING REGIONS

Group	*Counties*
I	Hunterdon, Sussex, Warren
IIA	Mercer, Middlesex, Monmouth, Passaic
IIB	Burlington, Camden, Gloucester
III	Bergen, Morris, Somerset, Union
IV	Atlantic, Cape May, Ocean
V	Cumberland, Salem
VI	Essex, Hudson

little public assistance to poverty families. Thus a rural northwest New Jersey region is defined by this cluster.

Group II: Burlington, Camden, Gloucester, Mercer, Middlesex, Monmouth and Passaic Counties

This is the most complex grouping that emerged in terms of spatial disparity, yet it is a valid typological category. Group II defines counties in the outer rings of the New York and Philadelphia metropolitan areas that possess similar variable profiles and similar relative spatial locations. Middlesex, Monmouth and Passaic Counties tend to mark the outer limits of the New York commutation ring. Correspondingly, Burlington, Camden and Gloucester mark the New Jersey limits of the Philadelphia region. Mercer is interpenetrated by and forms a disappearing buffer between these growing regional systems. Group II really comprises two subgroups of counties that probably perform similar functions within their respective metropolitan areas. Hence, each subgroup should constitute a sampling area. These counties are rapidly suburbanizing with young families, and have disproportionally low numbers of older people. Most of their taxable ratables are in residential structures.

Group III: Bergen, Morris, Somerset and Union Counties

The wealthy New Jersey portion of the inner ring of the New York metropolitan area is included within this clearly defined group of counties. The defining profile for this category is as follows: highly suburbanized, wealthy, a low proportion of minority group residents, minimal poverty, a low proportion of welfare families and a high proportion of residential ratables. All of these counties are among the 50 wealthiest counties in the nation.

Group IV: Atlantic, Cape May and Ocean Counties

These three contiguous counties lie along the southern Jersey shore. Still not heavily developed, these shore counties have little manufacturing employment and a generally low income population, of which a high proportion is elderly, retired and on social security. Most of the taxable ratables in this region comprise vacant land and residential structures. The region's principal focus is a resort-retirement orientation. However, Ocean County may be tending toward year-round residential development.

Group V: Cumberland and Salem Counties

A southwest New Jersey region is defined by these two counties. While a degree of manufacturing employment exists, and most ratables are in commercial and industrial land use, the resident population is generally low income, with a high proportion of minority group representation and a large number of poor families on public assistance.

Group VI: Essex and Hudson Counties

These two counties comprise New Jersey's portion of the core of the New York metropolitan region. The principal defining elements of this cluster are that it is highly urbanized and dense, with high proportions of minority group citizens, poverty and public assistance families, and a significant commercial and industrial base. The problem of using a heterogeneous area such as a county for the basic unit of observation is emphasized in the case of Essex County, where the wealthy suburbs are obscured by the over-whelming poverty of Newark. The reader should bear this problem in mind.

Sample Universe

As discussed earlier, the sample universe was defined by county cluster, municipality and housing type. A list of housing develop-ments and the number of dwelling units for three housing types was secured from the local building inspector's office for principal municipalities in each sampling area (county cluster). For single family homes, the sample universe was drawn from a larger list of new subdivision developments advertised in local and regional news-papers from June 1, 1970 to July 1, 1971.[5]

One must distinguish between the known sample universe and the effective sample universe. Because of management refusals and developments that were unusable for other reasons, the number of usable developments was considerably smaller than the number of known developments. An explanatory letter was initially sent to the manager or owner of each garden and high rise apartment develop-ment selected for sampling, in order to obtain permission to interview. (It is recommended that a letter be sent to all poten-tial sample developments to prevent any possible lag time when a new development has to be selected to replace a refusal or other lost development.) After a few instances of refusal on-site in the field, permission was confirmed by telephone before an inter-view team was sent.

The number and the percentage distribution by housing type of developments in the known and effective sample universes are pre-sented for comparison in Exhibit A-4. The percentage distribution by housing type shows a considerable difference. The largest loss rate was clearly in high rise apartments. (The reasons for this

high loss rate will be explored later.)   There was some loss in
garden apartments.

EXHIBIT A-4.   KNOWN AND EFFECTIVE SAMPLE
UNIVERSES

Housing Type	Known Sample Universe		Effective Sample Universe	
	Number	Percent	Number	Percent
Garden Apartments	97	52.7	79	56.8
Townhouses	10	5.4	9	6.5
High Rise Apartments	38	20.7	13	9.4
Single Family Homes	39	21.2	38	27.3
Total Developments	184	100.0	139	100.0

There is no feasible way to estimate the possible biases introduced
into the survey results by these differences. We can merely detail
the known sample universe, the developments eliminated because of
refusal or other reasons, and the resulting effective sample universe.
Hence, we must exercise some care when extending results based on
the sample developments to the real (but unknown) sample universe
of housing developments in New Jersey. The sample universe defined
here was never intended to be an exhaustive list of all housing
developments in New Jersey.

There is no reason to believe that the final samples are not reasonably representative and typical. The survey procedures and results
are the basis of this belief. However, the reader must remember
that the difference between the known and effective sample universes
is principally that the latter does not include developments which
refused permission to interview. We do not know the configurational,
market, demographic or attitudinal characteristics of such developments except in the case of two developments successfully surveyed
by telephone, using reverse directories or tenant lists.

Using the known sample universe, we can examine the distribution of
the four housing types in New Jersey. The distributions of the
known and effective sample universes by sampling area are given in
Exhibits A-5 and A-6 respectively. Garden apartments are distributed

EXHIBIT A-5. DISTRIBUTION OF KNOWN SAMPLE UNIVERSE BY SAMPLING AREA

Sampling Area	County	Garden Apartments Number of Developments	Garden Apartments Number of Units	Townhouses Number of Developments	Townhouses Number of Units	High Rise Number of Developments	High Rise Number of Units	Single Family Number of Developments	Single Family Number of Units	Total Number of Developments	Total Number of Units
I	Hunterdon	7	647	---	---	---	---	---	---	7	647
	Sussex	---	---	---	---	---	---	1	400	1	400
	Warren	---	---	---	---	---	---	1	58	1	58
	Total	7	647	---	---	---	---	2	458	9	1,105
IIA	Mercer	8	2,366	1	608	---	---	---	---	9	2,974
	Middlesex	7	715	3	880	2	413	---	---	12	2,008
	Monmouth	---	---	1	164	---	---	---	---	1	164
	Passaic	---	---	---	---	---	---	---	---	---	---
	Total	15	3,081	5	1,652	2	413	---	---	22	5,146
IIB	Burlington	---	---	2	682	---	---	7	1,015	9	1,697
	Camden	9	1,603	---	---	13	1,756	3	724	25	4,083
	Gloucester	---	---	---	---	---	---	4	1,042	4	1,042
	Total	9	1,603	2	682	13	1,756	14	2,781	38	6,822
III	Bergen	28	6,937	---	---	21	4,543	---	---	21	4,543
	Morris	1	369	---	---	---	---	---	---	28	6,937
	Somerset	---	---	---	---	---	---	---	---	1	369
	Union	---	---	---	---	---	---	---	---	---	---
	Total	29	7,306	---	---	21	4,543	---	---	50	11,849
IV	Atlantic	---	---	1	75	---	---	7	241	8	316
	Cape May	---	---	---	---	---	---	---	---	---	---
	Ocean	15	1,136	2	333	---	---	14	3,497	31	4,966
	Total	15	1,136	3	408	---	---	21	3,738	39	5,282
V	Cumberland	21	1,717	---	---	---	---	2	165	23	1,882
	Salem	---	---	---	---	---	---	---	---	---	---
	Total	21	1,717	---	---	---	---	2	165	23	1,882
VI	Essex	1	243	---	---	2	525	---	---	3	768
	Hudson	---	---	---	---	---	---	---	---	---	---
	Total	1	243	---	---	2	525	---	---	3	768
	TOTAL	97	15,733	10	2,742	38	7,237	39	7,142	184	32,854

EXHIBIT A-6. DISTRIBUTION OF EFFECTIVE SAMPLE UNIVERSE BY SAMPLING AREA

Sampling Area	County	Garden Apartments		Townhouses		High Rise		Single Family		Total	
		Number of Developments	Number of Units	Number of Developments	Number of Units	Number of Developments	Number of Units	Number of Developments	Number of Units	Number of Developments	Number of Units
I	Hunterdon	4	339	-	-	-	-	-	-	4	339
	Sussex	-	-	-	-	-	-	1	400	1	400
	Warren	-	-	-	-	-	-	1	58	1	58
	Total	4	339	-	-	-	-	2	458	6	797
IIA	Mercer	5	1,635	1	608	-	-	-	-	6	2,243
	Middlesex	7	715	2	58	1	263	-	-	10	1,036
	Monmouth	-	-	1	164	-	-	-	-	1	164
	Passaic	-	-	-	-	-	-	-	-	-	-
	Total	12	2,350	4	830	1	263	-	-	17	3,443
IIB	Burlington	-	-	2	682	-	-	6	1,000	8	1,682
	Camden	9	1,603	-	-	9	835	3	724	21	3,162
	Gloucester	-	-	-	-	-	-	4	1,042	4	1,042
	Total	9	1,603	2	682	9	835	13	2,766	33	5,886
III	Bergen	-	-	-	-	2	544	-	-	2	544
	Morris	27	6,807	-	-	-	-	-	-	27	6,807
	Somerset	1	369	-	-	-	-	-	-	1	369
	Union	-	-	-	-	-	-	-	-	-	-
	Total	28	7,176	-	-	2	544	-	-	30	7,720
IV	Atlantic	-	-	1	75	-	-	7	241	8	316
	Cape May	-	-	-	-	-	-	-	-	-	-
	Ocean	7	336	2	333	-	-	14	3,497	23	4,166
	Total	7	336	3	408	-	-	21	3,738	31	4,482
V	Cumberland	18	1,377	-	-	-	-	2	165	20	1,542
	Salem	-	-	-	-	-	-	-	-	-	-
	Total	18	1,377	-	-	-	-	2	165	20	1,542
VI	Essex	1	243	-	-	1	250	-	-	2	493
	Hudson	-	-	-	-	-	-	-	-	-	-
	Total	1	243	-	-	1	250	-	-	2	493
	TOTAL	79	13,424	9	1,920	13	1,892	38	7,127	139	24,363

uniformly across the county groups. Townhouses, by contrast, are concentrated in county groups IIA, IIB and IV, the southern coastal and middle counties of New Jersey. Although few in number, such developments are an increasingly prevalent form of residential construction. High rise apartments - typically luxury units - are concentrated in Bergen and Essex (Group III) and Camden (Group IIB) Counties. Bergen and Essex are peripheral to New York City, and Camden borders Philadelphia. There are two known high rise developments in Middlesex County (Group IIA). New single family homes selling for less than $30,000 are a rare phenomenon in northern metropolitan New Jersey. There are two such developments in northwest Sussex and Warren Counties (Group I). Most are to be found in four southern counties: Burlington and Camden (Group IIB) and Atlantic and Ocean (Group IV).

Sample Size

The sample size of a survey is the desired number and distribution of households by housing type. For our purposes, a household consists of all persons resident in a dwelling unit. We shall use "household" and "dwelling unit" interchangeably. In order to secure the necessary demographic data for the calculation of the multipliers, 7,500 households were sampled in the four housing types previously mentioned: garden apartments, townhouses, high rise apartments and single family homes selling for under $30,000. This total sample size was effectively dictated by the resources available to the study. The price limitation on single family homes was introduced to permit direct comparison to relatively similar housing expenditures in the other three housing types. It should be emphasized, therefore, that the single family homes referred to in this study are highly atypical of New Jersey. Generally, such housing costs considerably more than $30,000.

The interviews were allocated among the four housing types according to the formula in Exhibit A-7. The garden apartment subsample was to include approximately 1,100 dwelling units which had originally been surveyed in 1963.[6] This replication permitted us to examine the question of change in demographic characteristics over time.

Sample size - and in this case its distribution by housing type - is determined by two factors, both of which are completely independent of the size of the sample universe. The first factor is sampling error. The sample size must be large enough to insure some predetermined level of accuracy in the interpretation of the results. In other words, how sure are we that the survey results are not simply random, the result of chance, and hence, inaccurate? The required sample size by level of accuracy can be found in virtually any textbook on survey research.

EXHIBIT A-7.   SAMPLE HOUSEHOLDS BY HOUSING TYPE

3,600	Garden Apartments	48.0%
1,700	Townhouses	22.7%
1,600	High Rise Apartments	21.3%
600	Single Family Homes	8.0%
7,500	Total Units	100.0%

The stipulated sample size and its distribution fall well within an acceptable level of sampling error. Exhibit A-8 reports the number of households which we attempted to sample and the field results (in terms of households successfully interviewed and not discarded from data analysis), as well as their distributions by housing type.

EXHIBIT A-8.   HOUSEHOLDS SURVEYED BY HOUSING TYPE

Housing Type	Attempted		Successful	
	Number	Percent	Number	Percent
Garden Apartments	3,611	48.2	1,852	44.8
Townhouses	1,709	22.8	1,144	27.7
High Rise Apartments	1,562	20.9	709	17.2
Single Family Homes	607	8.1	426	10.3
Total Units	7,489	100.0	4,131	100.0

Notice that the percentage breakdown of households actually surveyed (Exhibit A-8) is virtually the same as that stipulated for the sample (Exhibit A-7). However, the percentage breakdown of successful

329

interviews retained for data analysis is different. The percentage
of garden apartments and high rise apartments is below that stipulated, while the percentage of townhouses and single family homes
is too high. These deviations are not particularly significant
problems for data analysis. The stipulated sample size is intended
as a guide rather than a formal design requirement.

The second factor affecting required size is the planned breakdown
of the survey results during tabulation. Each statistical technique has its own requirements for number of cases. These considerations may require a sample size larger than the minimum required by the laws of sampling error. In data analysis using the
number and distribution of successfully interviewed households reported, we encountered no difficulties at the housing type level.
Inevitably, there were some difficulties at the municipality and
development levels. For individual questions in the survey instrument, there were, of course, analysis problems. For example, there
are not really enough Spanish-speaking or black households in the
sample to permit much useful analysis of their characteristics and
attitudes. This problem is not due to an error in the survey design
but more properly reflects the fact that developments in New Jersey
suburban communities generally do not contain enough such households
for analysis.

Sampling Procedure

In principle, the general aim of the sampling procedure should be
to provide for an adequate representation of each housing type from
each sampling area. In fact, however, the non-uniform geographic
distribution of all housing types except garden apartments did not
permit such a sampling procedure. Therefore, we selected municipalities from the sampling areas which had the appropriate housing
types. Different sampling procedures had to be employed for each
housing type, and these procedures are discussed below. The distribution of the sample is given by sampling area in Exhibit A-9 and
by municipality in Exhibit A-10.

A. Garden Apartments

This housing type is fairly uniformly distributed across the county
groups. Therefore, the developments sampled in each municipality
were randomly selected so that the number of units to be sampled in
that community approximated the desired proportional representation.
In almost all instances, management cooperation was essential for
door-to-door interviewing in garden apartments. If the management
denied us permission to interview, another development was randomly
selected. If, at the end of the sampling, we found that we still
needed the refused development, we attempted to employ reverse

EXHIBIT A-9. DISTRIBUTION OF SAMPLE DEVELOPMENTS BY SAMPLING AREA

Sampling Area	County	Garden Apartments		Townhouses		Single Family		High Rise		Total	
		Number of Developments	Number of Units	Number of Developments	Number of Units	Number of Developments	Number of Units	Number of Developments	Number of Units	Number of Developments	Number of Units
I	Hunterdon	2	171	-	---	-	---	-	---	2	171
	Sussex	-	---	-	---	-	---	-	---	-	---
	Warren	-	---	-	---	1	58	-	---	1	58
	Total	2	171	-	---	1	58	-	---	3	229
IIA	Mercer	3	353	1	608	-	---	-	---	4	961
	Middlesex	7	715	-	---	-	---	1	263	8	978
	Monmouth	-	---	1	164	-	---	-	---	1	164
	Passaic	-	---	-	---	-	---	-	---	-	---
	Total	10	1,068	2	772	-	---	1	263	13	2,103
IIB	Burlington	-	---	1	604	1	104	-	---	2	708
	Camden	3	254	-	---	-	---	4	505	7	759
	Gloucester	-	---	-	---	1	77	-	---	1	77
	Total	3	254	1	604	2	181	4	505	10	1,544
III	Bergen	-	---	-	---	-	---	2	544	2	544
	Morris	8	996	-	---	-	---	-	---	8	996
	Somerset	1	369	-	---	-	---	-	---	1	369
	Union	-	---	-	---	-	---	-	---	-	---
	Total	9	1,365	-	---	-	---	2	544	11	1,909
IV	Atlantic	-	---	-	---	1	98	-	---	1	98
	Cape May	-	---	-	---	-	---	-	---	-	---
	Ocean	2	262	2	333	2	105	-	---	6	700
	Total	2	262	2	333	3	203	-	---	7	798
V	Cumberland	4	248	-	---	2	165	-	---	6	413
	Salem	-	---	-	---	-	---	-	---	-	---
	Total	4	248	-	---	2	165	-	---	6	413
VI	Essex	1	243	-	---	-	---	1	250	2	493
	Hudson	-	---	-	---	-	---	-	---	-	---
	Total	1	243	-	---	-	---	1	250	2	493
	TOTAL	31	3,611	5	1,709	8	607	8	1,562	52	7,489

EXHIBIT A-10. DISTRIBUTION OF SAMPLE DEVELOPMENTS BY MUNICIPALITY

Municipality	County	Garden Apartments		Townhouses		High Rise Apartments		Single Family Homes		Total	
		Number of Developments	Number of Units	Number of Developments	Number of Units	Number of Developments	Number of Units	Number of Developments	Number of Units	Number of Developments	Number of Units
Brick Twp.	Ocean							1	45	1	45
Cherry Hill Twp.	Camden					4	505			4	505
Collingswood Boro.	Camden	2	177							2	177
Dover Twp.	Ocean	2	262					1	60	3	322
East Windsor Twp.	Mercer	3	353	1	608					4	961
Edison Twp.	Middlesex	2	40							2	40
Flemington Boro.	Hunterdon	2	171							2	171
Fort Lee Boro.	Bergen					2	544			2	544
Franklin Twp.	Somerset	1	369							1	369
Freehold Boro.	Monmouth			1	164					1	164
Gloucester Twp.	Camden							1	104	1	104
Haddon Twp.	Camden	1	77							1	77
Highland Park Boro.	Middlesex	5	675							5	675
Lakewood Twp.	Ocean			2	333					2	333
Lopatcong Twp.	Warren							1	58	1	58
Monroe Twp.	Gloucester							1	77	1	77
Newark City	Essex	1	243			1	250			2	493
New Brunswick City	Middlesex					1	263			1	263
Northfield City	Atlantic							1	98	1	98
Parsippany-Troy Hills Twp.	Morris	8	996							8	996
Vineland City	Cumberland	4	248					2	165	6	413
Willingboro Twp.	Burlington			1	604					1	604
TOTAL		31	3,611	5	1,709	8	1,562	8	607	52	7,489

directories. Given the necessity of saturating the entire development - all dwelling units in the complex had to be contacted - the
actual number of units contacted in a particular municipality was
often a few units below or above the pre-interview sampling totals,
which were based on proportional representation by municipality of
the total number of garden apartments in the subsample universe for
that housing type.

We included a replication of a 1963 study of garden apartment developments (1,100 dwelling units or 30.6 percent of the subsample).
The developments involved are described in Exhibit A-11. All are
located in Middlesex County (Group IIA), except Pine Grove Manor,
which is in Somerset County (Group III). We also stipulated that
a NJHFA 236 project be surveyed. University Court in Newark was
chosen for this purpose.

The refusal rate by management varied considerably by community.
There was a particularly high refusal rate in Flemington Borough
and Dover Township. In Flemington, three (308 units) out of seven
developments (647 units) refused (47.6 percent of the units). In
Dover Township, we were denied admission by six (832 units) out
of 14 developments (1,136 units), or 73.2 percent of the units.
Also in Dover, two other developments were seasonal and another
development (or its management) simply could not be located, for
a total of 184 units (16.2 percent). Hence, we were left with
only 74 units (6.5 percent) in four small developments that could
be sampled using door-to-door interviewing. These few units were
not sufficient; we had already sampled one development there
(Princess Jane Apartments with 46 units or 4 percent) and felt
we had to interview in this township because of its growth characteristics. Dover had been programmed as one of several case
studies of growth pressures and municipal finance. Therefore, we
sampled a large development in the community (Presidential Apartments with 216 units or 19 percent) entirely by telephone using
reverse directories.

In Vineland, two large developments (232 units) refused, and we
sampled four smaller developments. We also discovered that Waldorf
Garden Apartments (108 units) was condemned. In East Windsor, one
development of 470 units refused. On the other hand, in Parsippany-
Troy Hills Township, out of 28 developments, only one refused permission.

B. Townhouses

This type of development is a relative newcomer to the New Jersey
scene, but is presently enjoying a construction boom. Our sample,
therefore, includes practically all of the completed developments.
Those excepted are the smaller or substantially unfinished developments in county groups where there was already adequate representation. In one case, only 23 out of 90 units were completed, and

EXHIBIT A-11. GARDEN APARTMENT DEVELOPMENTS SURVEYED IN BOTH 1963 AND 1972

County	County Type	Municipality	Development	Number of Units Contacted in 1963	Number of Units Contacted in 1972*
Middlesex	IIA	Highland Park Borough	1. Orchard Gardens	209	201
			2. Montgomery Apartments	192	185
			3. Adelaide Gardens**	200	198
			4. Old Queens (Levy Apts.)+	30	46
			5. Riverview Apts.++	48	45
		Edison Township	6. 311 Division and Green-wood	20	20
			7. Penn and Ovington	20	20
Somerset	III	Franklin Township	8. Pine Grove Manor	398	369
		TOTALS		1,117	1,084
		Totals Excluding No. 8		719	715

Notes: *Differences in number of units between 1963 and 1972 is due to different field procedures.

**Management refused cooperation in 1963.

+This development was called Levy Apartments in 1963 but was later renamed Old Queens. It had 46 units in 1963, but only 30 were complete at the time of that survey.

++Cooperation was refused by the management in 1972 and interviews were conducted using telephone numbers obtained through reverse directories.

334

even these were not yet fully occupied. The other excluded developments were of 35, 75 and 78 units each. Since townhouses are individually owned, generally no prior arrangements had to be made for interviewing. However, in one major development of 822 units, we did require permission which was refused. The development is an elderly retirement village restricted to occupancy by those 55 years of age or older. Entrance is strictly controlled.

C. High Rise Apartments

The sampling procedure used for this housing type was similar to that for garden apartments. The developments sampled in each municipality were randomly selected. There was, however, an extremely high management refusal rate for high rise developments which required us to alter our technique. The results are comparable, however, with some communities oversampled (the number of dwelling units sampled in Fort Lee and Cherry Hill is approximately the same). Zion Towers in Newark was selected because it is an NJHFA 236 project.

High rise developments proved to be by far the most difficult housing type in which to conduct door-to-door interviewing. These generally luxury developments typically have strict management security and doormen. Management cooperation was imperative for interviewing because of the security system. The refusal rate was extraordinarily high. For example, in Fort Lee, 15 (3,119 dwelling units) out of 21 (4,543 units) developments (that is, 68.7 percent) refused us permission to interview. In addition, one development had not been completed and three others could not be located (880 units or 19.4 percent). In Cherry Hill, four (921 units) out of 13 (1,756 units) developments (52.4 percent) denied permission. In New Brunswick, one of the two high rise developments (150 units) refused. The other development would not permit door-to-door interviewing but did provide a tenant list for telephone interviewing.

D. Single Family Homes

The sampling of single family homes was restricted to units with base selling prices of less than $30,000. Due to the time lags between advertisement of sale, construction and occupancy, the sample was drawn from a comprehensive list of such New Jersey developments with houses for sale between June 1, 1970 and July 1, 1971.[7] This procedure was followed to insure that, by the time of our interviewing, homes would have been occupied for some time, and residents would have some basis for evaluating municipal services. In several instances, these developments were still in the process of construction. Developments were randomly selected for sampling, subject to two conditions:

1. No development with less than 20 finished and occupied homes could be surveyed because of time and financial constraints;

2. No development which was a new section of an older development (e.g., new sections of Levitt's development in Willingboro) would be interviewed because of the difficulty of separating sections.

This housing type was the easiest to survey. There were no major problems encountered in the field administration of the questionnaire schedules. Because of individual ownership, there was no need to obtain prior approval. Typically, highly cooperative housewives were found at home during the door-to-door interviewing.

QUESTIONNAIRE DESIGN

The concept and structure of the questionnaire (or interview schedule) to be administered in the field depends upon what information the surveyor wishes to collect. The coding procedures used should be determined in advance to facilitate analysis of the data. A sample of our questionnaire is included as an addendum to this appendix. We sought to obtain nine general kinds of information. We wanted to know about: (1) dwelling unit characteristics (number of bedrooms, rent or market value, etc.); (2) household formation and mobility; (3) household demographic characteristics; (4) number of school age children and their distribution by school level; (5) respondent attitudes toward municipal services; (6) respondent satisfaction with the quality of their housing; (7) household shopping patterns (intended as a possible measure of the secondary impact of housing developments on the local economy); (8) household income and employment characteristics;[8] (9) household work-trip patterns. In addition, certain basic questionnaire identification material was included on the interview form.

Questionnaire Identification System

In any survey accounting system a reliable questionnaire identification system must be established. In this case, an identification system consisting of three types of codes was used. The system served to identify questionnaire, housing type and housing development. Each questionnaire form was given a unique four-digit identification number (question 1 on the interview schedule) which was repeated on the cover sheet. The number sequence started from 0001 (we expected a total of about 7,500 questionnaires). A one-digit code was used to identify the housing type of the dwelling unit surveyed: 1 for garden apartments, 2 for townhouses, 3 for high rise apartments, and 4 for single family homes (question 2 on the interview schedule). Each housing development was assigned a unique two-digit code starting from 01 (question 3 on the interview schedule).

The underlying principle of the identification system is that these three codes are used in conjunction. Every dwelling unit surveyed is identified uniquely, as well as by housing development and housing type. A system of this sort is imperative and must be strictly adhered to for efficient record-keeping and proper conduct of field surveying. Otherwise, there is a definite possibility of missing or reinterviewing large blocks of dwelling units. The same information is also important in data processing.

The actual identification system roughly approximated this ideal but a number of errors occurred, which is inevitable when three items of information are being recorded on 7,500 questionnaires which are in the hands of a large number of different persons. Errors result primarily for the following reasons: (1) accounting mistakes on the part of the control staff; (2) mistakes in the administration of the survey by the field staff; (3) changes in developments surveyed.

The Interview Schedule

As already indicated, the first three questions on the interview schedule contained questionnaire identification material. An additional piece of identification information was recorded in question 30. The interviewer was asked to check the method of interview (whether field canvass or telephone callback).

Dwelling Unit Characteristics

The first block of substantive data was concerned with dwelling unit characteristics. We were primarily interested in the number of bedrooms in each dwelling unit (question 4), which is essential for the calculation of household size and school load multipliers. Efficiencies were distinguished from one-bedroom units. For garden apartments and high rise apartments, we obtained the respondent's estimate of monthly rent without utilities (base rent), recorded in question 5a as a three-digit number or as "no response/don't know." Estimated market value for townhouse and single family homes was recorded in question 5b using $5,000 categories up to $50,000.

Household Formation and Mobility

Information about household formation and mobility may be important in predicting the socioeconomic composition and demographic characteristics of alternative housing proposals for particular geographic

areas of New Jersey. Question 6 recorded how long the household
had been at its present address in number of years. Zero to 11
months was recorded as zero years, 12 to 17 months as one year,
18 to 29 months as two years, 30 to 41 months as three years and
so on. A two-digit number (00, 01, 02, etc.) was recorded to permit long-term residents (ten or more years at the same address)
to be identified. The city and state where the household previously
resided was obtained (question 7 of the interview schedule). A
previous residence was identified as the same municipality, a major
city in New Jersey (defined as Newark, Jersey City, Paterson,
Elizabeth, Camden and Trenton), the balance of New Jersey, out
of state or outside the continental United States.

In question 8, the previous type of housing occupied by the household was recorded. The category "other" (to be specified) was used
for respondents who indicated that they had lived with relatives
or in-laws, in institutions, government or company housing, or under
other atypical circumstances. The category "group quarters" included
barracks, dormitories, fraternities and similar housing. Single
family houses included both attached and unattached owner-occupied
structures, while 2-3-4 family houses was intended to apply only
to rental units. We also determined whether the household had
owned or rented that previous housing (question 9 of the interview
schedule). The category "other" was again intended for respondents
who had lived with relatives or in-laws or in some similar circumstances.

Household Characteristics

The next block of information in the questionnaire concerns household demographic characteristics. We were most interested in the
total household size ("the total number of people living in the
household") recorded in question 10. For the purposes of this
survey, a household was defined simply as all persons residing
together in a single dwelling unit. It is important for the interviewer to establish whether the respondent has included children
temporarily away at college, work, in the army, etc. Such persons
should be included as members of the household if they permanently
reside at that address. The sex of head of household was reported
in question 11. We defined the head of household as the primary
wage earner. The marital status of the head of household was also
determined (question 12). The category "other" (to be specified)
was used to indicate related persons residing together who were not
married, separated, divorced or widowed. The category "non-related"
includes any two or more non-related single individuals sharing a
dwelling unit (such as students, secretaries or airline stewardesses).

Later in the questionnaire, we obtained the age of head of household
by category (question 21) and his highest level of education by
category (question 22). Junior college was defined as two or more

years of college without a B.A. or B.S. degree; high school was
defined as high school diploma or less than two years of college.
College included working on master's degree; Ph.D. or equivalent
included medical and legal degrees. In question 29, we inquired
as to the ethnicity of the respondent. The category "other" (to
be specified) included anyone who was not black, white or Spanish-
speaking (an important minority group in some New Jersey municipalities).

School Age Children

Another primary concern of the survey was the estimation of school
load (number of public school children per dwelling unit). This
information was recorded in questions 13 a-e and 14. First, we
determined the total number of children under 18 years of age in
the household, whether in school or not (recorded as a two-digit
number in question 13a). Then, in succession, we broke the total
number of children into prekindergarten, public kindergarten, public
grammar school (grades one through eight), and public high school
(grades nine through twelve) grade categories (questions 13b-f).
Finally, we asked how many children attended private or parochial
schools at any level (question 14). These data permit us to determine the number and distribution by school level of school age
children in public and private or parochial schools. If desired,
of course, the surveyor could obtain the name, age and grade of
each child under the age of 18. More precise data could be obtained in this manner.

Consumer Satisfaction with Municipal Services

A large block of information concerning respondent attitudes toward
the delivery of municipal services was requested in questions 15
(which had seven parts) and 16. For each of seven municipal services, the respondent was asked to state his attitude according to
a five-point scale: very good, good, neutral, poor, very poor (or
don't know). The seven services were in sequence: public education,
police protection, fire protection, recreation, sanitation and
street cleaning, libraries, public health and emergency services.
Notice that public transportation was not included in this list of
services. The "no answer/don't know" category was used for persons
who had had no experience or contact with a particular municipal
service or could not decide the issue. Clearly, however, there is
a difference between one's evaluation of a particular service and
his willingness or perception of the need to put money into improving that service. One may think that recreational opportunities
are dreadful but want to allocate even more of a limited budget to
an already high quality police department because the highest return
to public expenditure is in police protection. Therefore, in question 16, we asked the respondent to choose which municipal service

339

"most pressingly needed" improvements. Transportation and the category "other" (to be specified) were added to the seven cited services.
It is important to realize that "transportation" and "public transportation" may not convey the same meaning to different respondents.
Transportation may well include street repairs, availability of high
speed and limited access roads, safety devices and so on.

Housing Satisfaction

In questions 17, 18 and 19, we inquired as to the respondent's
satisfaction with the quality of his housing. Question 17 simply
asked the respondent to rate his housing satisfaction according to
the five-point scale: very good, good, neutral, poor, very poor
(or don't know). In the next two questions, he was asked to specify the major defect in, respectively, his dwelling unit and his
housing development.

Shopping Patterns

One possible measure of the secondary impact of a housing development on a local community's economy is the percentage of shopping
for basic consumer items that is done in the local community.
Question 20 asked the respondent to report what percent (by quar-
tiles) of shopping he did in the municipality for food, clothing,
house furnishings and gasoline. This information is, of course,
unspecified as to dollar value, but it provides some indication of
whether a housing development provides only a little or a good deal
of business for local retail establishments.

Income and Employment Characteristics

Several questions dealt with household income and employment.
Questions 23 and 24 ascertained the specific occupation (title
and precise description) of both the primary wage earner (head
of household) and any second wage earner in the household. Unemployed, student, retired, housewife, etc., were acceptable occupational categories. Occupational descriptions must be specific;
for example, "working in a hospital" is not sufficient. The
appropriate answer should be the kind of work the respondent is
doing in the hospital. Is the respondent a doctor, nurse, secre-
tary, janitor or what? In question 24, a "yes" or "no" response
was recorded for whether there was another wage earner in the
household and then the specific occupation was obtained. Total
household income (for all members of the household) was recorded
by $5,000 categories up to $50,000 in question 26. Then we sought
more specific income data for the elderly (defined as 65 years of
age or older) and for residents of Zion Towers (the 236 high rise
project in Newark). Elderly respondents were asked what percentage of their total household income was derived from social security
benefits (question 27). Zion Towers residents were asked the same
question (question 28a). In addition, they were asked how long

they had been receiving welfare payments (question 28b). For both, zero to 11 months was recorded as zero years, 12 to 17 months as one year, 18 to 29 months as two years, 30 to 41 months as three years, and so on.

Work-Trip Patterns

Household work-trip information was obtained in question 25. The respondent was asked to state his place (city) of employment and the estimated mileage traveled from home to work for both the principal and average secondary worker. Distance was recorded in five-mile categories up to 15 miles.

Master Coding Form

In conducting a large-scale survey of this sort, a master coding form is essential. Our questionnaire, for example, permits "other" responses and certain open-ended questions. In such cases, coding decisions must be made before the questionnaires can be keypunched and tabulated. A master coding form is necessary to coordinate decisions taken in coding, especially when several coders are involved. Exhibit A-12 presents our master coding form.

The occupation of the head of household (primary wage earner) and any secondary wage earner were recorded as open-ended responses in questions 23 and 24, respectively. Each interviewer was instructed to obtain as precise a title and description of the actual job as possible. As explained previously, occupational descriptions must be specific in nature. These open-ended responses were then hand coded.

We employed a modified version of a U.S. Bureau of the Census format used at the state level for all male and female workers over the age of 14, and used it to categorize primary and secondary workers, males and females. Generally speaking, we divided all occupations into seven groups: professional, technical and kindred occupations; managers, officials and proprietors; clerical, sales and kindred occupations; craftsmen, foremen and kindred workers; operatives and kindred workers; service workers; and laborers. As mentioned, this approach is a modification of the Census system. We discovered no farmers or farm managers and no farm laborers and foremen. Then we added categories for retired persons, students, unemployed persons, housewives and non-respondents. Due to the wording in question 24, an additional category was used to cover "not employed," a category which did not exist in question 23.

Question Number	Question Description	Column Number	Variable Number	Code Number and Description
1	Interview ID Number	1-4	1	Four-digit interview identification number
2	Type of unit	5	2	[1] Garden apartment [2] Townhouse [3] High rise apartment [4] Single family home
3	Development name	6-8	3	Column 6 should always be blank! Always two digits!

[01] Highpoint
[02] Kingsley Square
[03] Twin Rivers
[04] Rittenhouse Park
[05] Coventry Square
[06] Orchard Gardens
[07] Montgomery Apartments
[08] Adelaide Gardens
[09] Pine Grove Manor
[10] Redstone Apartments
[11] Partridge Run
[12] Knoll Manor
[13] University Court
[14] Wayne Gardens
[15] Marina Park Apartments
[16] Park Lake Village
[17] Chestnut Willow
[18] Hampton Arms
[19] Beverwyck Gardens
[20] Clearview Gardens
[21] Lincoln Gardens
[22] Riverview Apartments A
[23] Old Queens
[24] 311 Division and Greenwood
[25] Park and Ovington
[26]
[27] Madison Arms Apartments
[28]
[29] Princess Jane Apartments
[30] Presidential Apartments
[31] Cuthbert Manor
[32] Windsor Castle
[33] Vineland Gardens
[34] Woodstock Village Apartments
[35] Thornberry
[36] Brentwood
[37] Horizon Towers North
[38] Somerset
[39] Plaza Towers
[40] Zion Towers
[41] Colonial East
[42] Provincial West
[43] Northbridge
[44] Colony House
[45] Brakeley Park
[46] Meadowbrook Gardens
[47] Flemington Arms
[48] Nob Hill
[49] Friar's Cove
[50] Drum Point Gardens
[51] Olympic Estates
[52] Kimberley West
[53] Brookside Farms
[54] Fox Chase

(Continued)

Question Number	Question Description	Column Number	Variable Number	Code Number and Description
4	Number of bedrooms	9	4	[0] Efficiency (studio) [1] One [2] Two [3] Three [4] Four [5] Five or more [9] No Response/Don't Know
5a	Monthly rent without <u>utilities</u>	10-12	5	Blank for single-family homes and townhouses unless rented; coded for garden and high rise apartments.
		13	6	[9] If No Response/Don't Know for a rented unit; otherwise blank.
5b	Estimated <u>present</u> market value	14	7	Blank if a rental unit. [1] Less than $5,000 [2] $ 5,000 - 9,999 [3] $10,000 - 14,999 [4] $15,000 - 19,999 [5] $20,000 - 24,999 [6] $25,000 - 34,999 [7] $35,000 - 49,999 [8] $50,000 or more [9] No Response/Don't Know

6	Number of years at present address	15-16	8	[0] Less than one year
				    (0 to 11 months)
				[1] 1 year
				    (12 to 17 months)
				[2] 2 years
				    (18 to 29 months)
				[3] 3 years
				    (30 to 41 months)
				etc.

7	Previous residence	17	9	[1] Same Municipality
				[2] Major N.J. City:
				    Newark
				    Jersey City
				    Paterson
				    Elizabeth
				    Camden
				    Trenton
				[3] N.J. Balance
				[4] Out of State
				[5] Outside the Continental U.S.

8	Previous type of unit	18	10	[1] Single-family house (attached or otherwise) [2] 2-3-4 family house [3] Apartment [4] Group quarters [5] Other (specify) [9] No Response/Don't Know
9	Previously owner or renter	19	11	[1] Owner [2] Renter [3] Other (specify) [4] No Response/Don't Know

(Continued)

343

Question Number	Question Description	Column Number	Variable Number	Code Number and Description
10	Number of people in household	20	12	Actual Number [1-9] 1-9 [A] 10 or more
11	Head of household	21	13	[1] Male [2] Female [9] Don't Know/No Response
12	Marital status	22	14	[1] Single or non-related household [2] Married [3] Separated [4] Divorced [5] Widowed [6] Other (specify) [9] No Response/Don't Know
13a	Children under 18 yrs. of age	23-24	15	Actual number coded [00] - [99]
13b	Prekindergarten age	25	16	Actual number coded [0] - [9]
13c	Public school kindergarten	26	17	"
13d	Public grammar school	27	18	"
13e	Public high school	28	19	"
14	Private or parochial school	29	20	"
15	Municipal services			
(a)	Public education	30	21	[1] Very good [2] Good [3] Neutral [4] Poor [5] Very Poor [9] No Response/Don't Know
(b)	Police	31	22	"
(c)	Fire department	32	23	"
(d)	Recreation	33	24	"
(e)	Sanitation and street cleaning	34	25	"
(f)	Libraries	35	26	"
(g)	Public health and emergency services	36	27	"
16	Municipal service most in need of improvements	37	28	[0] Transportation [1] Public education [2] Police [3] Fire department [4] Recreation

344

(Continued)

Question Number	Question Description	Column Number	Variable Number	Code Number and Description
				[5] Sanitation and street cleaning
				[6] Libraries
				[7] Public health and emergency services
				[8] Other (specify)
				[9] No Response/Don't Know
				[10] No improvements needed
17	Overall housing satisfaction	38	29	[1] Very good
				[2] Good
				[3] Neutral
				[4] Poor
				[5] Very Poor
				[9] No Response/Don't Know
18	Housing unit defect	39	30	[9] "No" defect
				[1] Dwelling unit too small
				[2] More backyard space
				[3] Utility systems faulty
				[4] Construction defects
				[5] Storm drainage defects (flooding)
				[6] Attached houses
				[7] Noise
				[8] Neighbors (people)
				[10] Maintenance
				[11] Landscaping
				[12] Poor building materials
				[H] Miscellaneous
				[I] No Response/Don't Know
19	Housing development defect	40	31	[9] "No" defect
				[1] Maintenance
				[2] Management
				[3] Insufficient recreational facilities
				[4] Poor parking (not enough)
				[5] Landscaping
				[6] More open space needed
				[7] Storm drainage defects (flooding)
				[8] Neighbors (people)
				[10] Construction
				[11] Density
				[12] Faulty sewage/septic system
				[H] Miscellaneous
				[I] No Response/Don't Know
20	Shopping %			
(a)	Food	41	32	[1] 0 - 25%
				[2] 25 - 50%
				[3] 50 - 75%
				[4] 75 -100%
				[9] No Response/Don't Know
(b)	Clothing	42	33	"
(c)	House furnishings	43	34	"
(d)	Gasoline	44	35	"

(Continued)

Question Number	Question Description	Column Number	Variable Number	Code Number and Description
21	Age (head of household)	45	36	[1] Under 21 [2] 21-25 [3] 26-35 [4] 36-49 [5] 50-64 [6] 65 and over [9] No Response/Don't Know
22	Education (head of household)	46	37	[1] Less than high school (diploma) (1-3 yrs.) [2] High school (diploma) (1 yr. of college) [3] Junior college (2-3 yrs.of college) (business or trade school) [4] College (BA/BS) (working on MA) [5] Masters degree (working on Ph.D.) [6] Ph.D. or equivalent
23	Occupation (head of household)	47	38	[1] Professional [2] Managerial [3] Clerical [4] Craftsman [5] Operatives [6] Service workers [7] Laborers [8] Retired [9] Students [A] Unemployed [B] Housewives [H] No Response
24	Occupation (2nd worker)	48	39	" [I] Not employed
25	Work travel distance			
(a)	Head of household	49	40	[1] Less than 5 miles [2] 5-10 miles [3] 11-15 miles [4] More than 15 miles [5] No travel [9] No Response/Don't Know
(b)	Second worker	50	41	"
26	Total house-hold income	51	42	[1] Under $5,000 [2] $ 5,000 - 9,999 [3] $10,000 -14,999 [4] $15,999 -19,999 [5] $20,000 -29,999 [6] $30,000 -39,999 [7] $40,000 -49,999 [8] $50,000 or more [9] No Response/Don't Know

(Continued)

346

Question Number	Question Description	Column Number	Variable Number	Code Number and Description
27	%. income from social security	52	43	[1] Less than 10% [2] 10 - 14.9% [3] 15 - 19.9% [4] 20 - 29.9% [5] 30 - 39.9% [6] 40 - 49.9% [7] 50% + [8] No Response/Don't Know [9] "No" income from social security
28a	% income from welfare payments	53	44	[1] Less than 10% [2] 10 - 14.9% [3] 15 - 19.9% [4] 20 - 29.9% [5] 30 - 39.9% [6] 40 - 49.9% [7] 50% + [8] No Response/Don't Know [9] "No" income from welfare payments
28b	How long? (welfare payments)	54	45	[0] Less than one year [1] 1 year [2] 2 years . . . [A] 10 years or more [B] No Response/Don't Know
29	Ethnicity	55	46	[1] Black [2] White [3] Spanish Speaking [4] Other (specify) [9] No Response/Don't Know
30	Method of interview	56	47	[1] Field canvass [2] Telephone callback

347

Criticism and Revisions

We encountered a number of difficulties in the administration and interpretation of the interview schedule. Additional problems appeared during the error elimination and data analysis phases. Each of these difficuties is discussed below.

Rent

Monthly rent proved to be a particularly difficult item to determine. Question 5a was designed to obtain monthly rent without utilities. In fact, the data recorded are a combination of rent with and without utilities included, depending on the respondent's knowledge. Tenants generally do not know how their monthly rent payment is broken down between base rent and utility charges. In order to calculate base rent from our data, one must develop procedures for allocating monthly utility charges to each dwelling unit's rent payment. Base rent could be calculated, for example, by subtracting dollar estimates of utility charges from reported rent.

The specific utilities included in the rent were identified by the management of each development. Some managements may keep accurate records of the dollar value of utility charges, but we did not find this to be the general case in New Jersey. Hence, estimates must be obtained in some other fashion, such as average estimates of utility charges. In our study, we did not make such estimates of the dollar value of utility charges. Our rent data, therefore, should be interpreted with this in mind.

Moreover, monthly rent was reported as a continuous variable, unlike estimated market value for owner-occupied structures, which was recorded in question 5b as a categorical variable in $5,000 increments up to $50,000. Interpretation of these rent data are difficult because possible rent categories may not have as much meaning as market value categories: much more variation may be exhibited in rental data for the same dwelling unit (defined in terms of housing type and number of bedrooms). Hence, median or average rents must be calculated and used, with the problems attending such summary measures.

School Age Children

In any replication of this study, the surveyor might want to consider changing questions 13a-f and 14 (school age children) as well. We obtained only the number of children under 18 years of age and their distribution between prekindergarten age, public kindergarten, public grammar school (grades one through eight in New Jersey), public high school (grades nine through twelve), and private or parochial school. Two possible changes are conceivable.

First, the counting procedure leaves room for error. It was intended that 13b through 14 should sum to the number of children indicated in 13a. Yet, in a significant number of cases the sum did not match 13a. The surveyor is left to guess whether the respondent or the interviewer made some error. Perhaps the names, ages and educational status of each child under 18 years of age should be recorded so that the interviewer can detect mistakes made by the respondent and the control staff can detect mistakes made by the interviewer. Second, for the purpose of analysis as opposed to error correction, the surveyor may wish to obtain the exact grade of each child.

Age

We have decided, on the basis of data analysis, that question 21 dealing with age of head of household, might bear changing. The information was obtained using precoded categories. It may be too vague because of the restrictive categories. It might be best to obtain the exact age (as estimated by the respondent) of the head of household.

Household Income

We encountered difficulty with all the income questions. There was a sizable "no response/don't know" group on question 26 (total household income), even though the response was a rough estimate in $5,000 increments. The problem was compounded on questions 27 (income of the elderly) and 29 (welfare recipients residing in Zion Towers). Here, most respondents did not know even approximately what percentage of their income was derived from social security or welfare payments or how long they had received welfare payments.

Ethnicity

An interesting problem arose in connection with the ethnicity of the respondent. Question 29 poses little or no problem in door-to-door interviewing. The polite interviewer ordinarily does not inquire unless in doubt and merely records the obvious (not only are blacks and whites distinguishable, but one usually has little difficulty identifying Spanish-speaking, Oriental, Arab or Indian persons). Over the telephone, however, one must ask the race of the respondent. A respondent rarely hesitates to give his ethnicity (in general categories such as black, white and so on), but the interviewer - especially if he is shy or inexperienced - may hesitate to ask a potentially embarassing question. To evade problems on either side, we placed this question next to last (the last question on method of interview does not involve the respondent). Even face-to-face, occasionally an individual cannot be identified from his physical appearance and must be asked. We found a distinctly higher incidence of no responses (typically the question was left blank rather than [9] "no response/don't know" being coded) for telephone callbacks than for door-to-door interviewing. Interviewers must be carefully instructed that generally respondents have no objection to such inquiries if they are intended only for scientific purposes, and that knowledge of a respondent's ethnicity is crucial to data interpretation.

No Response

It is important, when designing a questionnaire, to work out the coding procedure completely in advance. Where precoded response categories are used, all possible responses should be anticipated (at the very least, additional categories should be available for unanticipated responses). For instance, we neglected to provide a "no response/don't know" category for several questions in the interview schedule although a definite possibility existed that some respondents might answer in such a fashion. The questions involved were numbers 6 (longevity at present address), 7 (previous residence), 10 (total household size), 11 (sex of head of household), 13a-e (various questions concerning school age children and their distribution by school level), 14 (children attending private or parochial schools), 18 (dwelling unit defect), 19 (housing development defect), and 20 (percentage of shopping for various goods).

In general, every precoded question addressed to the respondent should have a "no response/don't know" category (questions 1, 2 and 3 had no such category because they were coded by the interviewer or the control staff.) Usually we employ the code [9] for "no response/don't know" replies.

Take question 11 (sex of head of household) as an example. We defined the head of household as the primary wage earner in the dwelling unit. This approach may not fit for two separate reasons. Who is the head of a household comprised of unrelated persons who do not combine their incomes (regardless of whether either or both sexes are represented), or who are cohabiting out of wedlock (and, of course, we occasionally interviewed such households)? One consequence of women's liberation is that even some married households regard themselves as cooperative units without a traditional head. Even using the criterion of a primary wage earner (as opposed to the traditional concept of a necessarily male head in a married unit or possibly a female head in some other kind of unit), does not always sidestep these problems. As a result, we encountered definite "no response/don't know" answers for which another code had to be added.

350

Unexpected Responses

In addition to the "no response" problem, we occasionally encountered answers to presumably fully precoded questions that were simply unexpected. In question 25 (distance travelled to work by primary and secondary wage earners), we had to add a category for persons who do not travel to work (persons working at home for whatever reason are covered by the category of less than five miles), primarily retired and unemployed persons. There was, in fact, a sizable number of such respondents. One advantage of systematically using code [9] (or some other high code) for "no response/don't know" is that such a procedure readily permits adjustments in the coding scheme. In this case, the coding scheme runs [1] to [4] and them jumps to [9]. We simply add by hand code [5] for "does not travel."

Such an oversight can occur even for a self-coded question, such as 10 (total household size). Only one column was assigned to this question on the computer card. Hence, no easy numerical method existed for indicating a household with ten or more persons. Alphabetic codes (say, A for 10, B for 11 and so on) are more difficut to handle in most computer programs and must be converted. It would have been simpler and more practical to provide two columns. We recorded all households of ten or more persons (of which there were only a few) using the single alphabetic code A. Naturally, using letters, we could have indicated the exact size up to 34 persons and 35 or more persons. For our data analysis, no such coding complication was necessary (in contingency table analysis or cross tabulations there were too few cases to justify adding more categories).

Another example of the importance of having an escape route occurred in question 16 (municipal service most in need of improvement). There was a category for "other (specify)" since we could not anticipate the full range of possible responses. Those responses that could be anticipated - public education, police, fire and so on - were precoded. We found a wide variety of unusual (and sometimes irrelevant) responses. Many respondents indicated that no improvements in any municipal service were needed. Such "other (specify)" categories were included in seven other questions. Such responses must be hand tabulated for analysis, and therefore, should be avoided wherever possible. (Hand tabulation of other responses is discussed below.)

Other Responses

Eight questions in the interview schedule permitted us to record "other (specify)" responses which were not included in one of the predetermined categories. The purpose of such a category has already been explained. These questions, in sequence, were previous housing type (question 8), previous occupancy status (question 9), marital status (question 12), municipal service most needing improvement (question 16), major defect in dwelling unit (question 18), major defect in housing development (question 19), education (question 22), and ethnicity (question 29). The following discussion of the hand tabulation of "other" responses provides examples of what must be done and shows the sorts of atypical responses that may be recorded. One function of such hand tabulation is to see how many unclassified responses can be placed by the coders into one of the predetermined categories. Interviewers may make recording or interpretative errors in filling out the questionnaire. Hand tabulation also permits us to determine whether significant patterns emerge in the other responses. As we shall see below, several important patterns did occur.

There were 41 "other" responses out of 4,131 for previous housing type, 298 for previous occupancy type, 10 for marital status, 130 for municipal services, 81 for dwelling unit defects, 106 for development defects, 11 for education and 48 for ethnicity. This final response set was significantly reduced from the original response set by recoding many answers into one of the predetermined categories.

Previous housing type was generally given as mobile homes, hotels, ranches or farms, and condominiums or cooperatives. There were relatively few other responses. Therefore, our general results are not compromised. Previous occupancy type had the largest no response component. Here, respondents generally had lived with relatives and in-laws or in government and company housing. Other responses for marital status simply identified related but unmarried households, only 10 in all.

A wide variety of "other" municipal services were cited as needing improvement. Some of the responses clearly do not constitute municipal functions as we know them: housing, mail service, shopping. But there are some genuinely interesting responses regarding rent control, flood control, taxation, day care centers, municipal government reform, utilities administration and the like. Most respondents, as anticipated, confined themselves to the specified major functions of municipal government.

"Other" dwelling unit and development defects are simply miscellaneous items that did not seem to fit into any of the specified categories. Insect and rodent nuisance, garbage collection, high rents, and traffic congestion and safety were most often mentioned. Many townhouse developments have community associations or trusts. Of the 43 other responses in townhouses, over half cited an ineffective community trust or association, or poor community participation as major development defects. An examination of the "other" response sets for dwelling unit and development defects reveals a possible confusion between such defects among respondents. These two questions may not be fully separable as a result.

Education and ethnicity involve respondents who fall outside the usual ranges for such characteristics. "Other" responses with regard to education revolved around foreign education, trade or technical schools, and hospital or musical training. "Other" ethnic group members were generally Oriental or Indian and were mostly concentrated in garden apartments. Only one such respondent was found in the single family homes which we sampled.

FIELD PROCEDURES

This section includes a discussion of the initial field survey, the telephone callbacks, the accounting procedures and the results of interviewing. Following the final selection of sample developments, door-to-door interviewing was commenced immediately. As was pointed out previously, saturation interviewing was required for economy.

Initial Field Survey

Teams of interviewers headed by a field group coordinator were sent by automobile to each development during normal working hours. The field work was performed by four field crews of five persons each. Interviewing at night - when people would be more likely to be at home - was not feasible on a statewide basis. Three developments could not be interviewed door-to-door and had to be surveyed entirely by telephone using reverse directories or tenant lists. The field work of door-to-door interviewing extended over a four week period (15 May - 9 June 1972).

Each field group coordinator was responsible for the completion of his assigned developments. His delegated function was to assign personnel, handle the requisite number of questionnaires, and arrange transportation. In addition, he interviewed the superintendent of each development to obtain certain structural and management information. This procedure, or one similar to it, is strongly recommended to anyone planning a replication of this statewide housing survey. The field group coordinator under the direction of the survey project head is a pivotal control element in the proper execution of the survey design. Each coordinator was given personnel, numbered questionnaires and specific completion targets.

If a dwelling unit refused to be interviewed or did not answer, the coordinator was responsible for trying to obtain the name and address of the resident to permit telephone callbacks. Monetary incentives were offered to coordinators and interviewers to encourage the acquisition of usable names. Excellent success was met using this procedure, greatly facilitating telephone callbacks.

Interviewing Techniques

Before interviewers went to the field, each was given lecture training in the structure of the questionnaire and how to complete it
accurately. In most cases, we discovered no serious or irreparable
deviations from the master coding form. Each interviewer was also
issued a brief interviewer's manual covering the main points explained to him. The training of interviewers and coordinators is,
of course, utterly essential for the timely acquisition of accurate
information.

Telephone Callbacks

As soon as practicable, a second team of interviewers was put to
work on telephone callbacks. Telephone interviewing began May 22
and ended in mid-September. The number of telephone interviewers
ranged from seven to seventeen. Telephone interviewing varies with
the level of staff. It is strongly recommended that such a tandem
procedure be followed, especially on a statewide basis. Approximately 7,500 dwelling units is a very large sample. Sometimes as
many as three telephone callbacks were required to obtain an interview. A good deal of time can be consumed in this fashion without
satisfactory results. Telephone interviewers can call 40-55 households per week depending upon the individual. The work is by
definition part-time during evening hours and weekends.

Since the households being called are basically field not-at-home's,
weekday morning and afternoon calling is worthless. In general,
our policy was to call each dwelling unit up to as many as three
telephone callbacks where necessary to insure enough interviews in
each development. On each occasion, the interviewer was expected
to call three or more times before giving up. We employed a rough
50 percent rule to implement this policy. Telephone callbacks
were generally halted when approximately 50 percent of the dwelling units in any development had been successfully interviewed
either during the field survey or by telephone callbacks.

The names were checked first through telephone directories
and then with the information operator. Dwelling units with
no names or common names were checked where feasible through reverse directories. Two garden apartment developments were attempted entirely by telephone using reverse directories when the
management refused to cooperate. The management of a high rise
development provided us with a tenant list including telephone
numbers. The rate of success in obtaining telephone numbers was
somewhat higher using reverse directories than using a combination
of standard directories and the information operator. Even though
reverse directories tend to lag behind current listings, our telephone callbacks would not have been successful without the use of
this invaluable technique. Nearly half of all telephone numbers
we used were obtained through reverse directories.

Configurational Data

Each coordinator was asked to interview the superintendent of the development at the time of field surveying for garden apartments and high rises. We wished to acquire structural data (such as size of development, year of initial occupancy, stages of construction), the utilities included in monthly rent, and the volunteer or nonvolunteer nature of fire protection and ambulance service. We discovered later that additional information was required for analysis, which was relatively difficult to acquire. It is strongly recommended that a decision as to what information is required be made beforehand so that all of it can be acquired when the interviewers are actually at each housing development. Basically the same information had already been gathered for single family homes, in an earlier study by the Center for Urban Policy Research.

We discovered near the end of the survey that not enough structural and management information had been collected in the field for the analyses which we wanted to undertake. The developer or owner or superintendent of each development, for all four housing types, was telephoned to obtain the additional information, especially the breakdown of dwelling units by bedroom type. This information was combined with the various identification codes (development, housing type, municipality, county and county type) to facilitate the weighting procedure employed to pyramid the sample from 4,131 units to some 7,500 units for the estimation of development school loads. As we discovered, field estimation of vacancy rates is quite difficult. The vacancy data obtained are not really usable, since vacancy rates were collected over a substantial period of time; instead, standard estimates of vacancy rates were used for school load multipliers. Similarly even complete knowledge of what utilities are included in monthly rent (for garden apartments and high rises) did not permit us to adjust reported rent figures. One must also know what dollar value to attach to utilities, and standard estimates are not readily available.

Records Management

Records management and questionnaire accounting are crucial elements in such a massive survey. A number of forms were employed to maintain close supervision over the field survey process, and to provide a basis for permanent records. Similar procedures are strongly recommended for other such surveys.

Each field group coordinator was given an assignment sheet which specified his name, the date of interviewing, the development or developments to be interviewed, and the sequential questionnaire numbers issued to him for each development. For financial administration, information was recorded on travel distances and turnpike tolls. Finally, for each development interviewed, the coordinator maintained a record of the number of units contacted and how many interview attempts were successful, refused or did not answer. In addition, the survey director completed a separate form for each field interview trip containing much the same information. The results of the superintendent interviews and the number of names (as distinct from completed interviews) were also recorded. These records were employed as immediate checks on the activities and progress of the field group coordinators. Each coordinator was given another assignment sheet for his own personnel, in which he recorded the questionnaire numbers given to each interviewer and the interviewing results. These records are necessary for financial administration and also permit an immediate check on the activities of each interviewer. From this form, an interviewer payment schedule was recorded by the survey director for each interviewer on each day he was employed. Additionally, a personnel work record was maintained for each field interviewer.

As in the case of the door-to-door survey, a series of records maintained by the survey director was used to establish control over the telephone callback procedure. Full and regularly updated records are essential to the successful execution and interpretation of such a procedure. A personnel work record was used similar to that for the field interviewers. Each telephone interviewer was issued an assignment sheet listing each questionnaire number with telephone attempts made and the result. A separate assignment sheet was issued for each group of questionnaires given to an interviewer. An exact duplicate of the assignment sheet was maintained in the files of the survey director. As the telephone assignment sheets were returned to the survey director along with completed questionnaires, the results were recorded separately in a telephone accounting record organized by development. Each assignment sheet was recorded separately.

Accounting Procedures

Most of the information required for calculating the results of the survey was recorded on a separate accounting sheet attached to each questionnaire. Each sheet contained a printed form and was color coded by housing type (garden apartment, townhouse, high rise or single family home). The same form was used to record the questionnaire number, field group coordinator, interviewers, development, address, result of field survey, name and address, telephone number and the result of as many as three telephone callbacks. Consequently, the accounting procedure became nearly unreadable in a significant percentage of cases. An alternative cover sheet specifically designed for direct keypunching is recommended. Such a form can be easily reproduced and will not be too difficult for interviewers if they are carefully instructed.

In such a form each slot of information (except names and addresses) would be assigned a number. These numbers are column identifiers for keypunching. Any good keypuncher can operate directly from such a form. All the pertinent information required for a complete and exhaustive analysis of survey results would be recorded on such a form. The interviewer at each stage of processing the questionnaire need only check the appropriate slots. Each field group coordinator and interviewer is assigned a code number which in a fully compu- terized survey procedure would permit even closer supervision of personnel and more exact administration.

For the present survey, the cover sheets had to be hand coded onto a different accounting form for keypunching. That form is highly similar to the recommended accounting procedure. Originally field results were hand calculated using the original cover sheet, and a good deal of information was, in effect, "lost." Moreover, hand computation of results proved increasingly difficult and erratic. As the recommended accounting form shows, there are ideally some 52 separate items of information that we might wish to record about approximately 7,500 questionnaires. A matrix of 52 x 7,500 pieces of data is little problem for a computer program but excessively dif- ficult to work by hand. Moreover, keypunching permits full-scale error checking by computer. In the record form proposed, columns have logical relationships to each other which can be exploited for computerized error checking and data cleaning at minimal cost and effort. The entire matrix of information was subjected to careful scrutiny on this basis.

WEIGHTING PROCEDURE

A data file of 4,131 usable respondents was created. This file was generally employed to analyze the social characteristics of respond- ents and their reported satisfaction with municipal services. It was also employed in certain pooled regression analyses (particu- larly the ethnic composition of housing developments and checks on the calibration of the household size and school load multipliers).

To estimate household size and school load multipliers, we pyramided, or inflated, these 4,131 respondents to the estimated total number of households in the developments surveyed. Estimates of household size and school load should be based on the entire development. Therefore, we presented such data as based on 7,500 rather than 4,131 households.

Pyramiding the survey results was complicated by the fact that we used both door-to-door interviewing and telephone callbacks. There proved to be significant differences between respondents interviewed at home during the day and those interviewed by telephone at night and on weekends. Thus, in order to pyramid the survey results, we weighted each household to compensate for such systematic differences. We assumed that households not contacted would most likely be similar to households interviewed in the telephone callbacks. Neither type of household was at home during the door-to-door survey.[9] Using this approach, each question in the survey instrument must be pyramided separately due to variation in the non-response rate. Therefore, the number of households in the pyramided data file varies according to each question.[10] Only those questions actually used for data analysis were pyramided.

Weighting was done for each bedroom type in a development. The distribution of successful field and telephone interviews for the bedroom type was used. Each weight was calculated according to the following formula:

$$\text{Weight} = \frac{\text{Reported Number of Dwelling Units} - \text{Number of Field Interviews}}{\text{Number of Telephone Interviews}}$$

The following example should serve to illustrate the application of this formula. In one development, there were no efficiency, three-bedroom or four-bedroom dwelling units. In one-bedroom units, there were 19 successful field interviews and 14 successful telephone callbacks for 92 reported dwelling units. In two-bedroom units, there were seven successful field interviews and eight successful telephone callbacks for 32 reported dwelling units. The weight for one-bedroom units is calculated as:

$$5.214 = \frac{92 - 19}{14}$$

The weight for two-bedroom units is calculated as:

$$3.125 = \frac{32 - 7}{8}$$

Occasionally, there was a zero value for either the field survey or the telephone callback in a bedroom type actually present in a development. The former case provided no problem as all units were weighted according to the telephone callback. The latter case constituted a problem because one would have to divide by zero in the formula given above. In such cases (seven in number), the weighting had to be done by the field rather than the telephone results. A weight could not be calculated otherwise. The overall results are not drastically affected because only seven weights were so calculated. Such weights were calculated according to the alternative formula:

$$\text{Weight} = \frac{\text{Reported Number of Dwelling Units}}{\text{Number of Field Interviews}}$$

These weights were employed to pyramid the sample using an SPSS (Statistical Package for the Social Sciences) subroutine designed specifically for pyramiding.[11] Each case was associated with a weight. For each bedroom type within a development, each field response (or telephone response for the few examples in which there were no field responses) was weighted and each telephone response was given its appropriate weight. Each response was counted the number of times necessary to expand the sample (twice for a 50 percent non-response rate, four times for a 25 percent non-response rate, and so on). Non-responses were similarly weighted and counted. The final sample size was obtained by subtracting out the inflated non-responses. The larger the non-response rate, the more influential it is. Hence, the larger the non-response rate, the smaller the final inflated sample size.

[1]David Harvey, *Explanation in Geography* (New York: St. Martin's Press, 1969) p. 339.

[2]*Ibid*.

[3]Brian Berry, "A Method for Deriving Multi-Factor Uniform Regions," *Prezglad Geograficzny*, t. xxxiii A, 2 (1961) 263.

[4]The program used in this analysis was extracted from: Donald J. Veldman, *Fortran Programming for the Behavioral Sciences* (New York: Holt, Rinehart and Winston, 1967) pp. 308-317, with modifications introduced by Professor D. A. Krueckeberg of Rutgers University.

[5]See Lynne Sagalyn and George Sternlieb, *Zoning and Housing Costs: The Impact of Land-Use Controls on Housing Price* (New Brunswick, New Jersey: Center for Urban Policy Research, Rutgers University, 1973) for a full discussion of the methodology.

[6]George Sternlieb, *The Garden Apartment Development: A Municipal Cost-Revenue Analysis* (New Brunswick, New Jersey: Bureau of Economic Research, Rutgers University, 1964). A condensed version was published in *Urban Land*, Vol. 23, No. 8 (September 1964).

[7]See Sagalyn and Sternlieb, *op. cit.*, for full methodology.

[8]For Zion Towers, the NJHFA 236 project in Newark, some information was obtained on the income of welfare recipients.

[9]The validity of this assumption can be checked in a simple, though tedious, manner. We weighted non-respondents according to telephone callbacks. Non-respondents could also be weighted according to door-to-door interviewing and an appropriate average of the two techniques. The various pyramided responses could be compared to see how the results vary.

[10]The number of households never varies in the first data file, although the number of households responding to a question may vary because of "no responses" and "don't knows."

[11]Norman H. Nie, Dale H. Bent, and C. Hadlai Hunt, *Statistical Package for the Social Sciences* (New York: McGraw Hill, 1970).

ADDENDUM

MUNICIPAL COST REVENUE QUESTIONNAIRE

1. Interview ID Number (1-4) _____

2. Type of unit

garden apartment	(5) [1]	_____
town house	[2]	_____
high rise apartment	[3]	_____
single family home	[4]	_____

3. Development name _____ (6-8) _____

4. Could you tell me how many bedrooms your apartment/house has?

Efficiency (studio)	(9) [0]	_____
One	[1]	_____
Two	[2]	_____
Three	[3]	_____
Four	[4]	_____
Five or More	[5]	_____
No Response/Don't Know	[9]	_____

5a. How much is your monthly rent without utilities?

$ _____ _____ _____
       (10)   (11)   (12)

No Response/Don't Know(13) [9] _____

IF RESPONDENT OWNS TOWNHOUSE OR SINGLE FAMILY UNIT, USE 5b.

5b. What is the estimated value of your house if your were to put it on the market today?

(14) [1] Less than $5,000	_____
[2] $ 5,000 -$ 9,999	_____
[3] $10,000 - 14,999	_____
[4] $15,000 - 19,999	_____
[5] $20,000 - 24,999	_____
[6] $25,000 - 34,999	_____
[7] $35,000 - 49,999	_____
[8] $50,000 or more	_____
[9] No Response/ Don't Know	_____

6. How long have you lived in your present apartment/house? (Number of Years)

(15-16) _____

7. Just before you moved to this address where were you living? (specify place)

City, State _____

Same Municipality	(17) [1]	_____
N.J. Major City	[2]	_____
N.J. Balance	[3]	_____
Out of State	[4]	_____
Outside the Continental U.S.	[5]	_____

8. Were you previously living in a house, an apartment, in group quarters, or some other type of unit?

Single family house (attached or otherwise)	(18) [1]	_____
2-3-4 family house	[2]	_____
Apartment	[3]	_____
Group quarters	[4]	_____
Other (specify)	[5]	_____
No Response/Don't Know	[9]	_____

9. Were you previously an owner or renter?

Owner	(19) [1]	_____
Renter	[2]	_____
Other (Specify)	[3]	_____
No Response/Don't Know	[9]	_____

10. What is the total number of people living in the household?

(20) _____

11. Is the head of household a male or female?

Male	(21) [1]	_____
Female	[2]	_____

12. What is the marital status of the head of household?

Single or non-related household	(22) [1]	_____
Married	[2]	_____
Separated	[3]	_____
Divorced	[4]	_____
Widowed	[5]	_____
Other (Specify)	[6]	_____
No Response/Don't Know	[9]	_____

13a. How many children under 18 years of age do you have?

(23-24) _____

13b. How many children are of prekindergarten age?

(25) _____

13c. How many children attend kindergarten in the public schools?

(26) _____

13d. How many children attend grammar school in the public schools? (1-8 grades)

(27) _____

13e. How many children attend high school in the public schools? (9-12 grades)

(28) _____

14. How many children attend private or parochial schools?

(29) _____

15. There are many services a municipality provides. How would you rate the following?

		Very Good	Good	Neutral	Poor	Very Poor	NA/DK
Public Education	(30)	[1] _____	[2] _____	[3] _____	[4] _____	[5] _____	[9] _____
Police	(31)	[1] _____	[2] _____	[3] _____	[4] _____	[5] _____	[9] _____
Fire Department	(32)	[1] _____	[2] _____	[3] _____	[4] _____	[5] _____	[9] _____
Recreation	(33)	[1] _____	[2] _____	[3] _____	[4] _____	[5] _____	[9] _____
Sanitation and Street Cleaning	(34)	[1] _____	[2] _____	[3] _____	[4] _____	[5] _____	[9] _____
Libraries	(35)	[1] _____	[2] _____	[3] _____	[4] _____	[5] _____	[9] _____
Public Health and Emergency Services	(36)	[1] _____	[2] _____	[3] _____	[4] _____	[5] _____	[9] _____

16. In which one of the previous list of services, including transportation, are improvements _most_ pressingly needed?

                    Transportation   (37) [0] _____
                    Public Education   [1] _____
                    Police   [2] _____
                    Fire Department   [3] _____
                    Recreation   [4] _____
                    Sanitation and   [5] _____
                      Street Cleaning
                    Libraries   [6] _____
                    Public Health and   [7] _____
                      Emergency Services
                    Other (Specify)   [8] _____
                    No Response/Don't Know   [9] _____

17. Overall how would you rate your housing satisfaction?

                    Very Good   (38) [1] _____
                    Good   [2] _____
                    Neutral   [3] _____
                    Poor   [4] _____
                    Very Poor   [5] _____
                    No Response/Don't Know   [9] _____

18. Is there any _one_ major defect in your apartment/house? If yes, please specify.

                    No   (39) [9] _____
                    Yes
                    Defect   _____

19. Is there any one major defect in your housing development?

                    No   (40) [9] _____
                    Yes
                    Defect   _____

20. What percentage of your shopping for the following goods do you do within the town?

Food (41)	Clothing (42)	House Furnishings (43)	Gasoline (44)
0- 25% [1] ( )	0- 25% [1] ( )	0- 25% [1] ( )	0- 25% [1] ( )
25- 50% [2] ( )	25- 50% [2] ( )	25- 50% [2] ( )	25- 50% [2] ( )
50- 75% [3] ( )	50- 75% [3] ( )	50- 75% [3] ( )	50- 75% [3] ( )
75-100% [4] ( )	75-100% [4] ( )	75-100% [4] ( )	75-100% [4] ( )

21. What is the age of head of household?

                    Under 21   (45) [1] _____
                    21-25   [2] _____
                    26-35   [3] _____
                    36-49   [4] _____
                    50-64   [5] _____
                    65 and Over   [6] _____
                    No Response/Don't Know   [9] _____

22. What is his/her (head of household) highest level of education?

                    Less than High School (46) [1] _____
                    High School   [2] _____
                    Junior College   [3] _____
                    College (BA-BS)   [4] _____
                    Masters Degree   [5] _____
                    Ph.D. or Equivalent   [6] _____
                    Other (Specify)   [7] _____
                    No Response/Don't Know   [9] _____

23. What is the occupation of the head of household?

                                             (47) _____

24. Is there another wage earner in the household? If so, what is his/her occupation?

No   (48) [9] _____
Yes   _____
Occupation _____

25. How far does the head of household travel (one way) from home to place of work? _____ Secondary wage earner? _____

		Principal worker		Secondary worker
Less than 5 miles	(49)	[1] _____	(50)	[1] _____
5-10 miles		[2] _____		[2] _____
11-15 miles		[3] _____		[3] _____
More than 15 miles		[4] _____		[4] _____
No Response/Don't Know		[9] _____		[9] _____

26. In which of the following brackets does your total household income fall?

Under $5,000	(51)	[1] _____
$5,000 - $ 9,999		[2] _____
$10,000- $14,999		[3] _____
$15,000- $19,999		[4] _____
$20,000- $29,999		[5] _____
$30,000- $39,999		[6] _____
$40,000- $49,999		[7] _____
$50,000 or more		[8] _____
No Response/Don't Know		[9] _____

27. FOR ELDERLY (65+) ONLY:
Is any part of your household income derived from Social Security benefit? If yes, what percentage?

                            (52) [9] No _____
                                      Yes _____

28. TO BE USED FOR #236 PROJECTS ONLY.
Is any of the household income derived from welfare payments? If yes, approximately what percent?

                            (53) [9] No _____
                                      Yes _____

28b. How long have you been receiving welfare payments?

                            (54) _____

29. Ethnicity

Black	(55)	[1] _____
White		[2] _____
Spanish Speaking		[3] _____
Other (specify)		[4] _____
No Response/Don't Know		[9] _____

30. Check only if successful interview: method of interview.

Field canvass	(56)	[1] _____
Telephone callback		[2] _____

                            (80) [1]

BIBLIOGRAPHY

MUNICIPAL COST-REVENUE ANALYSIS

COMMUNITY GROWTH AND NEW RESIDENTIAL DEVELOPMENT

GENERAL

Adams, Charles S. Land Use and Municipal Finance (West Hartford, Conn.: Town Plan and Zoning Commission, 1960).

Alcaly, Roger E. and Klevorick, Alvin. "Food Prices in Relation to Income Levels in New York City," (April 1970) Cowles Foundation Discussion Paper.

Barnes, Ralph M. and Raymond, George M. "The Fiscal Approach to Land Use Planning," Journal of the American Institute of Planners (Spring-Summer 1955).

Beck, Morris. Property Taxation and Urban Land Use in Northeastern New Jersey: Interaction of Local Taxes and Urban Development in the Northeastern New Jersey Metropolitan Region (Washington, D.C.: Urban Land Institute, 1963), Research Monograph 7.

Bureau of Business and Economic Research, University of Maryland. Industry as a Local Tax Base (College Park, Md.: 1960).

Clark, William H. "An Area of Need for Cost-Revenue Studies," Municipal Finance (May 1964).

Dodge, Homer K. Framingham, Ten Years of Planned Growth: A Study and Report of the Growth of Framingham From 1950 Through 1960 (Natick, Mass.: Eastern Planning Associates, 1962).

Elias, C.E., Jr. "Land Development and Local Public Finance," in Essays in Urban Land Economics (Los Angeles: University of California, Real Estate Research Program, 1966).

Finkler, Earl. Nongrowth as a Planning Alternative - A Preliminary Examination of an Emerging Issue Chicago, Ill.: American Society of Planning Officials, (September 1972), ASPO Report No.283.

_____, "Can a Twist Turn the Tide on the Islands," Planning-The ASPO Magazine (November 1972).

Isard, Walter and Coughlin, Robert. Municipal Costs and Revenues Resulting From Community Growth (Wellesley, Mass.: Chandler-Davis, 1957).

Lansing, John B., Clifton, Charles Wade, and Morgan, James N.
New Homes and Poor People - A Study of Chains of Moves
(Ann Arbor, Mich.:Survey Research Center, Institute for Social
Research, University of Michigan, 1969).

Mace, Ruth L. Municipal Cost-Revenue Research in the United
States: A Critical Survey of Research to Measure Municipal
Costs and Revenues in Relation to Land Uses and Areas,
1933-1960 (Chapel Hill: Institute of Government, University
of North Carolina, 1961).

_____, Costing Urban Development and Redevelopment:
Selected Readings on -- Costs, Revenues, Cost-Benefit and
Cost-Revenue Analysis -- In Relation to Land Use (Chapel
Hill: Institute of Government, University of North Carolina,
July 1963).

_____, Industry and City Government (Chapel Hill: Insti-
tute of Government, University of North Carolina, 1963).

_____, "Cost-Revenue Research and the Finance Officer,"
Municipal Finance (May 1964).

Margolis, Julius. Land Use Related to Selected Fiscal Issues
(Berkeley, Calif.: Real Estate Research Program, Bureau of
Business and Economic Research, University of California,
(1957). Includes "On Municipal Land Policy for Fiscal Gains,"
National Tax Journal (September 1956).

Mitchell, George W. "The Financial and Fiscal Implications of
Urban Growth," Urban Land (July and August 1959).

Sacks, Seymour and Campbell, Alan K. "The Fiscal Zoning Game,"
Municipal Finance (May 1964).

Schelling, Thomas. "On the Ecology of Micromotives," The Public
Interest (Fall 1971).

Simon, Herbert A. Fiscal Aspects of Metropolitan Consolidation
(Berkeley, Calif.: Bureau of Public Administration, University
of California, 1943).

Sternlieb, George and Beaton, Patrick W. The Zone of Emergence:
A Case Study of Plainfield, New Jersey (New Brunswick, N.J.:
Transaction Books, 1972).

Sternlieb, George and Hughes, James W. "A Profile of the High
Rent Center City Resident," Real Estate Review (Fall 1973).

Urban Land Institute. The Dollars and Cents of Shopping Centers
(Washington, D.C.: 1961 and later volumes).

Wheaton, William C. and Schussheim, Morton J. The Cost of Municipal Services in Residential Areas (Washington, D.C.: U.S. Government Printing Office, 1955).

Wheaton, William C. "Applications of Cost-Revenue Studies to Fringe Areas," Journal of the American Institute of Planners (November 1959).

ALL HOUSING TYPES

General

Holley, Paul. School Enrollment By Housing Type, (Chicago, Ill.: American Society of Planning Officials, May 1966), ASPO Report No. 210.

Lansing, John B., Maranz, Robert W., and Zehner, Robert B. Planned Residential Environments (Ann Arbor, Mich.: Survey Research Center, Institute for Social Research, University of Michigan, 1970).

Norcross, Carl, Open Space Communities in the Market Place: A Survey of Public Acceptance (Washington, D.C.: Urban Land Institute, 1966), Technical Bulletin 57.

California

Mountain View City Planning Department. Insight (Mountain View, Calif.: 1964).

Georgia

Georgia Institute of Technology, Graduate City Planning Program. Report of a Study of Housing Developments and Their Effect on County Fiscal Capacity (Atlanta: 1970).

Illinois

Barton-Aschman Associates, Inc. The Barrington, Illinois, Area: A Cost-Revenue Analysis of Land-Use Alternatives (Chicago, Ill.: February 1970). Summarized in Stuart, Darwin G. and Teska, Robert B. "Who Pays for What: A Cost-Revenue Analysis of Suburban Land Use Alternatives," Urban Land (March 1971).

Hetrick, Charles B. Residential Land Use and Schools: A Study of Current Relationships for Park Ridge, Illinois (Park Ridge, Ill.: 1964).

Maryland

Maryland National Capital Park and Planning Commission. "Dwelling Unit Density, Population and Potential Public School Enrollment Yield By Existing Zoning Classification for Montgomery and Prince George's Counties" (Silver Spring, Md.: 1965).

Prince George's County Economic Development Committee. A Study of Income and Expenditures By Family Dwelling, Apartment and Business Units and Individual School Children for the Fiscal Year 1963-1964 (Hyattsville, Md.: 1963).

New Jersey

Catlin (Robert) and Associates. Comprehensive Plan for the Development of the Village of Ridgewood, Bergen County, N.J. (Rockaway, N.J.: 1964), prepared for the Ridgewood Planning Board.

Miller, William. Revenue-Cost Ratios of Rural Townships With Changing Land Uses: A Report of a Study for the Rural Advisory Council of New Jersey (Trenton, N.J.: New Jersey Department of Agriculture, 1965).

New York

Westchester County Department f Planning. School Taxes and Residential Development (White Plains, N.Y.: November 1971).

Pennsylvania

Pennsylvania Economy League. Fiscal Planning for an Urban Community: A Study of Public Finance in Pittsburgh and Allegheny County, Pennsylvania (Pittsburgh, Pa.: Urban Redevelopment Authority of Pittsburgh and Redevelopment Authority of Allegheny County, 1965).

Virginia

Fairfax County Planning Department. The Housing Study for Fairfax County, Virginia (Fairfax, Va.: 1964).

_____. Student Contribution From Apartments and Mobile Homes (Fairfax, Va.: 1966).

MULTI-FAMILY HOUSING

General

"Apartments in Suburbia.", in Planning 1964 (Chicago, Ill.: American Society of Planning Officials, 1964).

Melamed, Anshel. "High-Rent Apartments in the Suburbs," Urban Land (November 1961).

Neutze, Max. The Suburban Apartment Boom: Case Study of a Land Use Problem (Baltimore: Johns Hopkins Press, 1968).

Norcross, Carl and Hysom, John. Apartment Communities - The Next Big Market - A Survey of Who Rents and Why (Washington, D.C.: Urban Land Institute, 1968), Technical Bulletin 61.

Syracuse, Lee A. Arguments for Apartment Zoning (Washington, D.C.: National Association of Home Builders, 1968).

_____. How to Get Apartment Zoning: A Guide to Argument Presentation at the Public Hearing (Washington, D.C.: National Association of Home Builders, 1969), Information Bulletin 4.

California

Aberle, John W. and Wang, Pe Sheng. The Characteristics, Preferences, and Home Buying Intentions of Apartment Residents in San Jose (San Jose, Calif.: School of Business Administration, San Jose State College, 1965), prepared for the Real Estate Commission, State of California.

Arcadia Planning Department. A Statistical Comparison of Multiple-Family Dwelling Units and Elementary School Enrollment (Arcadia, Calif.: June 1970).

Colorado

Denver Planning Office. Apartment Growth in Denver: A Guide for Zoning Policy With Emphasis on the Southeast Area (Denver, Colorado: 1961).

Massachusetts

Newton Planning Department. Apartment Study (Newton, Mass.: April 1971).

Michigan

Ann Arbor City Planning Department. R4 Multiple Family Density Study (Ann Arbor, Mich.: 1965).

Missouri

Kaplan, Ethan Z. Multi-Family Housing in St. Louis County: A Survey and Evaluation Report (Clayton, Mo.: St. Louis County Planning Commission, 1965).

Saint Louis County Planning Commission. Multi-Family Housing (St. Louis, Mo.: 1965).

New Jersey

Clark, William H. "Apartments and Local Taxes: Are Apartment Projects Really Good Ratables? " New Jersey Municipalities (October 1963 and November 1963).

Fullerton Planning Commission. Fullerton Apartment Survey (Fullerton, N.J.: 1971, 1972).

Monmouth County Planning Board. Multi-Family Housing in Monmouth County (Freehold, N.J.: January 1973).

New York

Nassau County Planning Commission. Apartments: Their Past and Future Impact on Suburban Living Patterns (Mineola, N.Y.: 1963).

North Carolina

Greensboro Planning Department. Apartment Resident Survey (Greensboro, N.C.: 1970).

Pennsylvania

Grossman, Howard J. Survey and Analysis of New Apartment Construction in a Suburban County (Norristown, Pa.: Montgomery County Planning Commission, 1965).

_____. "Apartments in Community Planning: A Suburban Area Case Study," Urban Land (January 1966).

Rhode Island

North Kingston Planning Department. Multi-Family Housing in North Kingston: A Need for Public Policy (North Kingston, R.I.: July 1971).

Rhode Island Department of Community Affairs. The Rhode Island Apartment Occupant: An Analysis and Review (July 1972).

Virginia

Falls Church Planning Office. Apartments: Analysis of Multiple Family Dwellings, The Prospects and Recommendations (Falls Church, Va.: 1962).

GARDEN APARTMENTS

General

Rolde (L. Robert) Company. Garden Apartments and School Age Children (Washington, D.C.: National Association of Home Builders, 1962).

"The Tenants' Point of View: A Survey of Garden Apartment Residents' Attitudes in Five Cities," Urban Land (February 1970).

New Jersey

Passaic Valley Citizens Planning Association. Garden Apartment Study (Bloomingdale, N.J.: Bloomingdale Planning Board, 1963). Also studies in Lincoln Park, West Paterson, Little Falls, and Nutley, N.J.

Sternlieb, George. The Garden Apartment Development: A Municipal Cost-Revenue Analysis (New Brunswick, N.J.: Bureau of Economic Research, Rutgers University, 1964); summarized in Urban Land (September 1964).

Woodbridge Township Department of Planning and Development. Garden Apartment Evaluation (Woodbridge, N.J.: August 1968).

HIGH RISE APARTMENTS

General

Del Guidice, Dominic. "Cost-Revenue Implications of High-Rise Apartments," Urban Land (February 1963).

Canada

Board of Education for the Township of North York. Township of North York High-Rise Apartments Development Study (Willowdale, Ontario: 1965).

TOWNHOUSES AND CONDOMINIUMS

Norcross, Carl. Townhouses and Condominiums: Residents' Likes and Dislikes (Washington, D.C.: Urban Land Institute, 1973), Special Report.

SINGLE FAMILY HOMES

General

Mace, Ruth L. and Wicker, Warren J. Do Single-Family Homes Pay Their Way? A Comparative Analysis of Costs and Revenues for Public Services (Washington, D.C.: Urban Land Institute, 1968), Research Monograph 15.

Syracuse, Lee A. The Single Family Home, A Financial Asset to the Community (Washington, D.C.: National Association of Home Builders, 1968), Information Bulletin 3.

New Jersey

Sagalyn, Lynne B. and Sternlieb, George. Zoning and Housing Costs: The Impact of Land-Use Controls on Housing Price (New Brunswick: Center for Urban Policy Research, Rutgers University, N.J.: January 1973).

North Carolina

Weiss, Shirley F.,et al. Lake Oriented Residential Subdivisions in North Carolina: Decision Factors and Policy Implications for Urban Growth Patterns (Chapel Hill, N.C.: Institute for Research in Social Science, University of North Carolina, November 1967).

Ohio

Robinson, Raymond C., Jr. Residential Subdivisions and Their Inhabitants (Akron, Ohio: Tri-County Regional Planning Commission, 1965), Regional Study 34.